SPECIAL MESSAGE TO READERS

I've travelled the world twice over,
Met the famous: saints and sinners,
Poets and artists, kings and queens,
Old stars and hopeful beginners,
I've been where no-one's been before,
Learned secrets from writers and cooks
All with one library ticket
To the wonderful world of books.

© Janice James.

The wisdom of the ages
Is there for you and me,
The wisdom of the ages,
In your local library.

There's large print books
And talking books,
For those who cannot see,
The wisdom of the ages,
It's fantastic, and it's free.

Written by Sam Wood, aged 92

FLOWER OF SCOTLAND

The Drummond family seemed to have it all, their whisky distillery providing a very comfortable lifestyle for Murdo Drummond and his four children. Daughter Charlotte is ecstatically in love. Peter, the eldest, is preparing for the day when he will take over the reins of the business. Gregarious Andrew is already turning heads. The youngest, Nell, daydreams about a handsome highlander. Even Murdo is considering future happiness with widow Jean Ritchie. That is the idyllic scene in the summer of 1912. But, no respecter of family life, the Great War brings death, devastation, revenge, scandal and suicide to the Drummonds . . .

Books by Emma Blair
Published by The House of Ulverscroft:

EMMA BLAIR

FLOWER OF SCOTLAND

Complete and Unabridged

CHARNWOOD
Leicester

First published in Great Britain in 1997 by
Little, Brown and Company
London

First Charnwood Edition
published 1998
by arrangement with
Little, Brown and Company (UK)
London

Jacket Illustration Melvyn Warren-Smith

British Library CIP Data

Blair, Emma
    Flower of Scotland.—Large print ed.—
Charnwood library series
    1. Domestic fiction
    2. Large type books
    I. Title
    823.9'14 [F]   —   6476

    ISBN 0–7089–9014–2

Published by
F. A. Thorpe (Publishing) Ltd.
Anstey, Leicestershire
Set by Words & Graphics Ltd.
Anstey, Leicestershire
Printed and bound in Great Britain by
T. J. International Ltd., Padstow, Cornwall
This book is printed on acid-free paper

Part One

Twilight

1

HE was quite simply the most gorgeous man she'd ever clapped eyes on. Just the sight of him had the amazing effect of sending a thrill through her entire body, a phenomenon she had never experienced before. She found the inside of her mouth had gone suddenly dry.

'Charlotte, may I introduce my colleague Second Lieutenant Geoffrey Armitage,' her brother Andrew said.

Geoffrey gave a small bow of his head, then held out a hand. 'Delighted to meet you, Miss Drummond.'

'And to meet you, Lieutenant.'

He smiled as they shook. 'Geoffrey please.'

'Then you must call me Charlotte.'

She reluctantly released his hand, furious with herself to find she was blushing, something she rarely did. And never where men were concerned.

Andrew Drummond noted her blushing with amusement. Well well, he thought. This was a turn up for the book.

He turned towards his younger sister who was standing a little apart. 'And this is Helen,' he declared.

Helen, shorter than Charlotte and plumpish, also shook hands with Geoffrey. 'May I too call you Geoffrey?'

'Of course.'

'And what's all this formal Helen nonsense? It's been Nell since I was a child,' she admonished Andrew.

'Nell's far nicer. More you somehow,' Geoffrey stated.

Nell beamed. 'Thank you.'

Andrew rubbed his hands together. 'Now what about a dram after that journey, Geoffrey. I know I could certainly do with one.'

'The family whisky naturally.'

'Naturally.'

Andrew moved to a long oak sideboard on top of which were various decanters and glasses. 'Girls, will you take sherry?'

Charlotte glanced at the ornate grandfather clock situated in a corner of the room. It was just past three in the afternoon. 'A little early for me, but why not?' She decided to shock this Geoffrey Armitage who had just walked into her life and from whom she could hardly tear her eyes. 'Make mine a dram as well.'

Geoffrey was momentarily taken aback, then laughed. 'By Jove!'

Nell wasn't to be outdone, emulating her elder sister as she so often did, or tried to do. 'Same for me, Andrew.'

Charlotte crossed to a red velvet-covered chaise longue and sat, her mind whirling and filled with confusion. There she rearranged the ankle-length skirt of the white cotton day dress she was wearing, already mentally flicking through her wardrobe wondering which gown she would choose for that evening. Something

4

stunning; she wanted to look her best for Geoffrey. She glanced coyly over at him. About five foot nine or ten she noted. With raven black hair and matching eyes. He was broad shouldered, his body suggesting exceptional physical strength. He appeared to be roughly the same age as Andrew, who was twenty-six.

Geoffrey produced a silver cigarette case. 'May I?' he asked Charlotte.

'Carry on. Pa smokes, though in his case it's a pipe.'

'Tried smoking once but found it beastly,' Andrew declared, handing Charlotte a cut crystal glass. He then gave a second one to Nell, now sitting on a chair adjacent to the chaise longue.

'Did McPhie pick you up from the station?' Charlotte enquired of the men. McPhie was the family chauffeur.

'No, we came in Geoffrey's car. It's quite a corker!' Andrew replied enthusiastically.

'A Humber T. Splendid machine,' Geoffrey declared.

'I'm going to ask Pa to buy me one. It would be so convenient to tootle around in,' Andrew said, passing Geoffrey his drink. He raised his own glass in a toast. 'Chin chin!'

'Chin chin,' Geoffrey echoed, and they all took a sip.

'I say, this is sheer ambrosia,' he declared, black eyes shining.

'Twelve-year-old Drummond single malt. Pa says there isn't another in all of Scotland to beat it.'

'I must agree. Wonderful stuff.'

'We've been brought up on it. It's like mother's milk to us,' Nell informed him.

'Really?'

'Oh yes. I can't remember when I had my first drop.'

Charlotte laughed. 'Nell, what will Geoffrey think of us after such a confession?'

Nell was instantly dismayed. 'But it's true.'

'That's all very well. But it makes us sound so . . . awful I suppose.'

'Not at all, Charlotte,' Geoffrey hastily reassured her. 'It is the family business after all.'

'And a damned good business it is too. We're all extremely proud of our whisky,' Andrew declared. 'As for the girls being brought up to take a dram, that's a family tradition. My mother had one every single night before going off to bed.'

His face momentarily clouded. 'God rest her soul.'

'She died in childbirth,' Charlotte softly explained to Geoffrey. 'A baby some years after Nell which was stillborn.'

'I'm sorry,' Geoffrey sympathised.

Andrew stared into his glass, then quickly saw off the remains of his drink. It was still painful for him to think of his mother of whom he had such fond memories. It hadn't been quite so bad for the girls who'd been extremely young at the time, but he, several years older than the girls, had known her a great deal better. In his mind's eye he quite clearly saw a vision of Louise

Drummond, she and Pa together, the pair of them laughing as had been so often the case. His father had been inconsolable when she'd died and had never looked at another woman since.

'How about the other half?' he queried of Geoffrey.

'Rather.'

'Not for me. One is quite sufficient at this time of day,' Charlotte smiled.

'For me also,' Nell said.

Geoffrey finished his dram, Andrew taking his glass and refilling it along with his own.

'Pa and Peter won't be home till six. You'll meet them then,' Andrew said.

'Jolly good. I'm looking forward to that.'

Peter Drummond was the eldest of the Drummond children and worked with his father at the distillery which he'd eventually run by himself and inherit.

'Pa has a car which he bought last year,' Nell piped up, making conversation. 'A Rolls-Royce.'

'I say!' Geoffrey exclaimed.

'A Silver Ghost tulip back limousine with a body by Lawton,' Andrew elaborated. 'It's his pride and joy.'

'I can well understand that.'

'He doesn't drive himself. McPhie does that.'

'Have you driven it?'

Andrew gave his friend a conspiratorial wink. 'Several times though Pa doesn't know. He'd have a fit if he did. As I said, it's his pride and joy.'

'How long are you home for?' Charlotte casually inquired of her brother, holding her breath as she awaited his reply. What she really wanted to know was how long Geoffrey would be with them.

'A week.'

A whole week! That was wonderful indeed. It would give her time to get to know the fascinating Geoffrey better. There would be walks, and conversations, and . . . She experienced an inner shudder of delight at the prospect.

'It's my first time in this part of the country,' Geoffrey stated. 'Perthshire is quite new to me.'

'And where are you from?' Charlotte asked.

Geoffrey pushed back his hair which had partially flopped over his forehead. 'Glasgow.'

'Oh?'

'I'm a town chappie, I'm afraid.'

'I went to Glasgow once,' Nell said.

'And what did you make of the Dear Green Place, which is what Glasgow means.'

Dear Green Place! That was a joke. She'd thought Glasgow horrid but of course couldn't say so as that would have been rude. 'Interesting.'

'Very different to what you're used to.'

'Very,' Nell agreed.

'I love it there. But it's what you're brought up to, I suppose. And you, Charlotte, have you been to Glasgow?'

'On several occasions with my father when he had business there. I enjoyed the shops.'

'What you really need is to be shown the city by someone who knows it back to front as I do.'

Her heart leapt. 'Is that an offer, Geoffrey?'

'It would be an honour to escort you,

Charlotte,' he beamed in reply.

'Perhaps some time then,' she murmured.

He nodded. 'I'll look forward to it.'

'Now,' Andrew declared, their glasses empty once more. 'How about a stroll, Geoffrey? I need to stretch my legs after that car journey.'

'Excellent idea,' Geoffrey answered, trying to put enthusiasm into his voice. He'd much rather have stayed with Charlotte, a spiffing girl if ever there was. Quite a stunner in his opinion. He was glad he'd come to Drummond House.

Charlotte was also disappointed, wishing him to remain, but at least his absence would give her a breathing space in which to regain her composure.

'Are you all right?' Nell asked when the men were gone. 'You seem somewhat flushed.'

Charlotte fixed her sister with a level stare. 'Do you believe in love at first sight?'

Nell gaped in astonishment.

★ ★ ★

'I must say, old boy, your sister Charlotte is a corker.'

The two of them had just left the house, an imposing edifice of grey stone topped with slate and many chimneys. Andrew glanced sideways at his friend. 'I thought you were taken.'

'Quite bowled over. Quite. Is she spoken for in any way?'

Andrew laughed. 'She's entirely free. Most of the eligible young bachelors in the area have been after her to no avail. She hasn't been interested in any of them.'

Geoffrey sighed with relief.

'Smitten, eh?'

'Smitten indeed.'

'And she seemed rather taken by you,' Andrew mused, remembering how she'd blushed.

'Do you really think so?'

'Believe me, I know my sister. She was interested all right. I've never seen her so thrown by an introduction to a chap before.'

Geoffrey couldn't believe his luck.

★ ★ ★

'And whereabouts in Glasgow do you live?' Murdo Drummond inquired of their guest, tucking into poached salmon which was a great favourite of his.

'Park Crescent, sir.'

Murdo nodded his approval. That was an excellent address. He turned his attention to Charlotte, resplendent in a black silk sheath dress inlaid with narrow strips of blue satin that fell elegantly to her ankles where it flared slightly. Directly below her bust was a matching blue ribbon tied at the back from where the remainder of the ribbon dangled. 'What's wrong with you, gel, you're not eating?'

'I don't have much of an appetite, Pa.'

'Unlike you. You usually eat like a horse.'

Charlotte blushed bright red, the second time in one day.

'Hate to see good food wasted,' Murdo grumbled.

10

'I'm sorry Pa.'

Murdo beckoned to the maid in attendance to replenish their glasses. 'And what does your father do?' he enquired of Geoffrey.

'Senior partner in an accounting firm, sir. He wanted me to follow him into the firm as Peter has done with you, but accountancy held no attraction for me.'

'Not exciting enough, eh?'

'That's right, sir.'

Murdo grunted.

'Would you like me to show you round the distillery tomorrow, Geoffrey?' Peter smiled. He too sported the auburn hair which ran in the family, the exception being Charlotte who was golden blonde, though in Peter's case it had begun to recede. He also had the beginnings of a double chin, unlike his brother who had a firm jawline and finely chiselled features. Peter's were becoming rounded and fleshy.

'I'd like that, thank you.'

'Not very exciting, mind,' Murdo said drily, a twinkle in his eyes. 'Though I've always found it so.'

'I'm sure I will too, sir.'

Charlotte found herself mesmerised by Geoffrey's hands, wondering what it would be like to be touched, caressed by them. What it would be like to . . .

Rousing herself from her reverie she had a sip of wine.

'Any news of the regiment being posted?' Peter asked Andrew.

'None. At least not that I've heard.'

11

'Let's hope it isn't India. That's a long posting,' Murdo said.

'Five years.'

Five years! Charlotte thought in alarm. An eternity.

'Did you go straight to the Watch from Sandhurst?' Peter queried of Geoffrey. He was referring to the Black Watch, Andrew and Geoffrey's regiment.

Geoffrey shook his head. 'I was with the Middlesex for some time and was only transferred several months ago. Much to my pleasure, I might add. Nothing wrong with the Middlesex but I'd far rather be with a Scottish regiment.'

'Well said,' Andrew declared.

Geoffrey glanced across at Charlotte who was being very quiet, having contributed hardly a word to the dinner conversation. Was she always this quiet? He doubted it. God, she was beautiful.

For a brief couple of seconds their eyes met and locked, then Charlotte, with a small cough, looked away.

★ ★ ★

'I made my mind up during dinner, I'm going to marry Geoffrey Armitage,' Charlotte informed Nell.

Nell was stunned. 'But you don't know him,' she protested.

'This is going to sound silly, I appreciate that, but it's as though I've known him all my life.

We were meant for one another, I truly believe that with all my heart.'

Nell shook her head. This was so unlike her sister. Charlotte was acting completely out of character. 'You're mad,' she said softly.

'No I'm not. I've never been saner in my life. It's as if I've been waiting for Geoffrey, and now I've found him I'll never let him go. He's mine, now and for ever.'

'He's certainly handsome, I'll give you that,' Nell conceded.

'Isn't he just!' Charlotte beamed.

'But what of his character? You've still to find that out.'

'His character's fine. A gentleman through and through. And I love him.'

'Suppose he doesn't want you?'

'Oh he does all right. I could see it in his eyes tonight.'

Nell had a sudden thought. 'It's possible he already has a girlfriend, he might even be engaged.'

'He isn't. I had a quick word with Andrew before dinner. Andrew thought it highly amusing and laughed, but I got the answer I was hoping for.'

'Will you like being an army wife, Charlotte? It can be quite hard by all accounts. You could end up in the most God-forsaken of places.'

'It won't bother me,' Charlotte declared defiantly. 'As long as Geoffrey and I are together, that's all that matters.'

'You won't always be together, there are

bound to be separations.'

Charlotte's lips thinned in a grim line. 'They'll have to be endured somehow.'

'Oh, Charlotte!' Nell sighed. 'In a way I'm quite jealous of you.'

Charlotte went to her sister and clasped her by the arms. 'Don't worry, dear Nell, your prince will come.'

'I've never had anything like the suitors you have. Just Willie McCall come to think of it, and he's awful with smelly breath.'

True, Charlotte thought. Willie's breath did stink.

'I'm plain Jane compared to you, and fat . . .'

'You are not fat,' Charlotte interrupted.

'I am. It's horrible.'

'A trifle chubby perhaps, but certainly not fat.'

Nell slowly exhaled. 'Chubby,' she muttered. That was a nice way of putting it. But there was more to it than chubbiness and being plain; she didn't have any allure. Men simply weren't attracted to her. She lacked that something which Charlotte had in abundance.

'You'll be my chief bridesmaid of course,' Charlotte said.

'I think you'd better get him to propose first before you start making plans like that,' Nell counselled.

'I'll get him to propose all right. You can count on it.'

She would too, Nell thought. Charlotte had a long history of getting what she wanted.

Nell woke with a start to find her face and forehead slick with cold sweat while her body was shaking almost uncontrollably. She'd come out of a nightmare that had been ghastly beyond belief.

She gulped in a deep breath, the scenes of carnage in her mind still crystal clear.

Men in khaki uniforms, thousands of them, engaged in a dreadful war. Men being blown to smithereens, men missing arms, legs, others shrieking in agony.

Guns flashing and booming, shells whistling through the air to land with mighty explosions. And hanging over it all a terrible pall, the rank smell of fear.

Nell shook her head and the ghastly pictures began to fade, till at last they blipped into nothingness.

'Dear God,' she whispered. What a nightmare. It had all been so very real, as if she had actually been there. What did it mean?

It resembled one of her waking visions, only this time she'd been asleep. Visions that had been with her for years but which she'd never told anyone about, not even Charlotte, in case they thought her insane.

Visions that had always been set in the past, unlike this nightmare which she was certain was of the future.

Reaching out she picked up the glass of water by her bedside and greedily drank, noting as she did that her shaking had subsided. As she

15

snuggled back down into bed a cold, dark tremor of deepest apprehension and despair ran through her.

It was hours before she finally drifted off again to sleep.

* * *

Charlotte didn't sleep well that night either, rising from bed and putting on her negligée as dawn was breaking. She shook out her long blonde hair that reached almost to her lips and crossed to the window.

'Geoffrey,' she murmured, and a smile crept onto her face. She'd never been more sure of anything than that she and he were fated. She wondered if he'd slept well and hoped he had.

What time would he go down for breakfast? she further wondered, for of course she wanted to take it with him.

'Mrs Geoffrey Armitage,' she said aloud, her smile widening. What a grand sound that had to it. 'Geoffrey and Charlotte Armitage.' That sounded even better.

It was going to be another fine day if she was any judge, a day with Geoffrey after he'd completed his visit to the distillery. Pity about that. But afterwards . . .

A plan began to form in her mind.

* * *

'This is a mash tun,' Peter explained to Geoffrey. 'The dried malt is ground into a coarse flour, or

16

grist as we call it, which is mixed with hot water as it is poured into the tun. The mash is then stirred helping to convert the remaining starches to sugars . . . '

Geoffrey was only half listening, though trying to give Peter the impression he had his full attention. He was really thinking of Charlotte who'd been absolutely radiant at breakfast.

He couldn't wait to get out of the distillery and back to Drummond House, and her.

* * *

'He seems a personable enough young chap,' Peter commented to his father on rejoining him in the large office they shared.

Murdo glanced up from the figures he was studying as Peter sat at his desk. 'It went all right then?'

'Oh aye. Gave him the usual tour and a dram afterwards. I have to say though, he did seem a bit keen to be on his way.'

Murdo couldn't resist the jibe. 'Maybe he found it boring.'

Both men laughed.

Murdo tapped the sheets of paper in front of him. 'If this keeps up, and I can't see why it shouldn't, 1912 is going to be our most profitable year in the history of the distillery.'

'We're only half way through the year, Pa, don't tempt fate.'

'Aye,' Murdo agreed. 'Maybe I am being a bit hasty.'

17

They fell silent as each got on with the work in hand.

* * *

Charlotte was furious with her brother who'd got to Geoffrey first on his return from the distillery.

'Fishing,' Geoffrey mused. That wasn't what he'd had in mind at all.

'There are some excellent salmon to be caught round here this time of year. I'll kit you out and have Cook pack a hamper. Now what do you say?'

'I, eh . . . don't fish, old bean. Never handled a rod in my life.'

Andrew was relishing this, having purposefully suggested the fishing expedition just to annoy Charlotte. The look on her face told him he'd succeeded.

'Not to worry,' he enthused. 'I'll soon teach you the rudiments. I'm certain I can promise you a fine day of sport.'

How could he get out of this? Geoffrey wondered. 'I'm not sure, Andrew, fishing has never really appealed.'

'How do you know you won't like it unless you try?'

He was sunk, Geoffrey thought disconsolately. He'd so wanted to spend the rest of the day with Charlotte. Now this damned fishing nonsense had been proposed. Damn and blast!

Andrew was laughing inwardly.

'What will you be doing, Charlotte?' Geoffrey

queried softly. Perhaps she might care to come with them.

'I had thought of having McPhie drive me into Pitlochry. That's a small town not too far away. I have a few things to pick up from the shops there.'

Geoffreys face brightened. 'I've heard of Pitlochry. It's supposed to be lovely.'

'Oh, it is.'

Geoffrey rounded on his friend. 'Look here, Andrew, don't take this amiss, but I'd much rather trot along with Charlotte to Pitlochry. If she doesn't mind that is.'

'No of course not,' she replied swiftly. 'I'd enjoy some company.'

'What about Nell?' Andrew suggested, keeping the pot boiling. Oh, this was fun.

'She's busy,' Charlotte snapped in reply.

Andrew pretended astonishment. 'You must do as you wish, Geoffrey, you're our honoured guest after all. But I find it incredible you'd rather go to some pipsqueak little town where there isn't all that much to see as opposed to an afternoon's salmon fishing. Particularly on such a perfect day, what?'

'I would rather,' Geoffrey replied.

'Oh well, that's up to you then.'

Relief washed through Charlotte. 'I shall leave in half an hour. Is that all right with you, Geoffrey?'

'I'll be ready and waiting. But say, instead of McPhie driving us, why don't we go in the Humber?'

Better still, Charlotte thought. That way there

would be just the two of them.

'Good idea. I'll meet you right here in half an hour.' And with that she swept from the room before there was any more discussion.

Andrew turned away so that Geoffrey couldn't see the broad smile he couldn't keep from his face.

★ ★ ★

Wonky was dumbfounded. 'She's what?'

'Intent on marrying this Geoffrey Armitage.'

Wonky sat and stared at her cousin who'd just dropped this bombshell. 'Are we talking about the same Charlotte?'

Nell nodded.

'I don't believe it. You're pulling my leg. It's some sort of joke. She only met the man yesterday.'

'Love at first sight, according to Charlotte.'

'But . . . the whole thing's preposterous!'

'I entirely agree. But you know Charlotte, once her mind's made up there's no changing it. She's adamant. She says she's in love and going to marry him.'

Wonky, whose mother was Murdo's younger sister and father the local minister in Dalneil, simply couldn't believe this. It had quite taken her breath away.

'Love at first sight,' she said slowly. Their Charlotte!

'What's he like?' she queried, thinking he must be really something to have swept Charlotte off her feet. She couldn't wait to meet him.

'Handsome of course.'

'He must be an Adonis.'

'Hardly that. But certainly handsome.'

Wonky listened wide eyed as Nell launched into a description of Geoffrey Armitage.

★ ★ ★

Charlotte had never felt so much at ease in a man's company as she did in Geoffrey's. Everything was so natural between them. It was as though she'd known him all her life.

When they reached Pitlochry they parked and together went shopping for the items Charlotte had referred to earlier. Items that weren't really urgently required but which Charlotte had used as an excuse to lure Geoffrey away from Drummond House and to be alone with her without fear of interruption.

'Well, that's that,' she declared eventually, handing Geoffrey the final parcel.

'I say, how about some afternoon tea?' he suggested.

Her eyes sparkled with pleasure. 'That would be most agreeable. There's a teashop just down the street that does mouth-watering cream cakes.'

'Then that's the place for us.'

In the Atholl they chose a table and sat, Geoffrey placing their order with the waitress who was almost immediately in attendance.

'So,' Geoffrey smiled when the waitress had departed.

Charlotte returned his smile. 'I want you to

tell me all about yourself. And I mean *all*.'

They remained over tea for two hours that flew by.

During the drive back Charlotte reflected that she couldn't remember ever being so ecstatically happy.

2

'AND this is our cousin Wonky Comyn,' Charlotte declared.

Charlotte and Geoffrey had just returned from their outing.

Geoffrey extended a hand. 'Delighted to meet you, Miss Comyn.'

He *was* a dish, Wonky thought. 'And I to meet you, Lieutenant Armitage.'

'Geoffrey, please.'

'And I'm Wonky.'

Geoffrey raised a quizzical eyebrow. 'It's a rather strange name, is it not?'

She laughed. 'My real name is Veronica which when I was small I pronounced as Wonky and it's stayed with me ever since.'

Not unattractive, Geoffrey mused, though not a patch on Charlotte. He could see the family resemblance, however.

Wonky noted how Charlotte was staring at Geoffrey. A look of admiration and far more. Yes, it was love all right. Anyone with two eyes in their head could see that.

'Wonky arrived earlier and is staying to dinner,' Nell announced. That at Wonky's insistence, as she had no intention of missing the chance to meet Geoffrey. 'I've already informed Cook.

'How did your trip to Pitlochry go?' Nell now enquired.

'Excellent. Tip top,' Geoffrey beamed, glancing fondly at Charlotte.

It had obviously gone extremely well, Nell thought. Just look at the pair of them, like a couple of love birds. She wouldn't have been at all surprised if they'd suddenly started billing and cooing.

'We took tea in The Atholl,' Charlotte stated.

'Ooh, those scrumptious cream cakes,' Nell sighed.

Geoffrey produced his cigarette case. 'May I?'

'Of course you may,' Charlotte replied, having to stop herself at the last moment from adding, darling.

'And what did you think of Pitlochry?' Nell asked Geoffrey.

'Charming.' In fact he'd hardly taken anything in having had eyes only for Charlotte. What a truly splendid gel she was.

After a while of idle chatter Geoffrey reluctantly excused himself to bathe and get dressed for dinner.

'Nell's told me your news,' Wonky declared excitedly when Geoffrey had left the room.

'And?'

'Not only cream cakes can be scrumptious.'

The three young women laughed.

'Did it really happen just like that?' Wonky queried, snapping her fingers.

Charlotte nodded. 'A bolt completely out of the blue.'

'Heavens,' Wonky breathed.

Charlotte had a sudden thought that made

her laugh again. 'Andrew wasn't the only one who went fishing this afternoon. I've well and truly caught my fish, now all I have to do is land him.'

She paused, then added, great determination in her voice, 'Which I most certainly will.'

★ ★ ★

Murdo was sunk deep into a leather chair, morosely puffing on his pipe, with a large whisky balanced on the arm. He was in his study which was forbidden to the rest of the household, with the exception of the maid who cleaned it. He was thinking of his wife Louise.

He glanced over at a photograph taken the year before she'd died, his most treasured possession. Picking up his glass he silently toasted her.

'To you, darling,' he whispered. And in his mind he heard her voice replying.

He'd never get over the loss of her. She hadn't only been his wife and lover, but dear friend and companion. He missed her dreadfully.

He suddenly gasped and clutched at his chest, spilling some of the whisky in the process. Damn these pains, crushing ones that always left him breathless afterwards. He felt sweat pop onto his brow.

He really should go and see Dr McAllister, he thought when the pains had finally subsided. They were becoming more frequent. When was the last attack? The previous month he recalled.

He decided to call on McAllister, a lifelong friend, during the next couple of days.

★ ★ ★

'Hmmh,' McAllister murmured on completing his examination. 'I think the best thing for you, Murdo, is for me to refer you to a specialist in Glasgow.'

Murdo frowned as he began rebuttoning his shirt. 'Is that necessary, James? Can't you do something to help?'

'It's your heart, Murdo, and dealing with that is beyond me. I'm only a simple country practitioner. Ask me to deliver a baby or deal with gout and I'm your man. But when it comes to what's ailing you specialist advice is required. There's a chappie in Glasgow who's top notch in his field. He's the one to speak to.'

Murdo sighed. 'Then you'd better arrange the consultation.'

McAllister was more concerned than he was letting on. The symptoms Murdo had described, and his subsequent examination, were very worrying indeed.

He'd keep this to himself, Murdo decided. There was no point alarming the children.

★ ★ ★

A full moon and a million glittering stars shone brightly above them. The mood couldn't have been more romantic.

'Andrew and I are leaving after breakfast

26

tomorrow,' Geoffrey stated quietly.

'I know.' That was something Charlotte was only too well aware of.

'I've, eh . . . come to think a lot of you, Charlotte. I appreciate it's only been a week, a short time really, but that's the truth of the matter.'

'And I of you, Geoffrey.'

He took her hand and gently squeezed it. 'Can I come back?'

'Whenever you wish.'

'Then I will. As soon as I can.'

He gazed deep into her eyes. 'You're beautiful, Charlotte, but there's more to it than that. I simply don't have the words to express what I feel.'

'I understand perfectly, Geoffrey.'

'Do you?'

'Very much so.'

'Good.'

'How long before you can get further leave?'

'I'm not certain. In the meantime may I write?'

'That would be lovely.'

'And you'll write to me?'

'Yes.'

He took a deep breath. 'That's settled then. In the meantime there's another matter. I don't know if Andrew has mentioned or not but there's a regimental ball next month. Would it be at all possible for me to take you to it?'

'You mean in Perth?'

'That's correct.'

'I'd love to go, naturally. But I'll have to ask

Pa. I'll need his permission.'

'Of course.'

A ball with Geoffrey! How truly wonderful. And Pa would agree, for hadn't she always been able to wind him round her little finger?

Geoffrey leant closer, drinking in the sweet smell of her. Dare he on such short acquaintance?

Guessing what was going through his mind Charlotte closed her eyes in compliance.

Their lips met, and then she was gloriously in his arms.

★ ★ ★

'I'll write tonight, that's a promise,' Geoffrey said.

'I wish you could stay longer,' she whispered.

'So do I. Oh, how I wish that.'

Andrew, lounging by the side of the Humber, watched their parting with amusement.

'Take care, my darling.'

'And you.'

He touched her gently on the cheek. A kiss in the circumstances, there being spectators, would have been quite out of order. Turning abruptly he jumped purposefully into the car.

A heavy-hearted Charlotte stood staring after the vehicle until it was finally lost to sight.

★ ★ ★

'I'm off to Glasgow on business next week,' Murdo announced at breakfast a few mornings later.

28

Peter frowned. He knew nothing of this. 'Business?'

'Nothing to do with the distillery. It's private.'

'Oh.' Peter couldn't think what that business might be but from his father's tone knew better than to inquire.

'Can I come with you, Pa?' Charlotte asked eagerly.

Murdo glanced at her in surprise. 'Why would you want to do that?'

'I need a new gown for the ball, Pa, I've simply nothing in my wardrobe that's suitable for such a grand occasion.'

'You've got masses of dresses and gowns, gel,' Murdo protested.

'But nothing suitable, I swear. You don't want me to look as if I'm straight off the farm, do you?'

Murdo laughed. 'I can't imagine anyone ever thinking that of you.'

'Well, they might.'

Murdo considered the idea. Why not? There couldn't be any harm in her accompanying him and he'd enjoy the company. She wouldn't find out about his visit to the specialist, he'd keep that secret, the 'business' that was taking him to Glasgow.

'And how much is this new gown going to cost me?' he queried lightly.

'Oh, lots, Pa. Lots and lots!'

He laughed again. 'Don't you know we Scotsmen are supposed to be a tight-fisted bunch?'

'Not you, Pa.' Rising, she crossed and kissed

him on the cheek. 'Please, Pa. Pretty please?'

'Couldn't you have it made locally?' he teased. 'As you and Nell have always done.'

Her face fell. 'It wouldn't be the same, Pa. I want something very special for this ball, right up to the minute in style. The Glasgow dressmakers will be far superior and knowledgeable than our local ones.'

'Oh, all right,' he conceded, a twinkle in his eye.

The previously long face now lit up with delight. She kissed him a second time. 'Thank you, Pa.'

Murdo harumphed and got on with his breakfast as Charlotte returned to hers.

Something very special indeed, Charlotte promised herself.

★ ★ ★

They were leaving the breakfast room when Charlotte had another idea. She flew upstairs where she wrote a letter to Geoffrey.

★ ★ ★

'There he is!' Charlotte exclaimed excitedly, and waved.

'Contain yourself, lassie,' Murdo muttered.

Geoffrey came striding along the platform to meet them. It hadn't been easy but he'd managed to get the day away from the barracks, arriving from Perth three quarters of an hour previously.

30

Murdo was beckoning to a porter when Geoffrey reached them. 'Hello, Charlotte,' he beamed.

'You made it then.'

She was even more beautiful than he remembered. 'With some difficulty. But I'm here now and that's all that matters.'

Murdo instructed the porter where to find their two overnight cases, then turned to Geoffrey who immediately extended his hand. 'It's good to see you again, sir.'

'Hmmh,' Murdo muttered, shaking with Geoffrey. It had been quite a surprise when Charlotte had informed him she hoped to meet up with the young man, he'd had no idea they'd formed a relationship. Anyway, it was harmless him escorting her round the city. If they wanted to spend time together then let them get on with it.

'Where are you staying, sir?'

'The Station Hotel. We will be going there to register and freshen up, I'm sure you won't mind waiting for Charlotte in the foyer.'

'Oh, Pa, I don't need to freshen up and you can register for me.'

'I see,' Murdo commented wryly.

'Is that all right, Pa?'

He exhaled slowly. 'It seems it'll have to be.'

'Now where do you wish to go?' Geoffrey asked her as their little group proceeded along the platform.

★ ★ ★

31

A thoroughly shaken Murdo faced Mr Gillespie, the specialist, across his large wooden desk littered with paraphernalia.

'I can prescribe pills,' Gillespie went on. 'They'll help. But the main thing is for you to take life a lot easier. Do you smoke?'

Murdo nodded. 'A pipe.'

'Well, that has to stop. Now what about drinking?'

'I'm a distiller, so of course I drink.'

'From here on it'll have to be very much in moderation, I'm afraid.' Gillespie made a face. 'I always hate saying that to my patients as I enjoy a decent dram myself.'

'What do you consider moderation?' Murdo queried.

'A dram a day, perhaps two. Certainly no more. I also recommend gentle exercise, a daily stroll of about half a mile would be ideal.'

Walking, he loathed walking.

'That's it, Mr Drummond. All the advice I can give you except cut back on work if you can. Better still, give it up altogether if that's possible.'

'Give up work,' Murdo muttered. The thought appalled him.

He needed time to come to terms with this news.

★ ★ ★

On returning to the Station Hotel the first thing Murdo did was go into the bar and order a large

32

Drummond which he despatched in a single gulp. The moderation could start tomorrow, he thought, ordering a second.

Should he put Peter in the picture? he wondered. He could do that and not tell the others.

No, he decided. He'd keep them all in the dark. Best that way.

★ ★ ★

The dressmaker was situated in Holland Street, just off Sauchiehall Street and was expecting Charlotte to call as she had made an appointment by telephone.

Geoffrey insisted on coming in with her where he had to wait patiently in an ante-room while Charlotte was measured and she and the dressmaker, a Miss Sinclair, fussed over patterns and fabrics.

'Well?' he demanded when she reappeared some while later, her face radiant.

'I couldn't be more pleased.'

'Good. Now what about a spot of luncheon? I know the very place. And then I'll give you that tour I promised you.'

★ ★ ★

'Everything hunky dory?' Murdo enquired when Charlotte joined him at dinner.

'The gown is going to be fabulous, Pa. It's — '

He held up a hand, silencing her. 'Spare me

the details. Women's fripperies aren't my line of conversation.'

'Sorry, Pa.'

'And what did you do with the rest of the day?'

He listened quietly as she rattled on about all the things she and Geoffrey had done.

★ ★ ★

'Tell us all about it, every single detail,' Wonky demanded.

'Was Geoffrey there to meet you?' Nell queried.

Charlotte nodded. 'He managed to make it after all.'

Nell clapped her hands with pleasure.

'What about the gown?' Wonky asked. 'What colour did you choose?'

'There were so many wonderful colours but in the end I settled for a pale green chiffon.'

'Lovely,' Wonky breathed. 'That'll beautifully complement your blonde hair.'

'And what about the style?' Nell prompted.

'Very full sleeves caught at the wrist, masses of material that ends in a train, otherwise simple and flowing. You'd have to see it to understand the overall effect. It's going to be simply divine.'

Wonky sighed. 'Expensive, I take it?'

'Extremely. Pa's going to have a seizure when the bill arrives.'

'And what about fittings, are you going to have to go back?' Nell enquired.

Charlotte shook her head. 'Miss Sinclair understood the situation perfectly. She'd have liked fittings of course but in the circumstances says she'll manage without which was why she was so particular about measuring me. The gown will arrive by post in plenty of time for the ball.'

'Now what about shoes?' Wonky asked.

'I've found a pair in matching green that I've left out in the hall.'

'I'll fetch them,' Wonky declared, and quickly left the room.

'Do you still feel the same about Geoffrey?' Nell asked quietly.

'Oh yes, Nell. Being with him again was quite exquisite.'

'Did you kiss?'

Charlotte nodded. 'Discreetly, mind. As he was leaving to catch his train.'

Nell briefly closed her eyes wishing she'd been to Glasgow to meet her prince, whoever he may turn out to be. Please God there would be one, she prayed.

Please God.

★ ★ ★

Murdo replaced the top of his fountain pen and laid it aside. 'I'm off for a walk,' he announced.

Peter stared at him in astonishment. 'A walk? But you hate walking. You've said so many times.'

'It's good for you at my age. I've been

suffering from indigestion recently and that's what Dr McAllister has recommended.'

'I see.' That seemed reasonable to Peter.

'Another thing, I'm taking the day off tomorrow to go fishing. I presume you can cope by yourself?'

Peter rocked back in his chair. 'But you never take a day off! Even when you're ill, which is rare, you insist on coming in.'

Murdo had known this was going to be difficult, and so it was proving. He was changing the habits of a lifetime after all. He was a grafter, and always had been, a trait Peter had inherited.

Murdo made a pyramid with his hands and gazed at Peter thoughtfully over the tips of his fingers. 'I'm not getting any younger, son, and some day you'll be taking over. It seems to me I should start easing off and delegate more. A wise man looks to the future. Besides . . .' He allowed himself a soft smile. 'Who knows? I might actually enjoy having some time to myself.'

Peter was mystified and confused; this was so unlike his father. 'Is there something you're not telling me, Pa?'

Damn! Murdo thought. 'Nothing,' he lied. Rising, he crossed to the door. 'I'll be gone about an hour, perhaps longer.' And with that he left, clicking the door shut behind him.

Peter shook his head. Wonders would never cease.

★ ★ ★

36

'Taking the day off tomorrow!' Charlotte exclaimed.

'That's right.'

Charlotte glanced at her sister, then back at Peter. 'But he never does that. It's unheard of.'

'That's what I said and his reply was that it was time he eased off a bit and delegated more responsibility to me in preparation for when I take over.'

'And he went for a walk?' Nell queried.

'Said McAllister had recommended it for recent bouts of indigestion.'

'He's never mentioned indigestion to me,' Charlotte commented.

'Or me,' Nell added.

'Cook won't be best pleased if she hears,' Charlotte said.

Nell laughed. 'She'll be downright furious.'

When Murdo joined them prior to going through to dinner he refused a dram which none of the children could remember him, at that time of night, ever having done before.

★ ★ ★

'We'll go to Perth together. McPhie will drive us,' Murdo declared, thinking how much he'd enjoy a pipe right then.

'Pa?'

'Oh don't worry, I won't get in the way. I haven't been to Perth in years and fancy seeing it again. Besides, I have friends there I'd enjoy calling on.'

37

'You're not doing this just for my sake, are you, Pa?'

'Not in the least.' He paused, then said, 'I'll book us into an hotel I know. We'll stay the night and then come back next day as we did in Glasgow. That all right with you?'

'Yes, Pa.'

'Good.'

'What about Jenny, can I take her? She's a marvel at doing my hair.' Jenny was one of the household maids.

Murdo nodded. 'She can travel in front with McPhie.'

Charlotte thought of her gown which had arrived that morning and was now hanging in her room. It had more than lived up to her expectations.

★ ★ ★

Charlotte swept into the hotel foyer where Geoffrey was waiting. He stared at her in open admiration.

'You look . . . incredible,' he breathed, hurrying over to join her.

She stopped herself giving a little twirl as she'd done when showing off the gown to Nell and Wonky. 'I'm glad you approve.'

'Approve! By Jove I most certainly do. I'll be the envy of every man there.'

'You look fairly dashing yourself.' The kilt suited him, she thought, he had the figure for it.

He extended an arm. 'Shall we? Your carriage awaits, Miss.'

She gave a low laugh as she accepted the arm. It was the start of what was to be a memorable evening.

* * *

'Murdo, how lovely to see you. It's been far too long.'

The speaker was Jean Ritchie, a school friend of Louise's who'd moved to Perth when she'd married. Forbes Ritchie had died four years previously and now Jean lived alone as they'd never been blessed with a family.

'You don't look a day older than the last time we met,' Murdo declared gallantly.

'You old flatterer. I'd forgotten that about you.'

His eyes twinkled. 'I don't need to use flattery in your case, Jean. Simply tell the truth.'

She laughed. 'You're incorrigible. Now come and sit down and give me all your news.'

Murdo stayed far longer than he'd intended. It was almost midnight before he left.

* * *

Charlotte and Geoffrey were in the middle of a slow waltz, the pair of them well aware that she'd been turning heads all night. On a number of occasions she'd been approached and asked to dance, her reply the same every time, her card was already full. She had no intention of dancing with anyone other than Geoffrey.

'You're the belle of the ball,' you know that?' Geoffrey smiled.

'Nonsense.'

'You are, darling.'

His use of that word thrilled her.

'Would you care for some punch after this? I'm parched.'

'That would be nice.' She paused, then added mischievously, 'Or how about a whisky? That would go down well.'

'Don't you dare even think of it!' he retorted. 'You'd cause a scandal.'

'Well, I certainly can't do that. It might adversely affect your career, Lieutenant,' she teased.

On they danced, she seeming to float over the floor as gracefully as thistle-down.

* * *

'What a night,' Charlotte sighed, as they once more stood in the hotel foyer.

'It isn't one I'll forget in a while.'

'Me neither.'

'I wish I could see you again tomorrow. But unfortunately that's impossible.'

'Never mind.'

He desperately wanted to kiss her, positively ached to do so. He drew her behind a pillar that masked them from reception, and there he got his wish.

And she hers. For it was what she too had desperately wanted.

* * *

Murdo lay in bed reflecting on how satisfying it had been to have good female company again, and Jean Ritchie was certainly that. Not that he lacked feminine company at home, but Jean was of his generation and that made all the difference.

It wasn't as though he was thinking of taking another wife, Heaven forbid. No one could ever replace Louise in his affections. But company and a right old blether was something else.

Yes, he thought. The evening had been most satisfying and uplifting.

3

WONKY laid aside the book she'd been trying to read, realising it was a hopeless business. She just couldn't concentrate. She gazed around the parlour in distaste, hating the manse in which she'd been born and brought up. It was so dark and gloomy, like a mausoleum. It exhuded an air of genteel poverty, her father's stipend being a fair rate of pay for the job, but nowhere near a fortune.

She thought with envy of Drummond House, wishing she lived there. There was nothing dark and gloomy about it and certainly no air of genteel poverty, for the Drummonds were rich. She was further envious of the fact her cousin Charlotte had a man in her life, and a handsome, well-off one at that. She'd have given anything to have gone to the regimental ball in Perth, for there must have been stacks of eligible bachelors present.

That was the trouble of living in the country — the opportunities to meet new people, and by that she meant men, were few and far between. If only she could go to one of the big cities and get a job, but her father wouldn't hear of it. She was a nice, well-brought-up young lady whose place was at home.

She laid her head back against the antimacassar and closed her eyes, thinking of the ball and what it must have been like, for

Charlotte had described everything to her and Nell in detail.

The gaiety, the glamour, the uniforms, which had apparently been a glorious sight as had the gowns and jewellery worn by the women. There had been a dance band and piping and a sumptuous meal washed down with oodles of wine.

Oh, why couldn't she have been born a Drummond and not a Comyn, getting all the things that Charlotte and Nell did. Why, that gown alone had cost the earth and Uncle Murdo, against all expectations, hadn't complained about the price. There again, why should he? He could well afford it. And it was well known he spoiled Charlotte and Nell rotten. Maybe he wouldn't if their mother hadn't died, but she had and he did.

'Veronica!' her mother trilled outside in the hall. Only her mother and father called her that. 'Where are you?'

Wonky rose and made for the partially open door. 'Here, Ma.'

Moira Comyn was in her late forties and had long since run to fat, in complete contrast to her husband Tom who was painfully thin.

Moira was holding a cloth-covered bowl. 'I want you to take this to old Mrs Murchie. It's a wee bit of potted hough.'

Wonky's face fell. 'But, Ma, you know what she's like. She'll want to talk and never knows when to stop. I'll be there for ages and she's so boring.'

'That's a most unchristian thing to say, dear.'

43

'But it's true, Ma. She can talk the hind legs off a donkey and half the time forgets what she's just said and repeats herself.'

'A little charity, darling. The poor soul is so terribly lonely.'

'I can't help that. Can't you take it yourself? You don't mind the way she goes on.'

Moira did but would never have admitted to the fact. 'I'm busy, Veronica. I'm baking.'

Wonky could see there was no way out of it. Reluctantly she accepted the bowl. 'Oh all right,' she conceded with bad grace.

'There's a good girl.' And with that Moira hurried back to her kitchen.

'Blast!' Wonky muttered.

★ ★ ★

Charlotte stared expectantly out of a front window. Geoffrey had written informing her he had a spot of unexpected leave and would like to spend it with her at Drummond House. She was awaiting his arrival which should be any time now.

'Any sign yet?' Nell queried, glancing up from her embroidery.

Charlotte turned to her sister and shook her head.

'No doubt he'll be along shortly.'

Charlotte suddenly squealed as the Humber came into sight. 'He's here,' she informed Nell, and hurried from the room.

What a to-do, Nell thought. Charlotte had been on tenterhooks all morning. There again, wouldn't she have been in the same state if it had been her young man who was due.

Geoffrey leant out the car and waved to Charlotte when he spotted her. It was going to take all his self control not to sweep her into his arms, but that would never do.

'Hello there,' he smiled when he'd brought the car to a standstill. 'How are you?'

'All the better for seeing you,' she admitted frankly.

He laughed. 'Exactly how I feel for seeing you.'

'Are you tired after your journey?' she asked as he got out the car.

'I was a bit so I stopped off at a pub and had a pint of beer. That soon put things right.'

He touched her on the arm. 'I say, you look positively spiffing.'

She was wearing a light rose-coloured day dress edged at the bodice and cuffs with cream lace.

'Why thank you, kind sir.'

'How are the family?'

'Fine, though Pa's been acting queer of late.'

'Oh?'

'Let's go inside and I'll explain.'

★ ★ ★

There was a tap on the office door.

'Come in!' Murdo called out.

It was Isobel, one of the staff, with their morning coffee and biscuits. Murdo took out his gold pocket watch and snapped it open. Dead

45

on eleven as he'd expected. He leant back in his chair and thought of the pipe he'd normally have had after the biscuits. He'd come to terms with only one or two drams a day, even the walking which was becoming more endurable, but his pipe! He still craved that.

Peter stretched and yawned after Isobel had gone.

'Tired, son?'

'Not really. It's just a bit close in here.'

'Then open a window.

'Tell me something,' Murdo said when Peter was reseated. 'What do you make of Charlotte and Geoffrey Armitage. Is it really serious?'

So, Charlotte hadn't spoken to her father about Geoffrey. He'd wondered about that. But it was hardly surprising she hadn't confessed to her father her love for the chap.

'I think it might be,' he prevaricated.

'Seems a decent sort, eh?'

'Seems.'

'Good family as well, by all accounts.'

Peter had a sip of coffee and nibbled at a digestive. He preferred fancy biscuits himself but they invariably had digestives as those were Murdo's preference.

'How long is he here for?'

'No idea, Pa. I don't think Charlotte knows either. Unless he's arrived and told her.'

'Hmmh,' Murdo mused. Perhaps it was time he had a chat with Geoffrey Armitage, found out what the lad's intentions were. He didn't want his daughter's affections being trifled with. On the other hand, it might be early days for that.

46

Perhaps it was best to let matters ride for the moment, see what happened. The whole thing might fizzle out after all.

'I've made a decision,' Murdo declared, changing the subject. 'As from next Monday I shall be working mornings only.'

Peter carefully replaced his cup on its saucer.

'Can you cope with that, son?'

Peter eyed his father speculatively. There *was* something behind all this, he was certain of it. But what, he had no idea. If and when Murdo wanted him to know he would say.

'I think I'm quite capable.'

'So do I.'

'And what do you intend doing with all this free time, Pa?'

'Well, for one thing I'm going to learn to drive.' He glared at his son. 'You seem amused?'

'I just . . . well, I suppose I am if I'm being honest.'

'And why's that?'

'You've never shown any interest before.'

'Well, I am now. McPhie can teach me.'

Murdo chuckled inwardly. McPhie wasn't going to be pleased, in fact he was going to be downright outraged as he regarded the Rolls as his own personal property. Not that McPhie would articulate his displeasure or outrage, he knew better than that.

Murdo couldn't wait to see McPhie's face when he told him.

★ ★ ★

47

'It's such beautiful countryside round here,' Geoffrey observed. It was the middle of the afternoon and he and Charlotte had decided to take a stroll. He glanced round to make sure they weren't being observed, then took her hand. 'I've missed you.'

'And I you.'

'Letters are fine, but they're a poor substitute for the real thing.'

'Well, you have ten days of that ahead of you.'

'Sheer bliss,' he smiled.

And for her, she thought.

His smile vanished. 'There's a rumour going round that we might be posted overseas soon.'

Her face darkened. 'Oh, Geoffrey!'

'It's only a rumour, mind. And it's only *might*. But if it does happen it can happen quickly.'

'Any idea where to?'

He shook his head. 'Not the foggiest. It could be anywhere.'

She'd known this could happen of course, he was in the army. But so soon after their meeting! She suddenly felt sick.

'Are you all right, Charlotte?'

'I've just come over a bit faint, that's all.'

'I say, I'm sorry.'

He had said *might*, she must cling on to that, she told herself. A rumour was hardly fact. Far from it.

'If you go you will still write?' she asked.

'You have my solemn word on that.'

She turned away so he couldn't see her face.

48

'Have you ever considered leaving the army, Geoffrey?'

'You mean resign my commission?'

'That's right.'

'No, I haven't. I intend the army to be my career.' He barked out a laugh. 'I don't really know what else I could do. I have no other training or skills.'

'I can't bear the thought of you going away,' she said huskily.

'Now that we've met the prospect would be pretty dreadful for me too.'

Damn his being an army officer! she thought. Of all things why did he have to be that? It so complicated matters. But it wouldn't change things, how she felt, not one iota.

'I'll wait for you,' she said, knowing she was being fast but not caring.

He took her by the shoulders. 'I was praying you'd say that. I didn't dare ask.'

'I'll wait, no matter what,' she repeated.

'I think I love you, Charlotte,' he whispered.

'Only think? Aren't you sure?'

'Yes I am. And how do you feel about me?'

'The same. I knew we were meant for one another the moment we met.'

'Oh, my darling.'

He closed his eyes, and she hers, as they kissed. And it seemed to her they were already one.

* * *

'May I speak with you, sir? Alone that is.'

It was after dinner that night and Murdo had intended going to his study to read the day's papers. He suddenly guessed what this was all about and it explained Charlotte's nervousness during the meal, an uncharacteristic mood he'd put down to the young man's presence. 'Come with me,' he said.

Geoffrey didn't know the honour he was being accorded when Murdo ushered him into his study, the holy of holies.

'Care for a dram, lad?'

'Yes please, sir.' That would help keep up his courage. When Murdo handed him his drink he swallowed half of it straight off.

'Well, Geoffrey, what can I do for you?'

'Sit . . . ' He took a deep breath. 'I'd like to ask for your daughter's hand in marriage.'

'I see. That would be Charlotte presumably.' He'd said the latter as a little tease.

'Oh yes, sir.'

'I presume she knows you're asking me this and have her agreement on the matter?'

'Indeed, sir.'

Murdo crossed to the fireplace to gaze at the photograph of his beloved Louise standing in pride of place on the mantelpiece. 'A bit sudden, don't you think? I mean, you've only known each other five minutes.'

Oh God, Geoffrey thought. He was going to be refused. 'That's true, sir, but we're very much in love.'

He'd wondered what the lad's intentions were, now he knew. But what to answer?

'I think we'd better have Charlotte in on this. Will you go and fetch her.'

'Certainly, sir.' Geoffrey rushed out to fetch Charlotte.

Marriage? He wasn't against that but it worried him they'd only been acquainted such a short time. Marriage was a lifelong commitment after all.

A few minutes later Geoffrey returned with Charlotte who halted in the doorway. 'Am I to come in, Pa?'

'Well, I'm not going to shout at you across the room.'

She entered hesitantly, closing the door behind her. This was the first occasion she'd ever been in the room. She glanced curiously about her.

'Drink, lass?'

'Please.'

He stared at her, noting how nervous she continued to be, a nervousness he now interpreted as a good sign. She wanted this marriage and was worried he might object or cause problems.

'Whisky please, Pa.'

'Geoffrey has just asked for your hand,' he informed her as he handed her her drink.

'I know, Pa.'

'Says you love him.'

'I do, with all my heart.'

Geoffrey beamed.

'I see,' Murdo mused. He sipped his own drink. 'As I pointed out to him it all seems a bit sudden. You hardly know one another.'

'When something's right it's right no matter

the time involved. And that's how it is with Geoffrey and me.'

True, he thought. Quite true.

'There's no doubt in your mind then?'

'None whatever, Pa. I want to marry Geoffrey.'

'And I Charlotte,' Geoffrey stated.

Murdo turned his attention again to Geoffrey who boldly stared him straight in the eye. 'And what are your prospects, Geoffrey?'

'The army, sir. My prospects are what I make of myself. As an only child I shall also inherit a considerable amount in due course when my parents pass on.'

'Hmmh.'

'I've given it careful thought, Pa. Being an army wife isn't ideal but if that's required to be with Geoffrey then I'll put up with it.'

'Even if it means long years in various stinking hellholes?'

Charlotte blanched, then stuck out her chin. 'Even so, Pa.'

That seemed to be that, Murdo thought. He wasn't one to stand in the way of his daughter's happiness. If she wanted Geoffrey Armitage, then so be it.

'When would this wedding take place?' he inquired.

'Oh, not for at least eighteen months, sir. I'm not allowed to get married, rules and regulations you know, until I'm thirty and I'm twenty-eight and a half now.'

Murdo replenished his glass thinking he'd have more than two that night. It was a

52

momentous occasion after all.

'Do we have your permission, Pa? I'll only elope if we don't.'

'Don't threaten me, gel,' he growled. 'I won't have it.'

'Sorry, Pa.' She wasn't sorry at all, she'd meant what she said. She would elope come hell or high water if he refused permission.

There was a few seconds hiatus, then Murdo said, 'Tell you what, let's play safe on this by having a breathing space.'

'Breathing space?' Charlotte queried quietly.

'It still worries me that you've known one another such a short while so I'm going to ask you to humour your old father by putting the engagement off for six months. Come to me again in six months, Geoffrey, and my answer will be yes. This way, should it so happen that either of you does change your mind there won't be any loss of face or embarrassment. Now what do you say?'

'You *will* say yes, Pa?'

'You have my word on that, Charlotte.' He stared from one to the other. 'Well?'

Geoffrey looked at Charlotte who nodded.

'Agreed, sir. Six months it is and you may rest assured that I will be back.'

'I think a top up is in order all round, eh?'

Charlotte went to her father and kissed him on the cheek. 'Thanks, Pa.'

'And no more talk of eloping. If a marriage is to take place I want it to be done in style as befits the daughter of Murdo Drummond.'

When their glasses had been recharged Murdo silently saluted the happy couple and they all drank.

★ ★ ★

Nell clapped her hands with glee when Charlotte and Geoffrey told her.

'Congratulations to the pair of you!' Nell swept her sister into her arms and hugged her tight.

'It's unofficial of course,' Geoffrey said. 'We can't make a formal announcement for six months yet.'

'That's Pa's suggestion as we've only known one another a short time,' Charlotte explained.

'Is it to be a secret then?'

Geoffrey's brow furrowed as he reflected on that. 'I suppose so. I presume that's what your father meant when he said about there being no loss of face or embarrassment.'

'We must let Wonky in on it though,' Nell said.

'I'm sure there can be some exceptions,' Charlotte mused.

'Your brother for instance. I shall jolly well want to tell him.'

'Wonky and Andrew then . . . '

'And Peter,' Nell added, interrupting her sister.

Charlotte nodded her agreement.

'I can't tell you how pleased I am for the pair of you. It's so wonderful.'

'To begin with I thought he was going to

refuse outright. It fair put the wind up me,' Geoffrey said.

Charlotte laughed and the other two joined in.

She'd said she'd land her man and so she has, Nell thought. How like Charlotte.

Wonky screamed with delight when told the next day by Nell and swore to keep the secret.

★ ★ ★

Murdo halted to lean on the stick he sometimes carried when out walking. He was doing a loop that would eventually bring him back to Drummond House.

He glanced up at the sky wondering if it would rain. He didn't think it would. Summer had definitely gone and now there was a nip in the air. He was thinking of Jean Ritchie and the most pleasant evening he'd spent with her. He'd been mulling over the idea of asking her to Drummond House for a spell. It would be a nice break for her and a pleasant interlude, he hoped, for them both.

Why not? he thought. He decided to write to her on his return.

★ ★ ★

Charlotte and Geoffrey were also out walking, following the bank of the burn that fed the distillery, hand in hand.

'Only a couple of days left, I'm sorry to say,' Geoffrey sighed.

'I know.'

'I'd give anything for it to be longer.'

As would she. 'Any idea when you might get some more leave?'

'None at all.'

They strolled a few steps in silence. 'Geoffrey, what happens if you are posted abroad before the six months is up? You can hardly speak to Pa if you're overseas.'

'I've already thought of that. I'll have to write to him.'

'And what if you're overseas for years and years?'

'You can join me and we'll marry wherever I am. But let's not worry about that. It's a bridge we'll cross if and when we come to it.'

'Look!' Charlotte exclaimed, pointing over to their left. 'A stag.'

Geoffrey had never seen a stag before. 'It's magnificent,' he breathed.

The stag raised its muzzle and sniffed the air. Then slowly, proudly, began walking away.

'He reminds me of your father,' Geoffrey stated.

Charlotte laughed.

'No really, I'm serious. He has that same regal quality about him. The same sort of bearing.'

'I'm sure Pa would be flattered to hear that.'

They resumed walking. 'Talking of fathers, you'll have to meet mine. Both my parents that is.'

'I suppose I shall.'

'They'll like you, I'm certain of it.'

'I certainly hope they do. It'll be awful if they don't.'

He patted the hand he was holding with his free one. 'The three of you will get on like a house on fire. I have no worries in that direction.'

Charlotte prayed he was right.

★ ★ ★

'Are you happy about this proposed engagement, Pa?' Peter asked, as he and Murdo took their morning coffee in the office.

Murdo, who'd been lost in thought, came out of his reverie to stare at his son. 'Perfectly. Why, do you have doubts about the match?'

Peter shook his head.

'Then why ask?'

'The six-month postponement. I wondered if there was more to it than the reason given?'

'There isn't. Geoffrey is a fine chap and they assure me they're very much in love. It was simply a case of being cautious, that's all.'

'Everything's all right then?'

'Quite.'

Murdo had a swallow of coffee and finished his biscuit. 'What this engagement business has made me think about is you, son.'

'Me?'

'Isn't it about time you started courting? *Tempis fugit* and all that, and none of us is getting any younger.'

Peter dropped his eyes to gaze at the papers on his desk, not wanting Murdo to see his alarmed expression. How did you explain to your father that you had no interest whatsoever in women, that they left you entirely cold. The thought of actually entering their bodies was totally repugnant to him, revolting in the extreme. He didn't mind them being around, or their company, but that was as far as it went.

Not that he was homosexual, he had no inclinations in that direction either. There had been one incident at school which had been nauseating in the extreme. He recalled it now with an inward shudder. Sandy McPherson had talked him into it and he'd hated the bastard ever since. He'd been physically sick afterwards and was convinced he'd have the same reaction if he was to go to bed with a woman. If he managed the act that was, which he doubted.

'Well?' Murdo queried.

Peter, mind racing, refocused on his father. 'It's important to you that I produce an heir, isn't it, Pa?'

'Very much so.'

'But you would want me to be happy, as Charlotte now is?'

'Naturally.'

'I couldn't marry just for the sake of it, Pa. I'd want to be in love as you and Ma were. Or as Charlotte and Geoffrey now claim to be.'

'I understand that,' Murdo conceded.

'I don't know when it'll happen, Pa, or indeed if it ever will. But I refuse to get wed simply to produce an heir. It has to be love or nothing.' He then added craftily, 'I learnt that from you.'

A lump came into Murdo's throat remembering

58

the day, that glorious day never to be forgotten, when he'd met Louise. A day that had changed his life for ever.

'I'll say no more on the subject, son.'

Peter breathed a soft sigh of relief. There never would be an heir from him, that task would fall to Andrew and would have to satisfy his father.

4

JEAN RITCHIE carefully folded Murdo's letter and replaced it in its envelope.

The contents had surprised her.

A visit to Drummond House for a break, as Murdo had called it, the prospect certainly wasn't unappealing. Her life since Forbes's passing had been humdrum to say the least.

Her brow furrowed in thought. Was there more to this than met the eye? Murdo had always been devoted to Louise, virtually worshipped her. But Louise had been gone a long time now and perhaps he was thinking of remarrying and she was a candidate. It was a possibility.

Marriage to Murdo? He was a fine, upstanding man whom she'd always admired. It wouldn't be difficult at all sharing the rest of her days with him.

Forbes would have approved, she was certain of that. He'd always spoken highly of Murdo Drummond.

But here, she mustn't get ahead of herself. Perhaps the proposed visit was simply that, a break and nothing else. She mustn't put two and two together and come up with five.

Naturally she'd go, it would be lovely seeing the girls again. Now they were grown up the three of them could have some right old blethers together.

She decided to wait a few days before replying. She didn't want to appear too eager.

★ ★ ★

Nell was staring out of her bedroom window when the familiar tingling took hold of her, and then the trembling of her hands. The amazing thing was these visions always occurred when she was alone and never when with others.

Her sight wavered and then cleared. The countryside she was now seeing wasn't that she'd been looking at before. The land was wild and heather covered, somewhere further north, though where she had no idea. There were mountains in the background, several of the taller ones with snow on their peaks.

And then *he* came into view, the same Highlander as in all her visions. Tartan wrapped and armed with broadsword, dirk and pistol, he was wearing a blue bonnet that sported the eagle feather which proclaimed him to be a chief.

There was no sound, there never was. All was silent in her vision as the Highlander's weary horse plodded stoically forward.

He was closer now and she could see his face more clearly. He appeared drawn and haggard, ill almost. He shivered and drew his plaid more tightly about him.

He'd lost the beard he'd had the last time she'd seen him, but of course she had no way of knowing whether or not these visions were in chronological order. He'd always appeared to be roughly the same age.

A group of men came into sight, Highlanders like himself but wearing a different tartan, and went hurrying towards him. He pulled up his horse and dismounted.

When they reached him a discussion took place with one, who gave the impression of being the men's leader, pointing off into the distance.

Her Highlander — oh how she wished she knew his name — nodded, said something further to the men and remounted. The group started off in the direction he had pointed to.

The vision faded and then suddenly blinked out of existence and she was left gazing at the usual view from her window.

Nell took a deep breath, turned and crossed to her bed where she sat, drained as she always was after a vision.

She had tried looking up the ancient tartans but had never been able to discover the one he wore, so even his surname, or the clan he belonged to, remained a mystery.

She knew he lived in a big stone house with his wife and children where she'd often watched him.

Nell shook her head in wonder. Why did this happen to her and what did it mean? Why was it this particular man she always saw? How did these visions come about?

At least she wasn't frightened any more as she'd been when the visions started all those years ago. The only thing that frightened her now was the idea of anyone finding out about them.

She didn't want to be thought of as mad.

'I'll drive, McPhie,' Murdo declared. He was setting out to pick up Jean Ritchie from Pitlochry station.

McPhie groaned inwardly. He'd thought this might happen. He hated it when Murdo drove, the man was a bloody menace.

★ ★ ★

'Jean! How wonderful to see you again.'

She pecked him on the cheek, then regarded him speculatively through new eyes.

'How was your journey?'

'Uneventful. A little boring really.'

Murdo had a swift word with McPhie who climbed into the carriage Jean had just emerged from to get her cases. Why pay a porter when McPhie was on hand?

'It's most kind of you to invite me, Murdo. I've been looking forward to it and meeting your family again.'

'They all know you were a good friend of their mother's.'

They proceeded towards the barrier. 'I've told Cook to hold luncheon until we arrive.'

'Will the girls and Peter be there?'

'Not Peter, he'll be at work in the distillery.'

'Of course.'

Murdo felt very relaxed with Jean as he'd known he would. 'I drove the car here,' he declared proudly.

'I didn't know you could drive?'

He can't, McPhie thought sourly following in their wake and party to the conversation.

'I'm learning. And coming along fine, eh, McPhie?' The latter he said over his shoulder.

'Handsomely, Mr Drummond,' McPhie tactfully lied.

'I've stopped working in the afternoons and decided to learn as a sort of hobby,' Murdo explained.

'Good idea.'

Bad idea, McPhie thought.

'Are you finding it easy?' Jean enquired.

'Oh yes. I have a natural ability with mechanical things.'

McPhie nearly choked. Talk about self delusion! He made a face remembering the gear-grinding on the way there. That and the few hair-raising moments when Murdo had very nearly lost control. Some natural ability.

When they arrived at the Rolls-Royce McPhie was extremely relieved when Murdo assisted Jean into the rear of the car where he joined her.

Thank you, God! McPhie silently prayed as he began loading Jean's cases onto the roof rack.

★ ★ ★

'My, what fine young ladies you've turned out to be,' Jean declared to Charlotte and Nell, thinking Charlotte prettier than her plumper sister. 'You were only bairns the last time I saw you.'

Charlotte and Nell had been discussing Jean

before her arrival, both puzzled as to why she'd been invited. She'd been a friend of their mother's, of course, but why invite her now after so many years? Was Pa up to something? they'd wondered.

'How do you do, Mrs Ritchie,' Charlotte replied, giving a small curtsy.

Nell merely smiled as she curtsied.

'I see their mother in both of them,' Jean proclaimed, which delighted Murdo.

'Peter's the one who takes most after Louise. You'll meet him at dinner.'

Jean gazed around her. 'This sitting room is exactly as I remember it. Why I do believe that even the aspidistra is the same.'

Murdo laughed. 'You're wrong about the aspidistra. That's a new one though bought some while back.'

'Well, it looks the same,' Jean said, and laughed with him.

'Now how about some luncheon. I don't know about you but I'm starved.'

Charlotte and Nell led the way to the dining room.

★ ★ ★

'He's done what!' Charlotte exclaimed that evening shortly after dinner.

'Taken her to his study,' Peter repeated, pouring himself a dram.

'But no one's allowed in there,' Nell protested.

'Charlotte went in with Geoffrey,' Peter commented drily.

65

'Ah yes, but that was different,' Charlotte retorted. 'It was an exception. And the only occasion I've ever been in there, I'll remind you.'

Peter's expression became thoughtful. 'Ma was allowed in. I remember that quite distinctly.'

Charlotte glanced at Nell who raised an eyebrow.

'Makes you think, doesn't it?' Peter said quietly.

★ ★ ★

'That meal was delicious. The beef quite superb,' Jean declared, sitting on Murdo's comfy club chair, the only chair in the study.

'We're very fortunate to have Mrs Clark for a cook. If she has a fault it's that she can be a little adventurous for my taste. But on the whole she's excellent.'

'Has she been here long?'

Murdo paused in pouring out the sherry he'd previously brought into the study, having noted in Perth that that was Jean's preference. 'Five or six years, I can't recall exactly. She came from the Duke of Strathearn's household. It seems she and the Duchess didn't see eye to eye which doesn't surprise me; I've met the Duchess on occasion and she can be something of a dragon to say the least. As Mrs Clark is a very self-willed woman I suppose a collision of personalities was inevitable.'

Jean laughed.

66

'Well, the Duchess's loss was our gain.'

He handed Jean her sherry then crossed to the mantelpiece on which he placed his own glass. 'I don't know if you've seen this,' he said, picking up Louise's photograph in its ornate silver frame and giving it to Jean.

Jean studied the photograph, a soft smile on her face. 'Louise was a good friend to me, I still miss her.'

'As do I,' Murdo declared, a catch in his voice.

'You two were so much in love.'

'So much,' he repeated in a whisper.

Jean regarded him keenly. 'But life goes on, Murdo, we must always remember that.'

'Aye,' he agreed.

'That's what I told myself after Forbes died. Life goes on and we must go with it. The past is the past which can never be taken away from us. But it is the past.'

Murdo sighed and sipped his whisky. It had recently become a pretence with him not to notice he was pouring larger measures than he'd done before his trip to Glasgow and consultation with Mr Gillespie, the heart specialist, since when there hadn't been any recurrence of the chest pains.

'Do you get terribly lonely?' Jean asked quietly.

He glanced at her in surprise. 'I suppose I do. There's work, and the girls and Peter of course, and Andrew when he's home. But yes, I suppose I do get lonely. I miss . . . well, the companionship of someone my own age. Just being able to relax and chat about the day's events.'

'I understand that perfectly. At least you're fortunate enough to have your family and the distillery. I have nothing apart from bridge and whist afternoons, and the occasional bit of charity involvement. The days can seem interminable at times.'

She returned the photograph of Louise wondering if she'd been a little too honest. Trouble was, it was true. They were both roughly in the same boat.

Murdo replaced the photograph on the mantelpiece and gazed lovingly at it for a moment. 'I have a favour to ask.'

'Oh?'

He cleared his throat. 'This is rather difficult, Jean. A trifle delicate, shall we say.'

'I'm all ears, Murdo. If I can help you in any way . . . ' She trailed off and waited for him to go on.

'Charlotte has a young man who was recently in this very room asking for her hand.'

Jean beamed. 'That's wonderful.'

'He's one of Andrew's fellow officers, a splendid chap called Geoffrey Armitage. They both assure me they're head over heels in love.'

'She's extremely pretty, Murdo. And by the by, you were quite right. Peter does take after his mother the most.'

Murdo glanced again at the photograph, then back to Jean. He explained about the six-month postponement in the engagement announcement.

'Very wise of you,' she nodded.

'The thing is, Jean.' He cleared his throat again. 'Charlotte doesn't have a mother to talk to her about . . . you know, the intimacy of marriage. What actually happens.'

'And you won't explain?' Jean teased.

'Heavens no! I couldn't possibly.'

'And you wish me to have a chat with her?'

'Exactly,' he smiled. 'Though not straight away. Get to know her first, and she you. Then possibly towards the end of your stay here you might have a word. I'd be awfully obliged.'

Murdo saw off the rest of his whisky, noted Jean's glass was still half full, and poured himself a second, even larger than the first. He was most uncomfortable about asking this particular favour, but had seen Jean's presence as the perfect opportunity to do what had to be done.

'Tell me, Murdo,' Jean asked softly. 'Was this the reason you wanted me here?'

'Not at all. I didn't get the idea until after you'd accepted my invitation.'

'I see.'

'Of course if you feel that you can't . . . '

She held up a hand to stop him. 'I shall, Murdo. If the positions had been reversed I'm sure Louise would have done the same for me.'

Murdo breathed a huge sigh of relief. 'Thank you, Jean. I'm in your debt.'

★ ★ ★

'Andrew!' Charlotte exclaimed.

'Five days' leave, sis. Didn't know until this

69

morning so it's been something of a rush. Took a taxi from the station.'

Nell popped her head round the door. 'Andrew! I thought I heard your voice.'

'It's me all right. Home for five days. Terrific.' His eyes twinkled mischievously as he turned to face Charlotte. 'I've got news.'

'Oh?'

'It was only announced just before I left.' He smiled. 'The Battalion's being posted.'

Charlotte's face fell and she was filled with dread. 'Where to?'

'Jolly old India which is what the majority of us expected. The Battalion will be gone for years.'

Charlotte swallowed hard, crossed to the nearest chair and sat. Nell hurried to her and put a consoling arm round her sister's shoulders. This was awful. Poor Charlotte.

It wasn't the end of the world, Charlotte told herself. It simply meant she and Geoffrey would get married over there.

'The second Battalion that is,' Andrew added quietly.

It took a few moments for that to sink in. 'The second Battalion?' Nell queried.

'That's right.'

'But you're in the first.'

'Yes, we're remaining. Geoffrey and I aren't going anywhere.'

Relief surged through Charlotte and she found herself breathing heavily.

'You horror!' Nell snapped. 'That was downright cruel.'

'Just my little joke, that's all.'

'Some joke,' Charlotte hissed, furious with her brother. Nell was right, that had been cruel.

'I didn't realise you'd take it so badly,' he protested.

'How did you think I'd take it,' Charlotte retorted, voice icy cold. 'You know the situation, Geoffrey's told you.'

'That's why it was so funny.'

Charlotte resisted the urge to go and slap Andrew, reminding herself he'd always had a peculiar, some might even say perverted, sense of humour.

'So it's wedding bells, eh? Ding dong and all that malarkey. Congratulations,' Andrew smiled to Charlotte.

'Would you like a drink?' Nell asked Charlotte, seeing how shaken she still was.

Charlotte shook her head.

'I'd like one,' Andrew said.

'Then pour it yourself and I hope it chokes you,' Nell riposted.

'Doubt it'll do that,' he replied, heading for the decanters and glasses.

Charlotte took a deep breath to steady herself. 'Those were a few very nasty moments,' she murmured, shooting Andrew a filthy look.

'Thought I'd pop over and see Pa and Peter,' Andrew declared, taking a deep swallow.

'Pa doesn't work afternoons any more. He's out somewhere with Mrs Ritchie.'

Andrew stared at them in amazement. 'Not working in the afternoons any more, what's come over the old bugger? And who's this Mrs Ritchie?'

'Mrs Ritchie was a friend of Ma's who's staying as a house guest. As for what's come over Pa, who knows! He even goes walking nowadays which was unheard of until recently.'

Andrew gaped at them. 'Walking? I simply don't believe it.'

'It's true,' Nell said. 'And he's given up his pipe.'

Andrew whistled. 'Well, I never.'

'You haven't been home for some time and a lot has happened in the meanwhile,' Nell went on.

'I'll say. You'll tell me he's stopped drinking next.'

'Not quite, but he has cut back considerably,' Nell informed him.

'This is serious. Something must be wrong for him to do all these things.'

'If there is he hasn't said.'

'Hasn't one of you asked him?'

'You know Pa. If he hasn't volunteered the information then he doesn't want to tell us. Asking him would be pointless.'

'Hmmh,' Andrew mused. 'What does Peter think?'

'He's as mystified as we are,' Charlotte replied. Then, eagerly, 'How's Geoffrey?'

'You should know, he writes to you almost every day from all accounts. Lover boy is fine, in the pink. Getting set to go out on some jolly manoeuvres which I'll also be doing when I return.'

72

At which point voices in the hallway announced the arrival home of Murdo and Jean Ritchie.

★ ★ ★

Jean crawled into bed and pulled the bedclothes up to her chin. What a stunning young man, she thought, like a Greek God descended. Amusing too; he'd made her laugh repeatedly over dinner and afterwards.

She then found herself thinking of him in a sexual way, wondering how he'd look undressed. How he'd make love.

Don't be ridiculous, she chided herself. She was old enough to be his mother — indeed, his mother had been her best friend. It would almost be like incest.

She smiled wryly. If Murdo did have marriage in mind that's exactly what she would end up, Andrew's stepmother. What a lark!

It had been so long, so very long, not since Forbes in fact. There had been times when she'd almost screamed from frustration. She was a passionate woman who needed a man in her life, desperately so.

Oh, the memories of the lovemaking with Forbes, he had been excellent in that department, a man who knew how to pleasure a woman.

She thought again of Andrew, that dear sweet boy. She groaned imagining him fondling her, moving within her. Those brown eyes boring into her, those finely chiselled features gazing down at her.

'God,' she moaned. She shouldn't be thinking

like this, it was all wrong. She'd come hoping for the father and now all she could think about was the son, and certainly not platonically either.

She couldn't help herself. She needed release. She pulled up her nightdress and then slid her hand between her legs.

And all the while until release came it was Andrew she thought of.

★ ★ ★

'She didn't!' Wonky gasped.

'She did, at Pa's request. I nearly died of embarrassment. Though I have to admit some of the things she had to say were pretty informative.'

Nell giggled.

'Well, come on, tell us everything,' Wonky urged Charlotte.

Charlotte became coy. 'I don't know if I can bring myself to repeat what she said.'

'Of course you can. I'll kill you if you don't.'

Nell, face a trifle red, giggled again.

'Well, she started off by asking me if I knew what a man and woman did in bed, how babies were made.'

'And?' Wonky's eyes were huge and she'd moved forward to sit right on the edge of her chair.

'I reminded her that I was a country girl and that one couldn't help but observe things.'

Nell covered her mouth with a hand. This was priceless.

Charlotte continued. 'She said that was good.

74

Then she said I wasn't to worry if Geoffrey was too nervous on our wedding night and nothing happened. That occurs quite frequently apparently. I simply wasn't to worry and that nature would take its course in due time.'

Wonky was fascinated. 'Go on.'

'She told me that making love should be a pleasure and not merely a duty. That the woman should enjoy herself as much as the man. She advised me to take a large white handkerchief to bed with me as lovemaking can be pretty messy at times.'

Nell's face was now almost beetroot. 'A large white handkerchief,' she repeated, thinking about that.

'So she advised. She also . . . ' Charlotte broke off and took a deep breath. 'She also said I wasn't to be scared when I saw a man's erect penis for the first time. Some of them can be rather large and give an unexperienced girl quite a fright.'

'How big?' Wonky demanded.

'She didn't exactly say. Only that I wasn't to be put off by size.'

'Anything else?' Wonky queried.

'Well . . . she did mention that it isn't always done in the same way. I mean, there are various ways of doing it.'

'No!' Wonky breathed.

'She didn't go into great detail but according to her some men like doing it like the animals.'

Wonky frowned. 'I don't understand?'

'Well eh . . . You must have seen a bull with a cow?'

Wonky nodded
'Like that.'

'Aaahhh!' Wonky exhaled.

'How demeaning,' Nell declared.

'Exactly what I thought. Quite humiliating. But not nearly as humiliating as what she said next. Even she was embarrassed when she told me, which is something. She was quite matter of fact about what she'd said previously.'

'And what was that?' Wonky queried.

Charlotte shook her head. 'I can't repeat it.'

'Please, cuz?' Wonky pleaded.

'It's too awful for words and doesn't bear thinking about. It had never entered my mind that men could do such a thing.' She shuddered.

'Charlotte!'

Charlotte stared at her cousin. 'Honestly, Wonky, you don't want to hear.'

'But I do. What if my future husband wants to do it to me? I should be prepared in advance.'

'I swear, Wonky, it's too awful to repeat.'

'Then whisper in my ear.'

Charlotte considered that. 'She said it was something boys sometimes did to each other at school and then got a liking for.'

Boys to boys? Wonky couldn't imagine what. Neither could Nell.

'Geoffrey's never doing it to me I can assure you of that,' Charlotte stated firmly, and shuddered again.

'Please, Charlotte?'

She sighed. 'Oh all right. But you'll be revolted, it's quite ghastly.'

Wonky went pale as Charlotte whispered in

76

her ear. Her eyes had been huge before, now they almost popped out of her head.

'That's disgusting!' she exclaimed in horror.

'Do you want to hear?' Charlotte asked Nell, for if she'd told Wonky she might as well tell Nell.

Curiosity got the better of Nell who nodded.

Charlotte crossed to her sister and repeated her whisper.

'Dear God!' Nell said in a strangled voice. 'Surely not?'

Now it was Nell's turn to shudder. The thought was horrendous beyond belief.

'What else did she tell you?' Wonky croaked.

'Nothing as bad as that.'

'Thank the Lord.'

5

TOM COMYN might normally be the dreariest of men but all that changed the moment he stepped into a pulpit where he was transformed into a hellfire preacher.

Murdo groaned inwardly. Would Tom never stop! His sermon, as usual, was going on and on, seemingly without end. Tom's voice reverberated round and round the church, at times a mighty roar as he condemned the sins of humanity.

Murdo glanced sideways at Jean, wondering what she was making of all this. She seemed transfixed.

Charlotte was bored to tears, she'd heard all this countless times before. She'd have done anything to miss coming to church but for her to do so, unless she was ill, wasn't allowed. Murdo, as a pillar of the community and believer, insisted they attended without fail.

Nell shifted on the family pew with the beginnings of cramp in her legs. Surreptitiously she reached down and massaged them through her dress.

Peter was thinking about business, pleased with himself at how he was managing without his father there full time. He wished he wasn't sitting beside Mrs Ritchie whose strong-smelling perfume he found irritating. She must be doused in the stuff he thought.

Murdo was wrong about Jean being transfixed, she was only giving the appearance of being so. She too was thinking, about Murdo.

So far, to her disappointment, nothing had happened between them and she was rapidly coming to the conclusion that her invitation to take a break at Drummond House had been precisely that with no ulterior motive. Murdo had been friendly enough, a perfect host, and they'd spent considerable time together, but conversation and company were all he appeared interested in.

Her thoughts then turned to Andrew sitting beyond the girls. How handsome and dashing he looked that morning, almost good enough to eat. A little shiver ran through her, and she quickly banished some carnal images from her mind; she was in church after all. No place to be thinking such things.

And then she had an idea that brought a soft smile to her face. She'd speak to Murdo about it later.

★ ★ ★

'Can I have a word with you apart, Murdo?' Dr McAllister requested on the way out. He had hung back to wait for Murdo.

'Aye, of course,' Murdo replied. To Jean and the others he said, 'I won't be a moment.'

McAllister and Murdo moved away from the congregation still streaming out of the church.

'As you haven't been to see me for a while

I presume you haven't had any more attacks?' McAllister queried.

'That's right.'

'You're still taking the pills and doing everything Gillespie advised you to do?'

'A pill every morning without fail and I walk miles every afternoon. I still miss my pipe dreadfully, mind, there isn't a single waking moment when I couldn't cheerfully light up. But I don't. And only a couple of drams a day as ordered.'

McAllister nodded his approval. 'How do you feel within yourself?'

'Never better. Fit as a flea in fact.'

'That's grand, Murdo. Just make sure you keep up the regime and hopefully these attacks will be a thing of the past. He's a good man that Gillespie, knows what he's doing.'

'You must come up to the house sometime soon, James, and we'll have those two drams together.'

'I will indeed.'

They shook hands and parted, Murdo rejoining his party and McAllister his wife and family.

★ ★ ★

The Comyns had come to Drummond House for Sunday lunch. Murdo felt obliged to invite them several times a year, occasions he didn't look forward to. What Moira saw in Tom Comyn was, and always had been, beyond him. The man was dry as a stick and humourless.

But there you are, who was to say what one person saw in another. And the pair were happy together, or so Moira had told him often enough.

'Perth is such a lovely city I always think, Jean,' Moira said. They of course knew one another from when Jean had lived in the area.

'It is.'

'I can well understand why you've never thought of moving back.'

'I might have done if I'd any relatives still here, but as you know my parents are both dead and my brother is in Australia.'

Moira nodded. 'Taken so young too. You never know the moment, do you?'

'Amen,' Tom intoned.

Moira's eyes flicked from Jean to Murdo, and she wondered about Jean's visit. Murdo had always sworn he'd never re-marry, but people, even her brother, had been known to change their minds. And Jean was such an attractive woman too, she'd worn well. Murdo could do a lot worse.

Murdo stared at his empty wine glass contemplating indulging himself. Then he remembered his conversation with McAllister and put temptation firmly behind him.

'And how's the army treating you?' Tom Comyn asked Andrew.

'Fine. Our second Battalion's off to India shortly while my Battalion, the first, is staying behind.'

'Exotic place India,' Tom commented. 'Lots of disease there though I believe.'

'So I understand.'

Jean glanced at Murdo and smiled, he smiling in return.

Smiles Moira didn't fail to note. Perhaps there was something in the wind.

'I'm told you have a beautiful house in Perth, Mrs Ritchie,' Andrew said. 'Pa mentioned.'

'It is rather beautiful. You must come and see for yourself one day. Bring a friend, I always have a bottle of Drummond in the house.'

Murdo beamed. 'Well said, Jean.'

'Well, I could hardly buy any other brand, could I?'

'Most certainly not. By the by, Andrew, Mrs Ritchie has suggested that you and she travel back to Perth together. Good idea I thought. You can keep each other company.'

Jean had presented her idea to Murdo before luncheon and he'd instantly agreed.

'I hope you don't mind, Andrew?'

'Not at all, Mrs Ritchie. It will be charming.'

She hoped they managed to be alone in their carriage and then she'd have him all to herself. She shivered at the prospect.

'I say, are you cold, Jean?' Murdo queried.

'Not at all.'

'Are you certain of that?'

'Absolutely.'

Murdo glanced over at the roaring fire and wondered if he should instruct more coal be put on. The dining room seemed warm enough to him.

'If you wish to come up this way again perhaps you'll stay with us at the manse, Jean,'

Moira said provokingly, watching Murdo for his reaction.

Murdo frowned.

'That's a very kind offer, Moira, which I shall perhaps take you up on sometime.'

'Nothing so grand as Drummond House mind, plain fare I'm afraid. But you will be welcome.'

Jean was also wondering at Murdo's reaction. He seemed none too pleased. She had no intention of ever staying with the Comyns whom she found boring in the extreme.

A little later, and not for the first time, Murdo marvelled at Tom's appetite. The man ate like a horse, several horses, yet never put on an ounce.

He watched as Tom waded through three helpings of pudding after having had two full helpings of the main course.

★ ★ ★

'Well, I did enjoy my time at Drummond House,' Jean declared to Andrew as their train pulled out of the station. As she'd hoped they were alone in the carriage.

'I know Pa enjoyed having you there.'

She thought of Murdo who'd come to see them off. She was now more or less convinced that there hadn't been an ulterior motive behind his invitation which was a great pity. Life with Murdo could have been most fulfilling.

'Tell me, Andrew, do you have a lady friend?'

He laughed. 'No such luck, Mrs Ritchie.'

'I find that surprising considering you're such a handsome young chap.'

He regarded her with amusement. 'Not that handsome,' he replied modestly.

'Get away with you, Andrew. You're hiding your light under a bushel. I'm sure you're well aware that you're extremely so.'

Andrew glanced out the window, suddenly embarrassed. There was something about Jean Ritchie which unsettled him. Something he couldn't quite put his finger on. Perhaps it was the way she had of staring so directly at him.

'You're a handsome woman yourself, Mrs Ritchie,' he replied gallantly.

'Ah! A flatterer just like your father,' she teased.

'He can be, can't he?'

'Like father, like son.'

Andrew decided to change the subject. 'Whereabouts in Perth do you live?'

She told him the area and her address. 'Which reminds me, don't forget I've invited you to call on me. I'll take great delight in showing you round my house.'

'I haven't forgotten,' he smiled. 'And there's always a bottle of Drummond in residence.'

And more, she thought to herself. Much more.

★ ★ ★

'This is a pleasant surprise, Moira,' Murdo declared, pecking his sister on the cheek.

'I hope I'm not intruding?'

84

'Not at all.' He'd been preparing to go out for his daily walk but that could now wait for a while.

Moira crossed to a comfy chair and eased herself into it. 'I suppose you're wondering why I'm here having had luncheon with you last Sunday.'

'You're not exactly a regular visitor, Moira.'

'Nothing personal, Murdo, as you're well aware. Being a minister's wife can be most exacting.'

'Quite.'

'So many good works to be done. A whole host of tasks that fall on my shoulders.'

She was becoming more and more pious with the passing of the years, Murdo thought. It didn't suit her. Where was the carefree laughing lassie he remembered? No more, unfortunately.

'So how can I help you?' he asked. 'I presume there's a reason for this.'

'I'm simply being nosy,' she stated baldly. 'Is there something going on between you and Jean Ritchie?'

He stared at her in astonishment. 'How do you mean?'

'It could be you're thinking of remarrying and I wanted you to know if that's the case you have my full approval. Jean Ritchie's a fine woman who'll do you proud. She also has the advantage of being wealthy in her own right so you can be assured it isn't your money she's after.'

Her approval! How bloody impertinent. 'Tom's approval too I take it?' he queried.

'Of course.'

'Well, I'm sorry to disappoint you, Moira. There's nothing of that nature between Jean and myself. I merely asked her to Drummond House because she's such damned good company.'

'Language, Murdo!' Moira exclaimed, wagging a disapproving finger at him.

'I don't know where you got such an idea.'

'I saw the way you two were looking and smiling at one another during luncheon. She's certainly set her cap at you.'

'That's preposterous.' Murdo protested.

'Why should it be? You're a widower, she's a widow. It would make complete sense for the pair of you to get together.'

'I swear to you, Moira, it never even entered my mind. I'll never remarry. Louise was the only woman I'll ever love.'

'Who's talking about love? You said yourself she's good company which means the two of you obviously get on well. Wouldn't another marriage make sense? Do you want to end up on your own in your old age?'

'Peter will never leave this house which goes to him. When he marries he'll stay here with his wife.'

'That's not the same, or won't be, as having someone of your own. Someone to share with.'

She had a point, he thought. It was a fairly grim prospect. But remarry? Never. He was adamant about that.

'And while I'm here, what's all this about you not working afternoons any more. Work is food and drink to you.'

Dammit he thought. He was going to have a

dram. 'Would you care for a drink, Moira?'

'No I would not. You know Tom disapproves of strong drink. A little wine from time to time, yes. But no spirits.'

'There is sherry.'

'No thank you, Murdo,' she stated firmly.

He poured himself a hefty one.

'Well?' she demanded.

'Well what?'

'Not working in the afternoons.'

He sighed. 'This is beginning to sound like the Inquisition.'

'I know you, Murdo. You're up to something. Come on, admit it.'

'I'm nothing of the sort. I simply want Peter to take more responsibility. It's common sense as he'll inherit one day.'

Moira harumphed. 'I don't believe a word of it. You're fibbing. Murdo Drummond.'

'Not so.'

'You've also given up your pipe I hear, and you go walking. *You* walking! I nearly fell over when I heard.'

'There's nothing wrong with walking. It's good for you.'

'But you *hate* walking, always have. It's a well-known fact. And now here you are, walking all over the place apparently. Being sighted everywhere, up hill and down dale. What's going on?'

'Suppose I told you to mind your own business?'

'You're my brother, that makes it my business.'

'I don't pry into your affairs.'

Her face softened. 'I'm worried, Murdo. What's wrong. Are you ill?'

'Do I look it?' he prevaricated.

'Not in the least. To be honest I've never seen you look so fit and well.'

'There you are then!' he declared triumphantly, swallowing the remainder of his dram and pouring another.

'That still doesn't answer my question. Why the changes in the habits of a lifetime?'

He eyed her over the rim of his glass. She was right about being nosy, and knowing Moira she'd persist unless he gave her an acceptable explanation.

'It's poor circulation,' he lied.

She studied him intently.

'I'm doing all this on McAllister's advice. He said I was sitting down too much and not getting enough exercise.'

'Ahh!' she exhaled, believing him.

'And don't you go saying anything to the rest of the family. I don't want them worrying. Have I your word on that, Moira?'

She nodded.

He decided to elaborate a little. 'I was getting pains in my legs which is why I went to McAllister in the first place.'

'Are you still having them?'

'Not a twinge for ages. Nor will I go back to working full-time. What I said about Peter is right enough, it was time I let go of the reins a little. This simply gave me a reason for doing so.' Murdo made a mental note to speak to McAllister, it would be just like Moira to quiz the doctor on his story.

'I still think you should reconsider remarrying, Murdo. I'm sure Louise would have approved.'

'No,' he stated defiantly. 'And that is an end of that. I'll hear no more on the subject. Understand?'

A few seconds ticked by, then Moira replied in a gentle, caring voice, 'I understand.'

'Good.'

Moira rose. 'Now that's settled I'd better be on my way. I have a great deal yet to do this afternoon.'

'I know, good works,' Murdo said, a trace of sarcasm in his voice.

'Precisely.'

He saw her out.

★ ★ ★

'I called you all in here because there's something I wish to clear up,' Murdo announced later that day after dinner. Towards the end of his walk he'd dropped in on James McAllister and put him in the picture. Moira would get nothing out of the good doctor other than affirmation of the poor circulation nonsense.

Peter, Charlotte and Nell looked at him expectantly.

'Your Aunt Moira was here having got some idiotic notion into her head about Jean Ritchie and myself.'

He glared about him. 'Just in case you too are fostering the same delusion I wish to state categorically that there is nothing between Jean and myself. Nothing whatsoever. I enjoy her company, nothing more, nothing less.'

Charlotte glanced at Nell. 'We had wondered, Pa.'

'Well, now you know. Your mother's memory is sacred to me and always will be. There will never be another Mrs Murdo Drummond.'

He paused as a lump came into his throat, and turned away.

'Never,' he repeated quietly.

★ ★ ★

'Are you awake?' Andrew queried, having crawled into the tent he was sharing with Geoffrey on manoeuvres.

Geoffrey opened his eyes. 'Yes.'

'It's damned cold out there. I think we'll have snow before morning.'

Andrew shivered. Another five days before they returned to barracks. It seemed a lifetime away.

Geoffrey closed his eyes again. He'd been thinking about Charlotte and wishing he was with her. The image in his mind was so clear and sharp he could almost smell her personal scent.

'Supper was appalling. Those cooks should be hung, drawn and quartered,' Andrew complained.

'They're doing their best, old boy.'

'Well, their best isn't good enough. I feel as though I've been poisoned.'

Geoffrey chuckled. 'It wasn't that ghastly.'

'To me it was. Muck, pure and simple. When we get back to Perth the first thing I'm going to do when I get the chance is go out for a slap-up meal. Want to come?'

Geoffrey thought how he'd love to go out for a slap-up meal, but with Charlotte not Andrew.

'Well?'

'Certainly.'

'We'll have champagne, the lot. Put this misery behind us.'

Andrew turned out the hurricane lamp and crawled into his cot. 'I'd give anything for a lovely hot bath.'

'Fat chance out here.'

Andrew yawned, thinking how the cold was really sinking into his bones. He was terribly tired.

'Turkey's not doing well. The Bulgarians and Serbs are giving them a proper pasting by all accounts.' He was referring to the current war between Turkey and the Balkan League.

'So I hear.'

'Thousands dead apparently. Poor sods.'

'Who do you think will win?' Geoffrey asked.

'Well, it won't be the Turks unless they buck their ideas up somewhat. Just shows you how an army can be overrated.'

'Do you think we are?'

Andrew laughed. 'Don't be daft. The British Army could take on anyone and win. And the Watch is one of its finest regiments. We're with the cream.'

They were, Geoffrey thought. They most

certainly were. A regiment to be proud of.

'I wonder when I'll get my next leave?' Geoffrey mused aloud.

'Straight to Drummond House and Charlotte, eh?'

'As fast as the Humber will take me.'

'Missing her?'

'Of course. She's the woman I intend marrying.'

'I hope you're going to ask me to be your best man. I'll be frightfully slighted if you don't.'

'I fully intended asking you, nearer to the date that is.'

'Then you're on. I accept.'

'Good show, Andrew.'

'Now let's get some sleep. We're up before the crack.'

'Goodnight, Andrew.'

'Goodnight, future brother-in-law,' Andrew teased.

Geoffrey smiled in the darkness.

★ ★ ★

Jean Ritchie opened a letter that had arrived with that morning's post, a smile coming onto her face as she read it.

The letter was from Andrew proposing a visit. If he didn't receive a reply from her he would know she'd agreed the arrangements.

She felt light as air and extremely happy as she refolded his missive.

'It really is a splendid house, Mrs Ritchie,' Andrew enthused. He and Geoffrey, whom he'd brought along, had just completed the grand tour.

'Why, thank you.'

She escorted them down to her drawing room. 'Now how about some of that Drummond I promised you?'

'Yes please,' both young men chorused in unison.

She gestured towards a solid oak sideboard. 'In the right-hand side, Andrew, perhaps you'd do the honours.'

'Of course.'

Geoffrey took up a position in front of the roaring fire.

'And what about yourself, Mrs Ritchie?' Andrew queried.

'A little sherry would be agreeable.'

Her heart leapt when, on giving her her glass, his hand brushed hers.

'Now tell me all about your manoeuvres, Geoffrey,' she smiled.

'Too boring for words. You don't want to hear about them. Ghastly things.'

'The food was awful,' Andrew chipped in. 'On several occasions I thought I'd been poisoned.'

Jean gave a tinkling laugh. 'Well, I hope my cook does better by you tonight.'

'She certainly couldn't do any worse, and that's a fact.'

This time they all laughed.

They continued making polite conversation until informed that dinner was served.

Jean hooked each by an arm as they went through.

★ ★ ★

Jean took her opportunity after dinner when Geoffrey excused himself and left the room.

'It's been delightful having you here tonight,' she purred.

'I can assure you, Mrs Ritchie, we've both thoroughly enjoyed ourselves. An enchanting evening.'

'I think you can call me Jean when we're alone.'

He sat further back in his chair and stared at her. The suggested informality surprised him, she was an older woman after all. There were conventions.

'If you wish.'

'I do.'

'Then Jean it is when we're alone.'

'I hope you'll come again soon, Andrew, I'd like that. And perhaps next time without the chaperone.' She emphasised the word *without.*

By God, she was flirting with him he realised with shock. He hurriedly glanced down into his drink.

'Well, Andrew?'

'That would be more pleasant.'

'These long winter evenings can be most tedious, don't you agree? Or perhaps you don't?'

'Oh but I do. Especially in the barracks.'

'Then you must think of this as your second home where you're welcome any time day or night.'

He was beginning to see Jean Ritchie in a new light. He had to admit she was attractive, still attractive, considering her age. He swiftly worked out how old his mother would have been. Forty-eight, he calculated which would make Jean Ritchie the same age. Old, but not impossibly so. And terrifically well preserved.

He glanced at her quizzically. 'The family thought there might be something between you and Pa, Jean, but he called us all together to refute that. Said mother's memory was sacred to him and there would never be another Mrs Murdo Drummond.'

There it was, she thought. Confirmation that Murdo was out of the question. So why not his son? A dalliance instead of marriage, if Andrew was interested that was.

She laughed. 'Murdo and I are friends and no more, I assure you, Andrew. I'm well aware he would never look at another woman. He worshipped your mother.'

'Yes,' Andrew agreed.

Jean heard the sound of approaching footsteps. 'Now remember what I said. A second home, any time day or night.'

She'd given Andrew a great deal to think about.

6

'HOW wonderful to meet you at last, Charlotte, Geoffrey has told us so much about you,' Mrs Armitage gushed. Geoffrey had decided it was time Charlotte met his parents and so it had been arranged she'd travel down to Glasgow by train where he'd be waiting for her at the station. She was nervous as a kitten.

Charlotte shook hands with Mrs Armitage while Mr Armitage smiled on.

'How was your journey?' he enquired politely.

'Uneventful, thank you very much. Quite pleasant really.'

'I believe you have snow in Perthshire at the moment.'

'That's right. The first flakes fell early last week.'

They were in the Armitages' parlour, a large room with heavy flock wallpaper and thick floral-patterned curtains. There was a welcoming, cosy atmosphere about it.

'Would you care to sit, Charlotte?' Geoffrey asked.

'Please.'

Mr Armitage rubbed his hands briskly together. 'I thought a little refreshment might be in order. Will you take something?'

Geoffrey shot her a warning glance. His parents would be shocked beyond belief if she asked for whisky and probably deem her a most unsuitable young lady for their son's affections.

'A small sherry would be nice.'

Geoffrey heaved an inward sigh of relief.

'Certainly. And you, Gillian?'

'The same thank you, Robert.'

Mrs Armitage sat facing Charlotte. 'Geoffrey informs us that he's already requested your father for your hand in marriage and that your father has asked he wait six months and then request again.'

'That's correct, Mrs Armitage,' Charlotte replied.

'A wise precaution,' Mr Armitage said, handing Charlotte her sherry.

'Most wise,' Mrs Armitage agreed.

'Better safe than sorry,' Mr Armitage went on. 'Marriage is a huge step after all.'

'We both love one another dearly and that won't change,' Geoffrey declared stoutly.

'I understand your mother has passed on,' Mrs Armitage said, sympathy in her voice.

'Quite some time ago. In childbirth.'

'Your father must have been devastated.'

'He was, Mrs Armitage. They were devoted to each other. He's never got over her loss.'

Mrs Armitage nodded her understanding.

'So your father brought you up,' Mr Armitage stated.

'Yes he did. There were various nannies along the way because of Pa's business commitments but he did the best he could.'

Geoffrey produced his silver cigarette case

which caused Mrs Armitage to screw up her nose in disgust. 'Dreadful habit, don't you agree, my dear?'

Charlotte smiled. 'I can't say it bothers me.'

'Well, I wish he'd stop. The house always reeks after Geoffrey's been home.'

Geoffrey lit up.

'Can't say I approve either. But there you are. Chap's too old now for me to forbid him.'

'So, Charlotte,' said Mrs Armitage, settling herself deeper into her chair. 'Tell us more about yourself. We'd like to know all.'

★ ★ ★

'Isn't she a stunner!' Geoffrey declared enthusiastically to his father, the women having retired and the men staying on for a nightcap.

'She is, I'll grant you that. But looks aren't everything, Geoffrey. They often fade all too soon.'

'There's more to it than her looks, Father, it's Charlotte herself.'

'Are you certain about that?'

'Indeed I am.'

'Hmmh.' Robert Armitage mused into his brandy glass. 'Have to admit I was taken by the lass as was your mother which she'll no doubt confirm when I join her shortly.'

'I have your approval then?'

'I can see no reason why not. She'll make a welcome addition to the family.'

Geoffrey beamed, which he'd been doing on and off all evening. That was that out of the way. Not that he'd doubted Charlotte would make a good impression on his parents. He hadn't. It was simply good, and a relief, to have his judgement confirmed.

★ ★ ★

Charlotte was sitting at a vanity table in the room she'd been allocated staring at her reflection in the mirror and thinking about the evening which had gone off even better than she'd hoped.

What a lovely couple the Armitages were, so kind and understanding. It was foolish of her to have been so nervous beforehand, but despite Geoffrey's reassurances they might have turned out to be complete horrors.

She wondered what Geoffrey and his father were saying. Talking about her undoubtedly, Geoffrey getting his father's reaction to meeting her. She was certain, and there was no arrogance about this, that it would be favourable.

She unpinned her hair and shook it loose, then slowly began brushing it. She'd considered bringing Jenny along but had decided against that. She'd just have to do her own hair in the morning.

How long she wondered before the taps on the door? For she and Geoffrey had agreed a code before entering the house. Two taps meant all was well, three and it wasn't.

She thought of the following morning when she and Geoffrey were going shopping before she took the train back to Pitlochry. There were all manner of items she wanted to buy and what fun it would be doing so, especially with Geoffrey accompanying her.

She wished there had been an opportunity for a goodnight kiss but that had been impossible. Closing her eyes she imagined it instead.

She didn't hear any footsteps but suddenly there was a double tap on her door.

Charlotte smiled at herself in the mirror. As she'd thought, they'd taken to her as she'd taken to them.

All was well.

★ ★ ★

Murdo paused beside a pile of wooden boxes to watch with approval the bottling taking place. The women, all local of course, were doing the menial tasks, the men the semi-skilled labour.

The gaffer in charge came over and touched the brim of his cap. 'Good morning, Mr Drummond.'

'And how are you today, Jamie?'

'Just dandy, sir.'

'Everything going well?'

'As you can see, sir. No problems here.'

Murdo cast his eye along the line of workers 'Where's Isa McFarlane? She appears missing.'

'Down with the flu, sir. I sent her home yesterday in a terrible state. Her cousin Mary says Dr McAllister has called and confined her to bed until better.'

Murdo made a mental note to send round a wee something. This common touch was one of the many things that endeared him to his workforce who considered him a good boss. It was often said that, as employers went, there didn't come any better than old man Drummond.

Not that he was a soft touch, far from it. And as he paid a fair day's wages he expected a fair day's graft in return. But fair was the operative word, Murdo Drummond was always that.

'Carry on then, Jamie,' Murdo instructed, and went on his way.

★ ★ ★

Andrew was surprised when Jean Ritchie answered the door herself. She smiled at him. 'Come in. Come in.

'I've given the staff the night off,' she explained, helping him out of his coat.

Andrew still wasn't convinced he was doing the right thing. What if he'd misinterpreted her? Whatever happened, he was determined not to make a fool of himself. Jean would have to make her intentions absolutely clear.

'You'll need a dram to warm you up. It's cold out there,' she said.

'It certainly is.'

They went through to her drawing room where a cheery fire blazed.

'I've had a little supper laid in the dining room for later,' she said, opening the door on the right-hand side of the oak sideboard.

'You look very pretty tonight,' he declared gallantly.

'Why, don't I always?' she teased.

That flustered him. 'Well yes, of course. I mean eh . . . ' He broke off in confusion.

'Prettier than usual, is that it? I have gone to a lot of effort.'

'Yes, precisely.'

She could see how nervous he was, and on edge. When she gave him his glass she noted the hand that accepted it was trembling.

'Now come and sit beside me here on the sofa and we'll talk,' she said.

Slowly she began to calm him and put him at his ease.

★ ★ ★

Andrew didn't know how it happened, one moment they were chatting, the next she was in his arms, the two of them kissing. She was an expert at that he soon realised.

'Why don't we go upstairs?' she suggested after a while.

His nervousness returned and he didn't reply.

'Andrew?'

'I, eh . . . I . . . '

'Tell me something, and don't be shy,' she said, taking his hand and placing it on a breast. She'd already guessed. 'You've never known a woman, have you?'

He shook his head.

'I thought as much. Well, you're not to worry. Leave everything to me. I have been married don't forget.'

'Jean, I'm not certain we should be doing this.'

'And yet you came tonight. You may be inexperienced where women are concerned but you're hardly naive, Andrew. You knew full well what I intended.'

He swallowed hard. 'Yes,' he whispered.

'Is it my age?'

'Partly, I suppose. And that you were a friend of my mother's.'

'The friendship is true enough. But I get so lonely, Andrew, so very lonely. Surely there's no harm in us seeing one another?'

'Seeing, no. But what you're proposing is beyond that.'

'You're a grown man, Andrew, and I'm a woman. Surely that's all that matters. A woman who wants you very much. And don't think our involvement will give you cause for concern. I know nothing can come of this in the long run but in the meantime why not just enjoy ourselves.'

'You'd be discreet?'

'Totally, I swear. I have my reputation to think about after all. I've presumed you'd be the same.'

'Oh yes,' he assured her.

He squeezed her breast and immediately felt his manhood twitch and start to rise. He knew then there was no drawing back, that he'd go through with it. Going to bed with a woman was something he'd dreamed of for a long time.

Jean lifted the hand from her breast and rose, drawing him off the sofa.

'You won't have any regrets, I promise you.'

And with that she led him towards the door.

‘It's not a race, Andrew, slow down,’ she whispered throatily.

‘Sorry.’

‘There's nothing to be sorry about. Just slow down, make the pleasure last.’

He stared down at the naked body writhing beneath him, unable to believe this was actually happening. What a figure, her breasts large and voluptuous. The first naked breasts he'd ever seen.

So long, so very long, Jean thought. How she'd missed this. And what a stallion Andrew had turned out to be. Oh, she would teach him, many many things that Forbes had taught her.

‘Stop for a moment,’ she instructed.

‘Can't.’

‘Yes you can, but stay inside me.’ She offered him a nipple which he greedily took into his mouth like a starving baby.

She smiled as she stroked the back of his head. Dear Andrew, dear sweet Andrew.

‘Now the other one,’ she said.

He groaned and, despite her having told him to stop, started to move again.

Her lips drew back and shudder after shudder racked through her. When they'd subsided she brought her legs up round his waist as he plunged, though far less vigorously than before, on and on.

Then Andrew cried out, arched his back and then collapsed onto her sweat-slicked body, his own heaving from exertion.

Jean closed her eyes, in seventh heaven. 'That was wonderful, darling,' she whispered.

Andrew pulled himself up and out of her.

'Well?' she queried, a smile of sexual satisfaction on her face.

'I can't describe . . . I can't even begin to describe . . . '

She gave a low laugh. 'Not as you'd imagined, eh?'

'Far, far better.'

He was hers, she thought. There was no saying for how long, but for now he was hers. That was all that mattered.

A little later he mounted her again.

★ ★ ★

'I've got news, Miss Charlotte,' Jenny the maid, eyes shining, stated. Picking up a silver-backed brush she began grooming Charlotte's hair.

Charlotte stared at her in the mirror she was sitting facing. 'Oh?'

'I'm to be wed, miss.'

Charlotte's face lit up. 'Congratulations, Jenny. Who's the lucky chap?'

'Hamish Bell, miss. We've been stepping out for a while now.'

That was news to Charlotte who'd had no idea the maid was courting. Rising, she warmly embraced Jenny. 'I couldn't be more delighted for you. I know Hamish, he's a splendid young man.'

Jenny giggled. 'The ceremony will be next June, miss, when I'll move into Hamish's cottage. Oh it'll be grand right enough.' The cottage came with Hamish's job — he's a ghillie.

'Have you told Pa yet?'

'No, miss. I wanted you to be the first to hear seeing how I'm more or less your personal maid and all.'

Hardly that, Charlotte thought. The majority of her duties were general ones.

'Will you come to the wedding, miss?'

'Wild horses wouldn't keep me away, Jenny. I expect we'll all be there if asked.'

'Oh yes, miss.'

Charlotte resumed her seat and Jenny her brushing. 'Now the dress, what will you do about that?'

'Well, miss, I thought . . . '

Jenny's plans tumbled out of her as she dressed Charlotte's hair.

* * *

'What's wrong with you today?' Geoffrey enquired casually having come across Andrew standing staring distractedly out across the parade ground.

Andrew blinked and brought himself out of his reverie. 'Pardon?'

Geoffrey repeated himself. 'You've been like it all day I've noticed. Something up?'

Andrew's expression became sheepish. 'I have got a lot on my mind I'm afraid.'

'Want to talk about it?'

Andrew shook his head. It was Jean he'd been

thinking about, Jean whom he couldn't keep out of his thoughts. His whole world had changed, a new dimension added, since taking up with her. He was rapidly becoming obsessed with Jean Ritchie. That body, that magnificent body. The experience of making love to her had been as though Heaven had come to Earth.

'Well I'd look a bit more lively if I was you, you don't want the C.O. breathing down your neck.'

'Yes, you're right.'

'Certain there's nothing you want to discuss?'

Andrew would have loved to tell Geoffrey about Jean and what it was like being with her. But discretion, discretion.

'I'd best get on,' Andrew declared.

'And so should I.'

They parted, each going his separate way.

★ ★ ★

Murdo was in the study savouring his second dram of the evening and thinking about Jean Ritchie. He'd always sworn . . . But was Moira right? It wasn't that he was after sex. But the company . . . Aye well, that was something else.

If he did speak to Jean, and it was a big if, the nature of the relationship would have to be clearly spelt out.

She was alone after all, and so was he.

★ ★ ★

107

It was Andrew's third visit alone to Jean and he'd only just arrived. He was impatient to get upstairs to the bedroom.

'I had a letter from your father today,' Jean announced.

That startled him. 'Really?'

'He's asked me to Drummond House for Hogmanay. Says your family always has a gathering at that time.'

Andrew nodded. 'We do.'

'Should I accept?'

Andrew considered that. 'I don't see why not. Though it's hardly my decision to make.'

'I don't want you feeling embarrassed in my presence.'

He grinned. 'What I'll be feeling won't be embarrassment, Jean, and I won't be able to do anything about it.'

'No?' she teased.

'Hardly in the family home. Wouldn't be right somehow. And what if I was seen coming or going? What a scandal! Pa would be outraged.'

'You could always be very careful coming and going,' she further teased.

'Not worth the risk, old thing.'

She wagged a finger at him. 'Less of the old if you don't mind. That's a touchy subject.'

He went to her and took her into his arms, thinking how gorgeous she smelled. 'I didn't mean it that way. Figure of speech that's all.'

'I should hope so too.'

'Oh, Jean,' he whispered, and then his mouth was on hers, she melting against him.

Hogmanay is Scotland's greatest festival and celebrated with enormous enthusiasm, the revelries always accompanied with copious amounts of alcohol. Murdo had already made up his mind that he wouldn't be sticking to his daily quota. 'To hell with it,' he'd muttered to himself on making that decision.

Andrew and, to Charlotte's enormous delight, Geoffrey had managed leave, so they were in the throng now filling the Drummond drawing room.

Also present were Geoffrey's parents who, at Murdo's written invitation, had travelled up from Glasgow and would be spending the entire holiday at Drummond House.

The Comyns were there and the McAllisters, the good doctor turning a blind eye and not making comment as dram after dram vanished down Murdo's throat. He understood, Hogmanay was Hogmanay.

Jean Ritchie was chatting to Donald Skene, a local landowner and widower like Murdo. His grown-up daughter Alison, a spinster in her late thirties, stood listening on. The reason she was a spinster, despite the fact her father was a wealthy man, was obvious. She was extremely unattractive to the point that not even her father's wealth had ever tempted a suitor.

Peter went over to talk to Jack Riach, a friend of his, now in conversation with Wonky. Jack and he often went shooting together.

'Enjoying yourself?' he asked Jack on joining

them. A glance at the clock en route had told him there was still a little over an hour till midnight.

'Extremely. A splendid 'do', but then it always is.'

Wonky had on a plainish blue taffeta dress that she'd worn countless times before and which she now hated. But, due to lack of family cash, her wardrobe was limited and would remain so. She looked over at Nell in a new cream-coloured gown. What she wouldn't have given for a gown like that! It not only suited Nell to a T, it somehow made her appear slimmer.

Wonky brought her attention back to the men and Jack in particular. She'd been wildly attracted to Jack, a bachelor like Peter, for years but so far he hadn't shown the slightest interest. She lived in hope.

'Go on, ask him now,' Charlotte urged Geoffrey.

'He's busy chatting.'

'He'll be that all night. You'll just have to break in.'

Geoffrey had a swallow of whisky to give him courage, then set his glass aside.

'Good luck,' Charlotte breathed, squeezing his hand.

Geoffrey headed for Murdo.

'Excuse me, sir, may I have a private word?'

Murdo noted the look of determination on Geoffrey's face. Glancing round the room he spotted Charlotte watching them intently. 'If you wish.'

'Thank you, sir. Could we go somewhere perhaps?'

Murdo guessed what was coming. 'Follow me.'

They went to the study where Murdo closed the door. 'Yes, Geoffrey?'

'Sir, I'll get straight to the point. I know I agreed to wait six months before again requesting Charlotte's hand which I will honour if you insist. However, I can assure you, sir, neither she nor I will change our minds no matter what.'

Murdo nodded. He fully believed that.

'The thing is, sir, tonight would be, with my parents here and your family present, an ideal opportunity to announce our engagement.'

Murdo nodded again. The lad was right. It *was* an ideal opportunity.

'There's such a short while left to the end of the six months?'

'Whose idea was it you speak to me?' Murdo queried softly.

'Charlotte's, sir.'

'I see.'

Murdo crossed to the mantelpiece and leant against it, gazing at Louise's photograph. He remembered only too clearly what it was like to be newly in love. 'Have you bought a ring yet?' he asked over his shoulder.

'No, sir.'

Murdo knew Louise would have approved of what he was going to do next. 'Would you humour an old man, Geoffrey?'

Geoffrey frowned. 'Yes, sir. Anything, sir.'

Murdo sighed and went to his bureau where he opened one of the drawers. He reached for a small black box that lay inside. Opening the box he stared at its contents. He sniffed.

Geoffrey was mystified. Whatever was going on? He waited patiently while Murdo continued to gaze into the box.

Murdo fumbled in the box which he then snapped shut and replaced in the drawer. Turning to Geoffrey he smiled.

'This was my wife's engagement ring,' he explained, showing it to Geoffrey. 'If you agree I would very much like it now to be Charlotte's.'

Geoffrey accepted the ring when Murdo handed it to him. When it caught the light it was a blaze of diamonds, a large centre stone surrounded by smaller ones.

'I, eh . . . I don't know what to say, sir.'

'Yes or no would do.'

'Oh yes, sir, thank you, sir. But are you certain about this?'

'Quite, Geoffrey.'

'Then thank you, sir. I take it we now have your consent?'

Murdo nodded, suddenly afraid to speak because of the huge lump in his throat. He turned away and waved Geoffrey to leave him.

'Thank you again, sir,' Geoffrey said at the door. 'I promise you I'll be a good husband to your daughter. She'll never have a moment's regret marrying me.'

Murdo found his voice again. 'Just one thing, don't say anything to anyone, except Charlotte of course, until I make the announcement.'

'I understand, sir.'
Geoffrey left Murdo alone with his thoughts.

★ ★ ★

Murdo had always had a theatrical streak. He waited till five minutes to midnight before calling the gathering to order and attention. He then broke the news.

Wild applause erupted as Geoffrey slipped the ring onto a blushing Charlotte's finger.

As he kissed her, the clock chimed the hour heralding the arrival of 1913 and the room erupted with cheers.

7

ANDREW couldn't sleep; for hours he'd tossed and turned and even tried his old childhood trick of counting sheep, to no avail. The trouble was Jean Ritchie who was in a bedroom a few doors down the corridor. He simply couldn't stop thinking about her.

He groaned with frustration. He'd had no idea her close proximity would affect him like this. Visions of her naked voluptuousness and of them making love kept flashing through his mind.

If he'd known this was going to be the case he would have told her not to come to Drummond House. And she was going to be with them for another three whole days and nights! The thought of that was . . . well almost unendurable.

The party had gone extremely well, he reflected. But then as Jack Riach had commented, their Hogmanay ones always did. And what a surprise Geoffrey and Charlotte getting engaged like that. It had certainly leant an added zing to the occasion.

What would 1913 bring for him? More of the same he supposed. His duties at the barracks and . . . Jean.

He drew in a deep breath. He daren't go to her, that would be foolhardy in the extreme. What if he was seen? Though that was highly unlikely on this morning of all mornings. It would be a lie-in for everyone, including the servants who'd had just as late a night as the family and guests. The whole house was undoubtedly fast asleep with the exception of him.

Dare he risk it? Even a short while with her would suffice, rid this fever that had gripped him.

'To hell with it,' he muttered through clenched teeth. He had to have her, simply had to.

★ ★ ★

Murdo woke with a headache and the desperate need to go to the toilet. He shivered as he slipped into his dressing gown. If it was cold in the bedroom it would be damned freezing in the toilet. But needs must.

Murdo paused outside Jean's door and frowned on hearing muted sounds coming from within. What was she up to? And then it dawned on him what those sounds were the product of.

Dear God, she had someone with her! The woman was being rogered, no doubt about it. He flushed with embarrassment when she gave a low moan of pleasure. The sort of moan he remembered only too well from his marriage.

But *who* with her? That was the question. It certainly couldn't be Robert Armitage, he was tucked up with Gillian. And it certainly wouldn't be Geoffrey. So, apart from himself, that left . . .

He swallowed hard. Peter and Andrew were the only other males in the house which meant it had to be one of them. That staggered him. Why, she was old enough to be their mother!

Murdo shook his head in bewilderment. How could he of all people so misjudge someone. He would never have believed Jean Ritchie capable of behaving like this. Not only sleeping with one of his sons, but under his own roof.

For a brief moment he considered throwing open the door and confronting the pair of them, finding out which one of his sons it was before ordering the baggage from his house. Then discarded that idea for what possible purpose would it serve.

Then, 'Oh, Andrew!' he distinctly heard.

Well, that was that problem solved. It was his younger son in there with Jean Ritchie. The thought of them together was obscene. He found the thought of a woman her age with his younger son quite repugnant.

And to think he'd actually considered marrying her, making her his wife while all the time she was sleeping with his son.

He moved silently on towards the toilet.

★ ★ ★

'You're quiet, Murdo,' Jean commented over breakfast.

He eyed her coldly. 'Am I?'

'Hardly a peep out of you.'

He grunted.

'Well, it is New Year's Day,' she burbled on.

'The morning after the night before.'

His fork halted halfway to his mouth. She was certainly right about that, though the party wasn't what he had in mind.

Andrew breezed in. 'Sorry I'm late. Just couldn't get myself out of bed.'

Murdo noted the look that passed between Andrew and Jean. A conspiratorial one if ever there was. His stony expression became even harder.

It wasn't that he disapproved of Andrew having a sexual relationship — young men had to sow their wild oats after all. He'd done so himself. There had been several women before Louise. It was the fact Andrew had done it under his roof with a woman who'd once been his mother's friend.

He glanced again at Jean. Just look at her, a picture of innocence, as though butter wouldn't melt in her mouth. And what, if he had taken Moira's advice, would have happened when they were married — he was fairly certain she would have accepted — would she, lovemaking denied her by him, continue on with Andrew? Would Andrew have continued with the affair, cuckolding his own father with his stepmother? The thought sickened him.

'Bit liverish today, Pa?' Peter asked. 'You took more on board last night than you have for a while.'

'A bit,' Murdo grunted.

'I say, these kippers are excellent,' Geoffrey enthused which won him an admiring glance from Charlotte.

117

Andrew sat facing Jean. 'And how are you this morning, Mrs Ritchie?'

'Couldn't be better,' she smiled in reply.

'I feel on top form myself.' His time with her had been wonderful, and he had been totally drained when he'd eventually crept back to his room where he'd instantly fallen into a deep sleep. He was already wondering if he dared a return visit that night.

'Pa.'

Murdo looked up at Charlotte who quite clearly was radiantly happy. 'I did say to you last night, but thank you again for Mother's ring.'

Murdo's expression softened. 'Been in my mind for years.'

Charlotte twisted the ring. 'It fits so perfectly And . . . ' She hesitated. 'I never knew you'd kept it. You've never once said.'

'I kept a number of your Mother's things that I've never mentioned. Personal things, you understand.'

'What about her wedding ring, Pa?' Nell queried.

He nodded. 'That's one of them.' It resided in the same black box from which he'd taken the engagement ring.

'Any other jewellery?' Nell further asked.

'Bits and pieces. Your mother was never a great one for jewellery.'

'She did have a beautiful pearl necklace. I recall that quite distinctly,' Jean said.

Murdo regarded her with an icy stare. When she left after her visit she would never enter his house again. Not while he was alive.

'That's in my study along with the other items,' Murdo said, directing his reply to Nell. What he didn't say was that he occasionally took out these various bits and pieces and fondled them in memory.

'I love pearls,' Nell declared.

It was daft keeping these things shut away, Murdo thought. Far better, now the girls were grown up, for them to have them. It wasn't as though they'd be leaving the family after all. With the exception of the wedding ring that is, he'd hold onto that.

'Then you shall have the necklace,' he stated gruffly.

Nell's eyes flew open. 'Oh, Pa!'

'And there's a cameo brooch she was fond of. You can have that, Charlotte, if you wish.'

'Please, Pa.'

Murdo pushed his plate away and laid his napkin aside. 'I'm going out for a walk to clear my head. I'll see you all later.'

He had to stop himself shooting Jean Ritchie a withering look as he left.

★ ★ ★

Murdo gasped and clutched his chest, his face screwing up in pain. It only lasted for a few seconds, and then the agony eased.

Murdo staggered over to a large rock and sat. He sucked in breath after breath.

'Damn,' he muttered. 'Damn damn damn.' This was because he'd overdone it the night

119

before, had to be. It was his first attack since seeing Mr Gillespie.

He'd have to be more careful in future he told himself. No more exceptions to the rule, not even at Hogmanay. He didn't want to be pushing up the daisies quite yet.

He sat for a good ten minutes to recover before getting to his feet again and returning the way he'd come.

★ ★ ★

'I wonder when I'll get engaged and who it'll be to?' Wonky mused to Nell. She'd come to Drummond House to have another look at Charlotte's ring only to find that Charlotte and Geoffrey had gone out for a spin in his car.

'Only time will tell,' Nell replied.

'Or when you'll get engaged and to whom,' Wonky further speculated.

Nell sighed, 'If I ever do get engaged that is.'

'Of course you will!' Wonky assured her. 'It's only a matter of when.'

'I sometimes wonder . . . ' Nell trailed off. Would her prince come one day? She fervently hoped so. It would be ghastly ending up as an old maid. She thought of Alison Skene, and shuddered. There was no doubt in Alison's case.

'When I get married I wish it to be to someone fabulously rich,' Wonky declared. 'And we'll have six children, three of each.'

Nell laughed. 'Does he have to be rich?'

120

'Oh yes, most definitely.' She became introspective. 'You forget I've been relatively poor all my life, Nell, a minister's stipend doesn't go all that far, believe me.' A trace of jealousy crept into her voice. 'Unlike you and Charlotte. You've had everything from a doting, wealthy father.'

True, Nell thought. Murdo had spoiled them, though the reason for that was obvious. 'And what about love?' she asked softly. 'Suppose you fall for a poor man?'

Wonky bit her lip.

'Well?'

'I shall try very hard only to fall for a rich man,' Wonky replied defiantly.

Nell had intended telling Wonky about the pearl necklace Murdo had promised her, but now decided not to. She didn't want to rub her cousin's face in it.

'Jack Riach would be perfect,' Wonky stated dreamily.

'He is a nice chap.'

'He's more than that. He's scrummy.'

Jack didn't appeal to Nell at all. Oh, he was pleasant enough, but that was as far as it went where she was concerned.

'Except he's never shown the slightest interest despite my making it clear I was interested in him,' Wonky went on.

'Not the slightest?'

Wonky shook her head. 'I obviously don't appeal to him. God knows why.'

'Why does anyone appeal to anyone else? It just happens that's all. It's either there or it isn't. Look at Charlotte and Geoffrey, that was love at first sight.'

'Lucky thing,' Wonky said, meaning Charlotte. 'Yes she is, I agree.'

'So handsome too,' Wonky mused, thinking what she wouldn't have given for it to have been her Geoffrey had fallen for.

'Oh, how I wish I could get away from here,' Wonky went on. 'But as you know, Father won't hear of it. I have to stay at home and be the dutiful, well-brought-up daughter.'

'There are worse things in life than being that.'

'Are there?' Wonky sighed wistfully.

* * *

Peter was standing staring out of his bedroom window when Geoffrey and Charlotte arrived back in the Humber. They were both laughing as they emerged from the car, Geoffrey dashing round to open Charlotte's door and assist her out. Geoffrey quickly pecked her on the cheek.

What made him so different to other men? Peter wondered. It wasn't as though he wasn't manly, no one could ever accuse him of that. But when it came to women . . . They simply left him cold.

Grizelda McPherson had been after him again the previous night. Grizelda had the sort of figure most young women would have died for. She was intelligent too, you could always have a good conversation with Grizelda.

At least he had his job, he thought. He enjoyed

hat. And his friends, Jack Riach for example. They were a spiffing lot. Great fun most of he time.

Ah well, he was as the good Lord had made 1im. He could only presume there must be a reason for that.

★ ★ ★

Murdo entered his study and sat down. He vas dying for a dram but forbade himself from 1aving one. That incident out on his walk had rightened him more than he cared to admit. He 1gain told himself he'd have to be more careful n future.

He thought again of Jean and Andrew. Should 1e say something to the lad? He pondered hat.

No, he decided. It might cause a rift between Andrew and himself which he didn't want. Best et things go on as they were.

How on earth had Andrew become involved vith Jean? he wondered yet again. And how :ould she possibly bring herself to go to bed vith her friend's son? Why, it was almost like ncest. Louise would have been horrified.

Had it happened during Jean's previous visit? Then he remembered they'd travelled back o Perth together. Had the relationship been parked off then? He supposed he'd never know or he'd never ask and Andrew would hardly rolunteer the information.

What, though, if the lad was serious? Surely 1ot. The age difference was far too great for anything to come of the relationship. It was a transitory thing, had to be.

Please God.

★ ★ ★

'I can't tell you how delighted we are with your engagement,' Gillian Armitage said to Charlotte, having found her alone in a small sitting room, Geoffrey temporarily off tinkering with the Humber.

'Why thank you.'

Gillian beamed at her future daughter-in-law 'Such a good match I think. The pair of you are so well suited.'

'I believe so.'

Gillian sat beside Charlotte on a floral-patterned sofa and took one of Charlotte's hands in hers. 'I'm looking forward to being a grandmother. I hope you won't keep me waiting too long after you're married.'

Charlotte blushed. 'That's entirely up to nature, Mrs Armitage.'

'Of course it is, but you know what I mean.'

'I will certainly be doing my duty, Mrs Armitage, you can rest assured of that.' She recalled her conversation with Jean Ritchie, not a duty but something to be enjoyed. However duty seemed the correct word to use in these circumstances.

'His father always wanted him to follow him into the firm you know, but Geoffrey had other ideas.'

124

'Yes, he's mentioned.'

'A very strong-willed person is our Geoffrey. And he adores the army. Simply adores it. Both Robert and I are quite certain he'll go far.'

Charlotte smiled. 'Andrew speaks highly of him. One who's well liked by his fellow officers and men alike.'

It pleased Gillian to hear that. 'It was so kind of your father to invite us here. We're both having a wonderful time. I must say, I like your family. All of them without exception.'

'And we all like you and Mr Armitage. Nell remarked on that earlier.'

At which point they were interrupted by Geoffrey's return.

After a further short conversation Gillian left the young lovers to themselves.

It was all very satisfactory, she thought. Very satisfactory indeed.

★ ★ ★

'I'll call in next Wednesday evening,' Andrew whispered to Jean as he escorted her to the Rolls-Royce which would take her to the station.

'I'll be expecting you.'

He wished he could kiss her goodbye, but that was out of the question.

Jean climbed into the Rolls to which her luggage had already been strapped. She waved to Andrew as the Rolls purred away.

She leant back against the leather upholstery and frowned. Murdo had wished her a gruff goodbye at the conclusion of breakfast and that had been that. His manner had been distinctly cold over the past few days, something she hadn't mentioned to Andrew and Andrew hadn't seemed to have noticed.

Did Murdo suspect, or even *know* about them. She couldn't imagine how. Andrew had only come to her room that one night and assured her afterwards he hadn't been seen.

So why the change in Murdo's attitude? Was he merely guessing or was there more to it than that? He'd been friendly enough when she'd arrived, and then the change.

Perhaps he wasn't feeling well. Perhaps ... No, it wasn't that, he'd been friendly enough to the Armitages. It had only been her he'd been chilly towards.

So why?

If he did know then how he'd found out was beyond her.

★ ★ ★

Charlotte found Miss MacQueen in the linen cupboard where she was counting out sheets. Miss MacQueen was their housekeeper, an austere woman in her fifties who ran the house smoothly and efficiently. The staff, with the exception of Cook and McPhie, were said to be terrified of her. A hard woman, though fair and not unkind.

Little was known of Miss MacQueen other than she came originally from the Isle of Skye, but rumour had it she'd had a beau in her youth, a fisherman who'd been drowned at sea.

A tragedy she'd never fully recovered from.

'How are you today, Miss MacQueen?' Charlotte enquired. As the elder female of the family it was her task to act as the lady of the house and deal with the housekeeper and cook.

'Fine thank you, Miss Charlotte. Though displeased with McPhie.'

Oh dear, Charlotte thought. Here we go again. Miss MacQueen and McPhie didn't get on.

'What is it this time?'

'I've asked him twice to mend the runny tap in the laundry room which he still hasn't done.' Besides being chauffeur McPhie was also the odd job man round Drummond House.

'I see.'

Miss MacQueen sniffed. 'He's a law unto himself that man.'

'Quite,' Charlotte agreed.

'Would you care to speak to him. He'll take far more notice of you than me.'

Which was true enough, Charlotte thought. 'I'll do that right away. I'll see if I can find him. Is there anything else?'

'Not for the moment thank you.'

'Right then,' said Charlotte, turning to go.

'Oh, Miss Charlotte!'

Charlotte stopped and turned again. Miss MacQueen's usually stern features softened. 'I haven't had a proper chance to congratulate you on your engagement. I'm very happy for you.'

For a moment Miss MacQueen's eyes took on a faraway look and Charlotte wondered if she was thinking of her long dead beau. Then the look was gone.

Charlotte smiled. 'Exciting, isn't it?'

'Very.'

Charlotte didn't know why she did what she did next, but somehow it seemed right. She went to Miss MacQueen and kissed her on the cheek.

'Thank you. I appreciate your congratulations.' And with that she hurried off to try and find McPhie.

When she was gone the faraway look returned to Miss MacQueen's eyes and it was some minutes before she returned to what she'd been doing.

* * *

'What do you think of women having the vote Pa?' Nell asked. The family were in the drawing room, Murdo reading while Charlotte and Peter played a board game.

Murdo glanced up at his daughter and frowned. 'I'm not certain really. One thing I am certain about is that I don't believe in violence.'

'You mean Mrs Pankhurst?' Emmeline Pankhurst was due in court the following day on bomb charges relating to the attack the previous week when an explosion had wrecked Lloyd George's new golf villa at Walton Heath in Surrey. No one had been hurt but workmen had been due to start only twenty minutes after the bomb went off. According to newspaper reports the explosion was so strong some local residents had thought it an earthquake.

Murdo nodded. 'Dreadful woman to have done what she did. A quite outrageous act. It's a mercy no one was killed.'

'There are many think she's a heroine.'

Peter glanced across at Nell. 'She could easily have been a murderess and there's nothing heroic about that.'

'It's what she stands for I'm asking about. Not the woman herself.'

'Women and the vote!' Peter laughed. 'Stuff and nonsense. What do women know about politics and the like? They should leave all that to men.'

Charlotte regarded him coldly. 'I don't see why women shouldn't have the vote. They comprise half the population after all. Your ideas are quite outmoded, brother dear.'

'Are they indeed,' he replied, voice dripping sarcasm.

'Pa, you haven't answered my question,' Nell prompted.

'It's something to which I haven't given a great deal of thought,' Murdo confessed. 'But yes, I believe the day will come when they will get the vote. Though I think that day is still far off. Considerably so in fact.'

Peter laughed again. 'They'll never get it, Pa. Not in a thousand years. You mark my words, it simply won't be allowed. The whole thing is quite preposterous.'

'I suppose you think we're all feather-brained idiots,' Charlotte accused hotly.

Peter shrugged.

'And I'm included in that generalisation.'

'And me,' pouted Nell.

'Maybe Mrs Pankhurst should have tried to blow up you and your beliefs,' Charlotte muttered.

'That's enough,' Murdo admonished her.

'Do we have a couple of budding suffragette here?' Peter teased.

'Fat chance we have of being suffragettes in Dalneil,' Nell retorted.

'You could always chain yourself to the distillery,' Peter further teased. 'That would be a fine sight. Or how about the pub? That would be a laugh.'

Charlotte and Nell glared at him. 'For someone who's reputedly, by gender that is supposedly so intelligent you don't half come out with some stupid suggestions,' Charlotte said.

Murdo sighed. 'I think we should terminate this conversation, don't you?'

Peter stood and crossed to the whisky decanter. 'I've had enough of the game, sis.'

'Only because I'm beating you.'

He smiled as he poured a dram. It was true he didn't like losing. 'No, because it's boring me,' he lied.

'Hah!'

Peter waved the decanter at Murdo. 'Pa?'

Murdo stared enviously at the whisky, but he'd already had his quota. 'No thank you son,' he replied reluctantly.

'If I lived in one of the big cities I'd be a suffragette,' Nell declared.

Murdo sighed again. 'Would you really?'

'Oh yes.'

'And so would I,' Charlotte added.

Peter regarded his sisters with amusement. 'I doubt Geoffrey would be pleased about that,' he said to Charlotte.

Charlotte had no idea what Geoffrey thought of the matter. It was a subject they'd never discussed. She didn't reply.

'Well?' Peter prompted.

'There are times when you can be quite horrid,' she snapped.

'Game, set and match I believe,' Peter murmured, and had a sip of his drink.

'Enough,' Murdo said sternly. 'Enough.'

'I think . . . ' Charlotte began.

'I said *enough*,' Murdo repeated in a voice that made Charlotte blink and shut up.

'I'm going to bed,' Nell declared.

'Me too,' said Charlotte, rising.

They heard Peter chuckling as they left the room.

8

'I SAY, you chaps, I'm drunk as a lord,' Bobby Baxter declared.

His three companions, out on the town celebrating Geoffrey's engagement, laughed.

Andrew knew he was fairly tipsy as well, but then he would hope to be considering the amount of alcohol he'd consumed. Geoffrey was in a similar state.

'Why don't we move on?' John Blair suggested. All four of them were equal-ranking officers in the Watch.

Bobby hiccuped. 'Jolly good idea. But where to?'

They all thought about that. They'd already done several pubs and were now in the bar of the St Johnstoun Hotel.

Andrew ran a hand through his hair and tried to think, a difficult process as his mind was quite muzzy.

John leaned across to Geoffrey. 'Enjoying yourself, old bean?'

'Thoroughly. Though the room keeps going round and round.'

They all laughed and Bobby slapped his thigh which caused several of the other patrons to glance across at them.

'Ssshhh!' John counselled. 'Don't want to get thrown out, what? Regimental honour and all that.'

The other three nodded sagely.

'I know where we could go,' Bobby declared.

His companions looked on expectantly.

'Mulligan's.'

Andrew rocked back in his seat. He'd heard of Mulligan's, a gaming salon, but had never been there.

'What do you chaps think?' Bobby queried.

'Mulligan's,' Geoffrey mused. 'Don't you have to be a member or something?'

Bobby tapped his nose. 'In the know, old boy. My father's a member and I've been a few times with him. They'll let us in all right. Might cost a couple of bob at the door, but so what.'

'Then let's go there,' John declared, finishing his whisky and standing up. The others did likewise.

'Cab or walk?' Andrew queried when they were outside the hotel.

'Cab, of course,' said John. 'We're officers and gentlemen, bad form to be seen staggering down the street.'

That produced another laugh for they all knew it would have been the case.

* * *

'Now sober up,' Bobby said when they arrived at Mulligan's, a detached house indistinguishable from any of the others in the area. There was no outward sign that it was a gaming salon. Stepping forward he tugged on the bell pull.

The man who answered the door was smartly dressed in a double-breasted pin stripe. His face had the battered look of an ex-pugilist. 'May I help you?' he asked in a gravelly voice.

Bobby explained who he was and enquired politely if he and his friends could come in.

The man's keen gaze swept over them. 'There would be an entrance fee, sir,' he said. And stated the amount.

'That all right, chaps?'

Wallets were produced and money changed hands. Then the man stepped aside and gestured they should enter.

Their coats and hats were taken by a maid who then disappeared off into a side room.

Bobby rubbed his hands and led the way while the man followed the maid.

The main room was formed from two large ones that had been knocked together. Andrew judged there to be roughly thirty patrons present, most of them at the various gaming tables. Elegantly dressed young women who Bobby explained worked for the establishment were there to assist or simply chat if that was what was required. One of these, a pretty dark-haired girl, now approached them.

'What would your pleasure be, sirs?' she asked.

'A drink to start with if you don't mind,' Bobby, who'd temporarily become their leader, replied.

'Certainly. Champagne?'

'That would be wonderful.'

'I shan't be long, sirs.' And with that she walked off.

Andrew gazed about him. The wallpaper was

flock and two large crystal chandeliers dangled from the ceiling. If it hadn't been for the gaming tables he might have been in a decent drawing room. He felt quite relaxed and not nearly as tipsy as he'd been earlier.

'These girls go upstairs if you wish,' Bobby whispered to them.

Andrew raised an eyebrow. He hadn't been aware *that* activity took place at Mulligan's. He glanced with new interest at the girls wondering what it would be like to go to bed with someone other than Jean. He had to admit he was tempted.

The girl returned with a silver tray on which there were four flutes of champagne. 'Will you be playing tonight, sir?' she asked Bobby as he took a glass.

'Certainly shall. Though not quite at present.'

'I understand, sir.' She gave them all a sweet smile and went off again.

'What a corker!' Geoffrey breathed.

'Down, boy, you're engaged,' Andrew, eyes twinkling, told him.

'Can still look though, can't I?'

'No harm in that, dear chap,' Andrew agreed.

They crossed to a sofa where they sat and observed the proceedings. After a short while Bobby declared he was going to play cards and John said he would join him.

'Are you going to play?' Geoffrey asked Andrew after they'd gone.

'Might do. You?'

'I fancy a couple of spins at roulette. I'm feeling lucky tonight.'

Andrew thought he might try that as well.

After another glass of champagne they rose and went to the roulette wheel.

* * *

Andrew collapsed onto his bed, rolled over onto his back and laughed. He'd won a hundred pounds, a whole hundred! He could hardly believe it.

What fun the evening had been. He'd thoroughly enjoyed himself. They all had. A spiffing celebratory night out.

As for Mulligan's, well . . .

His head dropped sideways as he abruptly fell asleep. Seconds later he began to snore.

* * *

Nell was returning from Dalneil where she'd been on an errand when the familiar tingling and trembling of the hands took hold of her. She came up short and stared out over the winter landscape.

Her sight wavered, and then cleared. There he was, the Highlander and his wife, in a room she recognised as belonging to his house. A door was thrown open and another man hurried in, obviously agitated.

The Highlander, who'd been sitting, immediately came to his feet and went to the newcomer. A short conversation took place during which the Highlander also became agitated. At the conclusion of the conversation he crossed to his wife, who had a tartan shawl draped round her shoulders, and warmly embraced her.

The Highlander's two young children came running into the room through another door that was open and were immediately scooped up by him who held one in each arm.

The Highlander threw back his head and roared with laughter. He was still laughing when the vision started to fade. And still laughing when it blinked out of existence and Nell found herself back in the present.

She shivered, a shiver that had nothing whatsoever to do with the extremely cold day.

★ ★ ★

It was a Friday night and Andrew was at a loose end. Normally he and Geoffrey would have gone out somewhere together but Geoffrey was on duty as was Bobby Baxter. He'd already knocked on John Blair's door, getting no reply. Nor could he find John anywhere else.

'Damn,' he muttered to himself. It would have been lovely to go and see Jean except it wasn't an agreed night for him to visit and he never called unless it had been arranged.

What to do? he wondered. He could go to the officers' mess, he thought, but that had been almost deserted when he'd looked in a short while previously.

And then he had an idea. Why not go to Mulligan's? The man on the door had already let him in once so why not twice?

Yes, he decided. Mulligan's it was.

Andrew reluctantly left the roulette table. Best to finish while he was ahead, he told himself. This time his winnings amounted to just short of a hundred and fifty pounds. He crossed to one of the sofas dotted round the room and sat.

'You did well again, sir.'

He'd been so bemused by the situation he'd neither seen or heard her approach. It was the same girl who'd greeted him on his last visit.

Andrew nodded. 'Yes I have. Jolly good, eh?'

'Jolly good indeed. Can I get you anything, sir?'

He could certainly use a drink. 'Champagne would be pleasant.'

'I'll fetch it for you.'

He studied her as she walked away and, to his surprise, suddenly found himself aroused. He again wondered what it would be like to sleep with someone other than Jean. He was still thinking about that when the girl returned.

'Will you join me for a while?' he requested with a smile.

'Certainly, sir.'

She sat beside him.

'I should have told you to get a drink as well.'

'I couldn't do that, I'm afraid. It's forbidden while on duty.'

He nodded his understanding. 'I'm Andrew by the way.'

'And I'm Tina.'

A somewhat common name he thought, though she was fairly well spoken. He wondered what her background was that it had brought her to work in a place like Mulligan's.

'I'm an army officer,' he explained.

'Oh?'

'With the Black Watch.'

'I must say you look the officer type. It's the bearing that gives it away.'

He gazed into her dark, intelligent eyes. 'How old are you, Tina?'

'Nineteen.'

He'd have thought older. 'Do you get many officers in here?'

'From time to time. It varies.'

He had a long swallow of champagne. 'I really enjoyed myself tonight.'

'I should hope so, winning all that money. You must be frightfully clever at roulette.'

He laughed. 'Lucky more like.'

'You're being modest now.'

He was still aroused, an arousal that had become a positive ache. He hoped it wasn't obvious.

'Are you going to become a member?' she asked.

'I hadn't thought about that. But yes, perhaps I shall.' Reflecting it would be easier that way, as he certainly intended coming again.

'I can arrange it for you before you go.'

'What's the subscription?'

She told him and he considered it reasonable.

Andrew cleared his throat. 'I, eh . . . I believe you girls go upstairs. Is that correct?'

She gave him a sweet smile and nodded.

'Can I ask how much?' He dropped his gaze. 'I'm afraid all this is rather new to me. Paying I mean.'

'There's no need to be embarrassed, Andrew. Now, which of the girls has caught your eye and I'll sort it out for you.'

'Why you, of course,' he replied hastily.

'I see.'

'How, eh . . . how much?'

'I'm not cheap, Andrew. None of us is.'

'How much?' he repeated.

'Do you wish it to be a short time or to spend the entire night?'

The ache became even more pronounced. 'All night,' he breathed, and drank more champagne. God, this was exciting. Going to bed with a tart. And such a gorgeous one at that. If he'd seen her in the street he'd never have guessed in a thousand years that's what she was.

'Again it depends on what you wish.'

He stared blankly at her. 'I don't understand?'

'Do you wish it straightforward or do you have something else in mind?'

'Like what?'

He blushed bright red as she explained. 'Straightforward,' he croaked. Sweet Jesus! Did people really get up to those sort of things? It was mind boggling to say the least.

Tina named a sum.

She was right, he thought. It was expensive. But what the hell, he was flush with funds. 'Agreed.'

'Then follow me, bring your champagne if you like.'

En route from the room Tina had a brief word with another of the girls.

In the hallway she slipped an arm round his. 'All night it is,' she said.

Andrew swallowed hard.

★ ★ ★

It had been different, Andrew reflected as he made his way through early morning mist back to the barracks. The same act of course, but different nonetheless.

Obviously her body had been younger than Jean's and she'd had far smaller breasts and a smaller bottom, the latter delectable to caress. She'd also been firmer than Jean who had an overall voluptuous softness about her.

He chuckled. Now a member of Mulligan's he'd be back there at the first opportunity.

For the roulette and Tina.

★ ★ ★

Wonky emerged from the local shop in Dalneil humming jauntily to herself. She felt it to be one of those wonderful days when it's glorious to be alive. She halted when Jack Riach rode up.

Jack dismounted and doffed his hat to her. 'Good morning, Wonky. You seem particularly happy today.'

She beamed at him; here was a piece of luck. 'I'm always happy, Jack. It's part of my nature.'

He laughed. 'I wish I could say the same.'

'And what brings you into Dalneil? The pub I'll be bound.'

''Fraid not, though it's a thought. No, I have to pick up a few items from the shop.'

'You should get married then you could leave that sort of thing to your wife,' she teased.

He laughed again. 'Are you trying to marry me off, Wonky Comyn?'

'Not in the least. Though I think it's high time you and my cousin Peter got round to it. You can't remain bachelors for ever you know.'

'Why not?' he replied, eyes twinkling.

'Because it would be a waste of two fine men. Besides, you want children, don't you? A son and heir for a start.'

'There is that,' he agreed.

'So what's holding you back?'

'My my, we are personal today.'

She blushed. 'Sorry, I didn't mean to be. Nonetheless, what I say is true.'

It amused him to see her discomfiture. She was a handsome young woman he thought. Now why hadn't he realised that before? Probably because he always thought of her as a child, being that much older himself, and had simply failed to notice she'd grown up. Good figure too. He wondered what her legs were like.

Wonky sensed something of what was going through his mind which thrilled her. Had she finally captured his attention at long last? She prayed she had.

Intelligent too, Jack was thinking. A quick mind, he liked that. He couldn't be doing with boring women, no matter how good looking.

'I suppose I've never married because I've never found the right person,' he said.

'Maybe the right person's been under your very nose all along,' she declared, amazed at her boldness.

'Could be,' he mused. 'There again, maybe I'm just shy.'

Now it was her turn to laugh. 'I don't believe that, Jack Riach. You shy! If you're that then I'm a blackamoor.'

He was though, but only with the fair sex. He liked them well enough, there was no doubting that. It was just . . . well he didn't know. All he could put it down to was the fact he was, beneath the outward bravado, shy.

'How's Peter?' he asked, changing the subject. 'I haven't seen him since Hogmanay.'

'He's all right. Same as usual.'

'I must go over to Drummond House and root him out one weekend. That'll be a night for the pub.'

She fervently wished Jack would take her to the pub, but that was totally out of the question. He could go there but certainly not a woman of her standing, far less the minister's daughter. The village would be scandalised.

'Well, it's been nice talking to you, Wonky. Now I'd better get on.' And having said that he tied his horse's reins to a pole situated for that purpose.

She made the first move. 'Bye bye then.'

'Bye.'

143

He watched her speculatively as she walked away. Wonky Comyn? Ridiculous nickname of course but it somehow suited her. It was a thought, he mused, entering the shop.

★ ★ ★

'You said what!' Nell exclaimed.

'That it was high time he and your brother Peter got married. And so it is.'

'Somewhat forward, wasn't it?' Charlotte smiled.

Wonky shrugged. 'He said I was being a bit personal. But there you are. The point is, I do believe he might be interested in me. I'm certain I detected something of that nature.'

'Are you sure you're not imagining things?' Charlotte queried.

Wonky frowned. 'I don't think so. It's so hard to explain. He was looking at me in a way he's never done before.'

Nell giggled.

'Anyway, we'll see what happens. If anything,' Wonky said, beginning to wish she hadn't confided in her cousins who'd put doubt into her mind.

'Well, I hope you're right,' Charlotte declared. 'Jack Riach is a good man and much respected.'

Wonky thought of being in Jack's arms, of him kissing her. Oh please please please . . .

★ ★ ★

'Fancy a drink in the mess tonight, old thing?' Geoffrey asked, the pair of them striding from the parade ground where they'd been putting a detachment of men through their paces.

'No, I've something else planned,' Andrew replied.

Geoffrey's gaze slid sideways to stare at Andrew. 'Do I detect a female in these proceedings?'

Andrew didn't want to tell his friend about Mulligan's and Tina, particularly the latter. He wanted to keep that to himself.

'Now why would you say that?'

'You've been so secretive lately. Always slipping off and not letting on where.'

'You're exaggerating, Geoffrey. Always indeed!' He laughed.

'There's something in the wind though. Bobby mentioned it only the other night. Not that I needed to be told.'

'Stuff and nonsense, I assure you.'

But Geoffrey knew better. Andrew was up to something, and if he wanted to keep quiet about it that was his business. He wouldn't pry any further.

'It should be a good night in the mess. It's Major Brown's birthday.'

'I'll be sorry to miss it.'

Geoffrey let the matter drop.

★ ★ ★

He sat disconsolately on a sofa in Mulligan's staring at the carpet underfoot.

145

'Andrew?'

He glanced up and smiled. 'Hello, Tina. How are you?'

'Fine. But you don't seem your usual cheery self.'

'I lost tonight. First time ever.'

She pulled a sympathetic face. 'I am sorry.' She sat beside him. 'Badly?'

'Twenty-odd pounds. Not a lot, but still a loss. I decided luck was running against me and got out.'

She squeezed his arm. 'You can't always win. It's gambling after all. Sometimes you win, sometimes you lose.'

'Oh well,' he sighed. 'I'm still quids up overall. That's the main thing. Where have you been anyway? I looked for you when I arrived but you were nowhere to be seen.'

Tina glanced away. 'Where do you think I was? You know what I do here. You're not the only client I have.'

He was suddenly covered with embarrassment. For some reason the obvious had never crossed his mind. He'd thought she might be ill.

'I see,' he murmured.

Tina bit her lip, having taken a genuine liking to Andrew. 'Will you play again tonight? Your luck might change.'

He shook his head.

'Well, I'm free if you have that in mind.'

Directly after another man? He wasn't too keen on that idea. There again, Tina looked gorgeous as usual. He felt a familiar stirring in his loins.

'Perhaps you haven't enough money with you?'

'Oh I have,' he replied quickly.

'Well then?'

He smiled at her, desire mounting within him. His gaze dropped to the deep blue dress she was wearing and he thought of what lay beneath. 'All right,' he replied softly.

'That's my boy.'

★ ★ ★

Jean came onto an elbow and stared in puzzlement at Andrew lying beside her. 'Where did you learn that little refinement?' she queried.

Andrew immediately tensed, his mind racing. 'What refinement?'

'You know very well what I mean.' This time her tone was accusatory.

Andrew pretended to think. 'Oh yes that,' he answered eventually. 'I didn't learn it anywhere. It just sort of happened naturally.'

Her gaze was level, her eyes now cold. 'You wouldn't lie to me I hope?'

He laughed. 'Don't be ridiculous, Jean. Why should I do that?'

'You might if there was someone else.'

God, he thought. How stupid of him. The refinement as she'd called it was one he'd picked up from Tina, employed with Jean in the heat of the moment.

'There isn't, Jean. I swear.'

Her eyes had become gimlets, boring into

him. 'If you wish to stop seeing me, Andrew, you only have to say.' That was the last thing she wanted.

Panic welled in him. 'I do want to keep seeing you, Jean. And there isn't anyone else. On my mother's grave.'

That reassured Jean. She believed him. Surely he wouldn't make an oath like that if he wasn't telling the truth. 'Come here,' she smiled, and drew him to her.

Andrew buried his face in the valley of her breasts, his heart beating wildly. That had been a near thing, too damn near. He'd have to be more careful in future.

★ ★ ★

Wonky had given Jack Riach something to think about. The lassie was right, it was time he got married. He poured himself a dram and sat, his mind roaming over the available girls in the area.

There was Winnie Urquhart, a possibility. Except for her temper that is, for which she was well known. He dismissed Winnie, he'd never get on with a woman like that.

Then there was Flora McEwan, a pretty little thing who nearly always made him laugh when they spoke. The trouble with her was her nose, a hooter if ever there was. Sweet personality though, that counted in her favour.

One by one he went through the list, leaving Wonky till last.

'Wonky Comyn,' he murmured, swilling the

whisky round in his glass, seeing her again as she'd been outside the shop. He hadn't felt shy with her at all.

'Hmmh,' he mused.

★ ★ ★

The Comyns' only maid answered Jack's knock. 'Is the minister home I wonder?' he smiled.

'He is, sir.'

'Do you think I might have a word with him? The name's Mr Riach.'

'I'm certain you can, sir. If you'd care to come in.'

Jack stepped into the manse's hallway.

9

NELL sat abruptly up in bed, her chest heaving. She'd been dreaming about the Highlander's wife, watching the woman going about her daily chores.

Such a vivid dream, everything crystal clear. Even now, awake, she could still see the woman's face with the blue eyes, the slightly aquiline nose, the full lips.

Nell frowned. In her dream the woman had reminded her of someone, someone she knew in the present. Or had it been merely her imagination?

Nell considered that. No, the woman had definitely reminded her of someone.

She laid her head back on the pillows, pulled the bedclothes up to her chin, and tried to think who.

* * *

'More tea, Mr Riach?' Moira Comyn asked politely.

'No thank you. I've already had three cups. Any more and I'd be awash.' He'd asked Tom Comyn's permission to call on his daughter and permission had been granted. This was his first visit as suitor and appallingly dreary it was proving to be.

'How about you, dear?' Moira queried of her husband.

Tom shook his head. 'But I will have another biscuit.'

Wonky rose from her chair and offered her father the large plate of assorted biscuits. Preceding those had been small, neatly cut triangular sandwiches with the crusts removed.

'Thank you, Veronica,' Tom murmured, making his choice.

Wonky returned the plate to the table and sat again. She wished her parents would leave her and Jack alone but there was no chance of that. Not on his first visit anyway.

'How are those sheep of yours coming along?' Tom inquired. 'You seem to have a fairly sizeable flock.'

'They're fine, minister, thriving. I have a little over two hundred.'

'Quite a job in the lambing season, I dare say.'

'I have two men working for me. We manage.'

'I'd love to see a lamb being born,' Wonky enthused.

Tom's eyebrows shot up. 'Hardly a sentiment to express over tea, Veronica. In fact, hardly a sentiment for a well-brought-up young lady to express in any circumstances. The very idea.'

Wonky's face fell. 'Sorry, Father.'

'I should say.'

'You like animals then?' Jack queried.

'Oh yes, very much so. I'm just an old-fashioned country girl at heart.'

Tom harumphed on hearing that.

A few seconds silence ensued. 'Those were lovely sandwiches,' Jack said to Moira, desperately trying to make conversation.

Moira inclined her head. 'Most kind of you, Mr Riach.'

'My wife is a wonderful cook and baker,' Tom commented, smiling warmly at Moira.

'I can imagine,' Jack said. She must certainly eat enough from the looks of her, he thought.

'You must come to supper one night and sample her cuisine.'

Jack groaned inwardly, he could well imagine what that would be like, tedious in the extreme. 'I shall look forward to it,' he lied. He turned his attention to Wonky. 'Are you also a good cook and baker, Veronica?' He'd realised early on that she was always referred to as Veronica by her parents and had thought it best to do the same while in their company.

'I have my moments.'

'Makes a succulent steak and kidney pudding,' Tom declared. 'And her apple crumble isn't bad either. Eh, my dear?'

Wonky gave him a thin smile.

More silence ensued, broken only by the steady ticking of the clock on the mantelpiece. Jack decided he'd have to get out of there or scream. A glance at the clock told him he'd been with the Comyns an hour; it seemed an eternity. He rose and placed his cup and plate on the table.

'Thank you for a delightful tea, Mr and Mrs Comyn, but I'm afraid I must go. I have animals to feed.' The latter a fib, the feeding would have already been done.

'So soon!' Moira exclaimed in disappointment. She wasn't half as disappointed as Wonky who knew the visit had been a total disaster. Why were her parents so formal and stuffy! For what might have been the millionth time in her life she wished she'd been born a Drummond.

Tom also rose and placed his cup and plate on the table, carefully aligning them alongside Jack's. 'I'll ring for Heather. She'll show you out.'

'I can do that, Father,' Wonky said hastily.

He frowned. That wasn't at all correct. Then he saw the pleading in his daughter's eyes and relented. 'Certainly, Veronica, if you wish.'

'I'm so sorry,' Wonky apologised quietly when she and Jack were in the hallway.

'That's all right.'

'I should have warned you but had no way of doing so.'

They reached the door which he opened.

'You will come again, Jack, won't you? Don't let my parents put you off.'

'I shall be in church Sunday morning. Perhaps I can walk you home?'

'Oh, yes please,' she smiled.

When the door was shut behind him Jack heaved a huge sigh of relief. He untied his horse and leapt into the saddle.

His next stop was the pub and a much needed drink.

★ ★ ★

153

'It's been so long, darling,' Geoffrey said throatily to Charlotte, who was in his arms. He had arrived at Drummond House only minutes before. A tactful Nell had left them alone when Geoffrey had joined her and Charlotte.

'I know.'

He gazed into her eyes, his own shining. 'I've missed you so much.'

'And I you.'

'You're even more beautiful than I remembered.'

She laughed. 'I think I've told you before, Geoffrey Armitage, flattery will get you everywhere. Now, how long have you got?'

'Five days only, I'm afraid. I was hoping for a week or even more but five days was all I could manage.'

'Don't worry, we'll make good use of every minute of them.'

He could contain himself no longer. His lips met hers and she melted against him.

'Oh, my angel. My wonderful, wonderful angel,' he breathed when the kiss was over.

★ ★ ★

Andrew accepted the glass of champagne he'd requested with a trembling hand. He'd just won three hundred pounds at roulette which more than made up for the few small losses he'd previously sustained. His luck had returned with a vengeance.

He caught Tina's eye, where she was sitting with a middle-aged patron, and nodded to the door. She got the message.

154

As soon as she could Tina excused herself and followed Andrew upstairs.

Paying beforehand, as was the custom, he delighted her by including a very large tip.

* * *

Peter placed the tray of drinks he'd fetched from the bar on the small circular table where he and Jack had decided to sit. They were in the Dalneil pub which both used frequently.

Jack lifted a pint and took a deep swallow. 'I was ready for that,' he grinned.

Peter removed the remaining three glasses then stood the tray by a leg of the table. 'Slainthe!' he toasted, taking a sip of whisky.

Peter glanced round the pub, knowing every face there. He'd always enjoyed its warm cosy atmosphere.

'So what's new with you?' Jack inquired amiably.

'It's not what's new with me, but you. I hear you've called on Wonky.'

Jack's grin widened. 'True enough.'

Peter leant back in his chair and studied his friend. 'When did this start?'

'It was something Wonky herself said about it being high time I was married. She also said the same about you.'

'Me!'

'That's right.'

'A bit cheeky of her I'd say.'

Jack swallowed more beer. 'I got to thinking about it and decided why not her? She's pretty after all and has a pleasant temperament. I could do far worse.'

'Hardly sounds like a love match,' Peter replied drily.

Jack shrugged. 'My father once told me they don't always turn out for the best. Love can die and then where does that leave you? His advice was to marry someone you got on with, that that was far more important. It's said you can love a person and not even like them. Well, I don't want any of that.'

'I take it then that you and Wonky get on?'

'That's what I'm trying to find out and why I'm calling on her. I'll know soon enough believe me.'

'She's very keen on you,' Peter stated quietly

One of Jack's eyebrows slowly rose. 'How do you know that?'

'The girls told me. Apparently she's been keen for ages and upset you've never taken any notice of her. Up until now that is.'

'Well, well,' Jack murmured. That was interesting.

'And she's worried she'll lose you because of her parents. Though there's nothing she can do about them. Her father rules her with a rod of iron.'

'Never liked the man,' Jack confessed. 'Even less now that I know him better.'

'He would be your father-in-law if you married Wonky,' Peter pointed out.

Jack chuckled. 'I can handle him. Contact between us would be kept to a minimum, I'd see to that. Anyway, what about you? If Wonky was right about me she's also right about you. It is high time you were married for the old son and heir if nothing else.'

'You sound just like my father, he was on about the same thing some months back.'

'And?'

Peter employed the same argument that he had with Murdo. 'Unlike you, and your father, I think a love match is the be all and end all. I won't marry unless I'm in love, and that hasn't happened yet.'

'What if it doesn't?'

Peter gazed down into his pint pot, not wishing Jack to read his expression. Should he be honest with Jack, tell him the truth that he never intended to marry. That women left him totally cold. He decided against it. That secret was one he'd keep to himself.

'I'm sure it will one day,' he lied.

'But what if it doesn't?' Jack persisted.

'Then I'll remain a bachelor.'

Jack saw off his whisky, then had another swallow of beer. 'You're being a bit hard on yourself, aren't you? I mean, we all have needs, dear chap.'

'Mind over matter, Jack. Mind over matter.'

Jack laughed. 'You sound like a papist monk or priest. They remain celibate but it would hardly do for me.'

Peter's expression became quizzical. 'Does that mean you've . . . ?'

Now it was Jack's turn to wonder if he should confess. And, like Peter, he decided not to. 'No, but as I said, we all have needs. Needs that aren't getting any easier to cope with as a single man.'

Peter nodded his understanding. 'When are you seeing Wonky again?'

'I walked her home from church last Sunday which was fine, away from Mater and Pater that is. I'm calling again for tea at the manse next Wednesday.' He pulled a face. 'God help me.'

Peter laughed. He couldn't have agreed more.

★ ★ ★

Murdo stopped just inside the malting house and drew a deep breath down into his lungs. This was his favourite part of the distillery. The odour that assailed his nostrils was one he'd known all his adult life, and one that never failed to delight him.

He watched Bill Murray and his brother Enoch, two of his maltmen, turning the germinating malt to aerate the grains, part of the whisky-making process.

Bill spotted Murdo and acknowledged him, Murdo replying with a finger wave.

Murdo stayed there for all of ten minutes, not checking up on the work but simply enjoying the experience, before moving on.

He felt quite buoyed up on leaving the malting house.

★ ★ ★

'Jesus!' Andrew exclaimed, rolling off Tina. 'That was amazing.'

She gave him a feline smile. 'I try to give money's worth.'

That irritated him for some reason. He hated the thought he was paying for it. Not that he was mean, not at all, it was just that he'd have preferred the relationship to have been a non-professional one.

'Where do you live?' he asked.

The feline smile vanished. 'Why?'

'Just curious, that's all.'

'I can't say, Andrew, it's against the rules.'

'Really?'

'Really.'

'But why?'

'You'd have to ask Mr Mulligan the owner that.'

He lay back and studied her naked form. 'Can you tell me something about yourself? I'd like to know.'

Tina sighed. 'Is this leading up to, what's a nice girl like you doing in a job like this?'

He reached across and stroked a coral-tipped breast, smiling with satisfaction when the nipple responded. She might only be nineteen, he thought, but she was all woman with a mind far older than her years. But then he supposed being a prostitute, for that's what she was, did that to a female.

'I'm one of five children, the eldest,' she stated suddenly. 'Da's a drunk and Ma's half blind with cataracts. I don't know where the family would be without me and this job.'

He took his hand away. 'I'm sorry.'

She shrugged. 'I don't come from the sort

of background you obviously do. This job is a Godsend. I make far more than I would in service or a factory.'

'I can imagine,' he murmured.

'It took a bit of getting used to I can tell you, but it isn't as bad as it might be. Most of the gentlemen I entertain are exactly that, gentlemen. Not one of them has ever mistreated me or refused to pay.'

She chuckled. 'Not that there's much chance of them not paying. A shout from me and they'd be in very big trouble indeed. Mr Mulligan looks after his girls.'

'I've got two sisters,' he declared.

'Oh?'

'Charlotte and Nell. Charlotte's engaged to a fellow officer, in fact it was that engagement we were celebrating the first night I came here.'

'As I remember they all seemed decent blokes.'

'They are, Geoffrey in particular. He's the one Charlotte's going to marry.'

She stretched out beside him. 'Can I ask *you* something?'

'What?'

'There's a girlfriend, isn't there?'

He stared at her, wondering how she'd worked that out. 'What if there is?'

'It's none of my business, Andrew. What you do is your own affair.'

He laughed. 'That's exactly what the girlfriend is, an affair. She's a lot older than me.'

'So it isn't serious then?'

'I like her well enough, she's good fun. But

fun is precisely what it is, she's too old for it to be anything else. She was a friend of my mother's who's now dead.'

Tina was visibly shocked. 'That's terrible.'

Andrew had the grace to look shamefaced. 'I suppose it is.'

'I mean, what would your mother think if she was still alive? And what about your father, what about him?'

'Well, he wouldn't be best pleased, that's for sure. But you see I . . . ' He cleared his throat. 'I hadn't been with a woman up until Jean. It seemed an ideal opportunity.'

'Still, your mother's friend. That is rather off.'

Andrew suddenly smiled. 'She suspected something recently. I was very stupid, used a 'refinement' she called it which I'd learnt from you.'

'Is she rich?' Tina asked.

'Considerably. She was left very well provided for.'

'Her husband's dead then?'

He nodded. 'She was lonely and . . . shall I say libidinous when we got together.'

Tina frowned. 'What's this libby thing?'

He gestured at his penis. 'To be blunt about it, she was missing that.'

A huge smile lit up Tina's face. 'I see.'

'Not that she's actually ever said, but I'm not daft. I can put two and two together.' He cradled his hands behind his head. 'Do you mind me talking like this?'

'It's part of the job, Andrew. Men will tell

women like me things they wouldn't to anothe
soul. It's amazing what some of them come
out with.'

'And you are discreet.'

'Completely. It would be more than my job'
worth to blab. What's said between these four
walls is strictly between us, you have my word
on that.'

Andrew had been certain that was the case
'Have you got a boyfriend, outside here tha
is?'

'No.'

'I'm surprised. You're not exactly a gargoyle
you know.'

She laughed softly. 'Thank you, kind sir. I'l
take that as a compliment.'

'It was meant as one. So why not?'

'A boyfriend? What decent chap would wan
someone like me? I'm somewhat shop soiled to
say the least. But perhaps one day, who knows
I won't be here for ever after all. Mr Mulligar
likes his girls to be young. After a while they're
simply let go.' Tina looked wistful. 'There was a
smashing woman here when I arrived, her name
was Jessica and we got on like a house on fire
But she was let go on account of her age.'

'What happened to her?'

'I've no idea. She walked out the front door
one day and that was that.'

'You've had a hard life,' Andrew sympathised

'So have many. I'm not complaining. I jus
wish my dad was different, that's all. He drinks
every penny he can get hold of. He's violen
in drink too, it wouldn't be the first time

he's smacked me almost senseless. Though he's stopped that since I came here, he's still got the sense to realise I can't do this job all battered and bruised.'

'Does he hit your mother?'

'Oh yes. Frequently.'

'Even though she's half blind?'

'That doesn't worry him. He's a brute. But he'll get his come-uppance some day.'

'Why don't you move out?' Andrew queried.

'My mother and brothers and sisters need me, it's as simple as that.'

He reached across and drew her into his embrace. 'I don't even know your surname. Is it permissible to ask or is that also against the rules?'

She smiled. 'It is. But I'll tell you anyway. It's Mitchell.'

'Tina Mitchell,' he mused.

'And your surname is Drummond. That's what you wrote on the membership form you filled in.'

'Correct.'

'Well, Andrew Drummond, you've paid for all night so what do you want to do next? Sleep or — '

'Or,' he interjected.

★ ★ ★

Murdo sighed as he studied the gold-rimmed invitation to the annual dinner of the Whisky Makers' Association in Edinburgh. Large amounts of their product were always consumed at the

163

event, that was de rigueur, which meant he couldn't attend. He knew he'd succumb to temptation if he did.

'Peter?'

His elder son glanced up at him.

Murdo waved the invitation and explained what it was. 'I think you should go in my place this year,' he proposed.

Peter stared at his father in astonishment, knowing how much Murdo enjoyed the annual dinner. 'Whatever for?'

'It'll be good for you, another step to taking over in time.'

Murdo rose from behind his desk, crossed the office and placed the invitation in front of a bemused Peter. 'You'll have a whale of a time, believe me. And you'd better put your drinking boots on, there'll be enough whisky there to sink the proverbial battleship.'

'If you're certain, Pa.'

Murdo was filled with nostalgia remembering past dinners. Yes indeed, the temptation would be too great and he didn't want another attack.

'That's settled then.'

★ ★ ★

Jack Riach took out his pocket watch and snapped it open. Hettie would just be finishing, time for the weekly assignation. He smiled in anticipation.

Hettie, Jack's dairy maid, was wiping her hands on her apron when Jack strolled into the byre.

'How are you?' he queried with a smile. She was seventeen years old and they'd been having their weekly assignation for almost eighteen months. She was a bonnie lass in a rustic way, well proportioned with generous hips and breasts.

Hettie moved away when Jack went to touch her.

He frowned. 'What's wrong with you?'

'I hear you're courting, Jack. The minister's daughter.'

'That's right,' he nodded.

She came straight to the point. 'Does this mean you're ending our arrangement?'

'Why should it mean that?' he queried.

'If you get married you won't want me no more. You'll be getting it at home.'

'I see,' he murmured. 'And that would upset you, Het?'

It damn well would, she thought. Part of their arrangement was, the most important part as far as she was concerned, that if she fell pregnant Jack would pay her off with a lump sum in return for which she wouldn't tell anyone he was the father. A sizeable sum that had been agreed on. A pregnancy Hettie was certain must happen in due course. With that lump sum behind her she wouldn't have any difficulty finding a husband, pregnant or otherwise, and would be able to afford the cottage she wanted. That was her dream which would blow away like so much chaff if Jack stopped seeing her before she fell pregnant.

'Yes,' she stated emphatically.

He laughed and chucked her under the chin. 'Not jealous, are you?'

'Might be.'

'I like that.'

'So?' she demanded.

'If I do get married to Miss Comyn, and nothing's certain, it won't be for some time yet. In the meanwhile let's just enjoy ourselves. Who knows what'll happen in the long term? I certainly don't.'

Jack was thinking he didn't want to burn any boats. He relished his weekly sessions with Hettie Campbell, she was a lustful lassie who knew how to pleasure a man.

Maybe she should try and see Jack twice a week, Hettie thought. That would double her chances. She *wanted* that cottage and hopefully a piece of land to go with it. It would be a big rise in the world for her.

Jack produced his wallet from which he extracted a pound note. 'Why don't you buy yourself a wee present, Het. That'll cheer you up,' he declared, slipping the note into her hand.

'You're good to me, Jack. Always have been,' she murmured.

The pound note vanished into her pocket.

'We're wasting time, Het. You go on to the barn and I'll follow in a minute.'

'All right, Jack.'

He watched her walk away, hips swaying provocatively. Once outside he glanced around checking that the coast was clear as it invariably was at that time on a Sunday.

In the barn he found Hettie already stretched out behind a stack of hay bales, her skirt up round her waist, her female nakedness revealed.

Standing over her he smiled as he began undoing his trousers.

10

ANDREW left the roulette table feeling sick to the very pit of his stomach. How could he have been so incredibly stupid! Of all the damn fools he was the biggest.

He sat and swallowed hard, noting that his hands were trembling. He should have got out far earlier but had kept telling himself that his bad run must end if he kept doubling up. Only it hadn't. And now . . .

'Christ!' he murmured, and closed his eyes. His senses were reeling. How could he possibly pay back that amount?

'Andrew?'

He blinked his eyes open to find Tina staring sympathetically down at him.

'How much?' she asked softly. She blanched when he told her the amount.

'Can you cover it?'

'I'll have to.'

'I have a message from Mr Mulligan. He'd like to see you in his office. I'll take you there.'

Andrew rose and teetered on the spot. What had started as a smashing evening had somehow turned into a nightmare.

He followed Tina from the room as he'd done so many times before, only this time it was different.

A helluva lot different.

★ ★ ★

'Please take a seat, Mr Drummond,' Mulligan said from behind a fog of cigar smoke.

Andrew sat facing the small man who, despite his Irish name, was in fact Jewish. Mulligan studied Andrew from behind a huge beak of a nose.

'You signed a number of IOUs tonight, Mr Drummond. I have them here.' Mulligan tapped the pieces of paper in front of him.

'Yes,' Andrew croaked.

'The first time you've asked for credit.'

Andrew nodded.

'It's quite a sizeable amount.'

Andrew licked bone-dry lips. 'Yes,' he said again.

'I allowed the credit because of your family connections. Your family owns Drummond whisky I believe.'

Andrew nodded a second time.

'There again, perhaps you're a man of means in your own right?'

Panic was threatening to engulf Andrew. He had to get out of there, he needed to think.

'You'll get your money, Mr Mulligan,' he replied coldly, avoiding the question.

'Oh I'm sure,' Mulligan said softly.

'If you could give me a few days, a week perhaps. Surely that's reasonable?'

'Quite. As a serving officer and gentleman I know you're a man of honour and his word. A week it is.'

169

'Thank you,' Andrew said through gritted teeth.

'A pleasure doing business with you, Mr Drummond. You're always welcome in my establishment.'

Mulligan rose and extended a hand. 'Goodbye for now,' he declared, slightly emphasising the 'now'.

'Goodbye.'

Andrew, still in a daze, left the office and collected his coat and hat.

He stumbled out into the night.

★ ★ ★

'I was thinking,' Hettie said to Jack, having just bumped into him in the yard.

He smiled. 'What's that?'

'You know what they say about choosing a wife. Always look to the mother to see what she might one day turn into.'

The smile vanished from Jack's face. Now why hadn't he thought of that! The thing was, he hated fat women and Moira Comyn was decidedly that. It was all right to be well built like Hettie but fat women revolted him.

It pleased Hettie to see the effect her words had had on Jack, who'd once made an offhand remark, which she'd remembered, about his dislike of female corpulency.

In his mind's eye Jack was picturing Wonky the size of her mother. He shuddered.

'I'd hate you to make a mistake, Jack,' Hettie crooned.

So would he. Particularly that mistake. The thought of going to bed with a tub of lard was . . . well, just too awful to contemplate.

'It's certainly something you should give consideration,' Hettie went on.

'Yes,' Jack agreed quietly.

Hettie walked away, waiting till she rounded a corner before bursting out laughing.

★ ★ ★

Peter stared at Andrew in disbelief. 'How much?'

'Sixteen hundred pounds.'

Peter swore, then crossed to the whisky decanter and poured himself a large one. 'You're an idiot. A total idiot. That's a small fortune.'

'I know,' Andrew replied miserably.

'But how?'

'In the end it all happened so quickly. I simply kept on losing.' Andrew took a deep breath. 'I've been going to Mulligan's for months, you see, and doing terribly well on the whole. Then this.'

'Does that mean you have some cash put by?'

Andrew dropped his gaze to stare at the carpet. 'The sixteen hundred is after I've deducted what I have in the bank.'

'And now you want to ask Pa to cough up for the remainder?'

Andrew shrugged. 'Who else can I ask?'

Peter stared at Andrew over the rim of his glass. 'He'll go berserk, have a heart attack,'

Peter said quietly, not realising how close to the mark his words were.

'How about you, Peter, can you lend me something?'

Peter barked out a laugh. 'I don't have any money of my own, you know that. All I have is my salary.'

Andrew went to the decanter and poured himself a dram as hefty as Peter's. 'What a mess. What a bloody awful mess,' he muttered, before taking a long swallow.

'Of your own making, brother. No one twisted your arm encouraging you to gamble.'

'Do you think that makes it any easier? It doesn't, I assure you.'

'Sixteen hundred pounds,' Peter mused, shaking his head.

Andrew felt tears come into his eyes which he brushed away with the sleeve of his jacket. He was terrified of facing his father. Scared witless.

'When will you speak to him?' Peter asked.

'Tonight, after dinner.'

'Well, good luck, you're going to need it.'

Andrew knew that only too well.

★ ★ ★

Dinner was over and the family had retired to the drawing room. Charlotte and Nell were embroidering while Peter was reading a newspaper. Murdo was sitting in a club chair clearly in a contemplative mood.

Andrew stared at his father, willing himself to

172

ask Murdo if he could have a private word. A dozen times during the past hour he'd opened his mouth to make the request, and a dozen times he'd closed it again.

Coward, he berated himself. And he was right. His father was a good man who'd have been the first to help in any other difficulty, but a gambling debt! That was something else entirely.

Peter glanced at the ashen-faced Andrew, partially amused to see his brother's funk, the rest of him sympathetic to what Andrew was going through. Andrew's fault mind, but nonetheless.

'Has he kissed her yet do you know?' Nell whispered to Charlotte who'd spoken with Wonky that afternoon. She was referring to Jack Riach.

'Apparently not,' came the whispered reply.

Nell giggled softly.

'She thinks he will soon. At least that's the impression she gets.'

'So it's all going well?'

'According to Wonky it is.'

Nell sighed. Lucky old Wonky, and lucky Charlotte. When was it going to be her turn?

'They have held hands. Only briefly though,' Charlotte confided.

'Is he getting on any better with Uncle Tom and Aunt Moira?'

Charlotte pulled a face. 'What do you think. But he's persevering.'

'What are you two whispering about?' Murdo suddenly demanded, causing Andrew to start.

'Nothing, Pa.'

'Well, it must be something.'

'Nothing important, Pa. Girls' talk, that's all.'

Murdo snorted and gazed enviously at the dram balanced on the arm of Peter's chair. 'Next week, Peter,' he said.

'What's that, Pa?'

'The Whisky Makers' Association dinner.'

'Oh yes, I'm looking forward to it. And Edinburgh, I always enjoy going there. A lovely city.'

'A lovely city,' Murdo agreed. His gaze focused on Andrew. 'What's wrong with you tonight? You're being very quiet, most unlike you, lad.'

'Nothing to say, Pa.'

Murdo barked out a short, sharp laugh. 'Well, that makes a welcome change.'

Ask now, Andrew thought. Ask now. He couldn't. It filled him with despair and shame.

'Ah well!' Murdo declared, rising. 'I'm off to bed. Want an early night.'

'Why's that, Pa?' Peter queried.

'Just do, that's all. No particular reason.'

'Old age I suppose,' Charlotte teased.

Murdo glowered at her. 'Less of your cheek, young lady. I'm not decrepit yet.'

Now, Andrew urged himself. Before it's too late. He said nothing.

'I'll see you all at breakfast,' Murdo declared, and strode purposefully from the room.

Peter glanced across at Andrew and shook his head.

Andrew willed himself to follow Murdo, to tell his father of his problem.

He remained sitting.

★ ★ ★

Andrew closed the bedroom door and leant back against it. Tomorrow night he promised himself, he'd speak to his father then. This had to be sorted out. But Christ, it was hard.

Sixteen hundred pounds, the figure was indelibly printed on his brain. And what if his father refused? The consequences to that were too awful to contemplate. Damn Mulligan and damn his salon. He wished with all his heart he'd never heard of the place.

It had all been so easy while he was winning, a few hundred here, a few hundred there. And where had most of it gone? Champagne and all the other luxuries he'd so lately enjoyed. Not to mention Tina.

'God,' he groaned. If only by some miracle the whole horrible episode could be washed away, made to vanish. He'd have given anything for that to be the case.

Tomorrow night, he promised himself, taking off his jacket. He couldn't delay the inevitable longer than that. It would have to be then.

He remembered Peter's contemptuous look when he'd announced he too was off to bed. Thankfully Peter hadn't made any comment, he'd been spared that.

He was hanging his jacket in the wardrobe — they hadn't dressed for dinner that night — when he noticed the letter he'd picked up at the barracks on his way out. In his anxiety he'd forgotten all about it.

He took the letter from the jacket's inside pocket and tore it open. He frowned as he read the official contents.

It was too good to be true. Too too good. Throwing back his head he roared with laughter.

Problem solved.

★ ★ ★

'Ireland,' Murdo repeated, sitting with the family at breakfast next morning.

'My posting order came through yesterday, Pa. I'm to join the First Essex as soon as possible. They're already there, in Dublin.'

'Well,' Murdo mused. 'That's a turn up for the book. I'd have thought they'd have given you more time to get your affairs in order.'

'That's the army for you, Pa.'

Peter was staring quizzically at his brother wondering about this turn of events since the previous evening. He was pretty certain he knew how Andrew would now handle the debt situation, and totally disapproved. However, Andrew was a grown man, entirely capable of making his own decisions. Though in this case Peter was convinced it was a mistake. The expression 'lack of moral fibre' sprang to mind.

'How long will you be away for?' Nell asked.

Andrew shrugged. 'Can't say. Could be a couple of years.'

'I wonder why you've been transferred?' Nell mused.

'Search me, sis. You're rarely given a reason. The First Essex are a decent bunch from what I've heard, though I'll be sorry to leave the Watch.' Not as sorry as he might have been, he reflected.

'So we won't be seeing you for a while,' Nell said.

''Fraid not. Will you miss me?'

'Of course,' she replied, pretending to be sarcastic. For she would, they all would.

Charlotte suddenly clattered her knife and fork on to her plate. 'Geoffrey didn't get a similar posting order, did he?' she inquired anxiously.

'No idea. But it's doubtful he would. Not two of us at the same time. That's highly unlikely in the circumstances.'

Relief welled through Charlotte. Thank the Lord for that. Although she couldn't be absolutely certain until she heard from him.

★ ★ ★

Andrew, having already packed, left directly after breakfast, the rest of the family seeing him off.

'Well, good luck, son, and take care of yourself over in Ireland, hear?'

'Thanks, Pa. I will.'

The two men shook hands as McPhie climbed into the Rolls-Royce which would take Andrew to Pitlochry station.

Peter's eyes bored into Andrew's as they

shook. 'I hope everything works out for you,'
he said.

Andrew knew to what Peter was referring. 'I'd
say things couldn't have worked out better,' he
replied jauntily.

Fool, Peter thought.

There were more farewells from Charlotte and
Nell, then Andrew was in the Rolls and waving
goodbye as it purred away.

Miracles do happen, Andrew thought, sinking
into the deep leather upholstery.

They really do.

★ ★ ★

'Ireland!' Jean Ritchie exclaimed.

'I'm leaving the day after tomorrow which is
why I sent round the note.'

'It's so . . . sudden, isn't it?'

'The army's like that.' He was about to say
he was looking forward to the adventure, then
thought the better of it. To have done so would
have been insensitive to say the least.

Jean put a hand to her forehead, for a moment
having felt slightly dizzy. This was awful.

'There's absolutely nothing I can do about it,'
Andrew declared softly.

'I appreciate that.'

'I'll be gone for quite some time. And when
I do return who knows where I'll be based.'

It was over, Jean thought in despair. What had
been wonderful would now only be a memory.
Nor could she take him to bed for one last
time. The servants were in the house. There

was her reputation. But oh she was tempted, so very tempted.

'Can I see you again before you go?' she asked.

He shook his head. 'Impossible, I'm sorry. Can't be done, Jean. I have no control over it, that's just the way it is.'

'I understand,' she said huskily, and sat. Although not yet noon she wanted a drink, and something stronger than her usual sherry.

'Could you pour me a gin and 'It'?' she asked Andrew. 'You know where it's kept.'

'Of course.' He decided to have one himself, to keep her company.

'How long can you stay for?' she queried.

'No more than half an hour.'

She stared at him, memorising every detail of his face, recalling the many nights of passion they'd shared together. 'I'm going to miss you dreadfully,' she stated honestly.

'And I you, Jean.'

'We didn't have long, did we?'

'No.' He hoped she wasn't going to break down, that would be embarrassing.

'Will you write?'

'I'm not much of a letter writer. But I'm sure I can manage a few lines from time to time.'

Letters she would treasure. If they came that was. 'How's everyone at Drummond House?'

'Fine. In the pink.'

'And how did they take the news?'

Andrew had a swallow of his gin. 'They were all right about it. They appreciate I'm in the army after all and that this sort of thing happens.'

'I'll miss you, Andrew,' she repeated in a cracked voice.

When he'd gone she went up to her bedroom, locked the door, laid on the bed and wept copiously.

* * *

Andrew stood at the ship's rail until the Scottish coastline vanished over the horizon. Then he smiled, for with it went Mulligan and his debt. He couldn't have been any happier.

He thought of the gold cufflinks in his suitcase, a last-minute present from Jean delivered to the barracks. That had been kind and thoughtful of her.

He then thought of Tina whom he'd also have liked to say goodbye to. But of course that had been completely out of the question.

Well, a whole new chapter in his life was opening up. What would it bring? It was going to be interesting finding out.

Putting Jean and Tina from his mind he went below.

* * *

As had become their custom Jack was walking Wonky home from church, and he was wondering how tactfully to broach the subject that had been plaguing him since his conversation with Hettie in the yard. Hettie whom he'd be seeing later on that day for the ongoing Sunday assignation. He was looking forward to that.

They strolled a little way in silence, Wonky revelling in his company, silent or otherwise.

'It was a particularly long sermon this morning,' Jack commented.

'Yes. I sometimes think Father doesn't know when to stop once he gets going.'

Jack laughed. 'It was real fire and brimstone stuff. I felt I was already roasting in hell.'

Wonky glanced sideways at him. 'Surely you haven't done anything that would put you there?'

'A few sins,' he confessed. 'Nothing major though.' He thought of Hettie, if that wasn't a major sin what was!

'Your mother seems to have lost weight,' he lied.

Wonky frowned. 'I can't say I've noticed.'

'Well, it seems to me she has.' He paused for several seconds, then asked innocently, 'Has she always been stout?'

'As long as I can remember. But I believe she had a lovely figure when young.'

Jack's heart sank.

'It started with childbirth you see. It affects some women that way, I'm told.'

Jack's heart sank even further. If that was what had happened to Moira Comyn with childbirth might it not also to Wonky, her daughter.

'Of course she eats a fair amount,' Wonky burbled on. 'But then so does Father.'

Jack had noticed that at the supper he'd had with them. And Wonky had eaten her fair share,

181

no demure picking with her.

'I'm not surprised considering how good a cook she is. The supper I had with you was delicious.'

Wonky beamed at him. 'You'll have to come again soon. And this time I'll make my apple crumble. *Lots* and *lots* of it.'

Those fateful words decided her fate with Jack.

He lapsed into a brooding silence for the remainder of their journey to the manse.

★ ★ ★

Jack put on his jacket, pulled out his wallet and extracted a five-pound note. 'For you,' he stated gruffly to Hettie who'd also come to her feet and was busy brushing straw from her clothes.

Her eyes snapped wide with delight. This was far more than he'd ever given her before. 'What's that for?'

'Saving me from what might have turned out to be the biggest mistake of my life.'

Hettie accepted the note, folded it and slid it safely into a pocket. 'Are you referring to Miss Comyn?'

Jack nodded.

'Have you told her yet?'

'That's still to come. It's going to be difficult, believe me. I'd rather have a tooth pulled.'

'Well, if you take my advice do it sooner rather than later. Best to get these things over as quickly as possible.'

She was right. Call at the manse or wait till

next Sunday? He'd have to think about that.

Hettie turned her back to Jack so he could brush off the straw she wasn't able to reach. This was something he did every week.

Hettie smiled. Her little scheme had paid off as she'd hoped it would. Jack was still hers and hers alone.

Before leaving the barn she kissed him on the cheek. 'I'm sure you're doing the right thing, Jack, feeling as you do. It would be awful for you ending up married to a tub of lard.'

Jack shuddered at the thought.

★ ★ ★

Jack slid from his horse and tied off the reins. He'd come straight from the pub where he'd consumed a number of large drams to give him Dutch courage. At that moment he wished he'd drunk more.

He knocked and waited.

'Why hello, sir,' said Heather the maid on opening the door.

'Is Miss Comyn at home?'

'She is indeed, sir.'

'I'd like a word if I may.'

'Certainly, sir. Come in.'

In the event it proved even worse than Jack had anticipated. On leaving the manse, and a sobbing Wonky, he returned to the pub where he stayed, sat by himself in a corner, for several hours.

★ ★ ★

'Broke it off!' Charlotte exclaimed.

Wonky nodded.

'The dirty dog,' Nell said.

'But why?' Charlotte demanded.

Tears welled in Wonky's eyes. She'd been crying more or less non-stop since Jack's visit the previous day. 'He said that, in his opinion, we weren't really suited and that it was in both our interests that he stop calling on me.'

'Oh dear,' Charlotte breathed.

'It's just not true!' Wonky wailed. 'We are suited. We get on terrifically together.'

'He obviously doesn't see it that way,' Nell commented.

'Perhaps it's simply funk on his part,' Charlotte mused.

Wonky's tears rolled down her puffed-up face. 'Do you think he might change his mind?'

Charlotte sighed. 'I have absolutely no idea. But would you want him back after this?'

'Oh yes.'

'I think you should put Jack Riach right out of your mind,' Nell counselled.

Wonky gave Nell a stricken look. 'That's just it, I can't. Not now, not ever. I know that for certain.'

Charlotte squeezed her anguished cousin's shoulders, imagining what it would be like if Geoffrey were to break it off with her. It didn't bear thinking about.

'I love him,' Wonky whispered.

'This is hard to say, and will cause you pain, but it would seem he doesn't love you,'

Charlotte replied in a sympathetic voice.

'Oh, Charlotte, oh, Nell, what am I to do? It's so horribly unbearable.'

Neither Charlotte or Nell had an answer to that.

11

MURDO rose to meet this man whose letter had arrived the previous week requesting an interview. The man had written that he had delicate business to discuss with him with no clue whatsoever as to what that business was.

Mulligan extended a hand. 'I'm pleased to meet you, Mr Drummond. It's most kind of you to see me.'

Murdo had been expecting someone Irish and was momentarily thrown to discover Mulligan was Jewish. 'How do you do,' Murdo replied a trifle formally as they shook.

'Beautiful countryside, a delight to drive through. You're very fortunate to be living here, Mr Drummond.' Mulligan sighed. 'I rarely get to leave Perth myself, the city itself that is. When I do it's a treat.'

Murdo gestured to a chair. 'Would you care for a dram, Mr Mulligan?'

'Not for me thank you. But don't let that stop your goodself indulging.'

There was something rather oily about Mulligan, Murdo thought. Good-quality clothes though, well cut. Mulligan was clearly a man of standing.

'I won't bother,' Murdo said, and sat facing Mulligan. 'Now how can I help you, sir? A delicate business matter you mentioned in your letter.'

Mulligan pulled a face. 'I'm afraid so. Not only delicate but embarrassing too.'

Murdo nodded and waited for him to go on.

'I have an establishment in Perth, amongst other interests that is, a gambling salon which bears my name.'

Murdo frowned. Gambling salon? What on earth could that have to do with him.

'One of my patrons is, or was, your son Andrew.'

Murdo digested that. Andrew a patron of a gambling salon? He'd had no idea his son gambled. He was suddenly filled with foreboding, half guessing what was coming next.

Mulligan sighed again. 'This is the delicate part. Unfortunately, during your son's last visit to my salon he lost heavily, a great deal of it on IOUs which I accepted and still hold.'

Mulligan fished in an inside pocket and produced the IOUs. Rising, he crossed and handed them to Murdo, then returned to his chair from where he regarded Murdo keenly.

Murdo's face was stony as, one by one, he examined the various notes. He had no doubt that the writing and signature were Andrew's.

'I see,' he said quietly when he'd finished his perusal.

'I spoke to your son on the night of his losses and it was agreed between us that he could have a week in which to raise the money. Unfortunately, which I learned from enquiries

I made, he was suddenly posted abroad during that period.'

Mulligan paused, then added with a smile, 'I'm sure that in the circumstances the matter simply slipped his mind and he had no intention whatsoever of welching on me.'

Murdo winced at the use of the word welch in connection with a member of his family.

'So I thought the best thing was to come to you,' Mulligan went on.

Murdo leafed through the IOUs again, adding the total. He paled when he arrived at it.

'A little over two thousand pounds, Mr Drummond. I'll happily round that figure off.'

If Andrew had been present in the room Murdo would have struck him. He then recalled Andrew's strange behaviour the night before he'd left, the uncharacteristic quietness of the lad. Now he knew why.

'And if I don't pay?' Murdo queried, already knowing he would. He was simply curious.

'Mr Drummond,' Mulligan replied in a sad voice. 'You must understand my position. I can't allow patrons to get away with matters of unpaid credit. There are ways and means depending on the person involved. In Andrew's case I would have to inform the army authorities which I'm certain would have unfortunate repercussions for your son.'

Cashiered, Murdo thought. Kicked out in disgrace. Officers had a code of honour to adhere to. A gentleman always paid his debts.

'I think I will have a dram after all,' Murdo declared.

Mulligan watched Murdo as he poured from the decanter and then had a large swallow. He didn't elaborate that if Murdo didn't pick up the IOUs then that would reflect on Murdo himself. He didn't have to.

Murdo finished his dram in a second large swallow. 'If you'd care to wait here, Mr Mulligan, I'll go to my study and write you out a cheque.'

Mulligan inclined his head. 'I knew you would resolve the situation, Mr Drummond. And I can assure you what has taken place will remain strictly between ourselves. You have my solemn word on that.'

'Thank you,' Murdo replied.

He paused at the door. 'Who or what shall I make the cheque out to?'

'Mulligan's will be fine.'

★ ★ ★

He was seething, raging. Two thousand pounds! How could Andrew be so irresponsible to do such a thing. It beggared belief.

Murdo poured himself a fourth dram, hardly aware that he was doing so. He continued to pace up and down the drawing room as he'd been doing since Mulligan had left ten minutes previously.

And then they hit him, the agonising pains in his chest. The glass spun from his hand as he staggered to the bell pull. He tugged it once and then sank to the floor.

Florence answered. 'Yes, sir — ' She broke

off and screamed when she saw a slumped, puce-faced Murdo. Turning she hared away to find Miss McQueen.

The pains lasted far longer than they ever had before, convincing Murdo he was done for. 'Get Peter and Dr McAllister,' he gasped to Miss McQueen, now kneeling beside him.

Miss McQueen rapped out an order and Florence bolted from the drawing room.

Thank God, the pains were easing. Murdo slowly drew in deep breath after deep breath.

'Can you make it to the chair, sir?' a very concerned Miss McQueen queried.

'In a minute, not yet.'

The colour in his face was beginning to fade when Peter crashed into the room. 'Get him a dram,' Peter instructed Miss McQueen, dropping down beside his father.

'No, I don't want that,' Murdo whispered.

'What is it, Pa. What's wrong?'

'I came over all funny. Some sort of turn.' Well that was true, if not the whole truth.

'Dr McAllister has been sent for,' Miss McQueen informed Peter.

He nodded his understanding and approval.

The pains were easing even further. Murdo was shaken to the very core.

Peter knew only too well what had caused this as Murdo had mentioned that a Mr Mulligan would be calling. He'd ring Andrew's bloody neck when he next saw his brother

Peter loosened Murdo's collar and tie, then between them he and Miss McQueen managed to get Murdo to the nearest chair.

'I'll fetch some water,' Miss McQueen said and, ignoring the water by the whisky decanter, hurried off to get fresh.

'Andrew, wasn't it?' Peter said grimly.

Murdo nodded.

'Little swine.'

'Did you know about it?'

'Yes, Pa, he spoke to me the day he came back. I told him you'd . . . ' He broke off in confusion.

'Well?'

'Have a fit,' Peter said hoarsely. 'I didn't think it would be a literal one though.'

Murdo managed a wan smile.

'Sixteen hundred pounds is a fortune.'

'Two thousand, Peter. That's what the IOUs amounted to.'

So Andrew hadn't even paid off what he had in the bank. That made it even worse.

Miss McQueen returned with a glass of water which Peter held to his father's lips. Murdo had a few sips and felt the better for them. 'Enough,' he croaked.

'If McAllister's out on his rounds he might be a while. I think we should get you to bed,' Peter stated.

Murdo closed his eyes. That had been a near thing, he was convinced of it. Damn Andrew.

'I didn't know Andrew gambled,' he said.

'Neither did I until he told me.'

Gambled and went to bed with Jean Ritchie. His second son was just full of surprises.

★ ★ ★

McAllister removed the stethoscope from his ears, rolled it up and replaced it in his bag. Peter looked on anxiously.

'Could you leave the doctor and me alone for a bit,' Murdo requested of Peter.

'But, Pa, I . . . '

'Please, son.'

Peter was displeased with that, and it showed. Nonetheless, he did as asked.

'He still doesn't know, I take it?' McAllister said.

Murdo shook his head.

'Is that wise?'

'It's what I wish, James. Let's just leave it at that.'

McAllister nodded. 'Now, can you tell me what happened? Was there anything specific brought this on?'

Murdo explained about Andrew, Mulligan's visit and the IOUs.

'Two thousand pounds,' McAllister mused. 'A tidy sum to say the least.'

'I was so angry, James, so bloody bloody angry. Well, you can imagine.'

McAllister could. He'd never particularly liked Andrew Drummond, there was something about the lad.

'I had a few additional drams after Mulligan left. But I've been good as gold otherwise, I swear.'

It was the combination, McAllister thought. There again, the attack might well have occurred without the whisky. He couldn't really say.

'It's bed for you for a couple of days, Murdo.

You can get up and go to the bathroom, and that's it. After that complete relaxation for at least a fortnight which means no work. Understand?'

Murdo nodded.

'You're still taking the pills I hope?'

'Every morning without fail.'

'Hmmh.'

'I swear, James. Every morning without fail. I'm not a complete eejit.'

McAllister laughed. 'You're many things, Murdo Drummond, but certainly not that.'

Murdo's eyes clouded. 'How could Andrew do such a thing. It's beyond me.'

'He must have got carried away. They say that happens in gambling. Though my own opinion is that anyone who gambles in the first place is a fool.'

Murdo didn't entirely agree with that, sometimes it was necessary to gamble in business as he well knew. But to throw your money away in a gaming salon, that was something else entirely.

'What do you want me to tell Peter?' McAllister asked.

They agreed on a story.

★ ★ ★

Nell was sitting quietly by herself reading a book, Charlotte was with Miss McQueen attending to some domestic matters, when it suddenly struck her who the Highlander's wife reminded her of.

193

Her eyes widened in shock. It was herself!

But that was silly, she didn't look at all like the woman, not in any way. And yet, it *was* herself she'd been reminded of.

How? Why?

And then it came to her, making her go cold all over. Had she been that woman in another life? Was that the answer?

Preposterous of course. Totally ridiculous. Laughable really.

Except . . . why did she have these visions of the Highlander and his family, mainly of him? Visions so realistic she might have actually been there?

Closing her eyes she envisaged the man, the face, the smile. And it seemed to Nell something stirred deep within her, though what she couldn't have said.

Her husband all those years ago?

She shivered.

★ ★ ★

'So how does it feel to be an old married woman?' Charlotte teased Jenny who'd just returned to work, having had a week off after her wedding.

Jenny beamed. 'It's wonderful, miss. Hamish and I are ever so happy.'

Charlotte couldn't have been more pleased for the maid. 'The wedding went extremely well,' she commented. 'You looked radiant.'

'It took me Ma and me ages to sew that dress. But it was worth it in the end.' Jenny giggled.

'Hamish told me afterwards that when I walked into church he thought me an angel down from Heaven.'

The dress had been a good effort, Charlotte thought, considering it had been homemade of course. The headdress, which had fallen to Jenny's shoulders, had been bedecked with wild flowers. The dress itself had been fairly plain with few frills which had suited Jenny. The material had been mousseline de voile, the additions cream-coloured lace.

'It was ever so kind of the family to give Hamish and me that canteen of cutlery,' Jenny enthused. 'We could never have afforded anything as nice.'

'Are you using it yet?'

'Oh no, miss, it's being kept for best. I wouldn't dream of using it every day.' There was something Charlotte was dying to ask, but found embarrassing. Nonetheless, curiosity getting the better of her, she did. 'And eh . . . you know. Is that all right between you?'

Jenny blushed bright red. 'Oh yes, miss.'

'There weren't any problems?'

Jenny's blushing deepened. 'None at all, miss.'

That was as far as Charlotte could go. 'Good, I'm pleased.'

'You'll be next I suppose, miss.'

'Probably,' Charlotte mused. She couldn't wait for that day. That day of days when she and Geoffrey, dear darling Geoffrey, would be joined.

★ ★ ★

Wonky stopped dead in her tracks on spotting a solitary figure on horseback. The horse was stationary, and the rider appeared to be staring out over the countryside.

It was Jack, she realised. A lump the size of an apple came into her throat. At least it felt that big.

'Jack,' she whispered. 'Oh Jack.'

Why oh why had he thought they were unsuited when it was so blindingly obvious to her they were a good match. What had she done to give him that impression? She couldn't for the life of her think.

Had he met someone else, was that it? Someone prettier than her, more witty. Someone rich while she was poor. If he had she hadn't heard.

How she missed him, his calling at the manse, their Sunday walks home. What joy he'd given her, joy that would have increased a thousandfold if they'd been married.

Now that would never be. Unless he came back to her that was, a hope she desperately cherished.

She stood watching Jack until he rode off.

★ ★ ★

Peter laid his pint and dram on the table then sat facing Jack who'd also called in for a quick one.

'So how are things, stranger?' Jack enquired amiably.

'I've been busy. Pa hasn't been well.'

'Oh? I hadn't heard.'

Peter had no intention of going into details, not even with Jack. Andrew's shame would remain a secret between him and Murdo.

'Nothing serious, but it's kept him off work which has put an extra load on my shoulders.'

'Well, I hope he's better soon. Give him my regards.'

'I will.'

Peter had a sip of whisky followed by a gulp of beer. 'I was sorry to hear about you and Wonky.'

Jack was immediately on the defence. 'How is she?'

'Still upset. As I said before, she's very keen on you.'

Jack shrugged. 'I don't consider us suited. It would have been a mistake.'

Peter studied his friend. 'Is that the real reason?'

'Of course.'

'Then why don't I believe you?'

That threw Jack into confusion which he did his best to hide. 'I've no idea.'

'The pair of you seemed very suited to me.' He paused, then added softly, 'She's broken hearted, Jack. And I mean that.'

Jack dropped his gaze to stare at the table. 'Better not to make a mistake than to make one and then have to live with it. She's a sweet lass who'll be a marvellous wife to someone, but not me.'

'The girls tell me, and this is in strictest

confidence, that she's hoping you'll change your mind . . . '

Jack felt wretched to hear that. 'I won't,' he mumbled.

'Absolutely certain?'

Jack nodded.

'Well then, there's no more to be said on the subject.'

Jack imagined Wonky like her mother, fat and gross. An appalling thought. 'She was good fun,' he admitted against his better judgement.

Peter raised an eyebrow.

'That doesn't mean to say we were suited. Merely that she was fun.'

Peter didn't reply.

Jack finished his dram and gestured to Peter's glass. 'Want another?'

'Why not.'

Jack rose and went to the bar where he thought about Wonky as he was waiting to be served. It was surprising him to find out how much he missed her. He'd only been calling on her for a short while but in that time had grown closer to her than he would have imagined possible.

He plonked himself down again at the table. 'If I give you the truth, Peter, she is your cousin after all and I suppose I owe it to you, you and I being friends, will you promise not to let on to Charlotte and Nell who'd be bound to tell Wonky?'

'I promise,' Peter nodded.

'It's her mother.'

'Aunt Moira! What's she got to do with it?'

'She's fat. Horribly so.'

'But it would be Wonky you'd be marrying, not her mother, for Christ's sake.'

'Do you know the expression, if you want to know how the girl's going to turn out look at her mother? Well I don't like fat women, Peter, never have. They repulse me. It would crucify me to be married to one.'

'I see,' Peter mused.

'I just can't take the chance.'

'But otherwise everything was fine between you?'

Jack nodded. 'We got on really well.'

'What a shame. And what happens if she doesn't turn out to get fat over the years?'

'Then it's my loss. But as I say, I can't take the chance.'

Peter could see his friend's mind was firmly made up. There would be no change of heart.

He felt dreadfully sorry for Wonky.

★ ★ ★

Murdo closed his eyes, and bent his head backwards a little, thoroughly enjoying the warm summer sun beating down on his face. This was the life, he reflected.

'Hello, Pa,' said Charlotte, joining him on the bench. 'What are you up to?'

'Precisely nothing, which is lovely.'

She laughed. 'Can't say I blame you on a day like today. I just hope this weather keeps up.'

'I should return to work you know, but somehow can't bring myself to do so. Peter's coping well enough on his own, he doesn't really need me.'

Charlotte gazed at her father, realising with shock that he'd aged considerably over the past few weeks. He'd lost weight on his face and neck and there were lines where there hadn't been any before.

'If that's how you feel I'd stay off if I was you,' she said softly. 'In fact, why don't you give up work altogether? As you say, Peter doesn't really need you.'

'It's funny you should say that, I've been considering it. Though I am young for retirement.'

'Would you be bored?'

There was a few seconds' pause while he mulled that over. 'I don't think I would, you know. I think I'd enjoy a life of idleness.' He laughed. 'My God, Murdo Drummond saying that. Me who's always thrived on hard graft.'

'Times change, Pa, and so do people.'

He wanted to live to see his grandchildren, he thought. That above all else. To dangle a bairn or two on his knee and spoil them. But with this heart thing, well you just didn't know.

'Maybe I'll speak to Peter this evening,' he declared.

'Why don't you? Hear what he has to say.'

Murdo closed his eyes again. 'If you don't mind, Charlotte, I think I'll have a wee sleep. It's so glorious.'

She pecked him on the cheek before leaving him to his nap.

'But you can manage by yourself, can't you?'

'Of course, Pa. If I have to.'

Murdo sighed. Was he doing the right thing or not?

'I just can't imagine you not involved in the distillery, that's all,' Peter stated. 'It's been part and parcel of you, and you it, since I can remember.'

'I think it's an excellent idea,' Charlotte said. 'If it's what Pa wants.'

'Me too,' Nell chipped in.

'The workforce won't like it,' Peter declared. 'You are the distillery as far as they're concerned. They idolise you, Pa, you know that.'

Murdo allowed a small smile of satisfaction to drift across his face. He'd always prided himself on the fact he was a good boss and popular with his employees. It was his belief that what you gave you got back double.

'There is an alternative,' Charlotte declared.

Murdo focused on her. 'What?'

'You don't have to retire altogether. You could go in two mornings a week, for example. That way you'd have the best of both worlds.'

'Hmmh,' Murdo mused. 'What do you think, Peter?'

'It's entirely up to you, Pa. I'll fall in line with whatever you wish.'

Two mornings a week? The best of both worlds as Charlotte put it. The idea appealed.

He made a decision. 'That's what I'll do then, starting Monday.'

'So be it, Pa,' Peter nodded. Then, eyes twinkling, 'Just think, McPhie will be delighted now you're going to have even more time to drive the Rolls.'

They all burst out laughing.

★ ★ ★

Tina Mitchell started on spotting the back of a familiar head. Andrew, he hadn't been to the salon in ages!

'Excuse me,' she said to the client she was with, and moved across the room. The client, an elderly gentleman who only dropped in occasionally, sadly watched her go. He'd been enjoying their conversation.

He'd put on weight, Tina thought as she drew closer. Then 'Andrew' turned sideways and she saw it wasn't him at all. She'd been mistaken which filled her with disappointment.

The man had an empty glass in his hand. 'Can I get you a refill, sir?' she asked.

'That would be nice.' He flashed her a smile. 'And who are you, young lady?'

'Tina, sir.'

'Well, Tina, I'm pleased to make your acquaintance.'

'Is it your first time here, sir?'

'That's right. I'm with a chum who's toddled off for the moment.'

'Will you be playing, sir?'

'Rather. A spot of roulette I think later on.'

Andrew's game. What had happened to Andrew? she wondered, unaware he'd been posted abroad.

She took the man's glass. 'I'll get that refill for you, sir.'

12

'I THINK we should set a date, don't you?' Geoffrey suggested to Charlotte.

They were sitting on a riverbank tucking into a picnic that Mrs Clark, the cook, had prepared for them.

'Oh yes,' Charlotte agreed quickly.

Geoffrey topped up her wine glass, and then his own. 'Any suggestions?'

'I'll leave it all to you, darling.'

He nodded his approval. 'I'll speak to your father this evening and start the ball rolling.'

Charlotte shivered in anticipation. It was her plan to use Miss Sinclair the Glasgow dressmaker. 'Nell and Wonky will be brides-maids, of course,' she said.

'Of course,' he echoed, thinking his intended had never looked lovelier. God, how he adored her! He was the most fortunate of men to have met Charlotte Drummond, not only to have met her but to have fallen for her and she him. Married life together would be sheer bliss.

'How is Wonky by the way?' he enquired. Charlotte had kept him informed about the Jack Riach business.

'She's slowly coming to terms with the situation. She's been hoping that Jack would change his mind but so far there's no sign of that happening.'

'Poor Wonky,' Geoffrey sympathised.

'She took it very badly. For a while she was quite inconsolable, forever bursting into tears. Thank goodness that stage is past.'

'And how about Andrew, have you heard from him?'

Charlotte, who knew nothing about the debt her brother had left behind shook her head. 'But then that's hardly surprising, it's rare for him to put pen to paper. We can only assume everything's all right.'

'I'm sure it is.' Geoffrey became thoughtful. 'I certainly miss him as do quite a few. His transfer was a loss.'

'The Watch's loss the First Essex's gain,' she laughed.

'Precisely.'

Geoffrey had a sip of wine. 'Dashed fine stuff this. Your father keeps a wonderful cellar for a whisky man.'

'Oh, he knows his wines as well, though he's never been a great wine drinker.'

Geoffrey listened to the nearby drone of bees, a soporific sound he found most pleasing.

'I wonder how he's getting on over in Ireland,' he mused. Then, with a wry grin, 'Whatever, he'll be enjoying himself. You can depend on that.'

'I'm sure,' Charlotte agreed, wishing Geoffrey would kiss her. She ached for his lips.

As though reading her mind Geoffrey laid his glass aside and squirmed over. 'Darling,' he crooned softly into her ear.

* * *

'A July wedding it is then,' Murdo declared. 'That gives us eleven months to get everything in order.'

Charlotte sighed with satisfaction.

'Now the venue, sir, what do you suggest?'

Murdo reflected on that. 'I have of course given the matter some thought. My initial reaction was to have it in Glasgow Cathedral, or Edinburgh. But then I changed my mind as so many of the locals would be terribly disappointed at not being able to attend. So what do you say we have it here with the reception held in a marquee in our grounds. Charlotte?'

'Sounds lovely to me, Pa.'

Murdo grunted. 'Geoffrey?'

'I'm in agreement, sir.'

'Good.' Murdo rubbed his hands together. 'I'll speak to Tom after church on Sunday.'

'And hopefully, if he can arrange it which I'm sure he'll be able to, Andrew will be my best man,' Geoffrey declared.

The smile vanished from Murdo's face. 'I see.'

'We had already decided that, sir, before Andrew was posted.'

'And if he can't make it?' Peter inquired casually, thinking of the almighty row that was going to erupt when Andrew next put in an appearance at home. Murdo would have the bugger's guts for garters.

'I'm sure it'll be all right considering the advance notice he'll be able to give them. But if there is a snag for whatever reason would *you* do me the honour?'

That surprised Peter. 'Well of course, old chap. I'd be delighted.'

'That's settled then.'

'You might pour us all a dram,' Murdo instructed Peter. Setting his elder daughter's wedding date certainly called for one.

Murdo wondered how long it would be before Charlotte became pregnant. Not too long, he hoped. He smiled in anticipation of the grandchild he'd dangle on his knee. Boy or lass? He didn't mind. As long as he or she was fit and healthy, that was the main thing.

★ ★ ★

The next months flew past and for Charlotte and Murdo there were a host of arrangements to be made for the forthcoming wedding. There were the trips to Glasgow and Miss Sinclair for a start, the three girls, Charlotte, Nell and Wonky going down and coming back together, for Miss Sinclair was also making the bridesmaids' dresses. What fun those trips were, the choosing of designs, materials, initial fittings. Then there were the accessories to find which involved numerous trips round the Glasgow shops and visits to restaurants where they'd discuss what they'd seen and what were possible buys.

In the meantime Murdo had put weight back on and hadn't suffered any more attacks. His two mornings a week at the distillery were just about right, he'd long since decided, thoroughly enjoying them when he went in, and thoroughly enjoying the free time he had to himself. To

McPhie's despair and chagrin he'd been doing more and more driving, not going anywhere in particular most times, just driving for the pleasure of it.

And then one day early in the new year Andrew showed up.

* * *

'Surprise!' an excited Andrew exclaimed to Murdo whom he'd found reading in the drawing room. 'I'm back.'

Murdo slowly laid the book he'd been engrossed in onto his lap and stared grimly at his younger son. 'So you are.'

Andrew put his hands on his hips. 'What kind of greeting is that? You don't look pleased to see me.'

'I can't say I particularly am.'

That shocked Andrew. 'Pa?'

'How's Ireland?'

'Some of it good, some bad.'

'Oh?'

Andrew went straight to the whisky decanter. 'I'm dying for some Drummond, you can't get it in Dublin. It's nearly all Irish muck.' He pulled a face. 'Dreadful.'

'I'd have thought you'd get plenty of Scotch whisky in the mess?'

'Oh you can, but unfortunately they don't stock Drummond either. No, I meant outside the mess.'

Have it out now or wait till later? Murdo wondered. Here and now he decided.

'Speaking of the Irish, I met a chap with an Irish name a while back who's an acquaintance of yours.'

Andrew had a deep swallow of whisky, and sighed. 'Who's that?'

'A Mr Mulligan from Perth.'

Andrew went deathly white. Now he knew the reason for the icy reception. He glanced away unable to hold Murdo's accusatory gaze.

'I can explain everything, Pa, honest.'

Murdo's lips thinned into a brittle smile. 'Well, this should be interesting.'

When Andrew left the drawing room fifteen minutes later he was literally shaking after receiving the dressing down of his life.

★ ★ ★

'Well, look what the cat dragged in,' Peter said to Andrew that evening on returning from work. He had come across his brother in an upstairs corridor.

'Now don't you start. I've already had enough from Pa.'

'Did he tell you he had an attack after this Mulligan was here and the doctor had to be called? It was a minor seizure brought on by anger and shock.'

Christ, Andrew thought. Murdo hadn't mentioned that. He shook his head.

'You could have killed him, you little swine!'

Andrew hung his head in shame.

'Did you actually think it was all going to disappear just because you'd been posted elsewhere? Of course it wasn't.'

'I honestly never thought he'd come to Pa.'

'Then you're a fool. Do you think he was just going to write it off? Those people aren't like that. And what, if instead of coming to Pa, he'd gone direct to the army? That would have been the end of your career, me lad.'

'It never crossed my mind,' Andrew mumbled. 'I was just so pleased to get out of the mess and not have to face Pa.'

Peter wasn't a particularly physical man, but what he did next was born of extreme anger. He lashed out, cracking Andrew across the cheek with an open palm.

Andrew staggered backwards. 'There's no need for that,' he protested.

'Keep away from me as much as possible during the rest of your leave. I don't want to know. Understand?'

Andrew nodded.

'And remember, the girls know nothing about what happened and that's the way it's to stay.'

'I won't say anything,' Andrew assured him.

Peter laughed scornfully. 'Hardly in your interest to let them see you in your true colours, is it?'

He strode past his brother, knocking Andrew aside in the process.

Andrew went to his bedroom where he threw himself onto the bed. It was going to be hell facing Murdo and Peter over the dinner table. But he'd have to.

He'd cut short his leave, he decided. He'd only stay a few days and then return to Dublin.

He'd think of some excuse to explain why his leave was so brief.

★ ★ ★

'He's seeing Grizelda McPherson,' a miserable Wonky told Charlotte and Nell. 'I only heard this morning.'

Charlotte didn't know what to reply to that. Wonky had been fine of late, and now this. 'I'm sorry,' was all she could think of to say.

Nell pulled a sympathetic face. 'There's plenty more fish in the sea, Wonky. Remember that.'

'Not like Jack Riach there isn't.'

'At least now you can stop holding out hope,' Charlotte said. 'If he's seeing Grizelda McPherson then he definitely hasn't any intention of coming back to you.'

Wonky nodded. 'I realise that.'

'Well, he's welcome to Grizelda. I've never liked her anyway,' Nell declared gallantly.

Wonky managed a small smile. 'I've never liked her either, and that's the truth.'

'She'll probably make his life a misery,' Nell went on.

'Nag him half to death,' Charlotte added.

'Drive him to distraction.'

'Up the pole.'

'Round the bend.'

'Spend all his money.'

'Put him in debt.'

'Be useless at nearly everything you can think of.'

211

'Soon lose her looks.'

'Develop pimples.'

'And warts.'

'And *sag*.'

Wonky threw back her head and laughed at the absurdity of all this. It was wonderful.

'Get flat feet,' Charlotte persisted, a twinkle in her eye.

'And go bald.'

That was too much for Charlotte and Nell who also burst out laughing.

'You girls are priceless. Thank you,' Wonky said, still laughing. It proved a turning point in how she felt about Jack Riach. After that her emotions truly began to mend.

★ ★ ★

'What's the verdict, James?' Murdo asked McAllister, starting to button up his shirt after the examination he'd just had.

'You're fit as a flea, Murdo, I'm happy to say.'

Murdo beamed. 'And the heart?'

'Banging away like a good one. Are you still walking?'

'Every day, hail or shine.'

'Well, it's certainly had an effect. Don't stop though, keep it up.'

'I will, James. Don't worry about that.'

'How are you off for pills?'

'I could use some more.'

McAllister sat and reached for his notebook. 'This semi-retirement business is ideal I'd say.

Enough to keep your interest with lots of time to yourself.'

Murdo re-did his tie. 'I still miss my pipe I have to confess. You'd think I'd have got over that by now, but I haven't.'

McAllister gave him a mock fierce glare. 'Well I don't want any relapses there. You stay off the tobacco.'

'Will do, James. Will do.'

McAllister completed the prescription with a flourish and handed it to Murdo. 'Any news of that boy of yours?'

Murdo shook his head. 'Not since I gave him merry hell over the debts he left. He only stayed home for three days before scampering off again with the lamest of excuses about a short leave. God mend him.'

'At least there weren't any repercussions from his visit. No more attacks I mean.'

'I kept my temper, James, though it was hard. And I'll tell you, the ticking off I gave him was probably the more effective for it.' Murdo snorted. 'Two thousand pounds indeed!'

'It doesn't bear thinking about.'

'No it doesn't.'

★ ★ ★

Hettie was furious. She'd managed to get rid of that Wonky Comyn and now Jack was stepping out with Grizelda McPherson. She could have spat.

Was there anything she could do to break up that little twosome?

She'd go and visit Granny Robertson she decided, and shivered. Granny frightened her, gave her the willies, which was why she'd so far avoided visiting the old crone. But Granny had potions and mixtures that did all sorts of things. Maybe one of those would do the trick.

She'd call on Granny at the first available opportunity. She wanted that cottage.

★ ★ ★

'I'm expecting, miss,' Jenny announced to Charlotte.

Charlotte clapped her hands in glee. 'That's wonderful. Are you sure?'

'Absolutely certain, miss.'

Charlotte hugged the maid. 'I'm so happy for you, Jenny. What does Hamish say?'

'He did a wee dance when I told him, miss. Then went straight down to the pub and got drunk as a skunk.'

Charlotte laughed. 'Quite right too. I suppose he's hoping for a boy?'

'You know men, miss, a son and heir's the thing.'

'Have you thought of any names yet?'

Jenny shook her head. 'I think that's bad luck. There'll be time enough for that after the bairn's born.'

'So you'll be leaving us then?'

'I'm afraid so, miss. But I'm hoping you'll let me stay on as long as possible.'

'Of course we will. Pa will insist.'

Charlotte took several steps backwards and

studied the maid. 'I swear you look pregnant,' she declared. 'There's a sort of glow about you that wasn't there before.'

Jenny blushed. 'Thank you, miss.'

'Am I the first in the household to know?'

'Yes, miss.'

'Then let's go and tell Nell. She'll be delighted for you.'

Chattering like two magpies they left the bedroom in search of Nell.

★ ★ ★

How's it going with Grizelda?' Peter asked Jack, as the pair of them enjoyed a Saturday night drink in the pub, their favourite meeting place.

'Fine.'

'No regrets about Wonky?'

Jack considered that. 'Yes and no if you know what I mean. She was good fun and would have made a lovely wife except . . . '

'She might have become fat,' Peter interjected.

'Precisely.'

Jack had a swallow of beer. 'I was a wee bit surprised that Grizelda allowed me to call on her. It was always you she was daft on.'

'Was she?' Peter countered, pretending innocence.

'Don't try that with me, Peter. You must have been aware, she made it obvious enough.'

'Not my type, sunshine. Simply not my type.'

'And what is your type?' Jack was curious.

'Don't know really, but not redheads like Grizelda. Redheads have never appealed.'

'You're auburn.'

'That's different. Different entirely.'

Jack shook his head. 'You're a funny old stick, Peter. I've known you all my life and yet there are times when I think I don't know you at all.'

Peter smiled. 'A mystery, eh?'

'Something like that.'

'Well, maybe that's a good thing. It wouldn't do, especially for a man of business as I am, if people could read me like a book.'

Peter lifted his pint. 'Here's to you and Grizelda. I hope it works out.'

'Thank you.'

Rather Jack than him, Peter thought, his face not betraying anything of what was going through his mind.

★ ★ ★

'Well, Miss McQueen, everything going all right?' It was precisely a week to the wedding.

'Still a great deal to be done, Mr Drummond, but we'll get there in the end.'

'Good,' he nodded.

'You must be very proud.'

'Very, Miss McQueen. I only wish . . . ' He broke off, having been about to say he only wished his wife Louise had been there to witness the occasion.

'I'm sure she too would have been very proud,' Miss McQueen said softly, having guessed what his thoughts were.

'Yes,' Murdo replied equally softly.

Miss McQueen smiled her understanding.

'Well, best be getting on. As I said, still lots to be done.'

She strode purposefully away leaving Murdo with his memories.

★ ★ ★

Murdo stood watching the marquee being erected. God, but it was huge. But then it had to be to accommodate all the people who'd been invited to the reception. It was all going to cost a great deal of money but well worth it as far as he was concerned.

'Hello, Pa.'

He turned to find Charlotte had come up beside him. 'How are you?'

'Fine.'

'Not nervous?'

'Not yet, Pa. But I'm sure I will be. It's such a momentous occasion after all. Frightening really.'

He frowned. 'Not having doubts, are you?'

'No, Pa, none at all. I love Geoffrey with all my heart.'

He patted her on the arm. 'You'll be all right, I promise you. Your ma was nervous as a kitten on her wedding day, her hand shaking when I slipped on the ring. But once the ceremony was over she was right as rain.'

He cleared his throat. 'There's nothing else troubling you, is there?' He averted his eyes. 'You did have that long chat with Mrs Ritchie?'

Charlotte smiled thinly. That was bothering her somewhat but she wasn't going to admit it. She only hoped she lived up to Geoffrey's expectations.

'No, Pa.'

He nodded. 'Right. Well I'm off for my walk while these chaps get on with the marquee.'

He kissed her on the cheek. 'See you later.'

★ ★ ★

Charlotte woke drowsily then, remembering that this was it, her day of days, was filled with sudden excitement.

Throwing the bedclothes back she swung out of bed.

★ ★ ★

Peter sat in the rear of the Rolls as it purred towards Pitlochry and the hotel where Geoffrey, his parents and other guests were staying.

He was to be best man after all, Andrew having written to Geoffrey a fortnight previously saying he couldn't make it as the regiment was going on manoeuvres, something he simply couldn't get out of.

Manoeuvres his backside, Peter thought grimly. He'd have bet a pound to a penny there weren't any and that Andrew had merely funked coming home. He thought it awful to have let a pal down like that, but that was Andrew for you.

★ ★ ★

Peter knocked on the bedroom door.

'Come in!'

Peter entered to find Geoffrey in his dressing gown, clearly in an agitated state. 'That bad, eh?'

'I've been awake for hours. Couldn't sleep. All manner of things kept going round and round in my head.'

Peter was suddenly alarmed. 'You're not thinking of calling it off I hope?'

'Of course not. That's the last thing I'd do or want.' He clutched his stomach. 'Wait here, Peter. Shan't be long.' And with that he bolted from the room.

Peter smiled. Nerves he thought. And that was the effect it was having on Geoffrey. Poor bugger.

He produced a hip flask when Geoffrey returned. 'Bit early I admit, but perhaps a swallow or two might settle that stomach of yours.'

Geoffrey shook his head. 'If I touched that it would be coming out both ends.'

They laughed.

'Let's get you dressed, old son.' He glanced at the uniform, Geoffrey's Number One Dress, hanging on the front of the wardrobe door. 'Though you're going to have to advise me as I help you.'

Geoffrey lifted the uniform down and placed it on the rumpled bed.

'Let's get started then.'

'Just don't worry, there's no rush. That's why I got here in plenty of time.'

'God, I hope the car doesn't break down on the way there. That would be ghastly.'

'A car looked after by McPhie break down? There's more chance of Andrew turning up than that.'

It was a private joke to himself as Geoffrey fully believed the manoeuvres excuse.

★ ★ ★

Murdo emerged from the Rolls, Geoffrey having been firmly ensconced in the church before the car returned to Drummond House for the bride, bridesmaids and himself. He helped Charlotte out, scooping up her train before it hit the ground.

Nell and Wonky were swiftly in attendance, Wonky smoothing down the dress while Nell took charge of the train.

'So how do I look, Pa?' Charlotte queried anxiously when they were ready to go in.

'Do you know how many times you've asked me that this morning? I've lost count. You look like a fairy princess and, believe me, that's the truth.'

He stared in open admiration at her dress, a confection created from the softest ivory silk, short sleeved with pleats folding to a high-waisted bodice. From there the skirt fell in folds to the ground. But the *pièce de resistance* was the three-foot train that would swirl in a soft ivory circle, echoing the embroidery of the bodice, where pearls were sewn into Buckingham lace.

The headdress had the same details, consisting of a delicate band worn across the forehead with the same ivory lace and pearls. The bandeau anchored two ostrich feathers, also ivory. Charlotte's bouquet was an elegant spray of red roses.

As for Nell and Wonky, their dresses, each with a short train, echoed the bride's in pale pink silk, falling from a high waist with short sleeves and a bodice with folded pleats over an overskirt. They carried tea roses to match their dresses. Both girls wore pearl necklaces to match the bodices of their dresses.

'Thank you, Pa,' she replied, smiling.

He gave her his arm while Nell and Wonky fell in behind them.

The organ struck up as they entered the church.

★ ★ ★

My my, that's a massive thing between your legs,' Jack Riach, there with Grizelda, teased Geoffrey. The 'thing' was Geoffrey's sporran.

Geoffrey, already flushed from alcohol, flushed even more. 'Here, steady on, old chap.'

Jack laughed. 'It's a wonderful reception, Geoffrey. Murdo has done you and Charlotte proud.'

Geoffrey gazed about him. There were throngs of people present, among them two Dukes and a Duchess.

'All set for tonight then?' Jack further teased.

'Jack,' Grizelda admonished. 'Leave the poor

man be. You're embarrassing him, not to mention me.'

'Have you had enough to eat?' Geoffrey politely enquired of Grizelda.

'More than enough, thank you. I shall be fat as a pig for weeks to come.'

Jack winced.

Charlotte joined them, slipping an arm through Geoffrey's. 'Enjoying yourselves?'

'I should say,' Jack replied.

'You looked wonderful coming down the aisle,' Grizelda said to Charlotte. 'When I saw you the breath caught in my throat.'

'Well, thank you.'

'I'm a lucky man,' Geoffrey declared.

'And I a lucky woman,' Charlotte added.

Grizelda caught sight of Peter whom she hadn't spoken to yet. Well, she thought philosophically, he'd had his chance. Now she was with Jack and that suited her fine. Peter Drummond could go fly a kite as far as she was concerned. She gave Jack her best smile.

'Quite a do,' James McAllister commented to Murdo.

'It should be, it's cost enough.'

'How many of those have you had?' McAllister asked quietly, nodding to the glass of champagne Murdo was holding.

'Och, man, don't play the doctor today. It's my daughter's wedding for goodness' sake.'

McAllister had a sip from his own glass, hoping that Murdo just didn't overdo it too much. He wondered where his wife was, last time he'd seen her she'd been talking to that dreary Tom Comyn.

'What'll you do if Jack speaks to you?' Nell asked Wonky.

Wonky shrugged. 'I doubt he will. But if he does I shall be nothing but pleasant.' She lowered her voice. 'I say, have you noticed what big feet Grizelda McPherson has?'

Nell giggled. 'Has she really?'

'Big as boats.'

They both laughed.

Peter glanced at his watch. Time to have a word with Geoffrey. He looked around trying to pick out the bridegroom. Peter accosted Nell and Wonky. 'They should be making a move to get changed.'

'Right then,' Nell said, looking for somewhere to place her empty glass.

She suddenly giggled. 'Sorry,' she apologised, placing a hand over her mouth. 'It's all that bubbly.'

The Duke of Strathearn beamed at Murdo. 'Haven't enjoyed myself so much in ages. It's all been absolutely first class.'

'Why thank you, Duke.'

'And where are the happy couple honeymooning?'

'I don't know. Geoffrey hasn't even told Charlotte that.'

They were joined by Sir Ian Murray whose glowing cheeks attested to the amount of alcohol he'd consumed. 'I say, there are some pretty fillies here this afternoon,' Sir Ian declared, giving Murdo a salacious wink.

That amused Murdo. Sir Ian was in his late eighties and had been married three times, losing all three wives through childbirth. It appeared there was still life in the old dog yet.

* * *

A crowd gathered to see the newlyweds off Murdo in the forefront. He kept sniffing, telling himself not to be such an emotional ass.

'You take care of her mind,' he said sternly to Geoffrey.

'I will, sir. You can rely on it.'

Gillian Armitage, resplendent in blue, was sobbing into a handkerchief while her husband Robert gazed proudly on. He and Geoffrey shook hands and exchanged a few words, then Geoffrey kissed his mother on the cheek.

More exchanges took place and more kisses then Charlotte and Geoffrey were climbing into the Humber T.

Before closing her door Charlotte purposely threw her bouquet to Nell who caught it with a squeal of delight.

Charlotte was waving, the majority of the crowd waving back, as the car drew away.

'That's that then,' Peter said to Murdo.

'Aye, son, that's that.'

Slowly they all trooped back to the marquee

* * *

Geoffrey and Charlotte returned from their honeymoon on 4 August, the day Britain declared war on Germany.

Geoffrey immediately left for his regiment.

Part Two

The Long Night

13

'JUST our luck to be stranded in bloody Ireland when there's a war on,' Lieutenant Billy Roberts complained to Andrew, as the pair of them were out riding.

Andrew was a far more experienced rider than Billy who'd only taken it up eighteen months previously. He glanced sideways at his friend, not at all sure he agreed with those sentiments.

'Think of the promotions that will be going,' Billy went on. 'There are bound to be stacks.'

Only because of casualties, Andrew thought grimly. He gazed about him. It was beautiful countryside, lush in the extreme. But he wasn't too keen on the climate — it rained even more often than Scotland.

'That Captain Kennington's a right bastard,' Billy said. 'I can't tell you how much I dislike him.'

Andrew smiled. He got on with Kennington well enough, it was simply a case of how you handled the man. Toadying, some people might have called it, but it worked and, as far as he was concerned, that was all that mattered.

'You rub him up the wrong way,' Andrew commented quietly.

'It's his attitude that gets me, supercilious swine.'

Andrew reined in on spotting another horse,

the rider a woman obviously in distress.

'I say, look at that,' Billy exclaimed, having also reined in. 'The beast appears to have bolted.'

'She needs help,' Andrew declared, kicking his horse forward. Billy immediately followed.

Andrew urged his horse, a powerful gelding into a gallop. Slowly he began to narrow the gap between him and the female.

The young woman heard their approach and turned her head towards Andrew and Billy 'Help!' she cried.

'Just hold on,' Andrew shouted back, thinking she could easily be killed or at the least badly hurt if she came off at that speed. He was well ahead of Billy whose horse wasn't nearly as fast as his.

Yard by yard, aided by some clever manoeuvring on his part, Andrew gained on the girl till at last his horse and hers were neck and neck. Leaning across he managed to grab the bridle.

For a few moments it was a fierce clash of wills between them, then the horse began to ease back and gradually slow.

When the horse finally came to a halt Andrew leapt to the ground and grabbed hold of its reins He then assisted the young woman down.

'Thank you,' she panted. 'That was truly frightening.'

'What happened?'

She gave a wry grin. 'I was stupid and arrogant enough to think I could control Midnight, which clearly I can't.'

Midnight was an apt name, Andrew thought

The animal was velvety black from nose to tail.

'Just let me catch my breath a minute,' the young woman said, placing a hand on her chest.

Billy came charging up, reined in and also dismounted. 'Everything all right?'

'I think so,' Andrew replied.

Midnight whinnied and threw his head, but Andrew had him firmly under control.

'Dashed large beast for a girl,' Billy commented.

'He's my father's horse,' the young woman explained. 'My own is lame and I wanted a ride. A mistake with Midnight as you witnessed.'

Andrew stroked a neck that was flaked with foam. 'There there, boy. There there,' he crooned.

'I'm Alice Fortescue by the way,' the young woman said.

'Andrew Drummond, Lieutenant in the First Essex based at Dublin Castle. This is my chum Billy Roberts.'

'Delighted to meet you, Miss Fortescue,' Billy declared, giving her a small bow.

'And I the pair of you. Who knows what the outcome might have been if you hadn't been on hand.'

'How far away do you live?' Andrew enquired.

'Several miles in that direction,' Alice replied, pointing off to their left.

'Well I think it best we walk the horses for a bit,' Andrew said. 'They all need a breather after that.'

Pretty girl, Andrew was thinking. He placed her in her late teens, possibly early twenties.

She was dressed in a black hunting jacket below which flowed an ankle-length grey skirt.

'I lost my hat somewhere along the line,' she explained. 'It just blew off.' She shuddered. 'I don't mind admitting that gave me quite a scare. Father will be furious if he finds out.'

'Well, we won't let on, will we, Billy?'

Billy grinned. 'Finds out what?'

Alice smiled. 'You're both very kind and gallant.' Pronouncing the latter in the French fashion.

'As every army officer should be,' Andrew retorted.

The three of them laughed at that.

Andrew could see she'd got her breath back. 'Shall we get started then?' he suggested. 'I'll lead my own horse and Midnight.'

'Fortescue isn't an Irish name,' Billy commented as they got underway.

'The family is originally English. We came over here in the seventeenth century when we were granted lands for services to the Crown. Lands succeeding generations have managed to enlarge considerably.'

'I see,' Billy nodded.

'We don't think of ourselves as English any more, but Irish through and through, albeit we're Protestants.'

That was interesting, Andrew thought. 'And what does your father do, if you'll pardon my inquisitiveness.'

'He manages our estate, which is a considerable task I can assure you. He'll be out now, doing whatever.'

Damn it, Andrew thought, when it started to rain. A light smir as the Scots call it, which nonetheless soon had them soaked. Alice seemed oblivious to it.

They made small chat as they proceeded in the direction of Alice's house till eventually Andrew decided they could remount. Alice was instructed to take Billy's horse, the smallest of the three, while Andrew took Midnight.

'Is this your land we're on now?' Andrew inquired as they proceeded onwards, keeping the horses to a walking pace.

'Oh yes. Everything round here is ours.'

Andrew wondered just how rich the Fortescues were. Considerably he reckoned, though owning land didn't always equate with having money in the bank.

Andrew reined in Midnight when the Fortescue house came into view. Dear God, he thought, it made Drummond House look like a cottage. It was vast.

'Greystones,' Alice smiled to Andrew.

'Very imposing I must say.'

'Far too big of course, costs an absolute fortune to maintain. We only live in the central part, both wings have been shut off for years.'

'You're not a large family then?'

'No, only my parents and myself. They'd hoped for more children but weren't blessed.'

'I have a brother and two sisters myself,' Andrew informed her. 'While Billy here is the youngest of five brothers. That right, old thing?'

'That's right,' Billy confirmed.

231

'I'd have loved to have had brothers and sisters,' Alice said wistfully. 'But it wasn't to be.'

They came onto a long drive that wound its way towards Greystones, the drive flanked by conifer trees. Then they were onto the driveway itself which, it seemed to Andrew, could have taken an entire regiment of cavalry.

They dismounted in front of terrace steps leading to a massive wooden door.

'Would you care to come in and dry out a bit?' Alice asked.

Andrew was about to accept when Billy produced his watch. 'I'm afraid that's impossible, Miss Fortescue. We really must be getting back.'

Andrew sighed. 'Duty calls I'm sad to say.' If Billy said it was time to get back then it was.

Alice's face creased with disappointment. She'd taken a shine to these two young, personable men. 'I can't thank you enough for what you did,' she said to Andrew.

'My pleasure. In every cloud, what? It gave us a chance to make your acquaintance.'

A smile replaced the look of disappointment. 'You're most kind. Perhaps you'll call another day.'

'Perhaps,' Andrew replied.

He formally shook her hand after which Billy did the same. Then he and Billy remounted.

'Goodbye, Miss Fortescue,' Billy said.

'For now,' Andrew added.

★ ★ ★

Murdo glanced up from his newspaper which he'd taken to reading at the breakfast table every morning. 'The war news is mixed again,' he said to Peter. 'Don't trust those Frenchies not to make a fist of it you know. Never did like the Frogs.'

'You said the same thing yesterday, Pa.'

Murdo snorted. 'Well, it's true. Just don't trust them.'

Charlotte looked on in concern. 'I do hope Geoffrey's all right. I haven't had a letter in over a week.'

'Oh, he'll be fine,' Peter tried to assure her. 'He'll know when to keep his head down.'

Murdo rapped his paper with a hand. 'This place Mons seems to be featuring a lot. It's been mentioned again and again.'

Charlotte wondered if that's where Geoffrey was. Closing her eyes she prayed he was safe.

★ ★ ★

John Blair was about to say something to Geoffrey when a bullet took him at the junction between nose and forehead. There was a momentary look of surprise on his face before he slumped to the ground.

Geoffrey knelt beside him. 'John? John?'

Blood oozed from the neat little hole. Through a haze of exhaustion and fear Geoffrey dimly noted that his friend was dead, the bullet on emerging having blown away the back of John's skull.

'Dear God,' Geoffrey whispered.

'A charge!' someone shouted. 'A charge!'

Geoffrey came to his feet and hastily reloaded his pistol.

The Watch were being mauled, but far from beaten. They'd been told to stand their ground and stand it they would to the last man if necessary.

A horde of grey uniforms appeared in front of them, the Germans shrieking and shouting as they advanced.

Geoffrey took careful aim and pulled the trigger again and again and again until his pistol was empty. He then snatched up a rifle and bayonet from a fallen comrade and seconds later was in hand-to-hand combat with a snarling German infantryman.

★ ★ ★

Granny Robertson frowned when, on opening her door to a knock, she discovered Hettie standing there.

'Well?' Granny snapped.

'You said to come back if your potion didn't work, and it hasn't.'

Granny grunted.

'And I paid good money.'

'So you did, lassie, so you did.' The ancient, wrinkled leathery face regarded Hettie keenly. 'You took it exactly as I said?'

'Yes.'

'You didn't forget at any time?'

Hettie shook her head.

'Then you'd better come away in and I'll see

what else I've got for you.'

Hettie's nose wrinkled in disgust as she stepped inside the hovel. The stench was unbelievable.

★ ★ ★

Geoffrey was incredibly tired, all he wanted to do was throw himself on the ground and fall asleep. But sleep was out of the question with the Germans hard on their heels.

It was a bitter pill to swallow that they were in retreat, but those were the orders. The entire British Expeditionary Force was falling back.

Geoffrey blinked and gazed about him. Christ, but the men looked more like ghosts than living soldiers. He presumed he was the same.

John gone, and so many others lying back there with a great many German corpses to keep them company. At least John's death had been instantaneous, he wouldn't have felt a thing, unlike some other poor buggers. He shuddered at the memory.

A single shot rang out and a man just ahead of him stumbled and fell.

'Sniper!' the cry went up.

Geoffrey could only wonder if he'd be next. Please God, not, he prayed. Please God.

Then another shot rang out, this one taking a soldier through the neck. The man, making terrible choking, gargling noises, fell to writhe on the ground.

A stretcher was called for but the man was dead before it reached him.

How much more of this could they take? Geoffrey asked himself. How much more?

On they went, stumbling southward towards the French frontier.

★ ★ ★

Wonky sighed and placed her knitting on her lap. 'It does get tedious after a while, doesn't it?'

Charlotte smiled her sympathy. It did. They were knitting socks and balaclavas for the men of the BEF.

'Just think how pleased the chaps will be to get these things. That's what you have to remember,' Nell said.

'I appreciate that,' Wonky replied. 'But it doesn't make it any the less tedious. I've never enjoyed knitting, though I don't mind sewing. Goodness knows why one and not the other, but there we are.'

'It's a real worry I still haven't heard from Geoffrey yet,' Charlotte said quietly a few seconds later.

'I've told you, he's probably someplace where it's difficult getting mail out,' Nell declared.

Charlotte glanced at her sister, fervently hoping she was right. That it might be other than that didn't bear thinking about.

'Why don't I ring for tea?' Wonky suggested. 'It's high time we had a break.'

'Good idea,' Charlotte responded. 'Would you?'

Wonky laid her knitting aside, rose and

crossed to the bell pull.

Charlotte gazed ahead of her, visualising Geoffrey as she'd last seen him. What a strange marriage it had been to date, she reflected. A honeymoon, and that was it.

But a wonderful honeymoon full of magic moments between the pair of them. She smiled in memory at their first night together. How nervous they'd both been, how coy and embarrassed getting into bed together.

'What are you day-dreaming about?' Nell asked. Then, with a smile, 'As if I didn't know.'

Charlotte nodded.

'It's only natural,' Nell further smiled.

'I didn't tell you but I bumped into Jack Riach the other day,' Wonky declared on rejoining them.

'And?' Charlotte demanded.

Wonky shrugged. 'I was cool but polite. Naturally I didn't mention Grizelda McPherson. He seemed relieved when we went our separate ways.'

'Hardly surprising,' Nell commented.

'How did you feel about him?' Charlotte asked.

Wonky considered that. 'Not at all as I would have imagined. It was as if . . . well as though I just didn't care. I was pleased about that.'

When Florence appeared in answer to their summons Charlotte requested that tea, cake and biscuits be brought.

★ ★ ★

237

Andrew lay on his bed with his hands clasped behind his head. He was thinking about Alice Fortescue.

There weren't any brothers or sisters which meant that, unlike him being a second son, she would inherit. Now that *was interesting, very interesting indeed. It would make her an extremely wealthy woman. Had to, with all that land, not to mention the value of the house.*

Did she already have a suitor? That was something else he had to find out. And if she didn't . . .

He smiled. He'd call on Alice as soon as possible.

★ ★ ★

To Geoffrey it felt as though he'd been punched very, very hard on the shoulder. I've been hit, he thought as he spun round and then collapsed to the ground.

The world went silent. And then darkness closed in.

★ ★ ★

There were thousands of Highlanders, a great army of them on the move. Some were on horseback, the majority on foot.

Was *her* Highlander there? Nell wondered. Surely he was, otherwise why would she be seeing this?

The army were in a jolly mood, many with grins and smiles on their faces. Although she

238

couldn't hear, it seemed to her there was a lot of banter taking place.

And then there he was, looking weary but as cheerful as the rest. One of the horsemen rode up and had a brief word with him.

A city came into view where it appeared they were headed. A city different to what it was now but essentially the same. A city she correctly guessed to be Edinburgh.

And with that the vision began to fade.

★ ★ ★

Charlotte knew the moment she picked the letter up off the silver salver that it was bad news. The letter almost smelt of it. With trembling hands she ripped open the envelope and began to read its contents.

It was from Geoffrey's C.O. He'd been severely wounded in the shoulder and was being shipped home to Britain for further treatment and recuperation. The C.O. had no way of knowing which hospital Geoffrey would be going to. He went on to reassure her that Geoffrey's life wasn't in danger.

When she'd finished the letter Charlotte clasped it to her bosom and let out a huge sigh of relief.

At least Geoffrey was out of it for now. Safe and sound, apart from his wound that was, and soon to be in England.

Thank the good Lord.

★ ★ ★

Andrew dismounted and tied off his reins. He then ran up the terrace steps that led to the massive wooden door.

A maid answered his ring. 'Yes, sir?'

'Is Miss Fortescue at home?'

'She is, sir.'

He handed the maid his card. 'Would you be kind enough to ask her if she'd receive me?'

'Certainly, sir.'

The maid closed the door and left Andrew waiting. He cast an appreciative eye over the grounds stretching away on both sides. They were sumptuous.

A few minutes later the maid reopened the door. 'Miss Alice will be delighted to receive you, sir. If you'll follow me.'

Andrew removed his cap and stepped inside.

The floor of the huge hallway was tiled with marble, the walls covered in heavy embossed paper. There were various portraits on the walls who he presumed were family ancestors. His footsteps echoed hollowly as he strode after the maid.

He was ushered into a magnificent drawing room where Alice was sitting on an emerald green chaise longue. By the fireplace stood a middle-aged man in the garb of country gentleman. Partially bald he sported a very thick and heavy walrus moustache.

Andrew went straight to Alice, took her extended hand and lightly brushed his lips over it. 'Miss Fortescue.'

'Mr Drummond, what a delightful surprise.'

'I was out this way and decided to take up

your invitation to call.'

'I'm pleased you did.' She turned her attention to the middle-aged man. 'Father, this is Mr Drummond whom I met when out riding recently. He's a Lieutenant with the First Essex.'

Andrew crossed and shook with Alice's father whose grip, he noted, was a particularly strong one.

'I'm Sir Henry by the way.'

A shrewd old codger, was Andrew's initial impression of Sir Henry. Nobody's fool.

'Perhaps we should ring for tea?' Alice suggested.

Sir Henry regarded Andrew keenly. 'Maybe the young man would prefer something stronger?'

Andrew guessed that's what Sir Henry himself wanted. 'Oh yes please, sir.'

'Whiskey or claret?'

'Whisky, sir.'

'Good chap. Just the ticket.'

Alice, looking on, was thinking what a fine-looking specimen Andrew was. There was something different about him, though she couldn't have said what.

Sir Henry opened a drinks cupboard and reached inside.

'Do you have any scotch whisky, sir? I'd prefer that if you have.'

Sir Henry frowned. 'You don't care for our Irish?'

'It's not that, sir, but I suppose what you're used to.'

Sir Henry nodded his understanding. He

produced a bottle and two glasses from the cupboard. 'I'll join you in that. I quite enjoy a drop of scotch myself. Though I have to admit, my own preference is Irish.'

'As I said, sir, what you're used to.'

Sir Henry poured out two stiff ones. 'Water?'

'Just a drop, please.'

He handed Andrew a glass and held his own up in a toast. 'Your very best of health, Lieutenant.'

'Thank you, sir. Isn't Miss Fortescue joining us?'

'Doesn't drink, silly girl. Doesn't know what's good for her.'

Andrew smiled at Alice.

'You seem to know your whisky, Mr Drummond,' Sir Henry said after having a swallow. He was simply making conversation.

'I should, sir, my family own a distillery.'

A hairy eyebrow shot up. 'Really? That's interesting.'

'Drummond whisky, sir. Have you heard of it?'

Sir Henry shook his head. 'Can't say that I have.'

'Then allow me to send you a case, sir. I'd value your opinion.' Masterly stroke, he thought.

Sir Henry's face lit up. 'Dashed decent of you, Mr Drummond. I'll look forward to that.'

'It may take a while, sir, but have it you shall.'

'And where exactly is this distillery located, Mr Drummond?' Alice asked.

'A small village called Dalneil in Perthshire. The distillery has been in our family for generations.'

Sir Henry saw off the rest of his drink, considered having another, then decided against it. 'Met out riding you said, Alice?'

'Mr Drummond was with a colleague. They asked me for directions.' The latter lie came out smoothly. She shot Andrew a glance warning him to support her story.

'Daft of course, two army officers getting lost. Though in truth, we weren't exactly that. Let's just say we needed confirmation of where we were going.'

Sir Henry laughed. 'I quite understand. And where are you based, Mr Drummond?'

'Dublin Castle, sir.'

'Aah, Dublin,' Sir Henry sighed. 'Wonderful city.'

'I concur, sir. I'm very happy to be there.'

'I don't get up nearly enough. Must make more effort in future.'

'Do you like Dublin, Miss Fortescue?'

'Very much so. Like Father, I think it wonderful.'

Andrew stayed for half an hour, long enough for a first visit in his estimation. He left, promising to return soon.

A good start, he thought as he rode away. A very good one. Though he still hadn't found out if Alice already had a suitor.

As for money, the answer to that seemed obvious enough.

14

MURDO read Andrew's letter a second time then laid it down. So, the lad had written at last and appeared most contrite about the Mulligan business. And so he should be, a disgraceful episode.

According to him he was now thoroughly enjoying Ireland and his new regiment. They were nothing like the Watch apparently, but a good regiment nonetheless.

Towards the end of the letter Andrew had mentioned meeting an Alice Fortescue whose father, Sir Henry, an extremely important and prominent person in the area, he'd promised a case of Drummond whisky to and could Murdo please arrange for a case to be sent to him at Dublin Castle.

A romance? Murdo wondered. It certainly sounded like the beginnings of one. Andrew wasn't in the habit of promising cases of whisky. Done in this instance to impress the father no doubt.

Another marriage in the offing? It was a possibility, though obviously early days yet.

In his last paragraph Andrew had enquired about Geoffrey, hoping that he was well.

Murdo decided to send the whisky and a letter in reply. He wanted to let Andrew know that Geoffrey had been wounded and was currently in an English hospital.

★ ★ ★

'What do you think about Kitchener's appeal for more volunteers?' Jack Riach asked Peter, the pair of them in their usual seats in the pub.

'He must need them.'

'I presume so. Doesn't bode all that well though, I should say.'

'Hmmh,' Peter grunted.

'We couldn't lose this war, could we?' That was a truly appalling and humiliating thought.

'I don't know, my knowledge of military matters is only what I read in the newspapers. And they tell us we haven't been doing all that well so far.'

Jack nodded. 'Mons appears to have been a disaster and now the Hun are advancing on Paris. I just can't believe that'll fall. It's unthinkable.'

'From what I understand men have been volunteering in their tens of thousands to date and yet according to Kitchener he still needs more.' Peter shook his head in bewilderment.

'Everyone said it would be over by Christmas,' Jack mused. 'It would seem now that's somewhat over-optimistic.'

'Several of the chaps at the distillery joined up last week. Pa wasn't best pleased, but understood. Told them he was proud of them and wished them the very best.'

'Did they indeed.'

'Chaps our age.'

Jack thought about that.

'It means we're short handed which is a

245

bugger. However, we'll cope somehow. Pa has the idea of asking old Ronnie Montrose who retired a few years ago to come back and help out, though he hasn't spoken to him yet.'

They sat in silence for a while, each lost in his thoughts. 'How are you getting on with Grizelda?' Peter enquired eventually.

'Fine. Things are progressing nicely.'

'I see.'

'How's eh . . . Wonky?' Jack flushed slightly on asking that.

'She's all right. She and the girls spend most of their days knitting for the troops.' He laughed. 'They're getting through mounds of wool.'

'Good for them,' Jack nodded.

'I must say I'm impressed. It makes one feel . . . ' Peter broke off and reached for his pint.

'Feel what?'

'That perhaps one should be doing something oneself,' Peter stated quietly.

'I've been thinking the same thing,' Jack confessed equally quietly.

'Have you now? But how would you possibly get away?'

'Arrangements could be made. Talking of bringing people out of retirement, my parents retired to Largs as you know. I'm sure they'd come back for the duration if necessary. In fact I'm certain of it, Dad has never enjoyed retirement. What about you?'

'Same here. Pa's on hand, he could easily go full time again.'

The two men stared at one another.

'It's a thought,' Jack murmured.

'Yes,' Peter agreed. It certainly was.

★ ★ ★

Charlotte gazed eagerly into the distance, down the platform at Pitlochry station awaiting the arrival of Geoffrey. He'd spent two days in Glasgow with his parents and was now en route to Pitlochry and Drummond House.

McPhie took out his watch and peered at it. 'She's late, only minutes so far mind, but still late.'

Charlotte tried to contain her impatience. Of all the trains to be late it had to be this one. She reminded herself there was a war on, trains didn't always run to schedule during wartime.

McPhie slapped his hands together. There was a nip in the air. Winter was just around the corner and was, according to all the signs, going to be a severe one.

'There!' Charlotte exclaimed, pointing to where a thin plume of smoke had appeared. 'That'll be it.'

How would he look? she wondered. Thin probably. She'd have to feed him up, take care of him.

'Aye, that's it all right,' McPhie confirmed.

Charlotte's hand went to her hair which she was wearing in a roll at the back. Everything was in place. Her hat, a black one, brimless with a cherry-coloured bow at the front from which a similar coloured feather swept backwards. It was a favourite of Geoffrey's which was why she'd chosen to wear it.

'Hurry up,' she murmured, almost shaking with excitement. 'Hurry up.'

McPhie glanced at her in amusement. It was her man coming home from the war, he reminded himself. No wonder she was beside herself. He'd probably have been the same in her place.

For a few moments he reflected sadly that he'd never married. Not that he had anything against marriage, nothing at all, it had simply never happened for him. Anyway, he was past all that now, well past it.

What if Geoffrey had missed the train? Charlotte thought in sudden alarm. What if something had happened to make him miss it?

You're havering, she told herself. Imagining things. Geoffrey was on the train, she just knew it.

And then the train was pulling into the station and windows were being dropped so that the passengers getting out could open their doors.

The train halted in a great whoosh of steam and people began alighting. Charlotte spotted Geoffrey almost at once. 'There he is!' she exclaimed, hurrying forward.

She stopped about a foot from him and they gazed hungrily into each other's eyes.

'I'll get your case, sir,' McPhie said, and dived into the compartment from which Geoffrey had emerged.

Geoffrey broke eye contact to instruct McPhie which one was his, then he had his good arm round Charlotte and, not giving a damn what anyone thought, was kissing her.

* * *

'I'd forgotten just how truly beautiful you are,' Geoffrey said to Charlotte as the Rolls purred away from the station.

'And I how handsome you are.'

He laughed. 'We sound like a mutual admiration society.'

Reaching out he clasped her hand. 'Oh, Charlotte, my darling. I've missed you so.'

'And I you. It's been like a physical ache.'

He kissed her hand.

McPhie was studiously avoiding looking in the mirror. The sliding glass panel was shut so he couldn't hear what was being said.

Charlotte's gaze slid to the arm in a sling. 'Is it still painful?'

He nodded. 'Though nowhere as bad as it was. I was lucky in a way. It could have been far worse.'

'When . . . ' She swallowed hard, 'Do you have to return?'

'When the shoulder's healed. Your Doctor McAllister will tell me when that is. A few weeks probably. Maybe more.'

A few weeks, so short a time. She vowed they'd make the best use of it.

'The hospital let me go because they need the beds. There have been an awful lot of casualties,' he said softly.

'Was it . . . really awful over there?'

His eyes clouded in memory. 'Yes,' he whispered.

'Oh, Geoffrey.'

'We lost a lot of men at Mons and during the retreat. Do you recall my friend John Blair whom I've mentioned to you in the past?'

She nodded.

'We were standing together when he was killed. It was horrible.'

'I'm so sorry,' she murmured.

'He was a good man. One of the best.' Geoffrey's voice choked on saying that.

He looked away to stare out over the passing countryside. In his mind's eye remembering . . . remembering . . .

★ ★ ★

'Well, let's hear all about it,' Murdo said, the family having just sat down to dinner. He beamed at Geoffrey.

Geoffrey dropped his gaze. 'I'd rather not, sir.'

'Rather not?'

Peter frowned. He'd been looking forward to this. 'Why, old boy?' he queried.

Geoffrey took a deep breath. 'It's certainly not the sort of thing to discuss at the dinner table.'

'I see,' Murdo mused.

'I'm sorry.'

'No need for that. I'm sure you have your reasons.'

'You're going to have to cut my meat for me

when it comes,' Geoffrey said to Charlotte sitting beside him.

'Of course, darling.'

'Thank you.'

Murdo saw a great change in Geoffrey. A young man had gone away to war, a mature one had returned. A mature man with a haunted expression in his eyes.

Murdo could only imagine what it had been like. He thanked God Andrew was safe in Ireland.

* * *

'I'll help you undress,' Charlotte said later when they'd retired.

'I'd appreciate that.' He paused, then said, 'I hope I wasn't too much of a damp squib over dinner, not wanting to talk about it that is.'

'I'm sure they understood.'

'Maybe sometime, but not now.'

'Not even to me?'

He smiled lovingly at her. 'Especially not you, my darling.'

She began to assist him with his clothes and soon he was standing stark naked before her. What a pity they couldn't make love she thought, desperately wanting to do so. But that was impossible with Geoffrey's arm in a sling.

As it transpired it wasn't impossible after all, Geoffrey having already given the matter some thought.

She'd never heard of such a thing when he explained it to her, but it did the trick.

Andrew rented a carriage to take the case o
whisky to Greystones having first written to
Alice to tell her when he would be arriving
A return letter had invited him to luncheon or
the proposed day.

The same maid as before answered his ring
and again he was ushered into the drawing
room.

'As promised, sir,' he smiled at Sir Henry
'Now where shall I put this?'

'On that chair, Mr Drummond.'

Andrew placed the case on the indicated chair
then dusted his hands off. 'All the way from
Bonnie Scotland compliments of my father and
Drummond whisky,' he declared.

'We'll have a drop of that right away, just to
ensure it hasn't 'gone off' in transit,' Sir Henr
said, eyes twinkling at his joke. 'But first I'd lik
you to meet my wife. Mr Drummond, this i
Lady Fortescue. Mr Drummond, my dear.'

Lady Fortescue was roughly the same age a
her husband, dark haired like Alice and gav
the impression of having a forceful personality

'Delighted to make your acquaintance, M
Drummond,' she said in a slightly husky voice

'And I yours, Lady Fortescue.'

'Now that the formalities are over I'll ring an
have one of the servants open this whisky,' Si
Henry said.

'No need for that, sir. I'll do it.'

Alice, who'd been sitting, rose and joine
them. 'Hello, Mr Drummond,' she smiled.

He gave her a small bow. 'Hello, Miss Fortescue. It's a pleasure seeing you again.'

She continued to smile, but didn't reply to that.

It was the work of a minute, with the help of his knife, for Andrew to open the case and extract a bottle from within. 'Twelve-year-old Drummond single malt,' he declared. 'My father insists there isn't another in all of Scotland to beat it.'

'Then let's judge for ourselves, eh?' Sir Henry rounded on his wife. 'Will you join us in a drink, my dear?'

'A glass of claret would be acceptable I think.'

'Then claret it shall be.'

Andrew moved closer to Alice. 'Shall I tell you something quite shocking?'

Her eyes widened while Lady Fortescue looked on in sudden concern.

'Both my sisters drink whisky. They were brought up to it, you see. It's a family tradition.'

'Gracious,' Alice breathed.

'It raises a few eyebrows at times I can tell you.'

'I'm sure.'

Sir Henry chuckled as he poured the claret. 'Women drinking whisky, whatever next!'

'I hear French women drink absinthe which is a filthy concoction, so why not whisky,' Andrew smiled.

'Tried absinthe once, and you're right, it is filthy,' Sir Henry said, handing his wife her claret.

'When did you do that, Henry?'

'Years ago, my dear, in Dublin. We all thought it rot.'

Andrew was aware of Alice studying him and wondered what was going through her mind.

Sir Henry opened the whisky bottle and sniffed its contents. 'Doesn't seem to have 'gone off',' he further joked.

Hefty measures were spilt into two glasses. 'Now what's that Scottish toast again?'

'*Slainthe*, sir.'

'Then *slainthe* it is!'

Sir Henry tasted the malt, rolling it round his mouth before swallowing. 'Capital stuff,' he declared.

'I'm glad you approve, sir.'

'Very much so, Mr Drummond. Though I have to admit . . . '

'You still prefer Irish,' Andrew finished for him.

They all laughed.

★ ★ ★

'It was most kind of you to get that whisky for my father,' Alice said later after luncheon, as she and Andrew strolled in the gardens.

'Not really. It was merely an excuse to see you again.'

She glanced sideways at him. 'You're being very forward, Mr Drummond.'

'Then I apologise. But I do believe that honesty, as they say, is the best policy.'

'Indeed.'

254

'And I *was* keen to see you again.'

She didn't reply to that, but her mind was whirling.

'May I ask you something?'

'That depends on what it is.'

'Do you already have a suitor, Miss Fortescue?'

She felt her heart begin to beat faster.

'It's just that I can't believe you don't.'

Alice stopped and stared out over the gardens, her emotions now mixed. On one hand she was pleased with Andrew's attentions, on the other . . .

'I did have up until last year,' she said softly. 'His name was Paul McLuskey and we were childhood sweethearts. Everyone expected us to eventually get married, which I'm sure we would have done. Except last year . . . ' Her voice trembled. 'He was killed in a hunting accident.'

Jubilation filled Andrew, the coast was clear. 'I'm so sorry,' he lied.

'It was a terrible time, for all concerned. I've been something of a recluse ever since.'

Andrew thought of how they'd met. 'I'm surprised, in the circumstance, that you took out Midnight.'

She sighed. 'Stupid I agree. But there you are, we Irish love our horses and Midnight was a challenge.' She paused, then added, 'One I shan't be repeating I assure you.'

'I'm glad to hear it.'

She gave him a wan smile. 'If it hadn't been for you I might have gone the same way as Paul.'

'Which would truly have been a tragedy,' he said sincerely.

They continued walking.

'Father likes you,' she said.

'Does he indeed.'

'Oh yes.'

'And . . . what about you, Miss Fortescue?'

Again she glanced sideways at him. 'You're very pretty.'

Andrew laughed. 'I've been called many things in my time but never pretty.'

'Well you are. You also have an easy manner about you which is attractive.'

'As do you, Miss Fortescue. May I confess?'

She slightly raised an eyebrow. 'If you wish.'

'I was extremely attracted to you the first time we met.'

'I'm flattered,' she replied.

He took a deep breath. 'Were you very much in love with this Paul McLuskey?'

She considered that. 'To be honest, I don't know about love. Though I probably was. There aren't all that many Protestants in this area you see, so we do tend to interbreed somewhat.'

'I think I understand.'

'Do you?' she queried.

'It must be difficult for someone in your position. Meeting the right sort of man, I mean.'

'It is, believe me.' She stopped again. 'I think we should turn back now, don't you?'

'Only if you'll allow me to call on you again.'

'If you wish, Mr Drummond.'

'Andrew when we're alone, please.'

She smiled, a smile that lit up her face. 'And you may call me Alice.'

'As you're such a keen horsewoman perhaps we can go riding together. Or would that be in bad taste?'

'I take it you're referring to Paul. No it wouldn't be in bad taste as I ride out all the time.'

They settled a date before returning to Greystones.

* * *

Nell found Peter alone and lost in thought. 'Penny for them?' she queried.

He roused himself from his reverie. 'Oh I was just thinking.'

'About what. Work?'

'Partially.' That was true enough, work did come into it. He motioned to the settee he was sitting on. 'Come and join me.'

'Why, thank you, big brother.'

He ignored the sarcasm in her voice. 'I suppose Charlotte's with Geoffrey?'

'Of course. They've hardly been apart since he arrived.'

'He still won't talk about his experiences over in Belgium and France. I tried again to tackle him on them the other day and again he shied away.'

'They can't have been very pleasant.'

'No,' Peter nodded. 'They can't.'

'Have you noticed that look he occasionally

gets in his eyes nowadays? It's scary.'

'Yes,' Peter replied softly. 'I have and it is.'

'Poor Geoffrey.'

Peter took out his handkerchief and blew his nose. He thought he had the beginnings of a cold coming on which was a nuisance. 'Pa seems in fine fettle of late,' he said.

'Yes he does. A life of leisure suits him. He never misses his daily walk you know. Not ever.'

Peter shook his head. 'I still can't get used to the idea of Pa taking up walking. It's amazing.'

'Not only taking it up but relishing it.'

Talk to Murdo before or after? Peter wondered.

Definitely after the deed was done.

★ ★ ★

'I'm going to miss that when you're gone,' Charlotte sighed, sliding off Geoffrey and snuggling up beside him.

'Just that. What about me?' he teased.

'You too, silly. You know what I mean.'

'I'll miss it and you too,' he declared.

'I'd hope so.' She ran fingers across his chest. 'When you do go back how long is it likely to be before you get a leave?'

'No way of telling, Charlotte. That's entirely in the lap of the Gods. One thing I do know, I don't want another leave because I've been shot a second time.'

She winced. 'Don't even think about that, Geoffrey.'

He wondered how the battalion was getting on. When he did return how many faces would he discover to be missing. Men dead and wounded. It was a gruesome thought.

Closing his eyes he saw John Blair being shot, and the momentary look of surprise on John's face before he slumped to the ground. Despite the warmth of the bed and Charlotte beside him he was suddenly cold all over.

'Darling?' Charlotte whispered.

He opened his eyes. 'Yes?'

'For a moment there I thought you'd dropped off.'

'No, I'm still awake. Tired though, but still awake.'

She giggled. 'Have I worn you out?'

'More or less.'

'That's good then.'

'And how about you, have I worn you out?'

'Very much so, my darling.' Her expression changed. 'I so want to please you in every way.'

'You do, Charlotte.'

'Swear?'

'I swear.'

She smiled, a smile of satisfaction. How she loved this man of hers. How she adored him. Life before Geoffrey had been comfortable but bland and colourless, now it was oh so very different. They fitted so well in every way together, like two pieces of a jigsaw.

Reaching under the bedclothes she sought and found his penis which she gently held in her hand. 'It's like a little mole,' she whispered.

He laughed. 'Really?'

'Oh yes, a little mole. My little mole.'

'It wasn't so little a few minutes ago,' he reminded her.

Her eyes sparked with amusement. 'That's true, as I'm only too well aware. And thankful for. But in this state it's a little, soft velvety mole.'

He wondered if other people said daft things like this to each other. Probably, he decided. It was perfectly natural in the circumstances.

'A little mole looking for its burrow,' he said.

She laughed softly as what she was holding began to harden. 'Not again?' she teased.

'It appears I'm not so worn out after all. What about you?'

'Funny that, but it's the same with me.'

She straddled him as his little mole continued to grow and grow.

She sighed with pleasure as the mole found its burrow.

★ ★ ★

'I think we can dispense with the sling now, Mr Armitage. You're coming along extremely well,' Doctor McAllister announced.

Geoffrey wished with all his heart that he wasn't. The sooner McAllister pronounced him fit the sooner he'd be back in France and what lay in store there.

Charlotte, he thought. Oh, my darling Charlotte, all I want is to stay here with you.

15

'JOIN up?' Grizelda McPherson repeated, eyes gleaming.

Jack nodded. 'So what do you think?'

'You must, if that's how you feel. I'm all for it.'

'You are?'

'Oh yes. Every able-bodied man should do his bit, as they're all saying nowadays. It's your duty.'

That was a relief, Jack thought. He'd been certain she'd be against it. Clearly he'd been wrong about that.

'You'll look wonderful in a uniform,' Grizelda enthused, voice filled with excitement. 'You have the build for it.'

'It'll mean being away for quite some time. And who knows what'll happen, there's always the possibility I won't come back.'

A tremor ran through her that was almost sexual in nature. 'You'll come back, Jack, I just know it. And come back a hero.'

He laughed. 'Here, steady on. I've no intentions of being a hero. Serving my country well, and by that I mean Scotland, is all I have in mind.'

'But a hero you'll be nonetheless. That's the sort of man you are.'

Was he? Jack wondered. Did Grizelda see something in him he didn't. He had to admit being a hero was a pleasant prospect. 'Peter Drummond and I are going to enlist together,' he confided. 'But that's something you keep to yourself for now. All right?'

She nodded.

'It rather upsets things between you and me, I'm afraid,' he said.

'Why?'

'Because I'll be away, that's why.'

She lightly caressed his cheek. 'Time spent apart won't matter. At least not to me. I'll be here waiting for you when you return.'

'Are you sure about that, Grizelda? What if you meet someone else in the meanwhile?'

She gave a scornful laugh. 'Is that what you think of me, Jack Riach, that I'd allow that to happen? Well it won't, I assure you. I'll be here waiting on your return, I swear it.'

'If you are we'll get married, after a suitable engagement of course.'

'Oh, Jack,' she breathed. 'Is that a proposal?'

'Sounds like one to me. Do you accept?'

'With all my heart, Jack. With all my heart.'

Pride swelled within him. 'Will you write?'

'Naturally I'll write, you silly man. Every single day while you're away. And I'll knit for you, and send you parcels. I understand parcels are very gratefully received over there.'

'It's settled then,' he declared. 'Enlist I shall.'

'Oh, Jack,' she breathed. Face flushed, she pressed herself closer to him and closed her eyes.

Jack, knowing what she wanted, kissed her.

'You what!' Murdo exploded.

'Enlisted, Pa. Jack Riach and I together.'

Murdo couldn't believe his ears. His face went puce as anger burst within him. 'I won't have it, Peter, I just won't! Not two sons in the army. You'll just have to unenlist, that's all.'

Peter, still tipsy from the Pitlochry pub he and Jack had repaired to after the recruiting office, shook his head. 'That's impossible, Pa, as you're well aware. Once you sign on the dotted line that's it.'

Murdo was sorely tempted to slap his son, but refrained from doing so. This was a bombshell. 'What about the distillery?' he demanded.

'You'll have to go back full time, Pa. I'm sorry about that.'

Murdo wheeled about, strode over to the whisky decanter and poured himself a huge one which he despatched in a single gulp. Christ but he was angry. He poured himself another.

'Why didn't you discuss this with me first?' he queried harshly.

'I should have thought that was obvious from your reaction.'

'I would have tried to talk you out of it. No, more than that, I would have forbidden you to go ahead.'

'I know, Pa,' Peter nodded.

Murdo's anger suddenly disappeared and he sagged like a balloon that's had half its air let out. Peter in the army during wartime, the thought made him want to vomit.

'Kitchener's been calling for more volunteers, Pa, the country desperately needs men like me.'

'Don't you think I need you here?' Murdo snapped in reply.

Peter sighed. He'd known this wasn't going to be easy and was in fact proving even more difficult than he'd anticipated. 'You can cope on your own at the distillery, can't you, Pa?'

'I can cope all right. I'm hardly senile yet.'

'Then there isn't a problem.'

Murdo ran a hand over his face, suddenly feeling dizzy. He prayed he wasn't going to have an attack. 'When do you leave?' he asked softly.

'I don't know yet. They'll notify me by post. Probably sometime within the next few weeks.'

The next few weeks, Murdo thought bitterly. The next few weeks and then what? The casualty lists in the newspapers were lengthening all the time. How long before Peter's name appeared on one of them?

He mustn't think like that, he told himself. He should think positively. That's the only way.

The girls were subdued when Peter informed them. An anguished look sprang into Geoffrey's eyes, before he simply turned and walked silently away.

★ ★ ★

Hettie collared Jack in the yard. 'Is it true?' she queried.

'If you mean about my enlisting, then yes.'

And she still wasn't pregnant. Damn! She saw her dream of a cottage and wee bit of land fading fast.

'It'll be a glorious adventure,' Jack declared. 'I can hardly wait.'

Bloody idiot, she thought. She needed him here to make her pregnant which he could hardly do if he was over in France or whatever.

'I'll see you right before I go, Hettie, I promise.'

That meant money, she realised, hopes rising a little. But how much? Certainly not enough for the cottage.

'Will it be this Sunday as usual?' she asked.

'Oh yes. And the Sunday after if I haven't already gone.'

She put her disappointment aside, for she was genuinely fond of her boss. Tears came into her eyes. 'I hope you'll be careful, Jack. I don't want anything happening to you.'

'I'll be right as rain, don't you worry about that.'

But she did, Hettie thought. She did.

★ ★ ★

Geoffrey opened the official army communication and read its contents. He'd been promoted to Captain, missing out the rank of First Lieutenant.

In other circumstances he'd have been cock a' hoop, except he realised the full import of his promotion. He'd gone up two full ranks because of losses, what other explanation could there be?

He felt his shoulder which was almost healed. Unless he pretended otherwise to McAllister he'd be on his way after his next visit to the doctor.

A week, ten days at most. And then France again.

'Charlotte,' he whispered with a choke in his voice. 'Oh, Charlotte.'

★ ★ ★

Andrew gazed round the drawing room that was jampacked with people. It was the Fortescues' anniversary party to which he'd been invited. He was having a marvellous time.

Alice joined him. 'Everything all right?' she asked.

'Fine.'

'Enjoying yourself?'

'Very much so. And you?'

'The same.'

He had a sip of champagne of which there seemed to be a never-ending supply. 'If it wasn't so cold tonight I'd ask you out onto the terrace,' he said.

'And if it wasn't so cold I'd accept.'

They both laughed.

'I haven't had the chance to say so but you look splendid,' he declared.

'Why thank you, kind sir.'

'No need for thanks, it's absolutely true.'

Her dress was a Worth in a very pale shade of mauve with a white trim. Its crossover bodice draped softly in front of a low square neckline and was high waisted. A small train fell gracefully from the skirt.

A choleric-looking man, Andrew judged him to be in his late forties or possibly early fifties, who'd clearly been imbibing heavily, came up to them.

'Why, Alice me darlin', aren't you the sight for sore eyes. 'Tis an angel I see before me.'

She smiled. 'How are you, Mr McGinty?'

''Tis dandy I am. And how about your good and charming self?'

'I'm dandy also.'

A pair of suddenly hostile black eyes fastened onto Andrew. 'And who might this soldier laddie be?' Andrew was in uniform.

'Mr McGinty, may I present Lieutenant Andrew Drummond of the First Essex. A friend of mine. Andrew, this is Mr McGinty, a neighbour.'

'Pleased to meet you, sir,' Andrew declared, and extended a hand which was ignored.

'A friend?' McGinty mused, glancing at Alice. 'Well well. And since when did you have friends amongst the British military?'

Alice flushed. 'Since recently, Mr McGinty.'

The hostile eyes fastened themselves back onto a now uneasy Andrew. 'One day, and it'll be sooner rather than later, you mark my words, young man, we'll have all you British out of Ireland. Now what do you think of that?' he said belligerently.

'Perhaps you're right, Mr McGinty,' Andrew replied softly.

'Right! Of course I'm right. You buggers

should never have been here in the first place Usurpers, that's what you are. Usurpers.'

'I don't think we should talk contentious politics at a party. It's rather rude.'

McGinty bristled. 'Are you calling me rude you whipper snapper?'

'Not at all, sir. Merely that talking contentious politics is.'

Sir Henry suddenly appeared beside them 'Are you up to your old tricks then, Seamus?'

McGinty glared at him. 'Nobody told me the British army would be here.'

'Andrew is my guest, Seamus. Just as you are. I would be most upset if there was any unpleasantness.'

McGinty snorted. 'You have a point there Henry. Where are me manners after all. I wouldn't be shaming you in your own house.'

Sir Henry took McGinty by the arm. 'I've had enough of this champagne, a woman's drink. Why don't you and I pop into my den where I have some of the best poteen you've ever tasted.' And while saying that he gave McGinty a conspiratorial wink.

'Poteen is it!'

'I swear it's probably the best you've ever tasted. Sheer ambrosia.'

'Then lead me to it.'

McGinty and Sir Henry moved off, Sir Henry steering his companion towards the door.

'What was all that about?' Andrew queried relieved that Sir Henry had intervened and defused what might have become a nasty incident.

'Mr McGinty is a Fenian.'

'Oh!' said Andrew. 'You mean a trouble-maker.'

She regarded him curiously. 'He doesn't view it like that. He considers himself a patriot.'

'Patriot or not, he certainly doesn't like us British.'

'That's putting it mildly. He detests you. And there are many like him.'

'So I've heard.'

'Anyway, let's forget him. I don't want the evening spoiled over politics.' She hesitated, then added, 'You won't mention to anyone about the poteen?'

He smiled. 'No, Alice, I won't. You have my word.'

'Good. Now let's mingle, there are some people I want you to meet.'

'More sympathetic ones I hope,' he joked.

'To be sure to be sure,' she joked in reply, using a broad accent.

★ ★ ★

'This is it then,' Geoffrey said as his train pulled into Pitlochry station.

She wouldn't cry, Charlotte told herself. She'd promised herself she wouldn't. At least not until he'd gone.

'I'll miss you so much, Geoffrey,' she said quietly in a cracked voice.

'And I you.'

'The time seems to have flown by.'

'Yes,' he agreed.

McPhie, standing close by with Geoffrey's case, was steadfastly looking away from them.

'I love you,' she whispered.

'And I love you.'

With a great whoosh of steam the train came to a halt.

He took her into his arms, her arms encircling him tightly, and kissed her. While they were doing that McPhie was attending to the case.

'Oh, my darling,' she whispered when the kiss was finally over.

He reluctantly released her and climbed into the carriage, McPhie closing the door for him. Geoffrey released the window and leant out. God but this was hard. Excruciatingly so.

They clasped hands, each drinking in the other. 'Chin up,' he said.

'And you.'

She somehow managed a smile. 'Remember to keep your head down.'

'I will, you can rely on it.'

The tears weren't far away but she struggled to keep them back. She was thinking of the previous night, their frenetic lovemaking that had eventually left them both exhausted. And again that morning, a tender sexual farewell.

She winced when the guard blew his whistle. 'Au revoir,' she said.

They released hands as the train juddered and slowly began to move.

His last sight of Charlotte was her groping for her handkerchief.

'I wish I was a man,' Wonky announced.

Nell stared at her cousin in astonishment. 'Why?'

'So I could go and fight. It's so frustrating not being able to do anything other than knit socks and balaclavas.'

'At least you're safe doing that. I shouldn't like to be in a position where I might get shot or blown up at any moment.'

A stricken expression came onto Charlotte's face. She quickly rose and dashed from the room.

'Blast!' Nell swore. 'Me and my big mouth.'

'The fault's mine, I'm sorry,' Wonky apologised.

Nell stared after her sister who'd understandably been in a right old state since Geoffrey's departure.

'I still wish I was a man,' Wonky stated forlornly. 'If I was I'd enlist like a shot if for no other reason than to get away from home. It's stifling at the manse, Nell. There are times when I feel I could scream.'

'It must be difficult for you.'

'You've no real idea. Stifling and suffocating in the extreme. In the past I've felt as though I was buried alive.'

'Poor Wonky,' Nell sympathised.

'If it wasn't for coming here I do believe I'd have gone mad years ago.'

'Well you're always welcome. Any time, you know that.'

Wonky smiled at Nell. 'Thanks, cuz.'

A little later a now composed Charlotte rejoined them and the subject of the war wasn't mentioned again that day.

* * *

'Will you see me off, Pa?' Peter asked. He and Jack were due to leave for officer training in two days' time.

'No,' came the curt reply.

Peter's disappointment showed on his face. 'Have it your own way.'

Murdo glanced up from his desk to glare at his son. 'You'll be back soon enough anyway. It's not as though they're sending you straight to France.'

'That'll come soon enough I suppose,' Peter said quietly.

Murdo lowered his gaze to hide the apprehension and fear for his son that were evident in his eyes. If it had been possible he'd gladly have traded places, he putting himself into danger while Peter stayed safely at home.

'Pa?'

'Yes?' Murdo snapped.

'When the time comes for me to go properly I'd prefer we parted on good terms. It would be awful if . . . well something happened and we hadn't.'

Murdo blanched.

'Don't you agree, Pa?'

Peter was right, he told himself. They mustn't

part with a rift between them. If anything did happen . . .

Murdo swallowed hard. 'I'll see you off then,' he stated gruffly.

'Thanks, Pa. I appreciate that.'

'Now get on with your work and stop all this chit chat. There's plenty to be done.'

★ ★ ★

McPhie heaved Jack's case onto the car rack and began belting it down. While McPhie was doing this Jack got into the Rolls.

'Today's the day,' Peter smiled.

'Nervous?'

Peter shook his head. 'Excited, but not nervous.'

'Exactly how I feel.'

'I only hope we get posted to the Watch. It would be ideal serving alongside Geoffrey.'

Jack nodded his agreement, he too was hoping to be posted to their local regiment. 'How was your father when you left?' he asked.

Peter pulled a face. 'Not exactly ecstatic. Though I have to say things have thawed somewhat between us. He'll come round, it's only a matter of time.'

McPhie climbed into the driving seat and moments later the Rolls purred into life.

'Here we go,' Peter declared as the car moved off.

Jack didn't realise it but their departure was watched by a heavy-hearted Hettie.

Murdo sighed and laid his pen aside. A glance at the wall clock informed him Peter would be on his way, providing the train had arrived on time.

What would be the outcome of all this? God alone knew. All he could do was hope and pray the war would end soon, though there seemed little likelihood of that.

There was Geoffrey too to worry about. Charlotte would be devastated if anything happened to him. He wondered if Geoffrey was back in France, Charlotte hadn't heard anything for over a week.

There was a tap on the door and Isobel entered with coffee and biscuits.

'He's away then, eh, sir,' she said brightly.

Murdo nodded.

'You'll have your work cut out for you while he's gone I'm afraid.'

'I will that, Isobel.'

'Och you'll manage, sir. You did in the past before Mister Peter joined you.'

He gave her a wry smile. 'I was a lot younger then don't forget. Time takes its toll you know.'

'You, sir! You've got lots of life in you yet.'

He drank his coffee and ate his biscuits in brooding solitude after she'd departed.

He missed Peter dreadfully already.

★ ★ ★

Geoffrey discovered the war had taken a different turn on his arrival back at the regiment. Both sides had dug in, the fighting now conducted from trenches.

'Well well well,' Bobby Baxter smiled at him as he entered the dugout. 'Stopped skiving then?'

Geoffrey laughed. 'It was hardly that.'

'Reported to the C.O. yet?'

Geoffrey nodded. 'It was he who told me to join you here.'

Geoffrey glanced round the dugout which contained four cots plus a rickety table and four chairs. There were also rudimentary cooking facilities over in a corner. 'I take it this is to be home from home,' he said, slightly sarcastically.

'Don't complain, it's a palace compared to what the men have to put up with. And it's a haven when the shelling, not to mention the whizz bangs and 'Jack Johnsons' start flying about.'

Geoffrey sat at the table beside his friend. 'So how have we been doing?'

'Holding our own just about. Remember Bob Reid?'

Geoffrey nodded.

'Gone west. Charlie McFarlane?'

Geoffrey nodded a second time.

'The same. Direct hit by a shell and blown to smithereens.'

Geoffrey listened to a list of dead and wounded that seemed interminable. 'Christ,' he muttered when Bobby finally stopped.

'And it's going to get worse,' Bobby added, a note of hysteria in his voice.

A soldier appeared at the entrance of the dugout. 'Ah, McMillan!' Bobby exclaimed. 'What's the news?'

'Bacon and tinned peaches for tea, sir.'

'Excellent, excellent.'

'Is this the new officer, sir?'

'Captain Armitage, McMillan.' To Geoffrey he said, 'I'd heard of your promotion. As you can see I'm a captain now myself.'

'Pleased to meet you, sir,' McMillan declared, coming to attention.

'McMillan's our batman, and a splendid chap he is too. Has a knack of 'acquiring' things which is most useful.'

'Like peaches for tea, sir.'

'Like peaches for tea,' Bobby agreed.

There was a rattle of rifle fire, followed by silence.

'Cut along then, McMillan,' Bobby said.

'Certainly, sir. All four gentlemen for tea, sir?'

'As far as I know. But that could easily change as has happened so many times.'

'I understand, sir. Thank you, sir.'

And with that McMillan left them.

Geoffrey pulled out his cigarettes, offered Bobby one and they both lit up. 'How's old Blighty then?' Bobby asked wistfully.

'The same, yet different. Half the people in my experience don't seem to really appreciate what's going on out here. They think we're having some sort of party.'

Bobby laughed. 'Some party! I can tell you, it's one to which I wish I'd never had an invitation.'

Geoffrey felt exactly the same.

'How's the wife?'

Geoffrey thought of Charlotte as he'd last seen her at the station and a lump came into his throat. 'Fine. Bearing up under the circumstances.'

'There's going to be a big push soon,' Bobby said softly. 'That'll be fun and games.'

'When?'

Bobby shrugged. 'Your guess is as good as mine. But soon. We'll know when the continuous shelling starts. That can go on for days you know and then at an appointed time it suddenly stops. That's when we go over the top.'

Geoffrey glanced away. 'Will it be bad?'

'In theory no. In practice yes. A lot of chaps will be going west.'

'We're being supported on our left flank by the Indians, top hole fellows. On the right by Australians and New Zealanders, cracking troops as well. No respect mind you, a difficult lot. But damned good men to have alongside you in a fight.'

'Who else is billetted here?' Geoffrey asked, gesturing round the dugout.

'Ronnie Bell, remember him?'

'Of course.'

'And Jim Massie. He's new, only joined us a fortnight ago. He replaced Danny Black whom I mentioned.' Danny had lost both legs and been

277

shipped home to Britain.

'Poor Danny,' Geoffrey murmured.

'At least he's still alive,' Bobby said, eyes glittering strangely. 'At least he's that.'

Geoffrey felt sick.

16

'I THINK I'm pregnant,' Charlotte announced to Nell.

Nell's face lit up. 'That's wonderful!'

'Only think, mind you, I'm not absolutely certain yet.'

'How many have you missed?'

'Only one, but I never miss. I'm regular as clockwork which is why I think I have to be.'

'Oh, Charlotte,' Nell breathed. 'I'm so deliriously happy for you. What do you want, a boy or girl?'

'A boy really, a little Geoffrey. But I won't complain if it's a girl. Just as long as whatever I'm blessed with is healthy.'

'That's the main thing,' Nell nodded.

A child, Charlotte thought with delight. Geoffrey if a boy and, providing her Geoffrey agreed, Louise if a girl, named after her mother. She knew Murdo would be ecstatic if the latter.

* * *

'I can't wait to see Jack in his uniform,' Grizelda McPherson gushed to the others who'd come to tea.

'He'll be ever so dashing I'm sure,' Harriet Henderson smiled. 'Uniforms really do something for a man. Even my brother Leo whom

279

you both know hasn't exactly got the best o
builds.' Leo Henderson was serving with the
Seaforth Highlanders.

Antonia Phillips, who had neither boyfriend
or brother to talk about, popped a piece o
chocolate cake into her mouth. 'Hmmh,' she
murmured appreciatively.

'Good, isn't it?' Grizelda beamed.

Antonia nodded. 'Scrumptious.'

'It's a new recipe of cook's,' Grizelda informed
them. Her eyes took on a faraway look. '
wonder what Jack's doing now? What he's up
to at his officer training.'

'Goodness knows,' Harriet said.

Grizelda shivered. 'Only another week now til
he's home. I can't wait to see him.'

'Will you go to the station?' Antonia asked.

'I'd like to. It depends on whether or not
know exactly when he's arriving back.'

Antonia helped herself to more chocolate cake
meanwhile eyeing the other cakes on offer. She
would definitely have some of the Dundee she
decided.

'I know he's going to be a hero when he see
action,' Grizelda stated. 'I told him that.'

'I think they're all heroes,' Harriet declared.

Grizelda gave her friend a withering look
'They can hardly *all* be that.'

Harriet shrugged. 'In my opinion they are by
just being over there in the first place. It mus
be ghastly. I mean . . . ' She giggled. 'Frightfully
awful thing to say, but can you *imagine* what the
sanitary arrangements are?'

'They are soldiers after all,' Grizelda reminded

her. 'And I hardly think you should be mentioning sanitary arrangements. It's so unladylike.'

'Sorry,' Harriet apologised.

'How long will Jack be home for?' Antonia enquired.

'He's not sure about that, but is hoping for a fortnight. We'll have a spiffing time together.'

'Lucky you,' Antonia said, jealous of her friend. A jealousy not lost on Grizelda who positively preened with smugness and self satisfaction.

'How's Peter Drummond doing?' Harriet queried.

Grizelda's face hardened at the mention of Peter's name. Now there was someone who'd never be a hero, not in a million years. How fortunate she was to have landed Jack. She could not imagine what had once possessed her to have been so keen on Peter.

'Jack has never mentioned him in his letters,' she replied rather tartly, a lie for Jack had written about Peter.

'I wonder when someone will catch *his* eye,' Antonia said, pretending innocence but knowing full well that Grizelda had previously set her cap at him.

Grizelda changed the subject.

★ ★ ★

A Very light sailed into the night sky and burst directly overhead. Seconds later a German machine gun opened up.

Oh my God, Geoffrey thought, they'd been spotted. He swiftly pulled himself towards a shell crater and dropped inside, swearing involuntarily when another body dropped on top of him.

'Sorry, sir,' Private McMillan apologised.

'That's all right.'

Someone screamed, the scream tailing off and then ceasing altogether.

One of them had bought it; Geoffrey wondered who. He and McMillan remained cowering at the bottom of the crater as the machine-gun fire continued.

★ ★ ★

An ashen-faced Geoffrey lurched into the dugout to find Bobby writing a letter by the light of a hurricane lamp. Ronnie Bell and Jim Massie were both asleep, Ronnie snoring loudly.

'How did it go?' Bobby queried, glancing up.

Geoffrey slumped onto a chair. 'We were spotted,' he croaked.

'And?'

'I lost three men. I was damned lucky to get back alive myself. There was one point where . . . ' He broke off and shuddered.

Bobby rose and crossed to his kit from which he produced a bottle of whisky. 'You'd better have some of this, old chap,' he declared, splashing a hefty measure into a tin cup.

Geoffrey's hands were shaking as he accepted the cup. 'I really thought my number was up that time,' he said, voice trembling.

'I know the feeling,' Bobby stated quietly. 'Who were the men?'

Geoffrey named them.

'No wounded?'

Geoffrey shook his head. 'Only dead.'

'Are you certain about that?'

'Yes,' Geoffrey breathed.

'Were you spotted on the way out or back?'

'Out.'

Bobby swore. 'Which means one of us will have to try again tomorrow night. That wire has to be reinforced.'

'I'm sorry,' Geoffrey mumbled.

'Not your fault, old bean. Hardly that.'

Geoffrey swallowed the whisky which immediately warmed the coldness of his stomach.

'You'd better get some shut eye,' Bobby advised.

Sleep! How could he do that feeling as he did. And yet he'd have to. 'Right,' he sighed, placing the cup on the table.

'Another two days and we're in reserve again. It'll go quickly enough,' Bobby said.

Two days, an eternity where they were, Geoffrey thought. He touched the pocket containing Charlotte's last letter. Would he ever see her again, ever again hold her in his arms?

'Thanks for the whisky,' he said, getting up.

'My pleasure.'

He did fall asleep, to dream, as he so often did, of Charlotte.

Peter stepped from the Rolls and gazed a
Drummond House, a lump coming into hi
throat.

The door flew open and Charlotte, Nell an
Wonky came tumbling out to stare at him whil
he stared back. McPhie began unloading his cas
from the car rack.

Peter had rather hoped Murdo would als
be there to welcome him, but of course h
father would be working. He'd stroll over t
the distillery shortly.

He went to his sisters and cousin and hugge
and kissed them each in turn.

'They posted you to the Watch I see
Charlotte said, having noted the tartan c
his kilt.

'They did indeed. And Jack. We'll be servin
together.'

'How long?' Nell asked.

'Ten days. We were hoping for a fortnigl
but ten days is all we've got. Then it's straigl
to France.'

'You've lost weight, cuz,' Wonky smiled.

'So would you if you'd been through what
have.' He laughed. 'I enjoyed it though. In par
it was quite fun.'

'Are you hungry?' Charlotte queried.

'I am, but couldn't eat anything right awa
I'm too excited at being home.'

He put an arm round Charlotte's shoulde
and the other round Nell's. 'So how have yo
two been?'

Nell caught Charlotte's eye. Would she tell Peter or not? The possible pregnancy was a closely guarded secret between the pair of them that hadn't even been confided to Murdo yet. Charlotte, correctly guessing what was in her sister's mind, imperceptibly shook her head.

'In the pink,' Charlotte replied.

'Knitting mainly,' Wonky said, pulling a long face.

'I'll take this inside for you,' McPhie declared, passing them with Peter's case.

Peter hugged his sisters again. Oh, but it was grand being home! It had surprised him how much he'd missed it.

'Let's go on in,' he said.

* * *

Murdo glanced up as the office door opened and there was Peter resplendent in his uniform.

'You're back then,' Murdo commented dourly.

'You might look just a little bit pleased to see me, Pa.'

Murdo was, but wasn't going to show it. 'How did you get on?' he queried.

'Fine.'

'You've lost weight.'

'That's what Wonky said, and it's true. I feel the better for it.'

Murdo grunted. 'So now you've come to pester me during working hours.'

Peter glanced around, all sorts of memories of the office flooding his mind. 'I could sit down and help out if you like?' he offered.

Murdo waved a dismissive hand. 'Don't be daft. I wouldn't dream of it.'

'It's good to see you, Pa,' Peter declared softly.

'And you, son. And you. Now bugger off and we'll talk over dinner.'

When Peter had gone Murdo produced a handkerchief and wiped his eyes.

Sentimental eejit, he thought.

It was a full minute before he could concentrate again on the invoices in front of him.

★ ★ ★

'It's not fair!' Grizelda wailed. 'I'm streaming with cold.'

Jack grinned, she was indeed a sorry sight. 'You look gorgeous to me,' he declared gallantly.

'How can I possibly look gorgeous with a runny nose and puffy eyes. I wanted to come to the station but how could I in this state?'

'Well I'm here now,' he said, and going to her took her into his arms. 'You certainly smell gorgeous.'

She sniffed. 'Do I?'

'Wondrously so.'

That consoled her a little. 'I had all kinds of plans which will now have to be abandoned.'

'Don't worry. You'll probably be better in a couple of days and then we can carry out those plans of yours. You'll see.'

'I only hope so.'

He pressed her tightly to him and began

stroking her hair. He hastily disentangled himself when he felt a distinct reaction between his loins.

'I'd love a cup of tea,' he declared.

She nodded, wiping her nose with a scrap of lace hanky. 'I'll ring for some.'

* * *

The shelling had gone on for forty-eight hours nonstop and now, precisely on the stroke of noon, it was about to stop. Geoffrey held his watch in one hand, revolver in the other. The men on either side of him had tense, expectant faces.

This was it, he thought. Any second now and . . .

The shelling stopped, leaving a strange, eerie silence that hurt the ears almost as much as the noise of the artillery barrage.

Next moment a whistle blew followed by many others up and down the line.

'Right, lads, here we go,' Geoffrey shouted. 'Over the top!'

Somewhere the pipes struck up, Hielan Laddie, the regimental tune.

Then, with thousands of others, he was advancing over No Man's Land towards the German trenches.

Halfway there the German machine guns began to chatter.

* * *

Bobby was shaking all over as he rummaged in his kit for the whisky. A shocked Geoffrey stood watching him.

'What a fucking disaster,' Geoffrey eventually choked.

Bobby didn't bother with the niceties of a tin cup, he simply took the cork from the bottle and upended the latter into his mouth.

'So many hanging on the wire,' Geoffrey whispered, his voice seeming to come from a long way off.

'Here,' said Bobby, thrusting the bottle at Geoffrey who followed Bobby's example of upending it into his mouth.

'I saw Jim Massie get it,' Bobby said. 'He was almost cut in half.'

'Ronnie bought it as well. His head just sort of exploded.'

'At least we won't have to put up with Ronnie's snoring any more,' Bobby said, and laughed hysterically.

'Hanging on the wire,' Geoffrey repeated. 'All those men hanging on the wire.'

Bobby threw up.

★ ★ ★

Charlotte had left Nell and Wonky knitting while she attended to some household duties with Miss McQueen. She was returning to the pair of them when she came across Peter standing at a window gazing out. He was clearly lost in thought.

'Peter?'

288

He blinked himself out of his reverie and turned to smile at her.

'You were miles away,' she stated.

'Yes.'

'Are you worried about France?'

He ran a hand over his face, and sighed. 'I suppose so, but that wasn't what I was thinking about. Or not exactly anyway.'

'Oh?'

'I can't say, Charlotte. It would sound so . . morbid.'

She went to him and hooked an arm round his. 'Can I help?'

'Not really.'

'It's sometimes best to talk things over, Peter. A problem shared and all that.'

He smiled again. 'You're a poppet at times. Geoffrey's a lucky man.'

'Well?' she persisted.

His expression became serious. 'You won't mention the following conversation to anyone. Promise?'

'You have my word.'

He gazed around him. 'I was just wondering if I'll ever see Drummond House and the family again.'

Her face reflected her concern.

'It's possible I won't you know. Anything could happen over there.'

She kissed him tenderly on the cheek. 'You're right, that is morbid. You'll be back, Peter, I'm certain of it.'

'And how can you be that?'

She touched her heart. 'I can feel it here. So

I'd stop worrying if I was you.'

He laughed softly. 'A woman's intuition, eh?'

'That's right, Peter. A woman's intuition.'

'Well if that's the case then I'm bound to be back. There can't be any doubts about it.' He took a deep breath. 'Thanks for cheering me up, sis. I feel a lot better now.'

'No more dark brooding?'

'Now you have *my* promise.'

'Good.'

She kissed him again before continuing on her way.

★ ★ ★

'Having a baby!' Murdo repeated, eyes shining.

Charlotte nodded.

He swept her into his arms. 'I couldn't be more pleased, darling. I'm delighted.'

'I thought you would be,' she smiled.

He released her. 'A grandchild. The first of many I hope.'

'In the summer, Pa.'

He nodded. 'Are you feeling all right? Your mother used to get terrible morning sickness remember.'

Charlotte held up crossed fingers. 'So far none of that. A couple of queasy moments, but no sickness.'

'This calls for a dram,' he declared, and strode to the decanter. 'You?' He realised what he'd said. 'No, I think that's unadvisable in the circumstances.'

'Quite.'

He chuckled as he poured his dram. 'A grandchild, well well well.'

'If it's a girl I thought I might call her — with Geoffrey's consent of course, which I'm sure he'll give — Louise.'

The glass stopped halfway to Murdo's mouth and he swallowed hard. A hint of tears came into his eyes. 'That would make me very happy, Charlotte. You've no idea how much. Thank you.'

'It might be a boy, mind.'

Murdo nodded. 'Of course. But there's bound to be a wee lassie along the way. I doubt you'll be stopping at one.'

Charlotte doubted that as well.

'Tell you what,' he said. 'We'll have a party tonight. Just us, the family, to celebrate. What do you say?'

'That would be lovely, Pa.'

'Then a party it is.'

He didn't add that it would double up as a party for Peter who'd be leaving for France in two days' time.

★ ★ ★

Murdo was drunk and didn't give a damn. It wasn't every day you were told you were going to be a grandfather. He beamed across the room at Charlotte who was eating a slice of cream sponge Cook had made especially for the occasion.

'Another dram, Pa?' Peter asked, he none too sober either.

Murdo held out his glass which Peter topped up, before doing the same to his own glass.

'The day after tomorrow,' Murdo said.

'That's right, Pa.'

'I'll be coming to the station with you. Can Jack Riach make his own arrangements? I'd prefer if it was just the pair of us.'

Peter nodded. 'I'll speak to Jack in the morning. Probably best he makes his own arrangements as Grizelda's going with him.'

'How are those two getting on?'

'Extremely well according to Jack. A right couple of love birds.'

'You'll be seeing Geoffrey I presume. Give him my regards, won't you.'

'I will, Pa.'

Murdo cleared his throat. 'This isn't easy for a man like me. But I was angry at you joining up because . . . well because you're my son and all that entails.'

'I understood that, Pa,' Peter replied softly.

'A parent tries to keep his children out of danger. It's only natural, as you'll find out for yourself one day.'

Peter glanced away. That was something that wouldn't happen. 'Of course, Pa.'

Murdo suddenly reached out and gripped Peter's arm. 'You will watch out for yourself, lad. No stupid heroics and any of that nonsense.'

'No stupid heroics, Pa. You can rest assured.'

Murdo squeezed Peter's arm, then released it. 'That's good then.'

'I have always loved you, Pa, remember that,' Peter said very softly.

This time there was more than a hint of tears in Murdo's eyes. He raised his glass in a toast. 'Here's to you, son. Here's to you.'

'And you, Pa.'

It was a golden moment to be treasured.

★ ★ ★

McPhie knew Murdo better than Murdo realised. He opened the car door when Murdo, having escorted Grizelda to her vehicle, came striding towards the Rolls. Murdo's face told its own story.

'I took the liberty of putting something inside for you, sir,' McPhie said when Murdo reached him.

Murdo glanced into the car where there was a bottle of whisky and a glass lying on the back seat.

'Thank you, McPhie,' he replied gruffly. 'And by the way, take your time driving home. I'm not in any rush.'

'I fully understand, sir. We'll go the scenic route.'

Murdo waited till they'd left the station well behind them before opening the bottle.

They were almost halfway to Drummond House when McPhie looked in his rear-view mirror to see tears streaming down Murdo's anguished face.

He thanked God he didn't have a son who'd just gone off to war.

★ ★ ★

Alice reined in her horse and waited for Andrew to catch up with her. 'You let me beat you on purpose,' she laughed when he drew alongside.

'I did not,' he protested.

'Liar!'

He pretended indignation. 'I am nothing of the sort. You outrode me fair and square.' She was right of course, he had allowed her to win.

'Let's walk for a bit,' she proposed, dismounting.

Andrew dismounted also, patted his horse, then fell into step beside her. 'I was just thinking earlier,' he said. 'I'd love to take you home to meet Pa and the girls. They'd adore you.'

She glanced sideways at him. 'I believe I'd rather enjoy that. I've never been to Scotland.'

'I have a decent leave coming up and might go myself. But taking you is out of the question.'

'Why?'

'U-boats, Alice, they're proving quite a menace. I doubt your father would allow you to take the risk. And even if he did I wouldn't.'

Something fluttered inside her. 'You're very protective.'

'Naturally, I don't wish you to come to harm.'

'That's kind of you.'

'Kind? I think it's more than that, Alice. I've told you before I'm very attracted to you. An attraction that keeps on increasing.'

The fluttering grew.

'And we have been seeing rather a lot of one another,' he went on.

'Yes, we've become good friends.'

'I was hoping it was leading to more than friendship,' he said.

So had she, very much so. 'Is there any likelihood of your regiment being posted elsewhere?' she asked, changing the subject.

He shrugged. 'Of course, eventually. Why?'

'I was thinking of France.'

Andrew sighed. 'There's always that possibility. They might well take troops out of Ireland and send them over there.'

'Would you wish to go?'

He laughed. 'No thank you. I'm perfectly happy with my billet here where there aren't bullets flying round my ears. Besides . . . ' His tone changed. 'That would mean being parted from you.'

She didn't want to be parted from him either, he had come to mean a great deal to her. 'Will you always stay in the army?' she queried.

'I am a career officer.'

'I appreciate that, but it doesn't mean you have to remain in the army until retirement.'

He guessed what she was getting at. 'I certainly couldn't resign my commission before the end of the war. But afterwards? Who knows. It all depends.'

'On what?'

'Whether or nor I had a reason to resign. I'm not entirely against it. I'm well aware there is life outside the army. Though what I'd do I couldn't say. I'm not trained for anything else.'

'That might not be a problem,' she said.

'Oh?'

She smiled enigmatically and didn't reply.

The fish was taking the hook, Andrew thought jubilantly. What she was presumably hinting at was that he could work for her father in some capacity or even, and the prospect thrilled him, be a man of leisure. But, on reflection, he doubted it was the latter.

'I wish you wouldn't go to Scotland. I don't want you taking any risks either.'

'I'm a soldier, Alice. It's our job to take risks.'

'But not unnecessary ones,' she argued.

He stopped and stared at her, she stopping also. 'All right,' he replied softly. 'I shan't go.'

Her face lit up. 'You could spend your leave with us.'

'Meaning you,' he smiled.

She didn't reply to that either.

He took her into his arms, noting there wasn't any hesitation on her part, and the next moment his lips were hungrily on hers.

It was their first kiss.

17

PETER took in Geoffrey's dreadfully drawn and haggard face. Christ, he thought, his brother-in-law had aged a good ten years if not more.

'Hello, old bean,' he smiled.

The two men shook hands.

'You look fit,' Geoffrey commented.

Peter could hardly say the same. He gave Geoffrey the parcel he carried tucked under one arm. 'That's from Charlotte and crammed with goodies including a couple of bottles of best Drummond.'

'Is it by Jove!' Geoffrey exclaimed, placing the parcel on the table. 'We'd best have some of that straight off.'

Peter frowned. It was nine o'clock in the morning. 'This early?' he queried as Geoffrey began ripping the paper.

Geoffrey gave a dry, cynical laugh. 'We don't worry about things like that out here. Any time, night or day, is right for a drink. We do a lot of that in the trenches, drink, I mean. When we can get hold of it. Stiffens the sinews you know.'

Dear me, Peter thought. Was it really as bad as that. There again, the sights he'd seen so far were pretty grim.

'When did you arrive?' Geoffrey asked.

'Yesterday afternoon. I'm billetted further

down the line towards Machelle.'

Geoffrey removed the lid from the cardboard box inside the wrapping paper and grunted. 'Charlotte's done me proud. I'll thank her in my next letter.'

He removed a bottle of Drummond and quickly uncorked it. There was still some tea left in the tins mugs which he threw onto the ground. He then poured two enormous drams and handed Peter one. 'Chin chin!' he toasted, and had a deep swallow.

Geoffrey closed his eyes and sighed with satisfaction. 'God that's good,' he whispered.

Peter wasn't so sure on sampling his dram, almost immediately feeling his head swim. He wasn't used to drinking at that hour.

Geoffrey had another swallow. 'Charlotte wrote they'd posted you to the Watch.'

'It's what I was hoping for.'

'Well, it's great having you here. Sit down.'

'I can't stay long,' Peter explained. 'I'm on duty in an hour.'

'What have they got you doing?'

'Observation work to start with.'

Geoffrey nodded. 'There's a great deal worse than that, I can assure you.'

He finished his whisky and poured himself another enormous one. 'You've joined us at a difficult time, the battalion's considerably under strength which means we're having to do all sorts of extra duties.'

'Why's that?'

Geoffrey regarded his brother-in-law with amusement. 'Why the hell do you think?

Dead and wounded, old chap, dead and wounded. We lost two officers alone out of this dugout only a few weeks back who haven't been replaced yet. I hope to God they are soon.'

Geoffrey scratched himself. 'I'd love a bath but won't manage that till we're in the reserve line again. Roll on, roll on.'

McMillan appeared at the entrance to the dugout and saluted. 'Shall I clear and wash the breakfast things, sir?' he asked, addressing Geoffrey.

'Not now, McMillan. I've got a guest, my brother-in-law, who's just joined us.'

McMillan saluted Peter. 'Welcome to hell, sir.'

'Cut along then, McMillan.'

'Yes, sir.' And with that McMillan disappeared.

'How is Charlotte?' Geoffrey queried softly, the hint of a catch in his voice.

'Doing well.'

'She hasn't said, so I presume there isn't any trouble with the pregnancy so far.'

'None that I'm aware of.'

Geoffrey nodded. 'If it's a girl she wants to call her Louise after your mother.'

'So I believe.'

'Your father must have been pleased about that.'

'Tremendously.'

Geoffrey chuckled. 'Liked him right from the off. Fine man.'

Bobby Baxter entered. 'I say, what's all this then. A flaming booze up?'

Geoffrey introduced Peter and explained about the parcel. He then waved a hand at the opened bottle. 'Help yourself, Bobby. Don't stand on ceremony.'

Bobby poured himself a dram as large as those Geoffrey had. 'Here's how,' he toasted and drank his dram straight off.

'Well,' commented Bobby, gazing into the box. 'How absolutely spiffing.'

Peter started when a single shell screamed overhead, followed shortly by an explosion.

'You'll get used to it,' Geoffrey smiled knowing that to be a lie as far as he was concerned.

He never had.

★ ★ ★

It was a grand gathering, Nell observed, a ball perhaps or something similar, many of those present bewigged. She focused on one female in particular, a youngish lass wearing a hooped purple gown, silk by the looks of it, woven through with scarlet flowers.

The men were a colourful lot, some in best Highland garb, others in Lowland attire. Everyone appeared to be having a wonderful time.

Edinburgh? Nell wondered. That would tie in with her last vision. Was this taking place in Edinburgh?

And then there he was, her Highlander, a glass of wine in hand talking to a knot of people.

A woman in the group threw back her head and laughed uproariously while another Highland gentleman clapped her Highlander on the shoulder. Obviously he'd just told a joke or funny story.

All conversation and merriment abruptly ceased when a young man, most handsomely dressed, entered the room, everyone bowing to him.

Bonnie Prince Charlie? Nell speculated, a thrill running through her. It could well be.

The prince, she presumed it to be he, progressed through the throng. A word here, a word there. His hand kissed by this one, then that, the ladies curtsying as he passed.

She watched as her Highlander took the prince's hand and kissed it. How radiant he looked afterwards, almost glowing with pride. She guessed he was thinking how he would describe the occasion when he got back home.

And then the vision began to fade.

★ ★ ★

Charlotte caressed her abdomen which had started to expand, mentally counting off the months that were left to her. Her pregnancy was going better than she'd dared to have hoped. It couldn't have been more smooth.

A long way yet, she warned herself. Still time for lots of trials and tribulations.

★ ★ ★

'What's wrong with you?' Wonky queried. Nell took a deep breath, having just come out of her vision. Had it ended because of Wonky's approach? She didn't know. All she did know was that she never had them when others were present.

'Sorry, I was day dreaming,' she replied.

'You seemed transfixed.'

'Did I?' she answered innocently.

'Quite.'

'I suppose I was.'

'Day dreaming about what?'

Nell smiled at her cousin. 'You wouldn't believe me if I told you.'

'Go on, try me,' a curious Wonky urged.

'Well, for some reason I was thinking about Bonnie Prince Charlie.'

Wonky stared at Nell in astonishment. 'You're pulling my leg.'

'No I'm not, honestly. I was thinking about the Bonnie Prince.'

Wonky shook her head in bewilderment. 'But why?'

'I've no idea, he just came into my mind. I was trying to imagine what it must have been like in those days. The clothes they wore, that sort of thing.'

Wonky smiled. 'It must have been ever so romantic. Until Culloden that is. It wouldn't have been very romantic after that.'

Culloden, Nell thought. The great battle the Scots and their prince had lost to the English after which the prince had eventually fled to France where he'd died in exile.

What about her Highlander, the man she now believed had once been her husband. Had he also survived?

She prayed with all her heart that he had.

★ ★ ★

Andrew snapped awake as his bedroom door creaked open. What on earth was going on?

The door closed again. 'Andrew?' Alice whispered.

He sat up in bed. 'What are you doing here?' he queried, also in a whisper when she perched beside him.

'Don't think badly of me. I'm not fast and don't want you to make love to me. I simply couldn't sleep and wanted to be with you.'

He immediately thought of Jean Ritchie and how he'd slipped into her bedroom at Drummond House. There had been no protestations of not making love then.

Reaching out he grasped Alice by the hand. 'This is madness, what if someone saw you? There are other house guests not to mention staff don't forget. That would be the end of your reputation.'

'I was extremely careful, I promise.'

He'd never have believed Alice capable of such a thing. It was so out of character. Unless he'd misjudged her that is.

'Come into bed, you'll catch your death out there,' he said.

There was a sigh of material falling to the floor and then she was snuggling up to him.

'Oh, Andrew,' she breathed.

Her scent was strong in his nostrils, her body a temptation alongside his.

'Why couldn't you sleep?' he asked.

'Because of you. I just couldn't get you out of my mind.'

The fish was well and truly hooked, he thought, smiling in the darkness. Hooked but not yet landed.

Dare he? She shuddered when his hand brushed her breast.

'Kiss me, Andrew.'

He did, a passionate kiss with an interplay of tongues. He could feel the fire of desire mounting within him. His hand now touched the same breast and cupped it.

The kiss continued, Alice writhing against him, he not knowing if he could stop from going further. He was hard as rock.

'Sorry,' she apologised, breaking the kiss. 'I'm not being fair.'

'That's all right.'

'I'm a virgin, Andrew.'

'I presumed that to be the case.'

'Can I be honest?'

'Of course.'

She took a deep breath. 'No man has ever affected me the way you do. I go dizzy sometimes just being in your company.'

He undid the top buttons of her nightdress and dipped his hand inside, she giving a small gasp as he slid fingers over her nipple.

'Please don't think less of me for being here, Andrew. I couldn't bear that.'

304

'I don't. I swear to you.'

'I . . . ' She broke off in confusion. 'No, I can't say.'

'Yes you can.'

'I can't. It wouldn't be right. The declaration has to come from you first.'

'Are you telling me you love me, Alice?' he queried softly.

She didn't reply.

'Because I love you.'

There was a sharp intake of breath. 'Do you, Andrew?'

'With my entire being. I don't know when it happened but it did. Perhaps it was that day I stopped Midnight and I just didn't realise until later.' He was almost bursting inside with jubilation.

'And I love you, Andrew,' she said with a tremor in her voice.

'Oh, my darling. My sweet sweet darling.'

His lips again fastened onto hers while the hand inside her nightdress gently kneaded and massaged. He knew, despite the protestation on her arrival about not wanting to make love, that she was his for the taking. Should he or shouldn't he? The decision, considering the state of arousal he was in, was an agonising one. Reluctantly he decided against it. Everything should, and would, be done properly. Oh, but the temptation!

'Will you marry me?' he asked.

'Yes.'

He removed his hand from her breast and smoothed it over a silken cheek. Greystones and all that went with it was as good as his.

'I'll speak to your father before I return to Dublin,' he promised.

Dawn was breaking before a still-intact Alice left him to go back to her own bed.

★ ★ ★

Andrew stood at a downstairs window watching Sir Henry clearly remonstrating with Seamus McGinty. Now what was that all about? He'd been hoping to catch Sir Henry on his own to ask for Alice's hand in marriage, but now obviously wasn't the time.

McGinty stamped off a few paces, stopped and turned to yell something at Sir Henry. Sir Henry's reply was vehemently to shake his head.

He'd try again later, Andrew decided, moving away from the window.

★ ★ ★

Peter knelt in the forward post he was manning staring through binoculars at the German line. Nothing was moving.

He sighed. God, but this was tedious. Hour in, hour out, waiting for something to happen. He'd have welcomed any diversion, no matter what.

A little later he glanced round when he heard the approach of his relief whom he smiled thankfully at. He couldn't wait to get back to his dugout for a bite to eat and a rest.

The relief was a Second Lieutenant whom he'd trained with. A chap called Matheson.

'What's happening?' Matheson asked on reaching him.

'Nothing.' He was about to add it was quiet as the grave out there then thought the better of it. That would have been in extremely bad taste.

Matheson yawned.

'Been asleep?'

'Sound. I was only wakened about ten minutes ago.'

Peter handed over the binoculars. 'Have fun.'

'Oh very droll!' Matheson grinned in reply.

Peter slid down the trench wall allowing Matheson to take his place, which Matheson did.

Peter undid his flies to urinate, having needed to go for some time. He was in mid stream when a single shot rang out.

Finished, he did himself up again and turned to Matheson. The shot had obviously come from a sniper.

'Did you manage to spot him?'

Matheson didn't reply.

'Well?'

Then Peter noticed that Matheson was in a curiously slumped position.

'Matheson?'

When he touched Matheson the man slid down the trench wall to fall onto his back.

Matheson was dead.

The steady tick tock of the clock was driving Wonky out of her mind. Another evening in, another evening of crashing boredom.

She stared at her father engrossed in his Bible which he read every night. Then at her mother dozing in a chair.

Tick tock, tick tock, tick tock . . .

Wonky ground her teeth to stop herself jumping up and screaming out her frustration.

★ ★ ★

'Engaged?' Sir Henry mused, stroking his moustache.

'Yes, sir. If you'll give us your permission.'

'I see.'

Sir Henry produced a leather case of cigars, took one out, clipped it and lit up. 'I presume Alice knows you've asked for her hand?' he queried eventually.

'Oh yes, sir.'

'Hmmh.'

Sir Henry regarded Andrew through a haze of smoke. 'I've nothing against you personally, Andrew, you're a decent chap from a good family by all accounts, but I can't say I'd be happy Alice marrying an army officer.'

'We've discussed that, sir. As you'll appreciate I can't resign my commission while there's a war on, but most certainly could when it was over.'

'And would you?'

'If that's what Alice wished, sir.'

'And then what?'

'Well I'm not trained for anything other than army life. There's always the distillery of course, I'm sure my father would find me something there.'

Sir Henry considered that. It would mean Alice living in Scotland which didn't please him one bit. He wanted his only child at hand, as would her mother.

'I won't give you an answer right away, Andrew, I'd like to discuss the matter with my wife first.'

'Naturally, sir. I fully understand.'

Sir Henry eased himself forward in his chair a fraction. 'I take it you love my daughter?' His eyes bored into Andrew's.

'Very much, sir.'

Sir Henry was only too well aware of how good a catch Alice was and how unscrupulous certain men could be where a fortune was concerned.

'You mentioned once that your brother inherits when your father dies,' he said.

'That's perfectly correct, sir.'

'And what about you?'

'I'm bound to come into some money, sir, though how much I couldn't say. Pa has never mentioned.'

'Uh-huh,' Sir Henry nodded.

'We're not exactly a poor family, sir. We are of some substance.'

'I appreciate that,' Sir Henry murmured. Nonetheless, he'd find out what he could about the Drummonds. Always best to be on the safe side.

'Thank you for your time, sir,' Andrew said. 'Now if you'll excuse me, Alice and I are going out riding.'

Sir Henry gazed speculatively at the door through which Andrew had left.

* * *

'Well?' Alice demanded eagerly.

'He says he wants to speak to your mother first. But I have the definite feeling it'll be all right.'

Alice, face aglow, hugged Andrew. 'I'm certain so too.'

As they rode off Andrew twisted in his saddle to gaze back at Greystones.

He smiled at the thought of it one day being his.

* * *

'Are you convinced you love him?' Sir Henry asked softly.

'Yes, Father, I am.'

'And that *he* loves you?'

'Yes again.'

Sir Henry grunted. His daughter wasn't a fool, surely if Andrew was pretending love she'd see through him. On the other hand she might not considering how she felt.

'He said he'd resign his commission after the war,' Sir Henry stated.

'We've discussed that. I thought . . . well maybe you could find him a position.'

'There is that possibility.' It would be more than that, he told himself. He'd do his damnedest to keep Alice close by.

'So what's the verdict, Father?'

'Your mother isn't against the match, I've already spoken to her. Therefore it's all down to me.'

'You wouldn't refuse us, Father, surely? As I said, I love him dearly.'

He'd never been able to refuse Alice anything which she was well aware of. Still, this was a momentous step and his instincts were to be cautious.

'Tell you what, Alice. Give me a few weeks and you'll have my answer. Let's say the next time Andrew visits. Now how's that?'

Her appointment clearly showed. 'If you wish, Father.'

'I think that's wise. There's no hurry anyway, is there?'

She smiled. 'Not really. Except . . . ' She trailed off.

'Except what?'

'I'd rather have liked a decision to have been made today.'

'On his next visit,' Sir Henry repeated. That would give him time to make a few enquiries.

★ ★ ★

Jack Riach lay back in the tin bath, luxuriating in the warmth of the water it contained. He was in a deserted farmhouse that had somehow remained intact. He and the rest of the Watch were in deep reserve miles from the front line.

Closing his eyes he started to sing a song currently popular with the British troops:

'I don't want to die,
I want to go home.
I don't want to go to the trenches no more,
Where the whizz bangs and shells do whistle and roar.

'I don't want to go over the sea,
To where the alleymen will shoot at me,
I want to go home
I don't want to die.'

Peter breezed in. 'What a bloody caterwauling. Whatever else you can do, Jack, you certainly can't sing. You've got a voice like a foghorn.'

Jack grinned at his friend. 'What's for lunch? I'm starving.'

'Bully beef.'

Jack pulled a face. 'Is that the best that can be done?'

'We can always call in on Geoffrey. That McMillan of his seems to do wonders where food is concerned.'

'Then call we shall, old bean. Call we shall.'

Peter sat on an upturned box. 'Was that letter I saw you reading earlier from Grizelda?'

Jack nodded. 'She's in the pink and wondering when I'm going to win the Victoria Cross.'

Both men laughed.

'She'll be lucky,' Jack commented wryly.

Peter's expression changed to one of introspection.
'What are you thinking about?' Jack queried softly.

'Home, Jack. Drummond House, Pa, the girls, the distillery. I miss them all dreadfully. I wish . . . ' He trailed off.

'What?'

'I could just transport myself back there for a few hours. That would be wonderful.'

'Yes,' Jack smiled in agreement.

'But no chance of that I'm afraid. Such magic doesn't exist.'

'Oh I don't know.'

Peter stared in puzzlement. 'What does that mean?'

'You can't do it in actuality of course, but the mind and imagination are marvellous things. You can always think yourself back.'

Peter sighed. 'There is that.'

Jack closed his eyes again and conjured up a picture of Grizelda. Silly female at times, but he adored her. They'd be a splendid couple together when married. When all this . . . awfulness was over.

'Right!' exclaimed Jack, suddenly standing upright in the bath revealing himself in all his naked glory. 'Dried, dressed and a trip to your brother-in-law.'

They both laughed.

★ ★ ★

'You're right as rain as far as I can ascertain,' McAllister declared to Charlotte.

'I must say if this is being pregnant then it's far easier than I'd ever imagined.'

McAllister smiled. 'You've been very fortunate, lassie. There are many who have a considerably hard time of it.'

'So I believe.'

'Aye.'

'Is there anything else I can do, doctor?'

McAllister shook his head. 'Just keep on the way you are, and come and see me again in a month's time.'

'I'm, eh . . . ' She blushed. 'A bit scared of the birth itself doctor. I've heard tales.'

McAllister snorted. 'It's painful, I'll grant you that. But every mother has to go through it. And in your case, from the way things have gone to date, you'll probably pop the bairn as easily as a pea from a pod.'

She grinned at him. 'You're very reassuring, doctor.'

'And I'll be there don't forget.' His eyes twinkled. 'I wish I had a pound for every baby I'd delivered. Why, I'd almost be as rich as your father.'

Murdo roared when Charlotte recounted that to him.

18

'SO how are you, Murdo?' McAllister enquired, accepting the dram he was handed.

'Oh, so so.'

'If I was honest I'd say you were looking tired.'

Murdo sighed. 'I am, James, I am. I suppose it's simply that I'm not the man I once was. Work you know.'

McAllister thought of Peter. Damn the lad for going off as he had. That must be a terrible strain on Murdo. There again, it was partially Murdo's fault for not confiding in his son.

'Any more attacks?'

Murdo shook his head. 'You'd have known if there had been, believe me.'

McAllister tasted his whisky, pleased to note that Murdo hadn't joined him. 'Are you keeping up your walking?'

'By the time I get home at night I'm buggered,' Murdo explained. 'All I seem able to do is eat and fall asleep in a chair afterwards. And sometimes I'm not too keen to eat either.'

'You must Murdo. You could be in real trouble if you let that slide.'

Murdo ran a hand over his face. 'I drag myself out of bed in the morning and it's a real effort to walk up the road, far less anything else.'

McAllister tried not to let his concern show.

'Can you get some help?'

'You mean at the distillery? There isn't anyone. It's all on my shoulders.'

McAllister swirled the whisky round his glass. 'Heard from Peter recently?'

'The other day. He's as well as can be expected being out there in that hell. He tries not to be too pessimistic but I can detect his real mood underneath the things he says. And it isn't good.'

'Aye,' McAllister murmured sympathetically. He reflected on the list of dead in the previous day's newspaper and inwardly shuddered. Thank the Lord he was too old to fight.

'What about Charlotte?' Murdo asked. 'She came to see you the other day I understand.'

'Och, she's fine. Apprehensive about the birth, mind, but that's only natural. I'll get her through it, don't you worry.'

'You're a true friend, James. And that's a fact,' Murdo said softly.

McAllister smiled. 'It cuts both ways as you're well aware. You've always been a good friend to me. There are things you've done in the past for me and mine I'll never forget.'

Murdo waved a dismissive hand. 'Stop your havering, man. If the positions had been reversed you'd have done the same.'

McAllister knew that to be true. 'Can I say something?'

'What's that?'

'I sincerely hope it is a lassie that Charlotte has. I know that would give you more pleasure than anything else.'

'Another Louise,' Murdo muttered. 'Aye, it would.'

McAllister toasted Murdo, and drank. 'I'd better be moving. I've other calls to make.'

Murdo saw him to the door.

★ ★ ★

Charlotte gave a sudden gasp and bent over in her chair.

'What's wrong?' Wonky queried in alarm.

Nell jumped up and went to comfort her sister. 'Are you all right?'

Charlotte took a deep breath. 'Indigestion I think.'

'Is it bad?'

Charlotte took another deep breath. 'Dinner was extremely rich last night. Perhaps that's the cause.'

It had been rich, Nell thought. Charlotte could well be right. 'Why don't you go and lie down for a while?' she suggested.

Charlotte considered that. It seemed a good idea. 'Maybe I will.'

'Do you want some help upstairs?' an anxious Wonky offered.

Charlotte shook her head. 'I can manage.'

She winced as another griping pain grabbed her insides. 'Do we have anything?'

'I'll speak to Miss McQueen,' Wonky replied and hurried from the room.

'I'll have to be more careful about what I eat in future,' Charlotte said. 'At least until the baby's born.'

Nell nodded her agreement.

Charlotte laid her knitting aside and came to her feet. It was so unlike her to suffer from indigestion, but then she'd never been pregnant before. She gave Nell a weak smile. 'If this is all I have to contend with then I'll have no complaints.'

'Do you want me to send for Dr McAllister?'

'Don't be daft. I'm not calling the doctor out because of indigestion. Heaven knows what he'd think.'

'Are you certain of that?'

'Absolutely. Now I'm off to bed.'

Within the hour Charlotte had rejoined Nell and Wonky with the declaration that her indigestion had gone.

★ ★ ★

Sir Henry laid down the letter he'd received from the lawyer he'd contacted in Scotland, which confirmed that the Drummonds were an honourable and much respected family, highly thought of in Perthshire. Also that their business was a successful one.

He took out a cigar, clipped it and lit up. That seemed to be that then. There weren't any reasons he shouldn't give his blessing to Alice and Andrew's engagement.

And yet, why did a niggle of doubt remain in his mind? He couldn't for the life of him think why.

He thought again of Andrew, picturing him, going over conversations they'd had together.

A totally personable young man in all respects, whom his daughter loved.

Perhaps it was the fact that Andrew was so smooth which disturbed him. He would have liked to have seen a bit more grit there, more solidness of character. A man he could have had a damn good argument with which he could never envisage being the case with Andrew.

He sighed. Children! You did everything you could for them but in the end you had to let them go.

Was it jealousy on his part? he wondered. Alice was their only child after all, and a girl at that. He knew that fathers often over-zealously protected their daughters, that fathers were often somewhat in love with them themselves.

Was that it? Was he simply digging in his heels not wishing to give Alice up, not wanting her to escape the family fold.

The truth was, he just didn't know.

Sir Henry leant back in his chair and blew smoke at the ceiling. The last thing he wanted was to hurt Alice which he would if he refused her and Andrew permission to get engaged. Permission he had no logical reason to deny.

No logical reason, he repeated to himself. Surely the real nub of the matter.

So be it, he decided.

So be it.

★ ★ ★

Andrew flushed on hearing Sir Henry's words, while Alice gave a small exhalation of relief.

'Congratulations, darling,' Lady Fortescue smiled.

'And congratulations to you, my boy,' Sir Henry said, striding to Andrew and warmly shaking him by the hand.

Andrew was exultant. Not that he'd been worried, but still, you never knew. He glanced at Alice, his wife to be.

'I think this calls for a celebration,' Sir Henry declared with a chuckle.

Alice went to Andrew and they stared into one another's eyes. Then he took her into his arms and held her tight. Kiss her in front of her parents? Why not!

Sir Henry tugged on the bell pull. 'Champagne I think. Don't you?' he beamed at his wife who nodded her agreement.

'One thing though,' Sir Henry said, addressing Andrew. 'You won't be wed until the war's over and you've resigned your commission. That's the way I want it to be.'

'Certainly, sir. I understand.' Sir Henry was worried about him being posted to France and killed, Andrew correctly guessed, which was fair enough. He prayed the First Essex wouldn't be sent to the front line. That would be a nightmare.

A servant entered the room and Sir Henry ordered champagne to be brought. After which he lit up a cigar.

'Happy?' Andrew queried quietly of Alice.

'You know I am. And you?'

'The same.'

What a lovely couple they were, Lady

Fortescue was thinking. They might have been made for each other.

Andrew wrote to his father that night telling him the news.

★ ★ ★

'Engaged!' Charlotte exclaimed across the breakfast table.

'So it would seem,' Murdo replied. 'To an Alice Fortescue of an old Irish Protestant family. The father's a knight of the realm.'

'Good for Andrew,' Nell declared. 'I wonder what she looks like?'

'They're not getting married till the conflict's over apparently,' Murdo went on.

'Are you going to reply to his letter, Pa?' Charlotte asked.

'Of course.'

'Then perhaps you'll suggest he sends us a photograph of his Alice. I'm sure we'd all love to see one.'

'Good idea,' Murdo nodded, he too curious about Alice Fortescue.

'And we'll have to send them an engagement present,' Nell declared, eyes gleaming at the prospect. 'Something decent, can't let the side down.'

'The three of us can go to Glasgow and shop there,' Charlotte said. 'You, me and Wonky. It'll be ever such fun.'

Nell laughed and clapped her hands together. It would indeed.

Murdo regarded his daughters with wry

amusement. Women, how delightful they could be. Then he had another thought. 'Will you be up to such a trip?' he queried of Charlotte.

'Oh, Pa, stop being an old fusspot. I'm pregnant, not terminally ill.'

He'd still consult McAllister on the matter Murdo decided. You couldn't be too careful after all.

★ ★ ★

Charlotte was with Mrs Clark, the cook, when it happened. They were discussing culinary matters when the pain hit her. She staggered and clutched the nearest level surface.

'Miss Charlotte?'

Charlotte felt the blood drain from her face as pain tore at her insides. This certainly wasn't indigestion.

For a moment Mrs Clark watched in horror as Charlotte slowly began to sink to the floor, then grabbed her.

'Get Miss McQueen!' she screamed to Florence standing transfixed nearby.

★ ★ ★

'Well?' Murdo demanded when McAllister entered the small sitting room where he'd been anxiously pacing up and down.

McAllister sighed. 'These things happen, Murdo. I'm so sorry.'

Murdo stared at him aghast. 'Are you saying what I think you are?'

'Aye, that's right. She's lost the baby.'

Murdo reeled on the spot. This was calamitous. 'How . . . how is Charlotte?'

'Sedated for now.'

'Does she know?'

McAllister nodded. 'Yes. She became quite hysterical which is why I sedated her. And a strong sedation too. The best thing for her is sleep and lots of it.'

Murdo stumbled to a chair and sat. 'What happened?' he croaked.

McAllister shrugged. 'I honestly don't know. The lassie hasn't done anything untoward as far as I can make out. It's simply, for whatever reason, Nature intervening.'

Murdo gestured towards the whisky decanter. 'Will you pour us out a couple, James. And no lectures please.

'Geoffrey is going to be devastated,' Murdo remarked quietly as McAllister did as requested.

As he himself was, McAllister thought, making the measures generous ones.

'Was it a . . . ?' Murdo trailed off as McAllister handed him his dram.

'I don't know,' McAllister lied. 'The foetus was too young for me to be able to tell.'

Murdo stared into his whisky, then wafted the lot straight down. 'Poor Charlotte,' he whispered.

'Nell's with her.'

'Aye. Is she asleep?'

'Sound.'

'I'll go to her myself in a few minutes.'

Murdo lurched to his feet. 'I need another,'

he declared, glaring at the doctor.

'Just don't overdo it, man, that's all,' McAllister cautioned.

'You're a friend, James, but away to hell.'

Murdo stood over the decanter and closed his eyes. What a rotten thing to happen. What bloody awful luck.

'I take it Charlotte will be all right?' he said after a while.

'As far as I can make out. There certainly doesn't appear to be any physical damage. If you're wondering if she'll conceive again I can't see why not.'

Murdo nodded. 'Thank you, James.'

'She's going to be extremely upset for some time to come, you do appreciate that? It's no small thing losing a baby.'

'I understand, James.'

'Lots of cosseting and spoiling is my advice.'

'She'll have it, I assure you.'

McAllister went to Murdo and put an arm round his shoulders. 'I really am sorry, Murdo. From the bottom of my heart.'

'I know,' came the whispered reply.

★ ★ ★

Peter and Jack both stood when the Colonel entered their dugout. 'Afternoon, sir,' they said in unison.

The Colonel sat and ran a weary hand over his face; he hadn't slept for more than twenty-four hours. He was dead beat. 'We need the information, it's as simple as that,' he stated.

Peter and Jack joined him round the table. 'We appreciate that, sir,' Jack replied.

'Someone has to go. It's only a pity it's you two.'

'Can't we make a surprise raid further up the line after dark?' Peter asked softly.

The Colonel shook his head. 'I've already spoken to the Brigadier about that and the answer's no.'

'The Boche are sitting over there with a dozen machine guns trained on that hole we broke in their wire,' Jack said. 'They're just waiting for us.'

The Colonel didn't reply. Personally, he didn't give their chances of survival a snowball in hell's chance. But orders were orders. If he'd been in their shoes he'd also have to have gone.

'I was a headmaster in civilian life,' he said hollowly.

'Oh?' That was Peter.

'So many of the fine young men I looked after are now in this war. I often wonder . . . ' He trailed off.

'If only the trench mortars could have blown more holes in their wire,' Jack said.

'It took three hours to blow the one you're going through. You see the problem, don't you?'

Jack nodded. He did, only too well. It was like being handed a loaded revolver and told to put it to your head and pull the trigger.

'Chosen the ten men going with you yet?' the Colonel asked.

'Yes, sir,' Peter replied. 'They're hand picked.'

'It's a sod, isn't it?' the Colonel said softly.

'Yes, sir.'

'A sod and a half,' Jack added.

The Colonel laughed and rose from his chair. 'Report to me personally when you return.'

Peter and Jack both thought how funny that was. Return!

Fat bloody chance.

★ ★ ★

Charlotte woke into a hazy world, her head seemingly filled with cotton wool. And then she remembered.

Murdo, who'd been dozing, came awake at the sound of her whimper. 'Charlotte?'

She turned a grief-stricken face to him. 'Pa?'

'I'm here, girl, I'm here.'

'The baby's dead, Pa.'

'Yes I know.'

'Oh, Pa!' she wailed, tears springing into her eyes. 'I so wanted that baby. I so wanted it.'

He sat on the edge of her bed and took her into his arms. 'There will be others in time. Doctor McAllister says so.'

'But this one. What about this one?'

He gently rocked her the way he'd done so often as a child. There were now tears in his eyes also.

'I feel so empty, Pa.'

'Yes.'

'As though my insides had been ripped out.'

He stroked her cheek, wiping away the streaming tears, thinking it was one of those occasions as a parent when you felt completely inadequate. Why had God done this to his lassie? Why? It was a question for which he hadn't an answer. Didn't even have the beginnings of one.

'There there,' he murmured.

She sobbed, a harsh choking sound from the back of her throat. 'I should never have named the baby in advance,' she said. 'That was bad luck.'

'I don't believe that,' he replied softly, trying to console her.

'I do. I really do.'

'Hush, ma wee. Hush,' he crooned.

Charlotte continued sobbing, totally and utterly bereft. In the space of a few short hours her world had collapsed. If only Geoffrey had been there to share her grief, to hold her as her father was. Just to be with her.

★ ★ ★

Peter glanced at his watch. 'It's time,' he said. 'The smoke bombs will have been laid down.'

An ashen-faced Jack nodded in reply having just finished writing two letters, one to his parents, the other to Grizelda.

'How do you feel?' Peter asked hoarsely. He knew how he felt, scared half to death.

'How do you think?'

Peter laughed. 'Same here.'

'I wish we weren't out of whisky,' Jack reflected. A large tot would have done him the world of good.

Peter rose. 'We'd best be getting on with it then.'

Jack also rose and extended his hand. 'Good luck, old boy.'

'And you.'

'It'll all be over before we know it.'

Yes, but how? Peter thought.

Outside they found the ten selected men waiting. More good lucks were given then Peter and Jack together led the party into a swirling smoke-filled No Man's Land.

★ ★ ★

How had all this happened? Murdo wondered, sitting in his study staring vacantly ahead. Charlotte's baby, Peter at the front, his damn heart. How had it all happened?

He sighed in despair. Another couple of hours and he'd have to go to work, but at least Charlotte was sleeping again. What a night, he never wanted to go through another like it. It had been his worst since Louise died.

He sucked in a deep breath, rose and crossed to the cabinet where he kept his pipe. The tin of tobacco was old and fairly dried out, but that didn't matter. All he wanted was a smoke. Camel dung would have sufficed.

He shouldn't be doing this he reflected as he packed the bowl. It was stupidity in the extreme. But there again, what the hell!

Moments later sheer bliss descended on him.

Suicide, Peter thought. Sheer bloody suicide and madness. It was exactly as they'd expected.

★ ★ ★

'These cream cakes are delicious,' Alice smiled to Andrew. She'd come to Dublin so the pair of them could choose the engagement ring — a single diamond surrounded by a cluster of smaller ones.

Andrew smiled in return. 'You look radiant, my darling. I must be the envy of every man in this tearoom.'

She tinkled a laugh. 'Flatterer.'

Crossing his heart he said, 'I swear I'm telling the truth.'

She lightly placed her hand over his. 'We're going to be so happy together, Andrew. I just know it.'

'I couldn't agree more.'

'I love you,' she whispered.

'And I you,' he whispered in reply.

She sighed with pleasure and happiness, thinking how lucky she was to have met Andrew. He was a dream come true.

'Are you going to flash it again?' he asked innocently.

'Flash what?'

'That ring. You've done nothing but since we arrived here.'

'Have I?' she queried, equally innocently.

'You know you have. Come on, own up.'

She laughed again. 'It's not every day a girl puts on an engagement ring. Let me enjoy myself.'

How pretty she was he thought. Was he actually falling in love with her? That was possible.

'Father has asked me to pick up a few things from a shop before I return home. You don't mind, do you?'

'Not in the least.'

'It won't take long.'

'The length of time doesn't matter, just as long as I'm with you.'

He wondered what she'd be like in bed. Whatever, he'd soon train her up the way Jean Ritchie and Tina had trained him. Once wed she'd find out what it was all about. He only hoped she liked 'it', he knew there were women who didn't. He was certain she would, there was a passionate side to Alice quite contrary to outward appearances.

'I think I'll be piggy and have another,' she declared.

He watched in fascination as she ate an éclair.

★ ★ ★

A trench mortar exploded throwing Peter sideways. He landed on all fours, his head reeling. A quick fumbling examination told him he hadn't been hurt.

The German machine guns were chattering incessantly sending streams of death in all directions. A man close to Peter gave a cry and threw his hands in the air, his rifle spiralling off, his chest a sudden flood of blood. The man pitched forward to lie half in, half out of a shell crater.

How long had it been? One minute, two, five? It seemed like eternity.

They'd never get those prisoners for interrogation, Peter thought. It was an impossibility. What had Command been thinking of sending them into this? But then, what were Command ever thinking of.

The smoke was thinning now, wisps of it floating past his face. He had to go on, he told himself. They had to at least try to get to the hole in the wire.

A soldier called McGillvary staggered up to Peter, smiled grotesquely, and died. Peter watched mesmerised as McGillvary slumped to the ground. He knew McGillvary to be eighteen years of age. A lad from Perthshire like himself.

Suddenly Jack was by his side. 'It's fucking murder,' Jack swore.

Peter realised he'd dropped his revolver and picked it up again. A useless action he vaguely thought. He'd never get close enough to the Boche bastards to fire the damn thing.

'Let's go,' Peter said, and started forward again, bullets whizzing round his ears like angry wasps. He was wondering how much longer he had to live.

Jack was numb all over, petrified from fright. But not funk; he was doing, and continuing to do, his duty. They'd never say he turned and ran.

And then a huge orange flame blossomed in front of him and the world went quiet. That was it, he thought before the blackness descended.

Peter saw Jack go down and immediately dashed to his friend. Jack's face was a mess but he was still breathing.

Peter pulled Jack onto his side then lifted him in a fireman's carry.

'Retreat!' he yelled. 'Retreat!'

The machine-gun bullets continued to hum and whizz as Peter stumbled back to their own line.

He and Jack were the only ones who returned.

19

ANDREW jumped up and began pacing. God but he was randy, incredibly so. All he could think of was Alice and imagine what it would be like being with her.

He flicked sweat from his brow, and swallowed hard. He was in a lather of sexual excitement.

He stopped by his room's window and stared out over Dublin. In his mind's eye . . .

He swung away again. That wasn't doing him any good, only making matters worse. Damn, but the woman was getting to him. He wanted her so badly it literally hurt.

He thought of Jean Ritchie, and groaned. He'd have given anything for Jean to have been there, to have stripped her naked, laid her on his bed and . . .

'Christ Almighty!' he swore. This was intolerable.

Or Tina. He recalled vividly what it had been like with her. The sweetness of her, the wildness. Her total lack of inhibition.

Taking a deep breath he made a decision. There was a place he knew by repute only, never having visited it before. He'd go there now and indulge himself. Find release.

He had to.

★ ★ ★

333

'Charlotte?'

Charlotte didn't respond, continuing to stare vacantly ahead.

Nell sat on the edge of her sister's bed. 'Charlotte, this isn't doing any good. You must know that.'

Charlotte's eyes drifted sideways and what might have been something of a smile came onto her face. 'Hello, Nell.'

'Why don't you get up? You can't stay in bed for ever. It's been days now.'

'Has it? Time seems to . . . have no meaning any more.'

Nell's heart was breaking for her sister. 'The doctor said you weren't to blame. That you didn't do anything wrong.'

'But I must have. Somewhere along the line I must have. That's why God punished me.'

Nell shook her head. 'You're talking tosh, Charlotte. You had a miscarriage, pure and simple. There was no punishment involved.'

The hint of a smile became wry. 'No?'

'No,' Nell stated emphatically. 'It just wasn't to be, that's all.'

'Easy for you to say, sis.'

'Because it's the truth.'

Charlotte sighed. 'I keep thinking . . . I keep . . . ' She trailed off and turned her head away.

Nell caressed her cheek. 'I know it's difficult but you've got to pull yourself together.'

'*Know*?' Charlotte replied scornfully. 'How would you know anything about this? You've never been pregnant and lost the baby.'

'We're all on your side,' Nell declared softly. 'There's not one of us wouldn't do anything for you.'

'Does that include you?'

'Of course.'

'Then write to Geoffrey for me. I can't.'

Nell was appalled. 'Write to Geoffrey?' she repeated, a catch in her voice.

'I'm not able to, Nell. And he should be told.'

Nell dropped her head and thought about that. What a letter to write. What a burden to set on her shoulders. 'Are you sure?'

'I simply can't, Nell.'

Nell, against her better judgement, nodded. 'I'll do it this evening. Any messages?'

'Only that I love and miss him.' She hesitated, then went on, 'Say that when he gets back we'll have another baby together.'

'I will,' Nell whispered.

Charlotte felt that was the hardest thing she'd ever had to say in her life.

Make another baby together. One to replace . . .

★ ★ ★

Geoffrey ducked into Peter's dugout, pleased to find his brother-in-law alone. 'How's Jack?' he queried.

Peter glanced up to stare at Geoffrey through red-rimmed eyes, 'Alive when he was stretchered off. His face was badly burnt.'

'I brought this,' said Geoffrey, holding up a nearly full bottle of whisky. 'Want some?'

'Please.'

Geoffrey slopped generous measures into a brace of tin mugs and handed Peter one. 'How bad was it?'

'That's a bloody silly question.'

It was too, Geoffrey thought. He'd only been trying to make conversation

They sat in silence for a bit, each preoccupied with his own thoughts.

'I miss Dalneil so much,' Peter said eventually in a small voice. 'I dream about it almost every night.'

'And I miss Charlotte.'

'I imagine you do.'

'I keep seeing her. It's uncanny, like some sort of ghost. I look up and there she is, smiling, laughing, sometimes waving. And when I'm in my cot I . . . ' He trailed off. 'This war's a bastard.'

'Yes,' Peter agreed hollowly.

'I hope Jack's going to be all right.'

'I'm not sure. It was a pretty awful burn. His face was all . . . ' Peter also trailed off.

Geoffrey slopped more whisky into their mugs. 'Whisky, best thing ever invented. Especially in a situation like we're in.'

Peter nodded his agreement.

'I hear you've been put up for a medal, old boy.'

Peter laughed, a terrible strangulated sound. 'What do I want with a bloody medal. Chunk of metal that's all it is. I wouldn't trade Jack's face for a dozen VCs.'

Geoffrey didn't have an answer to that.

'How are things at your part of the line?'

'The same basically.' Geoffrey paused, then said, 'I believe there's to be another push shortly. That's on the QT for now.'

'A big one?'

'So I understand. That's one of the reasons they wanted those prisoners so badly. Find out exactly which units are facing us.'

That was some consolation, Peter thought. At least there had been a viable reason behind the raid. One he could understand.

'Jesus, I'm tired,' Peter said.

'Aren't we all. Still, there's only two days left till we're pulled back into reserves.'

'I never thought it would be like this,' Peter said morosely, staring into his mug.

'All honour and glory, eh?'

Peter smiled cynically. 'Not really. But I never thought it would be like this.' He hesitated, then went on. 'I don't think any of us will ever leave here you know. For each and every one of us it's only a matter of time. Hours, days, perhaps months. But only a matter of time.'

★ ★ ★

Captain Kennington came striding into the mess where Andrew, Billy Roberts and a few others were taking their ease.

'All right you lot, get kitted up straight away. There's some sort of disturbance this side of Halfpenny Bridge and the police have requested assistance.'

Andrew glanced at Billy. What was this all about?

'Snap to it!' Kennington barked, and left the mess as quickly as he'd entered it.

Everyone present leapt to his feet and hurried after him.

★ ★ ★

There were dozens of them, maybe a hundred, all milling about, their mood an ugly one. A howl went up as the various detachments from the First Essex took positions.

This could turn nasty, Andrew thought, unloosening the snap to his revolver holster. He noted that behind the mob several shop windows had been broken.

'Go home, you English bastards. You're not wanted here!' a rough Irish voice called out.

Next moment a brick flew through the air to land harmlessly in front of Andrew's platoon.

'Fix bayonets!' Captain Kennington yelled.

The mob quietened at that, though continuing to stare malevolently at the soldiers.

'Take your man's advice and go home. Leave Ireland to the Irish,' another voice shouted.

Scouring the crowd Andrew recognised Seamus McGinty.

'Disperse quietly and all will be well,' Kennington bellowed.

'Away to fuck, you English jackal,' came a stentorian reply. That raised a few laughs amongst the mob.

Kennington went puce with rage.

'Ireland for the Ireland. Up the Fenian cause!' yet another voice shouted.

Andrew slowly took his revolver from its holster, wondering what Kennington would do next. This needed delicate handling and he wasn't known for it.

Kennington seemed to regain control of himself. Taking several paces forward he put his hands on his hips. 'I warn you, if necessary we'll shoot. Make no mistake about that. Now disperse I say or take the consequences.'

The angry mood of the crowd suddenly subsided into muttering truculence and the danger was over.

Thank God, Andrew thought, who'd hardly been relishing the idea, no matter how in the wrong they were, of firing upon these people.

He made a mental note to mention McGinty to Sir Henry next time they met.

★ ★ ★

Peter was directed to Jack's bed by a nurse who then went off about her duties. Jack's head was swathed in bandages.

'Is that you, Peter?' Jack queried, having recognised his friend's voice.

'It is. We're in reserve and I managed to get away to come and visit.'

Peter sat on the chair beside Jack's bed. 'I'd have brought you some grapes but they're in short supply at the moment,' he joked.

Jack chuckled.

'So how are you, old thing?'

Jack eased himself slightly further up the bed. 'Have they told you?'

Peter's expression became grim in the extreme. 'Yes,' he replied quietly. 'I'm sorry.'

'You saved my life, Peter. To be honest I don't know whether to thank you or not.'

'You're still here. That's the main thing.'

Jack laughed bitterly, a sound that tore at Peter. 'Alive, but blind.' His voice cracked. 'They had to remove what little was left of my eyes. Fried in my head they were.'

Peter couldn't think what to reply to that.

'And my face . . . God alone knows what that'll look like when it heals. A gargoyle's no doubt.'

Peter took a deep breath. 'It's what's inside a man, Jack, not the outside that counts.'

'Is it really?' Jack replied dully. 'I wonder if Grizelda will agree.'

'I'm sure . . . ' Peter broke off. How could he say he was sure when he wasn't at all.

'Anyway, for what it's worth, thanks for pulling me out, Peter.'

'You'd have done the same for me.'

There was a hiatus between them, then Jack said, 'I understand you and I were the only survivors.'

'That's right.'

Jack swore. 'Suicide mission, that's all it was. They knew we never had a chance.'

'It was an important raid, Jack. I've since found out the reason behind it.'

'Oh?'

He glanced around to ensure they weren't

being overheard then repeated what Geoffrey had confided to him. 'And keep that strictly to yourself. This next big push is strictly hush hush.'

'I see,' Jack murmured.

'Geoffrey's had some bad news I'm afraid. Charlotte's lost the baby.'

'That is rotten luck. How's he taking it?'

'Better than might be expected. But there again, being out here does alter one's perspective. He's upset for Charlotte of course.'

There was another pause between them. 'So it's Blighty for you,' Peter said.

'In time.'

'Then home to Dalneil.'

Blind men without tear ducts don't cry. At least not outwardly.

* * *

Murdo joined Charlotte who was sitting on a bench outside the house, staring far into the distance.

'It's a beautiful summer's day,' Murdo commented.

'Yes,' she murmured in reply without looking at him.

'I wish you'd gone to church this morning.'

Her lips thinned into a cynical smile. 'I'm not in the mood for churches at present, Pa. They seem a rather sick joke really.'

'I understand.'

'Do you?'

'Don't forget I lost your mother. Someone I

loved and lived with, who bore my children. Her loss was awful.'

Charlotte snapped out of her reverie. 'I apologise, Pa, I shouldn't have said that. Of course you understand.'

He placed a hand over hers. 'These things are just something you have to come to terms with. Life goes on regardless. And at least, small comfort though it might be, you can always have other children That must be some consolation.'

If Geoffrey came back, she thought. *If* he came back. The casualty lists were horrendous.

'You're right of course, Pa. As you usually are.'

'Now let me make a suggestion. Why don't you and I, just the two of us, go for a nice walk. Stretch the legs a bit.'

She put a cheek on his chest and encircled him with her arms. 'That I would be lovely.'

'It isn't easy, girl. I know only too well.'

At that moment he felt closer to Charlotte than he'd ever done. Her pain was his, as was her loss.

They sat there in silence for a few minutes, then Charlotte roused herself.

'Where shall we go?'

'Who cares. As the mood takes us.'

'Then come on.'

After a few minutes he actually got her to laugh.

★ ★ ★

There had been a battle of some sort and the Highlanders had clearly won. Laden with booty they were in obvious high spirits as they marched.

There was her Highlander astride a spirited horse, laughing as he cantered past men who waved and appeared to make ribald remarks to him.

Nell shivered, and didn't know why. It didn't fit with the mood of the scene she was watching. It was as though . . . She felt tragedy, death, destruction. Her own mood was one of terrible foreboding.

The Highlander reined in his horse and swung from the saddle, laughing as he led the horse forward.

The countryside she could see was different somehow. Certainly not Scotland, it simply didn't have that 'feel' to it. England she surmised. The army was somewhere in England.

Her Highlander leapt back into the saddle and galloped off, waving his bonnet to the men he'd been talking to as he went.

Be safe, she thought. Oh, be safe, my bonnie laddie.

★ ★ ★

'I'm sorry, sir, but that's the way of it,' Enoch Murray, the maltman, said to Murdo.

Another one gone, Murdo thought in despair. How in God's name was he supposed to keep the distillery turning over when he was becoming more and more short staffed. He stared morosely

343

at Enoch whom he'd known all his life.

'What about your brother?'

'Och he's married as you know, sir. He'll hang on for a while.'

'And you haven't actually signed up yet?'

Enoch shook his head. 'Out of respect I considered it only polite to speak to you first, Mr Drummond.'

Murdo sighed. 'I don't suppose I can talk you out of this?'

'No, sir, my mind's made up. They need men and I'm not one to shirk my duty.'

Murdo sighed again. Damn and blast this war! It was turning into a total nightmare. Suddenly he felt incredibly tired, not the tiredness that comes from lack of sleep but the sort that comes from the very heart and soul.

'Have I your good wishes, sir?'

Murdo rose and came from behind his desk. He'd manage somehow, he'd have to. Extending a hand he said, 'You have my very best wishes, Enoch, though I can't say I'm happy to lose you. You're a good chap, one of the best. I hope and pray nothing happens to you and that one day you'll be back here at the distillery.'

'Thank you, sir.'

'Now you'd better be off, I've work to be getting on with.'

'I'll stay with you until the moment I have to leave, Mr Drummond. I owe you that.'

'Fine then.'

Murdo sat again after Enoch had gone feeling as though he had the weight of the world on his shoulders.

Closing his eyes he prayed for the umpteenth time that Peter was all right and would come through unscathed.

★ ★ ★

Hettie came up short in the hallway when she heard the sound of sobbing. Now what was that all about? She was in the Riach house on an errand.

She tapped the door from behind which the sobbing was coming. 'Hello?'

The sobbing continued unabated. What to do? She was only a servant after all, but someone was in distress. She tapped again.

The door opened to reveal Mrs Riach. 'Yes, Hettie?' she choked.

'Sorry to bother you but . . . can I help at all?'

Mrs Riach waved her into the room, crossing to a settee onto which she slumped. 'I've had some awful news, lass, and I don't know how I'm going to tell my husband.'

Fear clutched at Hettie. 'Is it about Mr Jack?'

Mrs Riach nodded. 'He's been wounded.'

Hettie took a deep breath, at least he hadn't been killed.

'I've had a letter from the hospital, written by a nurse. He was unable to write it himself.'

'How bad is it?' Hettie asked softly, picturing Jack in her mind. Remembering the times they'd had together. The lovemaking.

'He's been . . . he's been . . . ' Mrs Riach

dropped her head and cried.

It didn't matter their difference in stations. It was one woman comforting another. Hettie sat beside Mrs Riach and put her arm round the older woman's shoulders.

'He's been blinded,' Mrs Riach whispered.

The breath caught in Hettie's throat. 'Permanently?'

'Aye, lass, permanently.'

Oh Christ! Hettie inwardly swore. For that to happen to Jack Riach. A chap like him.

She hugged the older woman whose shoulders were heaving, her own tears not far away. 'Is there anything I can get you?'

Mrs Riach didn't reply, too overcome by grief.

Hettie thought of Grizelda McPherson and wondered how she'd react to this news.

'Is he coming home?' Hettie asked.

Mrs Riach nodded. 'When he's fit to travel which won't be for some while yet. He's still in France though expecting to be shipped to England before long.'

'It could be worse, Mrs Riach,' Hettie said. 'He could have been killed.'

'Aye, there is that.'

'At least he's coming back. There's that to be thankful for.'

'But blind,' Mrs Riach choked. 'My boy blind.'

Hettie stayed with Mrs Riach until the older woman had recovered enough to go in search of her husband.

At midnight precisely the guns started. Geoffrey lay on his cot listening to the sound of shells screaming overhead. It was to be the longest barrage of the war so far, and when it stopped he and everyone else would be going over the top.

They'd all be going, but how many would be coming back?

Closing his eyes he thought of Charlotte, wishing . . . wishing . . .

★ ★ ★

'I'll stand by him of course,' Grizelda declared to Harriet Henderson and Antonia Phillips who both nodded their approval.

'Good for you,' Harriet replied.

'Well, I mean, what else can I do. I love him after all.'

They were interrupted by a servant girl bringing in coffee and cakes, Antonia noting with pleasure there were chocolate ones among the latter.

'My hero,' Grizelda breathed, eyes shining.

'It will be difficult for you, mind,' Harriet said.

Grizelda snorted. 'Nothing I can't cope with I'm sure. It's not as though he has to work for money, he has plenty of that. More than enough for the pair of us to live in style.'

'How brave of you,' Antonia murmured, itching to get at the cakes.

'Shall I be mother?' she offered after the servant girl had left them.

'Please,' Grizelda beamed.

'I must say I admire your fortitude,' Harriet declared as Antonia busied herself with the coffee pot. 'If Jack's a hero then you're a heroine and no mistake.'

'How kind of you to say so, Harriet.'

'Kindness has nothing to do with it, it's true. I admire you tremendously.'

'Cream?' Antonia asked Grizelda.

'Please, but no sugar. I always watch my figure, as you know.'

Grizelda accepted the cup given her as did Harriet. Antonia helped herself to a chocolate cake before passing the plate round.

'I can't wait to see him again,' Grizelda went on. 'I shall welcome him with open arms and have already written telling him so.'

'You'll be wanting to start a family as soon as possible,' Antonia commented.

Grizelda blushed. 'Of course.'

Harriet sighed. 'You know, it's ever so romantic when you think about it. In a tragic way that is.'

Which was precisely what Grizelda thought, though she refrained from saying so.

Antonia reached for another chocolate cake.

★ ★ ★

Murdo noted his hands were shaking from fatigue as he poured himself a large dram. God but he was tired.

Charlotte entered the room and stared at her father. 'You look exhausted,' she commented.

'I am.'

'This is getting ridiculous, Pa. You can't keep working the hours you have.'

He leant against the sideboard for support. 'I have to, there's nothing else for it. I'm not only running the business but helping out with the men as well. It's necessary because we're so short staffed.'

'Come and sit down before you fall down.'

He sank into a comfy chair and closed his eyes, thinking he could happily have gone to sleep there and then.

'Mrs Clark has put something by for you as you missed dinner yet again.'

He considered that. 'I couldn't eat. I honestly couldn't.'

'Pa, you must! You'll make yourself ill.'

He drained his glass. 'Could you get me a refill, lass?'

She took his glass and crossed to the decanter. 'At least try and have a few mouthfuls of food. That'll be better than nothing.'

'But I'm not hungry.'

'Pa!'

'All right, all right,' he sighed wearily. 'If it'll stop you nagging.'

She handed him his refill. 'There must be some answer to the problem.'

He shook his head. 'If there is I can't come up with it. There simply aren't any suitable men available to take on. If there were I'd snap them up.'

'Oh, Pa,' she whispered sympathetically.

'I'll get by, Charlotte. You'll see, I'll get by.'

Not for long he wouldn't, she thought. Not at this rate. He was on the verge of collapse.

'I'll get that food,' she said, and strode from the room.

When she returned it was to find Murdo snoring.

20

MURDO looked up in surprise when Charlotte breezed into the office.

'What are you doing here?' he queried.

She glanced about her. Typical untidy male room she thought, and it smelt.

'I've come to help.'

'Help?'

'That's right. Anything Peter can do I can do as well, given some guidance and experience that is.'

Murdo leant back in his chair and studied his elder daughter. 'But you're a lassie.'

'So? I can read, count and I've got a brain in my head. What else is required?'

He tried to digest that.

'There are all sorts of women going out to work who never have before,' she went on. 'And doing pretty hard work at that. The munitions factories for instance are full of them.'

Murdo was flabbergasted. 'But they're working class, not like you,' he protested.

Charlotte crossed to his desk and stared him straight in the eye. 'Are you saying because I've had a privileged upbringing I can't do my bit? For that's how I see replacing Peter.'

'No, I, eh . . . '

'Because I fully intend to,' she interrupted. 'I have no intention seeing you come home night after night the way you have of late when I could be here easing the burden.'

How like Louise she could be at times, he thought. But working in the distillery!

'You're my daughter,' he stated.

'That's correct.'

'It's not right or proper.'

Charlotte gave a scornful laugh. 'The world's gone topsy turvy, Pa. The old rules don't apply any more. As far as I'm concerned, given the circumstances, it's quite right and proper for me to lend a hand where it's needed. And needed it most certainly is.'

He shook his head. 'I won't have it, lass. I thank you for the offer, but the answer is no.'

She'd always been able to twist him round her little finger, and would do so now. For his own good. 'If I help you, Pa, you'll be helping me.'

He frowned. 'How so?'

'It would take my mind off things. Stop me brooding.'

'Oh!' he exclaimed softly, all resistance to her idea completely melting away. 'I understand.'

She went to a window and opened it. 'A little fresh air would be a good thing for a start. Now where and how do I begin?'

⋆ ⋆ ⋆

'Cognac I'm afraid, no whisky,' Peter apologised to Geoffrey who'd come to visit. The other officer present was fast asleep.

'Better than nothing, eh?'

352

'It is that.'

They both had a sip from their tin mugs. 'Any news of Jack?' Geoffrey asked.

'None.'

'At least he's out of it, lucky sod.'

Peter laughed. 'I'd hardly call him lucky, but there we are. As you say, he's out of it.'

'Two days from now,' Geoffrey stated softly.

'Yes I know.'

'It'll be a bastard.'

They sat in silence for a few minutes listening to the sound of shells screaming overhead. A barrage that was into its third week.

'I don't know how I sleep through this bloody noise but I somehow do,' Peter commented.

'It'll be strange when it stops, that's for sure.'

Peter drank some more of his cognac which he didn't really like, thinking of the French further down the line who'd be attacking with them. Funny blokes the French, he didn't particularly like them either. Their officers could be exceptionally arrogant, brimming over with self importance. Thankfully his contact with them had been minimal.

'My father's unwell,' Geoffrey suddenly said.

'Oh?'

'Pleurisy according to Mother. But he'll come through it all right, he's a tough old nut.'

'I watched an aeroplane come down yesterday,' Peter said. 'All I could think of was the poor bugger trapped inside. That must be an awful way to go.'

Geoffrey nodded his agreement.

'The ones that do survive are usually terribly burnt. Hideously so in some cases.'

They both thought of Jack.

Geoffrey finished his cognac and rose. 'I'd better be getting along. Duty calls and all that.'

Peter also rose and extended his hand. 'Best of luck for the day after tomorrow.'

'And you.'

They stared at one another, wondering if they'd ever see each other again.

Geoffrey patted his brother-in-law on the shoulder, smiled and left.

★ ★ ★

'Pa, I don't understand this. Can you explain?' Charlotte said.

She really was doing extremely well, Murdo thought. Picking things up very quickly.

He came round from behind his desk and crossed to hers. 'Now what's the problem?'

★ ★ ★

'Lucky old Charlotte working at the distillery,' Wonky said, setting her knitting aside for a few moments.

Nell also laid hers aside, it was time for a breather. 'I'd offer to help there myself but I'm a dunderhead when it comes to facts and figures. I'd be a hindrance more than anything else.'

'If I suggested it to Father he'd have a fit,'

Wonky declared with a sigh. 'You know what he's like. His precious daughter over there with all those rough men. He'd have the vapours.'

Nell laughed. 'I don't think men have the vapours, do they?'

'Well, you know what I mean.'

'Charlotte's certainly the better for it,' Nell went on. 'She said it would take her mind off things and it has. She's enjoying it too apparently. Told me only the other evening it can be quite fascinating.'

'I saw Grizelda McPherson in the village,' Wonky stated. 'From what I hear she's all of a burble awaiting Jack's return.'

'Poor Jack,' Nell said, pulling a face.

'Yes.' Wonky thought of the past. It might have been her in Grizelda's shoes. If things had been different that is. If Jack hadn't preferred Grizelda to her.

'When will it all end?' Nell mused aloud. 'When will it all end?'

'When we've won,' Wonky stated emphatically. 'That's when.' There was no doubt in her mind that they would.

★ ★ ★

Geoffrey slid into the trench unable to believe he was still alive. How had he possibly come through that hell? That armageddon?

He'd seen 'Pop' Smith go down, and Charlie Abercrombie. Major Allan also, like a puppet whose strings had suddenly been cut.

As for the men, hundreds of them, thousands, all dying like heroes if you could possibly call it that.

Geoffrey dropped his head and put his hands to his face, desperately wanting to vomit and willing himself not to.

A private he didn't know collapsed into the trench beside him. 'Dear God!' the soldier breathed.

The German machine guns were still chattering which meant there were still men out there. Geoffrey shuddered.

More chaps tumbled into the trench, one of whom started to howl like a banshee. The lad had gone mad, Geoffrey thought. Stark staring mad. And who could blame him? Certainly not he.

Another great push that had ended in massacre, Geoffrey thought bitterly. How much more of this senselessness before it was his turn to die out there in No Man's Land? For die he would, he was convinced of it.

'Water, sir?'

Geoffrey focused on the speaker, a plain-faced boy with red hair and freckles. The boy had a deep gash on his left cheek but otherwise appeared unhurt.

'Thank you.'

He accepted the already open canteen and drank. Tepid water that was still welcome beyond belief. He hadn't realised how parched he was.

'It was a disaster, sir. A sheer bloody disaster.'

Geoffrey returned the canteen. 'Yes,' he agreed softly. That's exactly what it had been.

He wondered if Peter had made it.

★ ★ ★

'McGinty, you're sure it was him?' Sir Henry Fortescue queried.

'Oh yes, sir, I saw him plain as the nose on your face.' It had been some weeks, due to duties and manoeuvres, since Andrew had last been to Greystones.

'Hmmh,' Sir Henry mused thoughtfully.

'I thought you should know, being a friend of his, that is.'

Sir Henry smiled. 'I wouldn't exactly call him a friend. No, that's going too far. Neighbour and acquaintance is more like it. Someone it's best to humour rather than alienate.'

'Well, he was there, sir, take my word for it.'

Sir Henry stroked his moustache. 'It doesn't surprise me really. McGinty's a Fenian and that cult have become stronger of late.'

'So I understand, sir.'

'Nationalists, Andrew, they want a free Ireland. In fact, are determined to have one. To their way of thinking it's only a matter of time.'

Andrew frowned. 'But surely that's impossible. They could hardly take on Britain and its Empire.'

'Under normal circumstances I'd agree, but don't forget Britain is at war. Britain *and* her Empire. Which means she's weak at the moment, weak in places like Ireland that is. And don't think the Nationalists don't know that. If there should be an uprising . . . ' He broke off and shook his head.

'Uprising, sir?'

'It's possible, entirely so. The Irish are a proud race, very proud indeed, and they're under the British yoke. What better time than now to try and throw off that yoke?'

Andrew tried to digest that. He knew something of Irish history, but not a great deal. To him Ireland was part and parcel of the homeland and that was that.

'A free Ireland,' Andrew mused. It would take fighting for that to happen, fighting he'd be in the thick of. He didn't relish the prospect.

'And what about yourself, sir. How do you feel?'

Sir Henry laughed. 'Good question. I consider myself Irish through and through, but I'm Protestant Irish, an import no matter how long my family has been here. Me and mine aren't native Irish stock. So I suppose I'm rather ambivalent on the nationalist question. With one exception that is. I wholeheartedly believe it would be financially ruinous for this country to break free and go it alone. It's basically a poor country, Andrew, and I don't see how that can possibly change. So in my opinion it's in Ireland's best interests to stay shackled to the mainland. Though I have to say that's not an opinion held by many. Pride again, Andrew, pride of which the Irish come stuffed full of, God bless and keep them all.'

'But Irishmen are fighting with our troops in France and Belgium,' Andrew said.

'Young blood,' Sir Henry replied. 'Young blood, hot blood and a sense of duty. But where does their first duty lie? Put it to the test and the answer will be Ireland. Put it to the test and those selfsame Irishmen will always come down on the side of Ireland before anything and anyone else.'

'I see,' Andrew murmured.

'So be careful, lad. Who knows what might happen in the near future. Who knows? And you'd be at the sharp end. I'd hate to lose a potential son-in-law whom my daughter loves.'

'So you think there might be insurrection, sir?'

Sir Henry thought of recent conversations he'd had, of the mood of the people. If McGinty and his like had their way . . .

At which point they were interrupted by a tap on the door and the appearance of Alice.

'Now what are you two talking about closeted away here?' she demanded.

They both rose. 'Politics I suppose,' Andrew answered.

She made a face. 'How boring!'

Sir Henry smiled. 'Not really. We've been having a very interesting conversation.'

'Which I'm now halting. Andrew's only here for three days and I want more of him to myself.'

Sir Henry shrugged. 'I can hardly argue with that.'

'Shall we go for a walk, Andrew?' Alice proposed.

He knew what that meant. An invitation for kissing and cuddling. 'Of course.'

'Good.'

'Enjoy yourselves,' Sir Henry declared, eyes twinkling, remembering only too well the joys of courtship. Sighing inwardly with nostalgia. Which made him think of his wife Sybil and the fact he had the rest of the afternoon free. Now that would be lovely, if she was of a like mind that was. Sybil wasn't always. But then they had been married a long time.

'Run along the pair of you. We'll all meet up again at dinner.'

When the youngsters had gone Sir Henry went in search of his wife whom he found in a most amiable mood.

★ ★ ★

'It's agreed then?' Wonky said.

Nell nodded.

Wonky took a deep breath. 'I'm so excited. We should have thought of this before.'

'How about your father?'

'That's going to be the hard part,' Wonky nodded. 'But I'll tackle him about it tonight.'

'And what if he forbids you?'

A determined expression came onto Wonky's face. 'This is my big chance to get away from the manse and Dalneil. At least for a while. He'll see it my way if I have to argue till the cows come home.'

Nell thought of her own father. He wasn't going to be best pleased either. There again, Murdo was a far more reasonable man than Tom Comyn.

At least he always had been in the past.

★ ★ ★

Geoffrey took Peter's hand and they silently shook.

'It's good to see you all in one piece,' Geoffrey said.

'And you.'

'I said it was going to be a bastard and that it most certainly was.'

Both men sat. They were in Peter's dugout, Peter now the sole survivor of the four officers who'd been billetted there.

'I've nothing to drink I'm afraid,' Peter apologised. 'We drank it all before . . . ' He broke off and looked away.

'It was the same in my dugout,' Geoffrey said softly.

They fell silent.

'Christ,' Peter muttered after a while. 'Christ!'

Geoffrey knew exactly what he meant.

★ ★ ★

Tom Comyn stared at his daughter, aghast. 'You can't be serious, girl.'

'But I am, Father.'

'It's preposterous, I won't allow it. You hear? I won't allow it.'

Moira Comyn stared at Wonky in consternation. This was terrible. A complete bolt out of the blue.

'A nurse!' Tom exclaimed, and barked out a harsh laugh.

'Not quite a nurse, Father, a Voluntary Aid Detachment. VADs they're called. You must have read about them in the newspapers.'

'Naturally I have.'

'And that's what I intend becoming. The country is crying out for them. They're desperately needed to help the proper nurses.'

'Have you any idea what it would entail? The sort of men you'd have to come into contact with. Ruffians, scum.'

Wonky's temper flared. 'I hardly think that's quite fair, Father. You're talking about men fighting for their country. Prepared to lay down their lives if necessary. And again, according to the newspapers, only too many of them have.'

Tom waved a dismissive hand. 'It's out of the question, Veronica, and that's an end of it.'

'No it isn't, Father,' she replied hotly. 'This is a terrible war we're fighting and I propose to do my bit. And don't forget Nell's joining up also.'

'Veronica,' Moira said.

'Yes, Mother?'

'Why don't you think on this further. There's no rush after all.'

'There's no more thinking to be done,' Tom declared. 'I have said no and will be obeyed.'

'I'm going, Father, with your blessing or not.'

He swung on her, eyes blazing with fury. 'You will do nothing of the sort even if I have to resort to locking you in your room.'

Wonky laughed which infuriated her father even more. 'Who knows how long the war will last. Are you going to keep me locked up for the duration? That's absurd and you know it.'

He snorted, unwilling to admit to himself she was right.

'You have your knitting,' Moira said. 'Surely that's enough?'

'No it isn't. It's far from enough. The country needs me and those like me and I intend to respond.'

Tom fought back the urge to slap his daughter. 'And what if you're sent to France, eh. Answer me that?'

'If I'm sent I'm sent. There will be no hesitation on my part.'

'But you could be injured, girl, killed even.'

'Aren't we all in God's hands, Father?'

That made him halt and think, for he was a truly religious man. 'Maybe so,' he admitted reluctantly. 'But that doesn't mean you have to put yourself at unnecessary risk.'

'I'm joining, with or without your blessing, Father,' Wonky repeated emphatically.

'I . . . ' He suddenly stopped and sagged, knowing he was beaten.

'You won't have my blessing,' he croaked.

Moira Comyn began to cry.

* * *

Murdo let himself into his study, closed the door behind him, and sat to stare vacantly into space.

That had been a bombshell. Nell joining the VADs which would mean her leaving home as well. Now only Charlotte would be left.

How empty the house would seem, he thought. When Andrew had gone it hadn't been noticed all that much with three children still remaining.

Then it had been Peter, and now Nell.

Leaning back in his chair he closed his eyes, remembering them all as children, how it had once been. The laughter, the fun. And the difficult times too. The childhood illnesses, the problems of growing up, the sibling rivalry.

The time . . .

His memories rolled on and on.

* * *

Peter stared up into a leaden grey sky from which rain was lashing down. Rain meant the return of the terrible mud which would make their lives even more of a misery.

He shivered with cold, thinking of the awful months that lay ahead until spring. At least there wouldn't be any more big pushes for the foreseeable future. The fighting would continue of course, the unremitting patrols and the like, but no more big pushes for now. Thank the Lord.

Faces swam before him, friends, acquaintances, men under his command. Faces now gone for ever.

Damn the Kaiser for starting this carnage, damn him to everlasting perdition. He hoped the bastard roasted for all eternity.

Peter trudged on his way, stooping as always to avoid sniper fire.

You never knew when . . . You just never knew.

★ ★ ★

After months in hospital Jack Riach was returning to Pitlochry. It was something he was in two minds about, nervous as a kitten at the prospect.

'It's your station, young man,' the kindly female voice said, a middle-aged woman he'd chatted to off and on since leaving Glasgow.

'Thank you.'

'Shall I help you with the door?'

'No, I can manage.'

He came to his feet and groped on the overhead rack for his suitcase. He didn't have to ask which side to get off knowing that from past journeys.

'I want to wish you all the very best,' the lady said.

'I appreciate that. And the same to you.'

The train came to a halt and Jack fumbled with the window, eventually getting it down allowing him to open the door. Suitcase in hand he carefully descended onto the platform from where he swung the door shut again.

'Jack!'

He placed his case on the platform and turned

to the sound of his father's voice.

Bob Riach swallowed hard as he came nearer, the sight of Jack's dark glasses like a punch in the stomach. He stopped in front of his son, tears involuntarily springing into his eyes at the close-up view of Jack's badly scarred face.

'Hello, son.'

'Hello, Dad.'

'You're home at last.'

'Aye, at last.'

Bob Riach wasn't a particularly demonstrative man but he now put his arms round Jack and hugged him tight. 'It's so good to have you back, Jack. Your mother's been on tenterhooks.'

'Is she here?'

'No, she's at the house preparing the fatted calf.'

Bob released his son and picked up the case. 'If you take my arm we'll be on our way. There's the taxi waiting.'

Jack's white stick tap tap tapped as they made their way up the platform.

★ ★ ★

Nell sank onto a chair beside Wonky, the pair of them enjoying a tea break. They'd been assigned to the Southern General Hospital in Glasgow.

'I'm exhausted,' Nell sighed. 'All I want to do is go to bed and sleep.' They both lived in the nurses' quarters where they shared a room.

'I never realised the work would be so hard or the hours so long,' Wonky stated.

'Me neither. It just goes on and on.'

'It's the bed pans I hate most. I'll never get used to those. They're disgusting.'

'How about the back rubs?' Nell teased.

Wonky gave a small laugh. 'That was a bit of a shock to start with. I'd never seen a man's bare bottom before, far less touched one.'

Nell grinned ruefully. That had been a shock for her also.

'There's another batch of war casualties arriving tomorrow,' Wonky said. 'Staff told me.'

'Many?'

'She had no idea but thought there probably would be.'

Nell thought of the never-ending stream of wounded men who'd passed through their hands so far, and the deaths. Hardly a day went by when there wasn't a death on the ward.

Another VAD came into the room carrying a huge teapot. 'It was a case of help yourself, everyone else is busy,' she declared

Nell lurched wearily to her feet. 'I'll get yours as well,' she said to Wonky. The tea was foul, as it always was. But at least it was hot and wet which was something.

Ten minutes later they were both back on duty.

★ ★ ★

Grizelda was waiting with Mrs Riach, her presence a surprise for Jack who wouldn't be expecting her. She was atwitter with excitement.

'They're here!' she exclaimed on hearing a car draw up.

Bob paid off the driver and led Jack inside. He hadn't warned Jack about Grizelda, having been told not to. He hoped he'd done the right thing.

'Well here he is,' he declared when the pair of them entered the front room where his wife and Grizelda were.

The huge smile Grizelda was wearing vanished when she saw Jack's face.

'Oh my God!' she breathed in horror.

21

'HELLO, Jack.'

He recalled the voice only too well. 'Hello, Hettie. How are you?'

'Never better. What are you doing standing out here all by yourself?'

'I've been cooped up in the house for four days. I wanted a breath of fresh air.'

She nodded her understanding. 'I heard you were back of course, I've been looking forward to seeing you.'

He smiled thinly. 'Seeing?'

'That's right.'

'Not a pretty picture I'm afraid.'

He could smell her acutely, a fresh country odour that brought back memories.

'It's not that bad,' she said.

He barked out a laugh. 'Come off it, Hettie. Grizelda keeled over in a dead faint when she saw my face.'

'Did she indeed!' That angered Hettie. 'And then what?'

'She came round, stayed for a short while and fled.'

'Grizelda McPherson is a silly, vain woman, I've always thought so. What a dreadful thing to do.'

'She said she'd return in a few days when I've had a chance to settle in. But so far hasn't. I can only presume it's all over between us.'

'And good riddance in my opinion,' Hettie snorted.

'I half expected as much, mind. I should have been more explicit in the letters I had written about the extent of the scarring, but somehow couldn't bring myself to do so.'

He paused, then said softly, 'It's like a nightmare that you keep hoping you'll wake up from. Only of course you won't. It's all too horrid reality.'

Hettie gently touched his face. 'Well you're not the good-looking young buck you once were and that's a fact, but you're still Jack Riach to me and anyone else with sense.'

'Thank you, Hettie,' he said with a small choke in his voice.

'Now why four days indoors?'

'Why do you think?'

'You can't stay hidden away for the rest of your life, Jack. That's nonsense.'

'I had thought of going to the pub with my father, but when it came down to it I couldn't. I didn't have the courage.'

'*You* lacking in courage, Jack? I can't believe that.'

'Well it's true.'

She sighed. 'You're going to have to come to terms with that reality you spoke of and the sooner the better in my opinion. Now, will you buy a girl a drink? If you're not ashamed to be seen out with someone of my station that is.'

'How do you mean?'

'Have you got money on you?'

He tapped his wallet. 'Yes.'

'Then we'll go to the pub together and you can have a pint.'

'You mean now?'

'That's right.'

He hesitated. 'I don't know, Hettie.'

'Is it me?'

'No, of course not.'

'Then let's go. The walk will do you good.'

Still he hesitated.

'Sooner or later, Jack. Sooner or later.'

He suddenly made up his mind. 'All right then. The pub it is.'

She hooked an arm round his and they set off.

* * *

'That wasn't so bad now, was it?' she said later when they emerged from the pub.

'They were very kind.'

'Kind my arse, Jack. You're a local whom they all know and respect. Certainly they were sympathetic but that's as it should be. And they're only too well aware how you came by your injuries, fighting for your country and freedom. If anything they respect you even more than before.'

'I don't want to be a figure of pity,' he said softly.

'You'll only be that if you keep on pitying yourself. If folk see you don't then they won't either. At least not for long they won't.'

'You're a good woman, Hettie,' he said.

Unlike some he thought to himself.

'Want to hear a joke?'

He nodded. She then proceeded to tell him the filthiest joke he'd ever heard which caused him to roar with laughter.

★ ★ ★

'Come in!' Sister McAuliffe called out when Nell tapped on her door. Nell and Wonky went into the office.

Sister looked up from the paperwork she was dealing with and smiled. 'I've got good news for the pair of you,' she stated.

Nell and Wonky glanced at one another, then back at Sister.

'You're being sent to France to work over there. A group of VADs from here and the other Glasgow hospitals will be leaving on the fifteenth of next month. You're to be included in that group. Unless you decline that is. You do have the option.'

France! Nell swallowed hard.

'Well? Or do you wish time to think about it.'

'I'll go, Sister,' Wonky declared.

'And me,' Nell added.

'Good, that's settled then. You'll have a week off before then to see your families, then back here and France.'

'Thank you, Sister,' Wonky said.

A somewhat stunned Nell and Wonky returned to their duties, this new development in their lives having not quite sunk in yet. There had always been the possibility of course, but now it had actually happened.

★ ★ ★

It took Grizelda three weeks to reappear at the Riach house where she was ushered into the room where Jack was and the two of them left tactfully alone.

'This is difficult, Jack,' she said, voice trembling.

He knew what was coming next. 'You want to break it off between us.'

'I'm sorry. Truly I am.'

'That's all right, I understand.'

'I thought I could, but I can't.'

'The face is pretty horrendous I'm told.'

She winced.

There was no need to prolong this, he thought. He may as well put her out of her misery. 'Goodbye, Grizelda.'

'I really am sorry . . . '

'Goodbye,' he interjected.

'Bitch!' was Hettie's sole comment when she heard.

★ ★ ★

The Post Office was blazing uncontrollably, the sky an enormous mass of flame. To the observer it seemed the entire Dublin city centre was on fire, though it wasn't. Somewhere off to Andrew's left the British artillery was booming.

Andrew leant against a wall and wiped his

373

sweat-streaked face. Christ, but he was tired, and scared. The insurrection he and Sir Henry had discussed had finally taken place and he was at the sharp end of quelling it.

A bullet hissed, knocking a chunk out of the wall about a foot away. Andrew was galvanised into action, ducking into a doorway which offered temporary cover. He was joined there by a private called Stockton.

'Fun and games, sir, eh?' Stockton grinned.

Idiot! Andrew thought.

'Rebels!' someone shouted. 'Coming this way.'

Andrew peered round the corner of the doorway and quickly spotted them. About a dozen in all, heading directly for his platoon's current position.

He yelled out an order and the platoon opened up. One rebel clutched his side and then pitched over. Others were also hit.

The first wounded rebel turned on his side, clearly in great pain, crossed himself and started to crawl away. He'd only gone a few yards when he collapsed and could go no further. Unknown to Andrew and his platoon the man was a leader of the rising, and now dead. His name was O'Rahilly.

The artillery, 18-pounders, continued to boom inflicting terrible carnage.

Sergeant Mills joined Andrew as bullets flew in both directions. 'What shall we do, sir?'

'Keep firing and let's see if we can get them on the run.'

Andrew glanced up at a window opposite and saw a frightened female face staring down at him. His orders were to make for Jacob's Biscuit Factory but he was having a devil of a time getting there. There were rebels everywhere.

It was Easter 1916.

★ ★ ★

'I've made a decision, Dad,' Jack Riach announced to his father.

'Aye, what's that, son?'

'I'm going to sell this place and move into a cottage where I'll be able to cope.'

'You mean the house and land. The whole kit and caboodle?'

'That's right, Dad. It makes sense when you think about it. You're doing a splendid job, but I've got to think in the long term.'

Bob considered that. The house, land and everything else were Jack's to sell, having been signed over to him years previously. But it had all been in the family for so long.

'I can keep on till the end of the war, Jack, and then you can get a manager. Selling's not necessary.'

'I want to sell,' Jack stated softly. 'It just wouldn't be the same with a manager. It would . . . hurt too much. Can you understand that?'

Bob wasn't sure he could.

'I've decided, Dad, and that's how it's going to be.'

'What about if you have a family?'

Jack laughed. 'I'll never have one of those. What woman is going to have me now? No, I'm afraid I'm the last of the Riachs of Dalneil.

I'll never have a son and heir.'

'You can't be certain . . . '

'Look at me, Dad! For Christ's sake, no woman in her right mind is going to take me on. Not unless she was blind like myself and there are damned few of those of marrying age around here.'

'You could come and stay with us,' Bob suggested. 'Your mother and I would be delighted to have you.'

Jack shook his head. 'It's best I'm on my own.'

'But what about cooking and cleaning? You can't do that.'

'I'll employ someone, a housekeeper. In fact I already have someone in mind, if she'll agree.'

'Who's that?'

'Hettie Campbell. I'm certain she'll jump at the chance as it's a step up from dairy maid. She'll take good care of me.'

Bob thought of Hettie whom he'd always found a personable lassie, conscientious in her work too. She'd be ideal.

'It's up to you, Jack. It's entirely up to you.'

'I'll get things started then,' Jack replied.

* * *

'Housekeeper?'

'With better pay than you're getting now. So what do you say?'

Hettie was thrilled. 'Of course I'll do it for you, Jack. But are you absolutely certain about selling?'

His expression became serious and wistful at the same time. 'There are too many memories here, Hettie, of which I don't wish to be constantly reminded. The old Jack Riach lived here, not the one who came back from the war.'

A lump came into her throat. 'Oh, Jack!' she whispered.

'My father proposed a manager but that wouldn't be the same at all. I don't want to be stumbling round the house while someone else takes care of things. I'd hate that.'

'But you'd be there to consult and advise.'

'To begin with yes, but I'd soon become redundant. No, Hettie, that's how it's going to be. A little cottage somewhere, a new start. I had thought of moving right away from Dalneil, but that would be too big a wrench. As you said, I'm known here, a local. I'd rather remain amongst 'my ain folk'.'

She wanted to take him to her bosom and hold him tight, treat him like a child, comfort and console him, but refrained, knowing that wouldn't be appreciated. As Jack had told her, he didn't want to be a figure of pity and that's how such an action would be construed.

'Are there any cottages available around Dalneil?' she queried.

'I'll have to make enquiries. I'm sure I'll come up with something given time.'

'And when will you go on the market?'

'Right away, though how long it will take to sell is hard to say. In normal circumstances there wouldn't be any bother, but with a war on who

377

knows? I'll just have to wait and see.'

He laughed. 'Wait and *see*. That's a good one.'

'Don't be too hard on yourself, Jack,' she whispered.

Jack thought of Grizelda keeling over at the sight of him. How could he not be hard on himself. To spend the rest of his life not only blind but hideously scarred. Not for the first time he wished Peter Drummond had left him to die, for in death there was peace which he certainly didn't have now. Despair welled within him. Terrible, terrible despair.

★ ★ ★

Wonky found Nell and Charlotte in the drawing room. It was the evening of the day she and Nell had arrived home from Glasgow.

'I've left my case in the hall,' Wonky announced. 'Can I stay here during my week off?'

'Well of course you can,' Charlotte answered, face registering her surprise. 'What happened?'

Wonky took a deep breath. 'What do you think? *Father*. He went through the roof when I told him I was going to France.'

'As bad as that,' Nell commiserated.

'Worse, I can assure you. He actually swore. Can you imagine? Father swearing, I believe it's the first time I've ever heard him do so.'

Nell hid a smile. Wonky was right. For Tom Comyn to swear was almost beyond belief.

'He wants me to remain in Glasgow,' Wonky

378

went on. 'Or better still give up the VADs and come home. I naturally refused to do either.'

'Good for you,' Charlotte said.

'Does he know where you've gone?' Nell asked.

Wonky shook her head. 'No doubt he'll guess when he's calmed down so I can expect a visit tomorrow. I expect support from you two!'

'Which you'll have,' Nell assured her. 'And I'm glad you've stood your ground. The man, albeit he's my uncle, is a tyrant.'

Charlotte rose from where she was sitting. 'It's not long till dinner so I'd better inform Cook there'll be four instead of three.'

'Now tell me all about it,' Nell requested when Charlotte had left the room. 'Word for word.'

★ ★ ★

Nell groaned — was she going to vomit again? She'd already done so twice.

'I can see land!' Wonky exclaimed excitedly. 'It won't be long now.'

Thank God, Nell thought. She couldn't wait for the boat journey to France to be over and to be on dry land again. This was awful.

Wonky turned a sympathetic gaze on her cousin, wishing there was something she could do other than just be there. She felt fine, the rough crossing hadn't bothered her in the least.

'I feel so . . . ridiculous,' Nell gasped.

'Well, you're not the only one being sick.

There are a number from what I've seen.'

Nell groaned again as the boat pitched.

'Listen!' said Wonky.

The wind had suddenly changed direction and now they could distinctly hear the sound of heavy guns. Wonky shivered in apprehension.

Nell closed her eyes, wishing the boat to go faster.

★ ★ ★

'I was worried half to death for you when I heard what had happened,' Alice crooned to Andrew. 'You must have been right in the thick of it.'

Was he falling in love with her? he wondered. It seemed so, which delighted him. He certainly missed her when they were apart and thought of her constantly. Was that love?

'I was,' he acknowledged, pretending to be humble. 'The Post Office, Jacob's Biscuit Factory, I was there.'

'Oh, my darling,' she whispered.

'At one point a rebel bullet missed me by . . . oh! that much.' He held two fingers about an inch apart. An exaggeration of course.

Her eyes widened.

'I was lucky.'

She touched his cheek, lightly running her fingers over it. If that bullet had been any closer . . . she shuddered at the thought.

'And then Pearse saw sense and surrendered. That was an enormous relief I can tell you. I was amongst those who escorted the prisoners down O'Connell Street to Richmond Barracks. They gave a great cheer when they saw the tricolour still flying over the portico of the Post Office, but that was soon hauled down.'

Andrew became introspective. 'Some of those chaps seemed quite reasonable really. It was hard to imagine we'd been trying to kill each other only a short while previously.'

'Well, you're here now, safe and sound,' Alice declared.

'And with you, my pet, which is the best thing of all.'

She gave him a radiant smile which quite melted him inside. His lips met hers, and then she was in his arms.

It would be a good marriage he thought. Especially considering all that came with it.

Lucky! He was that and no mistake.

★ ★ ★

'It's strange there just being the two of us again,' Murdo said to Charlotte sitting beside him at the dinner table.

'Yes, Nell and Wonky certainly livened things up a bit.'

Murdo gazed about him. 'It's like living in a mausoleum.'

'It's hardly that grim, Pa!'

Murdo grunted.

Charlotte laid down her soup spoon. 'Why don't you go for a walk tomorrow afternoon? I'll be all right on my own for a while.'

He frowned. 'That's out of the question.'

'No it isn't,' she insisted. 'And you came to

enjoy your walks so much. I know you miss them.'

He did, he thought. He most certainly did. He didn't feel nearly as well as he had when taking them.

'Well?' she demanded.

'I'll think about it.'

Charlotte smiled, knowing she'd won and that he would. 'I wonder how the girls are getting on in France?' she mused.

'Probably up to their eyes in it. God help them.'

'Amen,' Charlotte murmured.

★ ★ ★

'Gas!' a lookout shouted. '*GAS!*'

Peter grabbed for his respirator which he quickly had in place. These gas attacks were increasing in frequency and a constant nightmare.

A young soldier who'd only arrived in the trenches for the first time that day froze with fear. Then he was fumbling with his respirator which, in his terror, he dropped.

He stared at the fallen respirator in horror as gas enveloped him and the others.

His first day in the trenches was his last.

★ ★ ★

Alice was laughing as she reined in her horse. 'You're letting me win again. That's not fair,' she called out.

Andrew reined in alongside her. 'No I'm not. I swear. It's simply that you're a far better rider than I.'

She gazed adoringly at him. 'Fibber.'

'Not so!' he protested.

Her face fell. 'I've just remembered you're returning to Dublin tomorrow.'

'Duty calls, Alice.'

'I wish you didn't have to go.'

'So do I, I assure you. I'd much rather be here with you.' He meant that most sincerely.

'Can I come to you tonight, be with you for a while? We could snuggle up.'

'No!' he replied sternly, the truth being he simply didn't trust himself.

'Please?'

'No, Alice. You know my feelings on that subject.'

She pouted. 'Spoilsport.'

'Indeed I am.'

As they rode on he thought of the brothel he'd been using and wondered if it would be safe to return there so soon after the rising.

★ ★ ★

'I don't think I'll ever get used to living in a tent,' Nell said to Wonky as she and the others present got dressed. There were six of them in the bell-tent to which she and Wonky had been assigned. This was the accommodation provided for the VADs by the 22 General Hospital, Camiers.

'It could be worse,' Wonky replied, thinking but not much.

Hope Langton, another of the six, laughed. 'Consider yourself fortunate, girls. You should have seen where I was before this. Now *that* was something to complain about.'

'I'm not complaining,' Nell retorted. 'Only remarking that I don't think I'll ever get used to it.'

'Can anyone lend me some hairpins?' Georgina Fletcher asked. 'I appear to have mislaid mine.'

'You're always mislaying things. I wouldn't be surprised if you mislaid yourself one day,' Rebecca Levi commented.

Georgina pulled a face. 'I can't help the way I am. I've always been the same.'

Rebecca sighed. 'Here, have some of mine.'

Georgina accepted the pins with a word of thanks and used them to secure the white cap which tailed down to her shoulders. Their white aprons were ankle length, full in cut, and held in place by a belt. Each apron sported a red cross on the bosom.

'Well I'm ready. I wonder what's for breakfast?' Wonky declared jauntily.

A few minutes later all six of them left together for the mess after which they started their shift.

★ ★ ★

'Yes!' Murdo called out when there was a rap on the office door, expecting it to be Isobel with their coffee and biscuits. He stared in astonishment when it was Miss McQueen who entered.

Miss McQueen's face was stone hard as she crossed to his desk. 'This came and I thought you'd better have it right away, sir,' she said, laying down an official telegram in front of him.

A mesmerised Murdo stared at the telegram. It might have been a hissing snake that had been put on his desk.

'Pa?'

Murdo didn't reply but instead continued to stare at the telegram. He'd heard of telegrams like these, who hadn't. And now one had been sent to him.

It took all his willpower to reach out and pick up the envelope. Slowly, unwillingly, he slit it open and took out the single sheet it contained.

Charlotte was on her feet now, the atmosphere in the office having changed to one of deep foreboding.

Murdo read the sheet and went white.

'Pa?' Charlotte repeated.

He looked at her through eyes filled with tears. 'Peter's been killed,' he stated simply.

'Oh, my God.'

Miss McQueen glanced away.

'Killed,' Murdo said again.

The pain that erupted in his chest was more intense than any he'd previously experienced. He gasped and clutched himself.

'Pa!' Charlotte screamed, rushing round from behind her desk. 'Pa!'

Miss McQueen got to Murdo first, cradling him in her arms. Then Charlotte was there also.

Murdo's colour changed from white to puce as he struggled for breath.

'Peter,' he murmured. 'Peter.'

'Get Doctor McAllister!' Charlotte ordered Miss McQueen. 'And hurry.'

Miss McQueen fled the room.

★ ★ ★

'It was a massive heart attack brought on by the news,' McAllister said to a distraught Charlotte. 'There was nothing you could have done. I'm truly sorry.'

Her brother and father in one day. Dear God.

'It's best Miss McQueen takes you home and I'll attend to what has to be done here. I'll be over later with a sedative.'

Before leaving Charlotte knelt and kissed her father on the lips. 'Goodbye, Pa. Say hello to Peter for me.'

Somewhere in her mind she heard his voice reply:

'I will, lass. I will.'

22

CHARLOTTE sat alone in the drawing room staring vacantly ahead, her mind in turmoil. She was racked with grief.

The funeral was in three days' time, she had to hold herself together for that. Andrew had been notified and was on his way home, as was Nell.

But what happened after the funeral, what then? She simply did not know.

* * *

'Hello, sis.'

Charlotte turned from the window through which she'd been staring to give her brother a wan smile. 'Hello, Andrew.'

He went to her and kissed her on the cheek. 'How are you?'

'Dreadful. And you?'

'Still in shock.'

She nodded her understanding.

'How was the trip over?' she enquired.

'Uneventful, thank goodness. There wasn't a moment went by when I didn't expect to be blown sky high. The U-boats are causing terrible carnage out there.'

'So I read in the newspapers.'

He went to the decanter and poured himself a dram. 'You?'

'No thanks.'

Andrew stared at her thoughtfully over the rim of his glass. 'Peter *and* Pa, it's hardly credible,' he said.

'Yes.'

'Right there in the office.'

'In my arms.'

'Christ,' Andrew muttered.

He gazed about him, thinking this was now all his. Who would have believed but he'd inherited after all. Not that that changed his plans for Alice, not a whit of it.

'Everyone has been so wonderful,' Charlotte declared. 'They couldn't have been kinder. The workforce in the distillery are soldiering on in the meantime. They're all coming to the funeral. Each and every one of them. Pa was so well liked.'

'When's Nell arriving?'

'Sometime today I believe. I just hope she isn't held up in any way.'

'I hope so too. It would be awful if she missed the funeral tomorrow. She'd never forgive herself.'

'Yes,' Charlotte agreed.

She shivered, she just couldn't seem to get warm since Murdo's death. Even in bed with a heavy quilt on top she was still cold. Reaction of course, she knew that.

'Have we heard yet what actually happened to Peter?'

Charlotte shook her head. 'There should be a letter from his C.O. I understand that's the procedure. But it hasn't come yet.'

'I hope this isn't tactless, but when's the will being read?'

'Monday of next week. You'll still be here I take it?'

'Oh yes. I've got a full fortnight's compassionate leave. By the way, Alice, my fiancée sends her condolences and hopes you're bearing up. So also do her father and mother, Sir Henry and Lady Fortescue.'

'You must tell me all about her before you leave.'

'I shall, sis. I shall.'

'Uncle Tom's taking the service. He and Aunt Moira are very upset.'

Andrew poured himself another dram.

'Jack Riach will be coming to the funeral. Did you hear about him?'

Andrew shook his head.

Charlotte told him.

'Poor bugger,' Andrew whispered, profoundly thankful he was in Ireland and not at the Western Front.

'He was supposed to marry Grizelda McPherson you know, but she broke it off when he got back. That caused a few comments I can tell you.'

'Is his face that bad?'

'Pretty ghastly. It was Peter who saved his life. Now Peter's gone.'

Two hours later Nell arrived home.

★ ★ ★

A huge turnout filled the church to capacity. There were people standing against the walls and a large number at the rear. Andrew spoke, doing justice to both his father and brother.

After Murdo had been interred those who'd been invited went to Drummond House where a buffet meal and drinks had been provided.

It was hours before the last mourner left.

★ ★ ★

'Sell the distillery!' Charlotte exploded, aghast.

Andrew shrugged. 'What else can I do? With Pa and Peter gone there's no one left to run the damn thing.'

'But it's been in the family for generations,' an equally aghast Nell objected.

'Nothing's for ever, Nell. And even if I could get out the army, which I can't for the present, I couldn't run it. I wouldn't even know where to start.'

'What about the house?' Charlotte queried.

'That'll remain the family home, for now anyway. I'd hardly toss you out onto the street.'

The will had been read that morning. As expected, with Peter's death, the main part of the estate had gone to Andrew. Both Charlotte and Nell had been well provided for.

'You can't sell the distillery. You simply can't,' Charlotte stated emphatically.

'Then come up with an alternative,' Andrew challenged.

She stared at her brother, eyes blazing. 'I'll run it.'

'You!' he scoffed. 'That's ridiculous.'

'Not as ridiculous as it might seem. I've been working with Pa there for some time now during which he taught me a lot. I believe I'm quite capable of taking over.'

Andrew leant back in the sofa and regarded Charlotte with amusement. 'Women don't run businesses, sis. It just isn't done.'

'There are lots of things women didn't do before the war which they're doing now, so why not this?'

'Hear hear,' Nell agreed.

'You're serious then?'

'I most certainly am. If you sell the distillery, Andrew, I'll never forgive you or speak to you again. You have my word on that.'

'And mine,' Nell added.

He frowned. He'd never considered this option. And the distillery might be difficult to sell during wartime. There was that.

'You've been working with Pa and he taught you a lot?' Andrew repeated.

'That's right. Pa took over again after Peter left, which you know, and was running himself into the ground because we're so short staffed. I offered to help to get my mind off losing the baby.'

Andrew dropped his gaze. 'Yes, Pa penned me a note about that. I'm sorry.'

'Not half as much as me. Anyway, those are the reasons I offered to help Pa and a great success my help has been, if I say so myself. Pa was coming to rely on me more and more.'

'I see,' Andrew mused.

'She's quite capable,' Nell said. 'I'd have every

faith in her if I was you.'

This was going to take some considering, Andrew thought. He wasn't about to rush into any decisions. Certainly not ones as important as this.

'Let me sleep on it,' he said with a smile.

Charlotte, after a few moments hesitation, nodded her agreement.

★ ★ ★

'I'm drunk as a lord,' Bobby Baxter declared to Geoffrey. The pair of them were in an Amiens nightclub, a husky-voiced female singer, on what passed for a stage, singing in French.

'Me too,' Geoffrey grinned back.

Bobby glanced about him. 'We could easily get fixed up you know, old bean. There are lots of ladies present who, for a price, would be most accommodating.'

Geoffrey shook his head. 'Not interested, Bobby. I'd never betray my Charlotte. She's the one and only for me.'

Bobby sighed. 'I envy you that. It must be an inspiration for you.'

'It is.'

'Someday . . . ' Bobby murmured. 'Someday.'

A waiter approached and spoke to them. 'Yes, another bottle of champers,' Bobby nodded. Then to Geoffrey, 'We may as well make a real night of it. Who knows when we'll get a decent one out again.'

The smell of cheap perfume, female flesh and sweat was almost overpowering, Geoffrey thought. It had a strange intoxicating effect that wasn't entirely unpleasant.

'Two more days and we're back in the frontline,' Bobby stated.

Geoffrey didn't reply to that. Two days could be a lifetime in their situation. You simply lived each day at a time and tried not to think of tomorrow.

The singer finished her song and was given a rapturous applause which she acknowledged flamboyantly

'Lovely pair of tits,' Bobby commented.

Geoffrey roared, for Bobby was right. They were lovely.

★ ★ ★

'I've decided to let you go ahead,' Andrew declared to Charlotte.

Relief surged through her. 'So you won't be selling?'

He turned away, not wanting her to see the expression on his face. 'Let's wait a bit and see how it all goes.'

She knew that was the best she could hope for. 'Thank you, Andrew.'

He shrugged.

'I won't let you down. I swear.'

'I'm sure you won't,' he replied. The only reason he'd agreed to her proposal was because it suited his purposes. For the time being.

'I'll be back to work tomorrow,' she stated.

★ ★ ★

The workforce had assembled as Charlotte had instructed. She now stepped forward to address them.

'As I'm sure you're all aware my brother Andrew has inherited the distillery. Unfortunately he can't leave the army with the war on to take charge, so in the meantime I'm going to run things.'

A muttering went up.

She raised an eyebrow. 'Any questions?'

Don McLeod, a stillman in his late fifties, held up a hand. 'That's ridiculous, lassie. Who's ever heard of a female boss?'

He laughed, as did many of the others present. 'You don't approve of the idea then?' she replied caustically

'No offence, Miss Charlotte, but the notion's a load of nonsense.'

'Really?'

'Oh aye,' he grinned.

'I see.' She paused. 'Well that's that then. I'll have to close the distillery down. There's nothing else for it.'

Don's grin vanished. 'Close down?'

'What else can I do? Nothing.'

She stared defiantly at him, then the others.

'Aye, well . . . ' Don muttered.

'And if I close down that means you're all out of work,' she pointed out unnecessarily. 'Is that what you want?'

Their faces reflected it was the last thing they wanted.

She softened her tone. 'I know I'm a woman and that might cause difficulties, not only with you but wholesalers and the like. Nor do I pretend to understand whisky making, I don't. But I am prepared to try to run the administration side of things if I can rely on your wholehearted cooperation. Without that we close and a For Sale sign goes up.'

The men glanced from one to the other.

'I'll tell you this,' she went on. 'My father would have hated the idea of the distillery being closed down and ultimately sold. You all know how much he loved this place. And how loyal he was to you and yours. Is it too much to expect a little of that loyalty back now that he's dead?'

Sandy McTavish raised his hand. 'May we speak amongst ourselves, Miss Charlotte?'

'Of course, Sandy.'

'Thank you, miss.'

The men conferred together, the women in the workforce excluded though the decision affected them also.

After a few minutes' consultation the men broke apart from the huddle they'd formed into.

'We're with you, Miss Charlotte,' Sandy declared. 'You'll get our full cooperation.'

'Does that go for everyone?'

'Everyone,' Don McLeod nodded.

She hesitated, then said, 'There are bound to be times when I have to come to some of you for advice. That seems inevitable. I hope you'll be patient with my lack of practical knowledge.'

'We'll be patient,' Sandy replied.

Jamie, the gaffer from bottling, raised his cap

aloft. 'Three cheers for Miss Charlotte. Hip hip . . . !'

'Now let's get on with it, myself included,' she smiled when the cheering had died away.

★ ★ ★

Wonky, having heard Nell was back, had sneaked away for a few minutes from the hospital. She found Nell sitting morosely in their tent.

'So how was it?' Wonky asked.

'Pretty awful.'

'I can imagine.'

'I still can't believe that Pa and Peter have gone. It's . . . ' She broke off and shook her head.

'Is there anything I can do?'

Nell took a deep breath. 'No. But thanks for asking. Your father did an excellent service by the way. It couldn't have been better if that's the right word to use for that sort of thing.'

Wonky placed a comforting hand on Nell's shoulder. 'They were both good men who'll be sorely missed.'

'Pa seemed . . . well indestructible somehow. A rock.'

'I know,' Wonky whispered.

'I could smell him everywhere in the house. And half the time expected him to come breezing in through the door. Charlotte said she felt the same.'

'How's Charlotte taking it?'

'As you'd expect. Andrew better than the two

of us, but then he's a man.'

'Andrew was there?'

'Oh yes. He got compassionate leave. He's agreed to let Charlotte run the distillery for now. I'm sure she'll make a success of it.'

'I agree, Charlotte's a very resourceful woman. Anyway, I'd better get back on the ward before. Sister realises I'm missing. I'll get a rocket if she does.'

Nell smiled at her cousin. 'Thanks for popping over.'

Wonky bent and kissed Nell on the cheek. 'Cheer up. We'll have a proper natter later.'

'All right.'

Wonky swished from the tent.

★ ★ ★

Wonky hadn't long gone when the familiar tingling took hold of Nell, followed by the trembling of her hands. It had been ages since she'd last had a vision.

The Highland army appeared to be in retreat, their mood one of utter dejection. They looked as though they hadn't eaten or slept in days.

Her Highlander was at the rear and seemed to be having trouble walking. His face was gaunt and unshaven, his shoulders drooping, and there was a blood-stained rag tied round his left arm.

Oh my poor darling, Nell found herself thinking. Her impulse was to rush to him and take care of him.

A horse stumbled and dropped to the ground

here it writhed for a few moments. Its rider, who'd jumped clear, wearily examined the animal, then took a pistol from his waistband, cocked it and shot the beast. Others, completely uninterested in the situation, continued to trudge by.

Her Highlander glanced up at the sky as though wondering if it was going to rain, then continued on his way.

It was still England, Nell thought.

The Highland army was still south of the border.

★ ★ ★

Andrew was sitting alone in the mess when he was joined by Billy Roberts. 'You'll never guess what happened when I was out on patrol?' Billy said.

'Somebody took a potshot at us. Luckily he missed.'

'A potshot?' Andrew mused.

'A Fenian of course. At least I presume it was.' Billy tasted his beer. 'I think we made a bad mistake executing all those rebels. We went overboard in my opinion.'

'I disagree. They were rebels as you say. They deserved what they got.'

'Maybe. But to execute so many? I'm certain that was wrong.'

Andrew leant back in his chair and closed his eyes.

'Something up?'

'I've been tired ever since I returned from

Scotland. Perhaps I'm coming down with a cold or the flu.'

'It could simply be reaction. Losing a father and brother at the same time must knock the stuffing out of you. I know it would me.'

'It certainly wasn't easy,' Andrew said. 'Nor was the trip over there and back. Rotten weather in both instances plus the worry about U-boats. There was a ship sunk on the day I made the return journey. It could easily have been the one I was on.'

'Still, you had to go. And take the risk involved I suppose.'

Andrew sighed. 'Anyway, it's all over and done with now, thank God.'

'And you've become a man of property and means,' Billy grinned.

Andrew's mood lightened. 'There is that. I only wish it wasn't at Peter's expense though. We were never the closest of brothers, but . . . ' He broke off. 'Well, you understand.'

'Of course,' Billy muttered.

'A potshot?' Andrew mused again thoughtfully. 'Well well well.'

He made a mental note to be extra vigilant while he was on patrol.

★ ★ ★

'How are you today, Jack?' Hettie enquired.

'So so. And yourself?'

'All right, bearing up. Any news of that cottage?'

He shook his head. 'There's absolutely nothing

going at the moment but something's bound to come up in time. It's simply a case of waiting.'

'I'm looking forward to being a housekeeper. It should be fun.'

'Fun,' he chuckled.

'Well, different anyhow.'

He sighed, a melancholy sound. 'I feel so useless, Hettie. I just wish I could do something. But what?'

She had no reply to that.

'You know what I miss most?'

'What, Jack?'

'Riding. I used to enjoy that so much. Now I'll never ride again.'

She bit her lip in consternation. 'Now don't take offence but you could always mount up and have someone lead you.'

That amused him. 'Not exactly the same, Hettie. Not by a long chalk.' He laughed bitterly. 'What would I look like? Ridiculous that's what. Completely ridiculous.'

'No you wouldn't!' she replied hotly.

'Well, that's how I feel.' He reached out and groped till he found her arm. 'I appreciate you're only trying to be helpful so thank you for that.'

'Been to the pub recently?'

'As a matter of fact I went last night with my dad. We had a smashing time. All sorts came over and joined us for a chat.'

'And what else have you been doing?'

'Nothing, Hettie, nothing at all. Thinking mainly, remembering how it used to be. I think of Peter Drummond quite a bit. We were great pals he and I.'

'I know,' she said softly.

'I miss the old bugger. At least . . . ' He trailed off.

'What?'

Jack spoke in almost a whisper. 'At least he didn't end up crippled or disfigured.'

'You're not crippled, Jack.'

'Then what do you call being blind? I'm a cripple as much as if I'd lost my arms or legs. Crippled,' he repeated.

Hettie swallowed hard, her heart going out to him. She was wise enough to know the last thing he needed was self pity, but how could she tell him that. It was something he had to learn for himself.

'I'd best be getting on my way, Jack. I still have lots to do.'

'Crippled,' he further repeated after she'd gone.

★ ★ ★

Isobel placed Charlotte's coffee and biscuits in front of her. 'Excuse me remarking, miss, but you look fair wabbit.'

Charlotte gave the girl a wan smile. 'I am, Isobel. Believe me.'

Isobel stared at her employer in concern. 'You're working too hard, miss. That's what folk are saying.'

Charlotte took a deep breath thinking how welcome the coffee was. 'There's a great deal to be done, Isobel, and I'm still learning the ropes. It isn't easy.'

'No, miss,' Isobel agreed.

Charlotte spooned sugar into her coffee, then added milk.

'Can I say something, miss?'

'Certainly, go ahead.'

'The workers all admire you, miss. They weren't sure about this to begin with but now they've come to respect and admire all you're doing. They're right behind you. Especially the women, they all think it's grand.'

That warmed Charlotte, as did the coffee when she sipped it.

'Is there anything else, miss?'

'No, Isobel. And thank you for your support.'

Isobel gave Charlotte a huge beaming smile. 'Not at all, miss. Not at all.'

Charlotte forced herself to take her time over the coffee and biscuits, before getting back to work.

★ ★ ★

'It's gorgeous!' Alice exclaimed, staring at the sparkling emerald necklace nestling on black velvet. She threw an arm round Andrew's neck. 'Thank you.'

'It'll maybe make up for the engagement ring I bought you. Money was tight then which it isn't now.'

'My ring is beautiful, Andrew. It's what it represents that matters, not the value of the ring itself.'

He *was* in love with her, he thought. He damned well was. He'd thought of her constantly, even through the traumas of Scotland, since their last meeting. Touching her, smelling her, gave him a thrill.

'Why don't you try it on,' he suggested.

She took the necklace from its box and he helped fasten it round her neck. 'There,' he declared. 'Perfect.'

Her eyes shone. 'Thank you again,' she whispered.

'Do I get a kiss?'

The kiss was long, deep and wonderful.

★ ★ ★

Sir Henry Fortescue was a worried man. He was pleased with Andrew's good fortune, albeit out of tragedy, but as Andrew now owned the Drummond distillery surely that meant Andrew, and Alice, would be residing in Scotland after the war. That was the last thing he wanted. What he did want was for Alice to stay nearby.

Sir Henry surveyed Andrew across the dinner table. 'And what are your plans for the future now, me lad?' he queried, trying to keep the anxiety out of his voice.

'How do you mean, sir?'

'The distillery of course. I presume you'll be taking over as soon as you can?'

Andrew glanced at Alice who smiled back at him. She was wearing the necklace which Lady Fortescue had cooed over.

'I'm not sure, sir.'

'Not sure?'

'I have a mind to sell it, sir. Though I haven't made a final decision yet.'

Sir Henry immediately brightened. 'And why would you do that?'

Andrew's reason was that it would give him enough money, if properly handled that was, to live a life of ease and luxury. After all, why work if you didn't have to? And then there was Greystones and the Fortescue inheritance. When they came Alice's way it would really be a life of luxury at the highest level.

'I've never really been interested in the distillery, sir,' Andrew said honestly. 'Perhaps things might have been different if I'd been the firstborn and trained into the business as my brother Peter was. But I wasn't and that's why I went into the army which appealed.'

'I see,' Sir Henry murmured, much relieved. 'I understand your sister is currently running it.'

Andrew smiled. 'A conceit on her part, sir. The idea of a woman in charge is absurd of course. But if she can keep things ticking over, till the end of the war that is, and perhaps somewhat beyond, then that suits me.'

'You're thinking of the price you'll get when you finally do sell?' Sir Henry asked shrewdly.

'Precisely, sir. To my way of thinking I should get a lot more after the war than I would now. So if I can hang on, thanks to Charlotte, then why not.'

Sir Henry chuckled. 'Good for you.'

Lady Fortescue frowned. 'Isn't that rather devious of you, Andrew? And what of your poor sister if she does make a go of it?'

'Devious perhaps, but then isn't that what business is all about? As for Charlotte, she'll lose interest when her husband Geoffrey gets back from the war and they start a family.'

'And what if he doesn't come back?' Alice queried.

Andrew had a sip of wine, a rather good Bordeaux. 'That'll alter things of course. In the short term, that is, for I'm certain after a suitable period Charlotte would marry again. She's a fine-looking woman and would not be one to remain a widow in my opinion.

'Anyway,' he shrugged. 'The decision of when to sell, regardless of the circumstances, is mine and mine alone. She has no say whatever in the matter.'

'So your plans are still to remain in Ireland?' Sir Henry asked, twiddling his moustache.

'Most assuredly, sir.'

'Aahhh!' Sir Henry breathed, and shot his wife a jubilant glance. That was excellent.

'There would naturally be trips to Scotland, but my home would be here.'

Sir Henry nodded his approval.

'Isn't he clever,' Alice beamed at her parents.

Sir Henry wasn't going to dispute that. 'Changing the subject. What have you heard about this torching in West Cork?' he asked Andrew.

'Torching? Nothing at all, sir.'

'Dreadful affair,' Lady Fortescue muttered.

Andrew was intrigued and waited for Sir Henry to explain.

'Two Protestant families were burnt out of their houses,' Sir Henry said. 'Luckily no one was injured.'

'Disgraceful,' Alice declared.

Sir Henry frowned. 'It's a worrying development for the likes of us who've managed to rub along with the Catholics all this while.' He shook his head. 'The majority of the populace weren't with the Fenians before the rising, but now . . . Well let's just say I detect a new mood in the land. One I don't like one little bit.'

Andrew recalled his conversation with Billy Roberts. 'Do you think we were too harsh with the rebel leaders, sir?'

'It's not what I think but the populace itself. And yes, I believe they do, that the British government went too far.'

He sighed. 'Who knows what the outcome will be.'

'Who knows?'

★ ★ ★

Andrew woke with a start when a body slipped into bed beside him.

'Ssshh!' Alice whispered.

'What are you doing here?'

'Don't be angry, darling, please? I just wanted to snuggle up for a while.'

'But you know . . . ' He was silenced by her hand being placed across his mouth.

'Instead of talking, kiss me.'

What else could he do? He couldn't exactly chuck her out of bed. That would have been a terrible insult. Besides, now she was here, why not make the best of it. Within limits that was.

Their lips met and his hand moved to her breast. She jerked slightly when he cupped it.

'You really are a hussy,' he whispered when the kiss was over.

'Only where you're concerned, Andrew. I'd do anything for you. Anything at all.'

His ego swelled. By Jove! he thought. Talk about a conquest. 'And I you. But this isn't right, Alice. You don't realise what a temptation you are.'

'Or what a temptation you are for me.'

Her hand wormed its way into his pyjama jacket and began roving over his chest. 'Stop it!' he hissed.

She didn't. Instead her other hand suddenly delved to encompass his bottom.

Andrew groaned. This was too much. He exposed the breast he'd been fondling and dropped his mouth to it.

All previous resolution he'd had evaporated. He lifted up her nightdress and squirmed out of his pyjama bottoms. He had to have her. He simply had to.

He must pull out in time he told himself. He must.

Alice gave a small grunt as he broke into her. And from then on it was sheer bliss for both of them.

★ ★ ★

'It's Charlotte Drummond to see you,' Bob Riach announced to Jack, sitting in a chair by the fire.

Jack immediately rose. 'Charlotte?'

She went to him and kissed him on the cheek. 'Hello, Jack.'

'You're brave to do that.'

'Am I indeed. I don't think so.'

He ignored her reply. 'Would you care for a dram. Or perhaps something else?'

'A dram would be lovely. It's been a long, hard day.'

'I'll get you one then.'

'Can I do it?'

He gave her a crooked smile. 'I can manage, thank you.'

She watched him go to a cupboard, open it and fumble inside. 'I'll sit down if you don't mind.'

'Please do.'

She further watched as he poured the whiskies then tentatively made his way back. 'Which seat are you in?' he queried.

She told him.

He came to her and handed her a glass. 'If you want water I'll have to shout for my mother or father.'

'Neat's fine.'

'Right then.'

He made his way over to the chair he'd been sitting in and sat again. '*Slainthe!*' he toasted.

'*Slainthe.*'

They both drank.

'Drummond,' she commented.

'Of course. What else?' He had another sip. 'Now why the visit, Charlotte. What can I do for you?'

'It's more what I can do for you.'

'Oh?'

'You know old Mrs Murchie?'

'Of course.'

She went on to explain to a delighted Jack the reason she'd called.

23

WONKY found the driver leaning against his ambulance smoking a cigarette. 'I'm the VAD for the CCS,' she smiled. The latter was short for Casualty Clearing Station where the wounded were taken from the frontline.

He had an open, intelligent face with deep blue eyes. 'Hi!' he replied. 'I'm Dale Kutchinsky.'

She frowned. 'Are you American?'

'Sure am. All the way from Albany, New York State. Hop aboard and we'll get underway.'

'An American,' she thought, going round to the other side of the ambulance. She'd heard there were some around, albeit America wasn't in the war, but this was the first she'd encountered.

She climbed into the passenger seat and closed the door. Moments later they moved off.

'New to this duty, eh?' he said.

'That's right.'

'Knew I hadn't driven you before. What's your name?'

'Wonky Comyn.'

He laughed. 'Wonky! What sort of name is that?'

'A nickname. My real name is Veronica.' She then went on to explain why she was called Wonky.

'Like it,' he declared. 'Never known a Wonky before.'

'Nor I a Dale.'

'That makes us even then.'

There was an easiness of manner about him which she liked, she decided. Not bad looking either, in a different sort of way. Now that she'd had something of a chance to study him he certainly didn't look British. Perhaps it was something to do with the relaxed way he carried himself.

'Been out here long?' she asked.

'Couple of months. You?'

'A little longer.'

He grunted, took a last draw on his cigarette then tossed it away.

'Are you a professional ambulance driver?' she enquired politely.

He laughed again. 'Hell no! I'm a lawyer, graduate of Harvard Law School. I haven't practised yet though, came straight over after graduation. Much to my folks' dismay. They sure were angry as can be when I told them my intention. Said I was stupid to put myself in danger when I didn't have to.'

She immediately warmed to him. 'It was the same with me. My father was beside himself when I told him I was joining the VADs, which was nothing to what he was like when I broke the news that I was coming to France.'

'Sometimes parents don't realise you've grown up and are capable of your own decisions,' he grinned amiably. 'They still think we're babies

411

in diapers who have to be looked after.'

She frowned. 'Diapers?'

'You know. Those things you put round a baby's a — ' He suddenly checked himself. 'Rear.'

'You mean nappies?'

'Whatever.'

Wonky flushed slightly. What a subject! 'Kutchinsky did you say?'

'Correct, maam. We're of Polish extraction. My grandfather and grandmother went to the States on an immigrant ship and made good. He was a tailor by trade.'

Wonky found that fascinating. 'And your other set of grandparents?'

'Oh, they stayed on in Poland. We lost touch with that side of the family long ago.

'Sorry,' Dale apologised as the ambulance bounced. 'These roads are a bitch.'

'So why did you decide to be in a war when your own country isn't fighting?' she asked, curious.

'Conscience, pure and simple. I'm also quite a Francophile, sure love those frogs. Their literature, art, cuisine.'

He took out a packet of cigarettes. 'You don't object I hope?'

'No I don't.'

'Do you?'

She shook her head.

He lit up.

'How long will it take to get there?' she inquired.

'Varies, maam. Depends on the roads and

other things. In other words we get there when we get there.'

He gave her a sideways glance. 'You English?'

'Scots.'

'I thought it wasn't an English accent. Leastways none of the ones I've heard.'

'What's Albany like? Sounds nice.'

He then proceeded to enthuse about his home town for the remainder of the bumpy ride.

★ ★ ★

'Wonky!'

She was supervising stretcher cases being loaded aboard the ambulance, and turned round in surprise at the sound of her name. She couldn't believe her eyes when she saw Geoffrey hurrying towards her.

He took her into his arms, a bemused Dale looking on, and kissed her on the cheek. 'Well isn't this a turn up for the book!'

'What are you doing here. You're not injured, are you?'

Geoffrey shook his head. 'Seeing a fellow officer who's been wounded. And you?'

She explained her new duty.

'You look wonderful!' he declared.

Which was more than she could say about him. How aged he was. There was even grey in his hair which hadn't been there before.

'How are you?' she asked with a smile.

'All right. Well, as right as can be, considering.'

'It was terrible about Peter.'

Geoffrey's face fell. 'Yes,' he agreed softly. 'It,

eh . . . well, best not speak about it.'

'I'll write and tell Charlotte I bumped into you. She'll be thrilled.'

'Quite a coincidence.'

'Quite.'

'Charlotte's doing awfully well in the distillery, I understand. I'm proud of her.'

She touched him on the sleeve. 'It was rotten about the baby, Geoffrey. Really rotten.'

He glanced away. 'So much death and destruction nowadays. It's all about us. A day doesn't go by but . . . ' He broke off and shrugged. 'Enough of that, have to look on the bright side, what?'

'That's the ticket.'

'Nurse, we need you,' Dale called out.

'I have to go,' Wonky apologised.

'Of course. You take care now.'

'And you, Geoffrey.' He kissed her again on the cheek, a misty look in his eyes. 'Ta ra for now.'

'Ta ra.'

He left her and strode away.

'Friend?' Dale enquired as she joined him.

'My cousin's husband.'

'Ah!'

Geoffrey turned and waved to Wonky but by then she was far too busy to notice.

★ ★ ★

'What's it like?' Jack asked.

Hettie glanced about her. They were in old Mrs Murchie's rented cottage which she'd

414

given up to go and live with her daughter and family. The cottage belonged to Charlotte who'd inherited it when Murdo died, being in that part of the estate which had come to her. She now intended selling it to Jack.

'Just as you'd expect of an old woman who's lived alone. It's going to need a lot doing to it.'

Jack nodded. 'I thought as much.'

'It appears solid enough, though no doubt you'll have that checked over.'

'I shall have everything ripped out and we'll start from scratch,' Jack declared. 'You'll do the choosing of carpets and curtains, those sort of things.'

That delighted Hettie.

'We'll go to Pitlochry when it's time and tour the shops there. How about that?'

'Sounds a real treat, Jack.'

If he could pluck up the courage to go to Pitlochry that was, he wasn't at all sure he could. 'How big is this sitting room we're in?'

Hettie gave him a rough estimate.

'Now take me to the kitchen.'

That was in an even worse state than the sitting room, and filthy in the extreme.

Hettie began the very next day to scrub out the cottage.

★ ★ ★

Charlotte coldly eyed Mr Strachan, her Glasgow and surrounding area's distributor, across his desk. The meeting was at her request.

415

'How pleasant of you to call, Miss Drummond,' he beamed. 'Can I offer you sherry?'

'No thank you.'

He made a pyramid with his hands. 'And to what do I owe the honour?'

'You've put up your prices.'

'That's correct.'

'I've been in touch with other distilleries you handle and you haven't done the same with them.'

His smile faded.

Charlotte arched an eyebrow and waited for an explanation.

'We will in time, Miss Drummond.' She could read in his face and from the fact he'd coloured that was a lie.

'Could it be you thought I was a soft touch being a woman?' she asked.

'Of course not!' he protested.

'No?'

'It is somewhat unusual I admit. I've never done business with a woman before.'

'There are other distributors in Glasgow, Mr Strachan, most of whom would jump at the chance of acting on my behalf. Perhaps I should get in touch with several of them.'

He stared grimly at her.

'Distributors whose prices would be more acceptable,' she added, driving the point home.

He rocked back in his chair. Lose the Drummond account! That was unthinkable. It may only be a small distillery but its account was prestigious.

'I'm sure we can come to some agreement,

416

Miss Drummond,' he said.

'The only agreement I'm interested in is the one we had before.'

He slowly nodded. 'Then that's what'll happen.'

'Good.'

She rose. 'Good-day to you, Mr Strachan.'

He also rose. 'Good-day to you, Miss Drummond. I'll see you out.'

'I'm perfectly capable of seeing myself out thank you very much.'

And with that she swept from the room.

★ ★ ★

Wonky had decided to go for a stroll after dinner, Nell declining to accompany her, and it was while out walking she came across Dale Kutchinsky sitting on a bale of supplies having a smoke.

'Hello,' she smiled.

'Come and join me,' he said, patting the bale. 'There's room enough for two.'

She sat. 'You looked as though you were deep in thought.'

'I was. Reminiscing you could say. Memories.'

'A girl perhaps?'

He shook his head. 'Oh sure there've been girls along the way, but no one in particular. There isn't anyone at home pining for me if that's what you mean. What about you?'

'Me neither.'

He studied her. 'I find that hard to believe, a gorgeous creature like yourself.'

Wonky blushed. 'Flatterer.'

'No, it's true. Honest!' he protested.

Her blushing deepened. 'There was someone once, but that didn't last.'

'What happened. Or am I being rude in asking?'

Wonky gazed up as a plane with French markings flew overhead. She could clearly see the pilot in the cockpit. From the direction he was taking he was heading straight for the German lines. She silently wished the pilot luck and a safe return.

She turned her attention again to Dale. 'I really don't know what happened. I thought it was good between us but apparently he took a different view.'

'I see. Do you still miss him?'

'No, I got over Jack long ago. He's home again after fighting with the Black Watch, a Scottish Regiment. He was blinded and left with a badly scarred face.'

'I'm sorry,' Dale sympathised.

'He was an extremely active man. The blindness must be terrible for him.'

'There are going to be a lot more like him when this war's finally over,' Dale murmured. 'Men with all sorts of horrible injuries.'

'Yes,' Wonky agreed, thinking of the many who'd already passed through her hands.

'Will you practise in Albany when you return?' she asked.

'That's the plan. What about yourself?'

Wonky thought about that. 'One thing for certain, I can't go back to the humdrum life

I had. Not after all this.'

'Did you work?'

'I only wish I had but my father would never allow it. No, I stayed at home with my parents and that was about it really. Too, too boring for words.'

'And what does your father do?'

'He's a minister in the Church of Scotland.'

'Really!'

'A very domineering man who likes to get his own way in everything, which he usually does.'

'I see.'

'And your father?'

'He's a lawyer too. He and I have always got on great, until I told him I was coming here that was. But even then he was only upset for my safety which is understandable. He writes all the time.'

Wonky thought of Tom and Moira and wondered what they were doing. Tom might be writing his next sermon, or there again he could be out on his rounds visiting people. As for Moira, who knew. Cooking or baking perhaps. Her mother always seemed to spend an awful lot of time doing that.

Wonky sighed, and stood up. 'I'd better get back. I'm on early shift tomorrow.'

'But you'll still be coming with me to the CCS?'

She nodded. 'I will that.'

He smiled. 'I shall look forward to it.'

What a nice chap, she thought as she walked away. She'd really enjoyed their conversation.

Sir Henry was fuming as he burst into the room and strode straight for the decanter.

'Something wrong, Henry?' Lady Fortescue queried in concern.

Andrew and Alice were also present in the drawing room, Andrew having managed to wangle a day away from Dublin.

'It's that damned McGinty,' Sir Henry retorted. 'Asked me again for a contribution, blast his eyes!'

'Oh dear,' his wife murmured.

Andrew looked to Alice for an explanation, which she wasn't about to give. In the event Sir Henry did.

He glared at Andrew. 'Wants me to give money to his Fenians, and me a Protestant. I ask you!'

'Was there a row?' Lady Fortescue asked.

'Of course there was. McGinty isn't a man to take refusal easily. He started shouting at me, the fool.'

'Was he involved in the rising?' Andrew asked quietly.

Sir Henry had a large gulp of whiskey. 'I can't say for certain, but I'm sure he was. All I do know is that he wasn't one of those arrested.'

Lady Fortescue went to her husband and put an arm round his shoulders. 'You shouldn't let him upset you so much. You look quite distraught.'

'That's because I am, Sybil. McGinty's put me in a dreadful position, and not for the first time either. He doesn't appreciate I have divided loyalties.'

Andrew felt sorry for Alice's father. As Sir Henry said, it was a dreadful position to be in. 'Would you like me to have him picked up, sir? It can be easily arranged.'

Sir Henry considered that. 'No, despite everything I rather like the idiot. Or eejit as we say here. His intentions are honourable, as he sees them that is. There isn't any real harm in the man.'

'There are a number of dead British soldiers killed in the rising who, if they were here, might not agree with that,' Andrew commented.

'I know, I know,' Sir Henry sighed, shaking his head. 'But I still don't want him arrested. At least not at my instigation. It would lie too heavily on my conscience.'

'So be it,' Andrew declared.

Sir Henry's eyes flashed fire. 'Had the impertinence to threaten me, the bounder.'

'Threaten?' Lady Fortescue queried in alarm.

'Oh don't worry, it was said in the heat of the moment. Not to be taken seriously. All bluster and wind in my opinion.'

A worried Andrew sincerely hoped that was all it was.

★ ★ ★

'You don't keep having to ask my permission to smoke, I've told you often enough I don't mind.'

Dale grinned at Wonky. 'I'm just trying to

be polite the way the British always seem to be. Those guys sure have manners.'

She grinned back. 'You mean Americans don't?'

'Not like you British. I think we cause offence at times without realising it. I guess we just do things a different way that's all.'

'I guess,' Wonky repeated, which made Dale laugh.

'Are you taking the mickey, Nurse Comyn?'

'Who me?' she replied, pretending innocence.

'It seems to me like you might be.'

She could see how amused he was. 'It's simply that you speak so strangely, to my ear that is. It's almost as though it's a different language.'

He thought about that. 'I suppose it is, or is becoming so. We may both speak English but American English is very different to English English.'

'Or Scottish English,' she smiled.

Next moment Wonky screamed as there was a huge explosion and their ambulance was thrown onto its side.

'Holy shit,' Dale swore, finding himself sprawled on top of her. They had to get out of there, he thought. 'You hurt, Wonky?'

She gulped in air, the breath having been knocked out of her. She was terrified and wondering if she was about to die.

There was a second explosion nearby followed by a third.

'We're being shelled goddamnit!' Dale exclaimed.

'I don't think I'm hurt,' Wonky said in a small voice.

Dale prised himself off her and reached for his door which was now above them. It took an effort but he managed to get the door open.

'Come on,' he urged.

He clambered onto the side of the ambulance and reached down for Wonky who grasped his hand. She could feel a trickle of blood on her face as he pulled her clear.

Dale glanced about them wondering where to take refuge. Another hit that close could send up the gas tank.

He spotted a deepish crater about ten yards away, the result of previous shelling. There wasn't any other cover he could see.

He dropped off the ambulance and beckoned her to follow suit, catching her when she did. Hand in hand they raced for the crater which they thankfully jumped into. All the while other shells had been exploding around them.

Wonky sobbed, her heart beating erratically.

'I don't know why these crazy Krauts are shelling here, it shouldn't be a target,' Dale said, wincing at another close explosion.

'Perhaps they're targeting the wrong area?'

That had to be it, he thought.

He threw himself on top of Wonky when there was the scream of an incoming shell that sounded as though it might be a direct hit. To their relief it landed far enough away not to be of concern, though the ground beneath them literally shook on impact.

How nice his body was, Wonky found herself thinking. Hard and taut, and she could feel his manhood pressing into her, the danger of the situation having aroused him. She didn't find the latter an unpleasant experience.

And then as suddenly as it had started the shelling stopped.

Dale waited for a bit to confirm it actually had stopped before getting off Wonky and dusting himself down.

'That seems to be it,' he declared. 'They must have realised their mistake.'

She touched the now dried blood on her face and he immediately bent to her in concern. 'Let me see,' he said.

His hands were warm and firm, his probing making her shiver slightly.

'You're OK,' he pronounced. 'It's only a small scratch.'

He helped her to her feet. 'Any other problems?'

She felt herself all over. 'No, I'm only shaken. How about you?'

'I'm OK as well. And shaken like yourself. That came out of nowhere.'

He lit a cigarette, inhaled deeply and then blew out a long stream of smoke. 'This butt sure tastes good,' he smiled at her.

'Butt?'

'Cigarette.'

'Oh!'

Her cap had come adrift and her apron was filthy beneath her cape. She would have to change when she got back to the hospital.

They climbed out of the crater, Dale helping Wonky, and stared at the ambulance.

'It's a long walk home,' Dale declared. 'You up to it?'

'I'll have to be I suppose.'

'That's the spirit.'

She smiled at him. 'Thanks for saving my life, Dale.'

'Hell, I did no such thing!' he protested. 'Certainly nothing that any other guy wouldn't have done.'

'That may be so, but I'm still thanking you for saving my life.'

There were a few seconds during which their eyes locked, then he glanced away.

'Shall we start hoofing it?'

'May as well.'

They started back down the road.

★ ★ ★

'Are you all right?'

Charlotte snapped out of her reverie and turned to Miss McQueen. 'I'm fine thank you. Just day dreaming, that's all.'

Miss McQueen moved closer. 'You looked like a lost soul there, if you don't mind me saying.'

A lost soul? How appropriate Charlotte thought. 'I suppose I am in a way,' she admitted. 'Outside work that is. It's so lonely living here all by myself. I miss everyone dreadfully. Pa, Nell, even Andrew albeit he hasn't lived at home for years. I just seem to rattle around.'

Miss McQueen nodded her sympathy. 'It must be difficult for you.'

'It is. There's you and the rest of the staff of course, which means I'm not entirely alone. Still . . . ' She trailed off.

'The war can't go on for ever, miss, and then Master Geoffrey and Miss Nell will be back. What a grand day that'll be.'

How she missed Geoffrey, desperately so. And worried about him. The lists of missing and killed in action printed daily in the newspapers seemed endless. Surely the war would stop soon, surely!

'Is there anything I can get you, a cup of tea or coffee perhaps?'

Charlotte shook her head. 'Some cocoa later would be nice. But not now.'

'And a bite of late supper?'

'No thank you, Miss McQueen. Cook's lovely dinner will see me through to breakfast.' She gave a low laugh. 'I do believe Mrs Clark is trying to fatten me up. The portion's she's serving are enormous.'

'We are all somewhat worried about you, Miss Charlotte. You've lost a deal of weight.'

Charlotte smoothed down her dress, a dress that had fitted perfectly a few months previously and now hung on her. She had lost weight, possibly more than she'd realised.

'Running the distillery takes it out of you,' she confessed.

'And thinking of Master Geoffrey no doubt.'

Charlotte glanced away. That most of all. The work she could cope with. But it was the constant worry about Geoffrey that was affecting her most of all.

Poor Jenny who'd worked for them as a maid had lost her husband Hamish only a fortnight ago. She'd gone and seen Jenny to offer her condolences — how distressing that had been! What could you possibly say to a young mother who'd lost her husband. Platitudes, that was all, mere platitudes.

'I think I'll try and read,' she said to Miss McQueen.

'Very good. I'll return later with that cocoa.'

'Thank you.'

When Miss McQueen had left her Charlotte did try and read, but it was useless.

She fell again into a reverie. Thinking, remembering, worrying.

24

'YOU appear to have taken a shine to that driver of yours,' Nell commented to Wonky, as the pair of them came off duty one night.

'Why do you say that?'

'You just do, that's all. I spotted the pair of you chatting earlier like the oldest of friends.'

Wonky coloured slightly. 'Dale's nice, very pleasant to be with. And yes we do get on.'

'Do I detect a budding romance?'

'Don't be silly, Nell. He's an American.'

Nell laughed. 'What on earth has that got to do with it? You can fall for an American as well as a Scotsman or Englishman you know. Perhaps more easily as they're so different and colourful.'

Was she falling for Dale? Wonky wondered. Or were they simply friends, pals? She wasn't sure. He certainly seemed very keen on her. There again, maybe he just enjoyed female company.

'Well?' Nell demanded.

'Of course not.'

Nell arched an eyebrow. 'No?'

Wonky thought of Jack Riach, the last thing she wanted was to be let down again. That experience had hurt her a lot more than she'd actually let on.

'He's a lawyer you know,' Wonky said. 'From

Albany, New York State.'

'America,' Nell mused. 'I'd love to go there. It must be such an exciting place.'

She'd love to go as well, Wonky thought. What a thrill that would be. So utterly different to Dalneil.

'Are you encouraging him?' Nell asked.

'I beg your pardon?'

'You know, giving off those little signals that tell him you're interested.'

'I'm doing no such thing.'

'I'll bet you are!' Nell teased.

'Can we change the conversation please. You're embarrassing me.'

She was, Nell thought, delighted for her cousin. 'He's certainly good looking, I'll grant him that. But what a peculiar surname.'

'I've told you before, he's of Polish extraction. It's like that in America, everyone, apart from the Red Indians that is, originally came from somewhere else, or at least their forefathers did.'

'There are a lot of Scots over there I understand, more so in Canada,' Nell declared. 'So no doubt you would feel right at home.'

'Will you stop it!' Wonky chided.

Nell grinned.

'I mean it. This nonsense has gone far enough.'

'OK,' Nell replied, purposely using the American expression.

Wonky glared at her. 'Very funny.'

Nell laughed.

That night Nell dreamed of her Highlander. She was in his arms, his hot breath on her cheek, her body pressed against him.

Their lips met in a kiss while his arms tightened even further around her.

Then he was leading her by the hand to a large bed which he stopped beside. Slowly, carefully, he began unbuttoning her dress.

The dress fell away to her hips and he started on her underthings. When her breasts were exposed his hands closed over them.

She was moaning at his touch, knowing what was to follow. He muttered love words as he fondled her, she eagerly responding.

And suddenly she knew his name. Rory.

The dress dropped to the floor, followed by her underclothes. Now she was standing naked in front of him, shivering in anticipation.

Rory.

Nell woke with a gasp to find herself covered in sweat, the dream vivid in her memory.

Good God, she thought. That had been so real. Better than a vision because she could hear, smell and touch him.

As for her, how brazen she'd been. How shameless. To stand before a man naked like that. She who was a virgin.

Nell gulped in a deep breath, trying to compose herself. Rory, she thought. A lovely name and so familiar, albeit she didn't know anyone of that name.

But she had once she reminded herself. For

back in time the Highlander had been her husband, she his wife.

'Rory,' she murmured aloud.

She could only wonder what it would have been like if the dream had continued.

The whole thing had been so real. So very very real.

★ ★ ★

'I don't believe it,' Billy Roberts exclaimed softly. 'I just don't believe it.' He and Andrew were sitting by themselves in the mess having a drink, and Billy had just glanced at the front page of that evening's newspaper.

'Don't believe what, old boy?' Andrew smiled.

'Wait a moment, let me read this through.'

Andrew sipped his whisky, wondering what had perturbed his friend.

Billy looked at Andrew, his expression grim. 'It's the Fortescues,' he said, voice tight.

'What about them?'

'They're dead!'

It was a joke, Andrew thought. Billy was pulling his leg. 'Oh yes? All three I suppose?'

'All three,' Billy nodded. 'Here, read for yourself.' And with that he passed the newspaper to Andrew.

The headline hit Andrew like a hammer blow. Greystones had been gutted by fire. He went white as he read through the report.

'I am sorry,' Billy murmured when Andrew, ashen faced, finally looked up from the paper.

Andrew was in shock, his mind reeling. This

couldn't be true. It had to be a lie. It had to be. Alice, his Alice, dead?

'Let me get you a refill,' Billy said, and picking up Andrew's glass he hurried to the bar.

Andrew started re-reading the article. The tragedy had occurred the previous evening according to the paper, the entire family perishing in the blaze as had some of the servants. Other servants had escaped to raise the alarm, to no avail. Arson was suspected.

Alice! Dear sweet Alice to whom he was engaged and was now in love with. Alice dead.

Billy was still at the bar as Andrew rose and stumbled from the mess. All he wanted was to be alone.

Alice dead. It was impossible. Impossible.

He managed to hold back the tears until his door was shut and locked behind him.

★ ★ ★

'Major Armitage, sir?'

Geoffrey glanced up at the officer who'd entered his dugout. He was in the middle of writing a report. 'That's correct.'

The officer snapped to attention and saluted. 'Second Lieutenant McKie reporting for duty, sir.'

How young he was, Geoffrey thought. No more than a boy really. Probably straight from school. They were getting younger and younger with every passing month, fresh faced and pimply, lambs to the slaughter. How long would this one survive? he wondered. For the last it had been a week before being blown to smithereens.

How old he felt himself, he thought. How dreadfully old. Methuselah had nothing on him. Old, drained and tired beyond belief.

Geoffrey returned the lad's salute. 'Nice to meet you, Lieutenant.'

'Thank you, sir.'

'Where are you from?'

'Perth, sir.'

Geoffrey nodded. 'I'm from Glasgow myself. Dirty place, but there you are. I like it.'

McKie beamed which depressed Geoffrey even further. 'First time in the frontline I take it?'

'Yes, sir.'

'You'll soon pick things up. Got your gas mask I see.'

McKie patted it. 'Yes, sir.'

'Well don't go anywhere without it. Take it to bed with you. You can need it at a second's notice.'

'I understand that, sir.'

'Straight from school, are you?'

'Yes, sir. How did you know?'

Geoffrey laughed inwardly. How did he know! 'Which school was that?'

McKie named a prestigious one.

'Age?'

Geoffrey winced when McKie told him. Dear God above! A year younger than his predecessor.

'What would you have me do, sir?'

'Find Captain McLennan and ask him to show you the ropes.' There was a recce party going out that night he thought. Put McKie on it, give him a taste of what it was all about? He decided against that. He'd give the lad a day before putting him into danger. Not that just being there wasn't danger enough.

'Remember to keep your head down when in the shallower trenches and saps,' he advised. 'That's important.'

'I understand, sir.'

'Don't and you'll get your head blown off. Now toddle along and find McLennan.'

McKie saluted again. 'Yes, sir. Thank you, sir.'

A weary Geoffrey returned to his report.

★ ★ ★

It was a combined funeral for Sir Henry, Lady Fortescue and Alice and the church was packed. Andrew was present with Billy Roberts there for support.

The hymn finished and they all sat. 'Now we will pray,' the minister announced.

Andrew didn't hear a word of the prayer. All he could think of was Alice and how desperately he missed her. He still couldn't really accept that he'd never see her again, that she was gone.

At the end of the prayer he looked up and the first person he saw was Seamus McGinty.

Was that the hint of a smile on McGinty's face? Surely not. It couldn't be. And yet . . . and yet . . .

Then Andrew remembered the conversation with Sir Henry when Sir Henry had mentioned the two Protestant houses in West Cork being torched by Fenians. And the row Sir Henry had had with McGinty and the fact McGinty had threatened him, a threat Sir Henry had dismissed.

Suddenly, and with absolute certainty, Andrew knew it was McGinty who'd torched Greystones. Or if he hadn't done it personally had been behind it.

Arson had been suspected but so far the police hadn't made an arrest. Their investigations hadn't come up with anything.

But Andrew knew who the culprit was.

Sitting there in church, consumed by grief and hatred, Andrew swore an oath to himself.

McGinty, the bastard, would pay.

An eye for an eye.

So it would be.

★ ★ ★

'I was wondering, would you like to go into town tonight for a drink?' Dale asked casually, as he and Wonky were en route yet again to the CCS.

She wasn't surprised, she'd been expecting as much. That or some other invitation.

'A drink?'

'Yeah, that stuff which comes in glasses and makes you feel good.'

She laughed. 'I don't know.'

'What do you mean, you don't know. You either will or won't.'

She didn't wish to appear too eager. 'How about transport?'

He snorted. 'Leave that to me. I'm a driver, aren't I? Transport won't be a problem.'

'I'm on duty till eight.'

'So?'

'I'd have to get washed and changed.'

'That doesn't bother me.'

'Would this be what you Americans call a date?'

'Damn right it would.'

'Dale, I . . . ' She trailed off.

'What, Wonky?'

What indeed. It was wartime and anything could happen. All she knew above all else was that she didn't want to be hurt again.

'I'd love to go for a drink,' she said in a small voice.

'Good. That's settled then.'

She wondered what she'd let herself in for.

★ ★ ★

Andrew had bided his time, now the score would be settled. He was standing in front of the McGinty farmhouse in the early hours of the morning, three full jerrycans of petrol at his feet.

The house was dark, the McGintys, he presumed, fast asleep. It was an overcast night with no stars or moon showing. Perfect for his purpose.

He thought again of all that he'd lost. Alice, Greystones and the fortune that would have come to her, and him eventually. All lost because of the Fenian bastard inside.

436

He picked up two of the jerrycans and walked softly towards the house. Stopping at the door he opened both cans. Then, using a knee to assist, he began pouring petrol through the letter box.

When the two cans were empty he took them back to the third with which he returned to the door and letter box. When that can was empty he took a deep breath, struck a match, dropped it through the letter box, picked up the can and ran like mad.

There was an enormous whoof! behind him which brought a smile of grim satisfaction to his face. He placed the can beside the others and turned to watch.

It didn't take long. Seconds later he could see flames licking behind the front downstairs windows and then wisps of smoke began to appear.

Would the smoke get them or the fire? Andrew wondered. If neither he had an alternative.

There was the sound of a small explosion. Now what was that? Could have been any of a dozen things.

Then he heard a female scream. Mrs McGinty or the daughter? He couldn't tell. Whoever, someone was now awake.

A young woman appeared at an upstairs window and threw it open, staring out in blind terror. She clearly considered jumping, then changed her mind and vanished from view.

Andrew took out his service revolver just in case it was needed. Using his thumb he slipped off the safety catch.

He wondered if they'd try the rear door. Well

if they did they wouldn't have any luck there, he'd jammed it. If they did come out it would have to be at the front.

The daughter, her name was Roisin and she was twenty-two years old — Andrew knew that from discreet enquiries he'd made, and the McGinty's only child, just as Alice had been the Fortescues' — opened the front door and rushed out, her long hair ablaze.

Andrew took careful aim and shot her through the head. She tumbled to the ground, hair still ablaze, where she lay still.

The entire house was now an inferno. Through the open door Andrew could see banks of flames leaping and dancing.

Mrs McGinty was the next to emerge, coughing and spluttering, her nightdress burning at the hem.

'For Lady Fortescue, you bitch,' Andrew muttered as he pulled the trigger a second time.

And then McGinty was there, stark naked which Andrew considered for some reason or other, an added bonus. McGinty stopped to stare at the bodies of his wife and daughter.

Andrew pulled the trigger a third time, only there was to be no quick bullet in the brain for McGinty. Andrew shot him in the stomach.

McGinty grunted and slumped to the ground beside his wife where he writhed in agony, blood dribbling from his mouth.

Andrew went and stood over him, smiling at the knowledge of how excruciatingly painful that particular death could be. McGinty stared up at him through bulging eyes.

'It's for my Alice and her parents, the Fortescues,' Andrew explained, wanting McGinty to know why he'd done all this.

'Protestant cunt,' McGinty croaked through a froth of pink-tinged bubbles.

'You're going straight to hell, and that's exactly where you belong. You're going to roast,' Andrew crooned in reply.

McGinty continued to writhe, all the while clutching at where he'd been shot.

Then Andrew had an idea. He put his revolver away and grasped McGinty by the shoulders. McGinty, too weak to resist, groaned as Andrew dragged him towards the doorway.

The heat was almost too much for Andrew but he was determined to do what he intended. Sweat rolled down his face as he hoisted McGinty to his feet and pointed him at the door.

'No . . . no!' McGinty choked.

'And the roasting starts here,' Andrew declared, pitching McGinty inside.

McGinty screamed and continued to scream until it was all over.

Andrew collected the three jerrycans and tossed them through the door as well, then beat a hasty retreat.

He walked away, not looking back. Alice, and his thwarted aspirations, had been revenged.

And sweet revenge it was.

★ ★ ★

'Shall we dance?'

Wonky giggled. 'I'm feeling tipsy from so much wine.'

'So am I,' Dale replied earnestly. 'Only in my case the wine is only part of it.'

What a lovely man, she thought. A lovely lovely man. She glanced at the three-piece band playing smoochy French music. It was all so terribly romantic.

She rose. 'Let's.'

He took her hand as they walked the few short yards to the tiny dance floor. 'I'm not much of a dancer I'm afraid. So I apologise in advance,' he said as she melted into his arms.

'I'm not so hot myself.'

'Anyway, with this sort of music all you have to do is shuffle.'

How warm he was, she thought. And how nice he smelt. Like . . . She didn't know what. And then she had it. Like an American. Though why they should smell differently to the British was beyond her.

'Enjoying yourself?' he asked softly.

'You know I am. And you?'

'I'm in seventh heaven, kid. And that's no lie.'

She laughed. How strangely he put things at times. American English again. It never ceased to fascinate her.

Wonky started when he licked her ear. No one had ever done that before.

'You can see why I'm such a Francophile,' he said. 'You wouldn't find a place like this in the States. Maybe down south, but not where I come from.'

Nor Dalneil, she reflected. Certainly not Dalneil. Dalneil was as far removed from this place as the moon was from earth.

The band finished the number and they stopped dancing. 'Will you stay up?' he queried.

'If you wish.'

'I wish.'

'Then I'll stay up.'

★ ★ ★

Dale pulled the car off the road. 'Before we get back I want to thank you for a wonderful evening.'

His eyes were glowing in the dark. Sensual, wonderful eyes. She shivered. 'It was wonderful for me as well.'

In the distance guns were booming but at that moment the war seemed a million miles away. All that existed was the pair of them.

'Shall we do it again sometime?'

'That would be nice.'

He grinned. 'Don't be too enthusiastic. Talk about British reserve.'

'Or American lack of it,' she countered.

He touched her cheek. 'You've come to mean a lot to me, Wonky Comyn.'

'Have I?'

'Darned tootin' you have.'

He was going to kiss her, she thought. And couldn't wait for it to happen. She wanted to kiss him too. In fact ached for it.

441

'Wonky?'

'Yes?'

'Nothing,' he whispered.

And then his lips were gloriously on hers.

★ ★ ★

Did he have any regrets? Andrew asked himself. And the answer was none at all. McGinty and family had deserved what they'd got. Those who live by the sword . . .

He pictured Alice the last time they'd been together and felt his throat clog with emotion. He'd come to love her, and she him. Now she was gone like so much smoke in the wind. And with her Greystones and the family fortune.

He understood there was a relative somewhere who'd now inherit, money and property that would one day have been his. At least he had the distillery, that was something. A great deal when you considered it. Not that it rivalled what would have come from the Fortescues, but he'd be comfortable for the rest of his days.

Good old Charlotte, doing a grand job. He'd been fortunate there.

He wondered how Geoffrey was doing? A major now, he understood. Poor sod out there on the Western Front. It must be a nightmare.

He shifted on his bed, smiling at the memory of McGinty's bulging eyes and how he had writhed in agony. 'And the roasting starts here.' He'd enjoyed saying that. Positively revelled in it.

His smile widened recalling McGinty's screams

as the fire had consumed him. He could almost imagine . . .

Andrew sighed in the darkness, his mind turning to the one and only time he'd made love to Alice. How enjoyable that had been, for her as well as him.

'Alice,' he murmured. 'Alice.'

★ ★ ★

'Finished at last,' Hettie declared as she and Jack emerged from the sixth shop they'd visited that day.

'Well thank goodness for that is all I can say. It was beginning to get tedious.'

She laughed. 'Shopping is never tedious for women, we adore it. I could shop all day.'

'Not with me in tow you wouldn't.'

'Now what, the train back?'

He stopped, which forced her to stop also, her arm hooked round his, and considered that. 'What time is it?'

'A little before one.'

'Then it's lunch. I'm starving.'

'I am too, but didn't want to say.'

'And while we're eating you can describe everything we bought to me again in detail.'

Hettie suddenly frowned and Jack, who'd now become used to picking up her moods, said, 'What is it?'

Hettie slipped her arm out of Jack's. 'Grizelda McPherson is coming this way.'

'Is she indeed,' Jack said softly. 'Is she alone?'

'No, she's with Harriet Henderson.'

'Ah!' Jack exclaimed.

Grizelda came up short when she spied Jack, her first impulse being to cross the road. But she realised she couldn't do so as that Hettie female had seen her. Imagine Jack consorting with someone as common as muck. What was he thinking of!

'I know just the place for lunch,' Jack declared to Hettie. 'We'll have a slap-up meal. We deserve it.' Not least for his venturing into Pitlochry he thought.

'Hello, Jack.'

'Hello, Grizelda. And you, Harriet. You both know Hettie my housekeeper of course.'

'Of course,' Grizelda replied disapprovingly, which neither Jack or Hettie failed to pick up.

What a bitch, Jack thought. She'd done him a huge favour in dropping him. The woman was shallow as a puddle.

They exchanged a few polite words and then Grizelda and Harriet moved on.

'The Lord truly moves in mysterious ways,' Jack commented.

'How do you mean?'

'If I hadn't been blinded and scarred I'd have ended up married to her. What a lucky escape.'

'Amen,' Hettie said.

★ ★ ★

Geoffrey was instructing Sergeant Smith about leading a probing party up one of the saps when the frantic cry went up that an attack was underway.

It was a foggy day, ideal for an attack which the Canadians had mounted that morning. Now the Germans were counter-attacking at their part of the line.

A fusillade of shots rang out, Geoffrey turning to the trench wall to assist when a potato-masher grenade landed on the far side of Sergeant Smith.

Geoffrey spotted it a moment before it exploded.

Part Three

A New Day Dawning

25

'IT'S Miss Drummond,' Hettie announced. Jack immediately rose from his chair. 'How are you, Charlotte?'

She went to him and kissed him on the cheek. 'Well, to be truthful I could be better which is why I've come to see you.' She glanced about her. The room was cosy in the extreme with a fine log fire burning in the grate. 'But first of all let me say how nicely you've done this place up. It has a lovely feel to it.'

Jack smiled. 'I've Hettie to thank for that. She chose and organised everything.'

Charlotte turned to Hettie hovering by the door. 'You've done a wonderful job. You must be proud.'

Hettie blushed. 'Did my best, miss.'

'Very tasteful. Congratulations.'

'Would you like some tea or coffee, Charlotte?' Jack asked.

'Coffee would be nice.'

'Hettie, would you?'

'Of course, Mr Riach.'

Hettie vanished from the room.

'Will you sit down,' Jack said, gesturing to a chair facing his.

'Thank you.'

'How are you getting on?' Charlotte queried when she'd sat.

'I have a buyer for the house and property

which is going through. As you probably know my mother and father have already returned to Largs.'

'Yes, I heard.'

Jack sighed. 'I miss them. I got used to having them around. But there you are. They have their lives to lead and I have mine.'

'And how are you coping?'

'You mean with blindness?'

Charlotte hadn't meant that at all. She'd meant being in the cottage. 'That as well,' she replied.

He shrugged. 'It's one of those things. To quote the Bard, 'What's done is done and cannot be undone'.'

How bitter he sounded she thought. But then that was only natural. She couldn't even conceive being blind herself. 'Hettie looking after you all right?'

'She's the proverbial treasure. I certainly couldn't manage without her. It was a wise choice on my part. There again, I knew her work from before. She's always been a grafter.'

Charlotte nodded her approval. 'How about meals?'

'Well I have to admit Hettie isn't up to Ma's standards, but then that would be asking something. She's very good nonetheless. I certainly don't have any complaints in that department.'

'You're looking fit.'

'I go for a walk every day, weather permitting, with Hettie of course. She guides me and we chatter along the way. She tells me what she sees and what's going on around us. It's the highlight of my day.'

Going for a walk reminded Charlotte of Murdo whom she missed terribly. She knew now why he'd started walking; Doctor McAllister had told her.

'And what else do you get up to?' she queried.

Jack ran a hand over his badly scarred face. 'Not a lot, there isn't much I can do. I sit and think a great deal I suppose, remembering.'

'The war?'

Jack's face clouded. 'Yes,' he whispered.

She studied him intently. 'Was I being insensitive in asking that question?'

'No, Charlotte. It's the past and we all have to live with that.'

Again she thought of Murdo, and her brother Peter.

'Have you heard from Nell and Wonky?'

'I had a letter the other day. They're both fine. Wonky's met a chap apparently, an American.'

'An American!' Jack exclaimed.

'He drives ambulances which is how they came to meet. According to Nell he's a lawyer in civilian life.'

'Well well well,' Jack mused. 'How about that.'

'As for Nell, she's happy enough, though no romance in her life yet. She says the work is hard and . . . not very pleasant. The casualties according to her simply mount and mount.'

A scene flashed into Jack's mind which made

him shudder. He knew all about casualties. The dead, dying and wounded. So many men he'd known, good men for the best part, who'd never be coming home again. And those who did . . . well he was testament to what they could be like. The whole thing was horrendous. No, worse than that.

Hettie reappeared with a tray. 'That was quick,' Charlotte commented.

'The kettle was almost on the boil anyway. I've put a few wee biscuits on a plate in case either of you is peckish.'

How nice, Charlotte thought. She wasn't peckish in the least but would have one just to be polite.

'Would you care to join us?' Jack asked Hettie.

That startled Charlotte. Ask the housekeeper to join them? How odd. Was there something going on here that she hadn't realised. She looked at Hettie through new eyes. A comely lass if ever there was, and certainly not unintelligent. Were they . . . ?

'I've got a pile of ironing still to do,' Hettie replied quickly. 'I'd best get on with that.'

'Fine,' Jack answered with warmth in his voice.

Hettie disappeared again.

'Will you play mother, as the English say,' Jack suggested.

'My pleasure.'

Charlotte did the necessary. 'Biscuit?'

'Not for me thanks. They are home made by the way, by Hettie.'

Charlotte leant back in her chair with one of the biscuits on her saucer. 'You and Hettie seem to be very close,' she ventured.

Jack laughed. 'Of course we are. I rely on her for nearly everything.'

'Yes, I can understand that.'

'You don't really. She's been a Godsend, Charlotte. I don't know what I'd have done without her. She makes my day-to-day existence, and I mean existence, somehow tolerable. She's a most compassionate woman to whom I shall be eternally in debt.'

Jack had a sip of coffee. 'Now enough about me, why the visit? Is there a reason?'

Charlotte glanced down into her own cup. 'I had a letter from Geoffrey yesterday,' she said in a small voice.

'Oh?'

'He's been wounded again.'

'Badly?'

'I'm not quite sure exactly. He said it's to his groin and that I'm not to worry. He's in hospital in France though shortly to be moved to England.'

Jack didn't reply, waiting for Charlotte to continue.

She sighed. 'I wanted to speak to you because you know what it's like over there. I can only imagine. And pretty horrible imagining it makes I can tell you.'

'It sounds like he's been lucky to me,' Jack replied. 'Anything that takes you out of the front line for a while is good fortune. A groin injury isn't so bad, not bad at all.'

'It's just . . . ' Charlotte trailed off. 'I don't know, I really don't. There was a tone to his letter that worried me. It's hard to explain.'

'A tone?' Jack mused in concern.

'As though he wasn't telling me everything. It wasn't like any other letter I've ever had from him. It was cold, distant somehow.'

Jack had a chilling thought. 'Did Geoffrey describe the wound?' he queried softly.

'Not at all. Only that it was to his groin.'

'He'll be fine,' Jack reassured her. 'He probably wrote while still in a state of shock. Besides, being out there does funny things to people. The sights they witness, what they themselves go through. You certainly can't expect the same Geoffrey to come home who went away.'

Charlotte nodded. 'That's probably it.'

'Don't forget the poor chap's been wounded, he'd hardly be in the mood to write you a love letter.'

Charlotte laughed. 'You're right of course. I'm just being silly.'

'No you're not. You love Geoffrey, so naturally you worry. It would be a poor show if you didn't.'

'I wish . . . oh how I wish he was home again and this entire ghastly business was over. It's a living nightmare.'

Too true, Jack thought. How true that was.

'Anyway, you've bucked me up as I knew you would.'

'I'm glad to be of some use,' Jack commented drily, something that was lost on Charlotte.

'So how's the biscuit?' he asked, changing the subject.

She had a bite and pronounced it to be delicious.

* * *

Wonky felt as though she'd just had a bucketful of ice-cold water poured over her. 'Transferred?'

'To number twenty-seven U.S. Base Hospital, Angers, I'm afraid. I leave the day after tomorrow,' Dale replied.

It had never crossed her mind that either of them might be transferred. She'd stupidly thought the pair of them would be together for the duration. 'I see.'

'There's nothing I can do about it, Wonky. If there was I would. You know what it's like.'

She did, only too well. 'It's a shock, that's all.'

Dale took her in his arms and gazed deeply into her eyes. 'I'll miss you, Wonky. You wouldn't believe how much.'

She'd miss him too, far more than she cared to admit even to herself. What rotten luck she had with men. First of all Jack, and now Dale. Her eyes welled with tears.

'Don't cry, honey, please don't cry.'

'I can't help it.'

'It isn't over, I swear. We'll meet up again. You'll see.'

Would they? Perhaps.

'I have a photograph I want you to have. Taken in the States.' He pulled out a wallet from his hip pocket and extracted a small photo which he handed her. It was one of him taken when graduating from Law School. He looked a lot younger.

'Thank you,' she whispered.

'I don't suppose you have one of yourself?'

She shook her head.

'No matter. I'll hardly forget what you look like.' He was trying to be jocular but for some reason it wasn't working.

'Day after tomorrow,' she said.

'That's right. Early.'

She mustn't blub too much, she thought. That would be awful. Let the side down and all that.

'I'll write as soon as I get there,' he promised.

'Will you?'

'On my word of honor. Will you write back?'

She forced a smile onto her face. 'You know I will, Dale.'

'I'm sorry, sweetheart, really I am. But I should have been with my own people all along. My being here with you British was purely by chance.'

She stared into his face, desperately memorising every line, every feature.

'Kiss me,' she whispered.

It was the sweetest, longest kiss she'd ever experienced.

★ ★ ★

'What's wrong?' Nell queried, Wonky having requested she leave the tent with her. Inside

456

Rebecca Levi and Hope Langton were chattering away nineteen to the dozen.

'Oh dear,' Nell replied when Wonky explained.

'I just can't believe it,' Wonky said, shaking her head.

They both paused to glance skywards as a flight of British planes flew overhead. They didn't get many pilots at the hospital, most of those shot down never survived as parachutes were forbidden them.

'Angers,' Nell said. 'Where's that?'

'A long way from here. Certainly too far for either of us to travel to see the other.'

Nell put her arms round her cousin and hugged her tight. 'You must feel pretty bloody.'

'I do, Nell,' Wonky whispered. 'I certainly do.'

'Was it that serious between you?'

'It was getting that way, Nell. If things had been different who knows?'

Nell released Wonky. 'Is there anything I can do?'

'Not really. Just being able to talk helps a little. Though not much I have to confess.'

A single artillery gun opened up, booming in the distance. Then another.

'I dream of home almost every night,' Nell said. 'Dalneil and our life there seems a world away.'

Wonky nodded. 'I know what you mean. I'll never be able to go back there, not permanently anyway. How stifling it all was, how very very insular.'

Nell thought of Drummond House and the

days, weeks, months they'd spent knitting for the troops. They'd been like children playing a game. What they were in now was deadly reality. Day after day of horrors. How it changed one. How precious every day now seemed.

How was the Highlander, Rory, faring? Nell wondered. Her husband in a different time. And the wife herself, how was she? It would only be a matter of time before she found out. The trouble was she was so rarely on her own nowadays and the visions only came when she was alone.

Rory, even to think of the name brought an excitement to her, made her pulse race. What a love that must have been to have survived over the centuries, to make her recall what she did. Was there a purpose to it all? She had no idea.

'Angers,' Wonky whispered. It might have been on the moon as far as she was concerned.

'Will you see him off?'

'If I can.'

In the event that proved impossible, for Wonky was on duty at the time.

★ ★ ★

Billy Roberts knocked on Andrew's door.

'Come in!'

'Lazy sod.' Billy smiled at Andrew, stretched out on bed reading the latest copy of *The Bystander.*

'To hell with you. I'm off duty and relaxing. Nothing wrong with that, old boy.'

Billy leant against a chest of drawers. 'The

458

word's just out. We've been posted.'

Alarm flared in Andrew. Not the Western Front! Anything but that. 'Where to?'

'County Cork. They're having a lot of trouble down there apparently and we're being sent to sort it out.'

'Fenians, I take it?'

'What else.'

Andrew laid *The Bystander* aside and thought about that. 'The back of beyond, I should imagine, populated by pig-trotter-eating Irish boggers.'

Billy raised an eyebrow, only too well aware how Andrew's attitude to the Irish had changed since the Fortescue fire. Not that he blamed him. 'I suppose so,' he replied.

'When do we leave?'

'A week this Saturday.'

Andrew grunted. That suited him just fine.

'I shall miss old Dublin town,' Billy commented.

So would Andrew, a certain house and lady in particular. He suddenly wondered how Jean Ritchie was doing, and Tina who'd worked at Mulligan's. Still, there were bound to be available women in County Cork, there always were no matter where you went. That was something he'd learned. Available for a price, and money was something he no longer had to be concerned about.

Andrew swung his feet off the bed. 'I think this merits a visit to the mess, what do you say?'

Billy nodded. 'My sentiments exactly.'

'And it's your round. You were one short the last time we were there.'

'Bloody Scotsmen, you never forget anything when it comes to money.'

Andrew laughed.

* * *

'Do you know what I miss most, colours,' Jack said to Hettie who was sitting across from him doing a bit of darning.

'Colours?'

'That's right. I can picture them in my mind of course, but that's not the same.'

'I can understand that,' she replied.

'Can you?'

She smiled. 'Now don't be patronising to me, Jack Riach. I won't stand for it.'

'Patronising,' he mused. 'A big word for an ex-dairy maid.'

'I may be an ex-dairy maid but I had a good Scots education until I left school. And I've been reading ever since to improve my mind.'

Reading, Jack thought. That was something else he missed. Not that he'd been a great reader but from time to time he'd enjoyed a book. Another thing denied him.

'What are you reading now?' he asked.

Hettie told him.

'Interesting?'

'Very. Well I find it so.'

Jack nodded. 'I've just had an idea. Why don't you read to me sometimes in the evenings? I'd enjoy that.'

'There's no reason why not. Any suggestions?'

'I've always liked the Waverley novels. Why don't we start with those?'

Hettie pulled a face. 'Not exactly my cup of tea.'

'Then what would you favour?'

She decided to tease him. 'How about Shakespeare?'

'Good grief,' he muttered. 'Surely you don't like that turgid stuff?'

'It's very good, I'll have you know. Especially his comedies.'

Jack laughed. 'I'd never have imagined in a thousand years that you'd read Shakespeare.'

'And Burns. Filthy bugger.'

He laughed again. 'Yes, Rabbie could be that. Have you ever come across 'Nine Inches Becomes A Lady'?'

Hettie blushed slightly. 'No I haven't. Though I've certainly experienced it.'

This time he roared. 'May I inquire from whom?'

Her eyes glittered with memory. 'You, Jack, you fool. Who else?'

He'd never thought of himself being that large. 'Really?'

'Oh yes,' she said softly.

'Well well. I'm a bigger boy than I realised.'

And probably a better lover, she thought. Jack had never failed to satisfy her. Either in size or anything else.

Jack's mood abruptly changed and he fell into a morose silence. He was remembering the times with Hettie, times that would never come again with her or any other woman. For who would

461

look twice at a blind chap with a face as scarred as his.

'Penny for them?'

He shook his head.

'Oh come on, don't be a spoilsport.'

He reached for his stick and rose. 'I'm off to bed, Hettie, Will you do what has to be done? I'll see you in the morning.' See you! Only an expression of course. His days of seeing anything were over.

'Are you all right, Jack?'

He could smell her across the distance between them, and how it made him itch inside. 'Fine, thank you. It's just that I feel a headache coming on and that it's best I go to bed.'

Hettie didn't believe a word of that. And furthermore had a fair idea of what was troubling Jack.

It was one subject never broached between them.

★ ★ ★

'Miss Charlotte?'

Charlotte was sitting gazing into the fire, lost in thought. She roused herself. 'Yes, Miss McQueen?'

Miss McQueen stared at her in concern. 'You seem so troubled. You were miles away.'

Charlotte gave her a thin smile. 'I was. I was thinking about Geoffrey.'

Miss McQueen considered that. 'It's hardly my place, but with your sister in France and your cousin there also you don't have anyone

to talk things over with. If I can be of help . . . '
She paused, then added. 'I'm most discreet as
I'm sure you're well aware.'

Charlotte gestured to a chair. 'That's kind
of you.'

Miss McQueen sat. 'Is it your husband, is
that it?'

Charlotte nodded. 'I haven't heard from him
in over three weeks now. I'm worried sick.'

'I take it you've written yourself?'

'Every other day. But no reply.'

Charlotte put a finger to her mouth and
chewed it. What was wrong with Geoffrey? This
was so unlike him. Had there been developments
of some sort that she wasn't aware of? That
could be the answer. There again, and this
terrified her, had he met someone else? A nurse
perhaps?

'Where's the hospital, miss?'

'Berkshire, in England.'

'Maybe you should take time off and pay him
a visit.'

Charlotte shook her head. 'In one of his letters
he asked me specifically not to do that. He said
I was to concentrate on the business and that
he would be fine.'

'I see,' Miss McQueen murmured.

Charlotte wrung her hands. 'I just don't know
what to do.'

Nor did Miss McQueen. If Geoffrey had
specifically asked Charlotte not to visit then she
shouldn't. He was a man, her husband after all.
His wishes should be obeyed.

'Have you any idea when he's expected

463

home?' Miss McQueen queried, presuming he'd be given leave after being wounded.

'No.' That came out as a whisper.

'Then I suppose you'll just have to wait until you find out. There's nothing else you can do.'

'No,' Charlotte whispered again.

'Now how about a nice cup of cocoa. Would that help?'

'Please, and thank you, Miss McQueen. I appreciate your concern.'

Miss McQueen left to make the cocoa.

★ ★ ★

It was a terrible battle. Nell stared on in horror as the English redcoats massacred the Scots. Nor was it only English against Scots, but Scot against Scot.

Men's faces contorted in agony as they died. Muskets flashed, bayonets lunged, broadswords and claymores whirled. Everywhere was death and destruction.

Nell knew with absolute certainty that she was witnessing the battle of Culloden, the last stand of Bonnie Prince Charlie before he took to the heather and exile.

Where was her Rory? She couldn't see him anywhere. Was he already amongst the fallen? Cold fear gripped her heart to think that might be so.

Blood spurted, fountains of it on both sides, but the English were clearly winning. They and the turncoats on their side. She grimaced as a head was cleanly lopped off to go spinning away.

And then there he was, targe in his left hand, broadsword in his right, fighting for his life against three English soldiers. She could almost hear him screaming at his adversaries.

One of the soldiers went down, and another, leaving it man to man.

Live, Rory, she pleaded inside her head. Dear God, live.

The third Englishman's eyes started as he was sliced neatly across the belly, then he was on his knees and Rory's broadsword was raised for the *coup de grâce*. The Englishman died from a thrust into his back.

Rory jerked his sword free and turned to face another onslaught, this from turncoat clansmen.

The battle continued to rage as it slowly faded from Nell's vision.

When it had blinked out of view she collapsed forwards in the chair with her head in her hands.

Had he lived?

Nell found tears streaming down her face.

★ ★ ★

'Well, it certainly isn't Dublin Castle,' Andrew pronounced, staring round the room he'd be sharing with Billy Roberts. 'The place stinks and it's filthy.'

'We'll soon get that sorted,' Billy replied, gazing about him in distaste. The house they were in had been commandeered.

465

Andrew went to the window and looked out. The countryside, in his opinion, was most uninspiring.

'Bloody Irish,' Andrew muttered.

'They're not all bad. You should know that.'

Andrew turned to his friend and smiled, a strange metallic glint in his eyes.

'I wonder what's for dinner,' he said.

★ ★ ★

Charlotte laid down her pen, deciding to take a few minutes' break. She had awful stomach cramp due to her period coming on which didn't help matters. If she could she'd have stayed home, but that was impossible with a business to run. As always when this time came round she felt dreadfully depressed.

She thought of Geoffrey, picturing him as she'd last seen him. How she missed him, how she craved his company.

The nights were so interminably lonely, her sleep almost always disturbed by dreams and half-waking memories. How many times had she reached out to touch him and he hadn't been there? Without number.

To snuggle up to him, smell him, hear him murmur to her. For him to caress her, put an arm round her neck and pull her close.

And why, oh why were the letters so infrequent. Why couldn't he write more often?

'Geoffrey,' she whispered. 'Darling, dear beloved Geoffrey. I so want you here with me.'

She closed her eyes, recalling their lovemaking, the sheer gloriousness of it. Sensations she'd never previously dreamt about. She missed those, but most of all she missed him. It was as though she'd lost an arm or leg.

At least he'd be coming back soon, and for good. Discharged on medical grounds, he'd said in his last letter, though unable at that point to give her a date for his arrival. He'd be staying in Glasgow first for a couple of days then travelling on. Only right he saw his parents of course, they being on the way. Only right . . .

The groin injury must have been worse than he'd said, otherwise why the discharge?

Charlotte smiled. Just like Geoffrey not to cause her too much concern, to minimise what had happened. At least it was over for him now, no more the horrors of the Western Front. That was history as far as he was concerned.

'Geoffrey,' she whispered again.

Her loving husband.

⋆ ⋆ ⋆

'We've got them cold,' Sergeant Plackett said with a smile to Andrew.

Andrew smiled also. Six of the Fenian bastards were in a gulley into which they'd scuttled after their truck had careered off the country road with its tyres shot out.

'So what do we do?' Plackett asked.

Andrew didn't reply straight away, thinking about that. The Fenians were armed and dangerous so all care had to be taken.

467

'I have twenty men under my command so it's best you show yourselves and surrender,' he called out.

There was no reply.

'I'll give you two minutes and then we move in!'

Again there wasn't a reply.

'Do you think they will surrender, sir?' Plackett queried.

'Oh yes,' Andrew replied softly. 'They're not eejits after all. Why die for nothing.'

He closed his eyes for a brief second, recalling Sir Henry using the word *eejit*. Sir Henry, Lady Fortescue and his Alice. Now all gone because of Fenians like those trapped in the gulley. Well, McGinty had paid the price of that episode, him and his family. But that wasn't enough, not by a long chalk. These murdering Fenians would also pay. That was only right.

A white handkerchief tied to a rifle was suddenly raised in the air. 'We're coming out, all peaceful like,' a thick-brogued Irish voice shouted.

'Drop your weapons then and proceed with your hands up. You've nothing to worry about,' Andrew yelled back.

The Fenians appeared one by one, a range of ages from an old man to a young boy who couldn't have been more than sixteen.

Andrew studied them as they came forward, hate aching in his heart. He slowly stood up revealing himself.

The rest of his detachment also rose, their rifles trained on the Irishmen, the only weapon carried by the latter being the rifle with the white handkerchief attached.

Andrew waited till they were halfway to him then raised his revolver.

'Fire!' he screamed, and pulled his trigger again and again till the weapon was empty.

All about him was the crash of rifles.

★ ★ ★

Sergeant Plackett stared aghast at the six dead bodies then up at a smiling Andrew. 'They were unarmed,' he whispered.

'Were they? That's not what'll go in the report.'

'But, sir . . . '

Andrew silenced him with a dismissive wave of the hand. 'We've been too soft for too long with these people, sergeant. Not any more.'

Plackett's expression became grim in the extreme. He didn't agree with that one little bit but would never have dreamt of voicing his opinion to a superior officer.

'We were attacked and defended ourselves, understand?' Andrew went on.

Plackett nodded.

'And make sure the men do as well. If any word of the truth gets out then we're all for the high jump. Not just me but them as well.'

Sergeant Plackett came to attention. 'Yes, sir.'

'Good. Carry on.'

'Yes, sir.' That with a salute.

Greystones, Andrew thought. Greystones and

Alice lost to him because of vermin like these now lying sprawled around him.

★ ★ ★

'Morning, miss,' McPhie said to Charlotte, opening the door of the Rolls. 'A big day for you.'

'It is indeed. Not every day your husband comes back from the war.'

'Indeed not, miss.'

Charlotte settled herself and McPhie closed the door behind her. She hadn't thought she'd be nervous, but was. It had been so long, so very long. She couldn't wait for Geoffrey to take her in his arms, for his lips to be on hers.

McPhie glanced in the rearview mirror as the Rolls purred away. The job wasn't the same any more, not since the old man died. Miss Charlotte didn't use the car nearly as much.

Charlotte stared out at the passing countryside, lost in thought.

★ ★ ★

Charlotte waved the moment she spotted Geoffrey stepping from the train. At last!

She flew along the platform and into his arms. 'Welcome home, darling,' she whispered.

She stared into his face, shocked at how he'd aged. She'd expected some of that but not as much. What he must have been through.

'Hello, Charlotte. It's good to see you.'

'And you, Geoffrey.'

470

He turned and instructed McPhie about his case, after which Charlotte linked an arm through his.

'Let's go home,' she said, wishing he'd kissed her.

'Let's go home,' he agreed.

26

'MRS CLARK excelled herself, that really was the most excellent dinner,' Geoffrey declared as he and Charlotte entered the drawing room.

Charlotte beamed. 'I'd have had something to say if she hadn't. It was quite an occasion after all.'

'Would you like something, a Drummond or brandy perhaps?'

Charlotte sat, puzzled by his behaviour. He seemed so distant somehow, as though there was a barrier between them. There again, perhaps he was simply finding it difficult being back.

'A Drummond I think,' she replied.

She watched him as he crossed the room, noting a slight stiffness in his walk. 'You said in your letters that you were treated very well in the hospital.'

'In Berkshire, yes. The one in France was rather more hectic. An awful lot of . . . ' He broke off, having been about to say deaths.

'Pretty nurses?'

He laughed. 'All sorts really. Pretty, plain and a few that were downright gruesome.'

'You must have become friendly with them.'

He turned and stared quizzically at her. 'To an extent. You can't help but get to know them and they you.'

'Of course.'

He poured them each a stiff one, remembering the vast amounts of alcohol he'd consumed in France. Alcohol that temporarily took away the fear and gave you some courage. Alcohol without which there had been many things he could never have got through

He handed her the drink, but disappointed her when he didn't join her on the sofa but instead chose a facing chair.

'So how are you really, Geoffrey?' she asked.

He dropped his gaze to stare into his glass. 'Not bad, considering.'

'And the wound?'

The hand holding his glass tightened. 'Healed sufficiently to let me come home.'

'Are you badly scarred?'

'Yes,' he whispered, wanting to jump to his feet and rush from the room. How was he going to tell her? It was something he'd agonised over for months.

She smiled. 'At least you're back in one piece.'

He blanched. Why couldn't she just shut up! He swallowed his whisky in a single gulp. 'It was dreadful about your father,' he said, changing the subject.

Now it was her turn to stare into her glass. 'It was,' she agreed softly.

'I liked him very much. He was a decent man. You must miss him a great deal.'

She nodded.

'Not easy for you either having to take over the business. That must have caused a few raised eyebrows.'

'More than a few. But what else could I do with Andrew in the army. I was capable and that was the end of it. Drummond survives with a Drummond at its helm.'

Geoffrey rose and returned to the decanter. 'Do you want me to try and help? I know nothing at all about that kind of thing but am willing to learn.'

She flashed him a grateful smile. 'I was hoping you'd suggest that.'

He shrugged. 'It seems the obvious thing to do. Just as long as you remember army life is all I know. It's going to be quite a change for me.'

'You'll cope, Geoffrey. I have no doubts about that.'

He hoped he would. A desk job was always something he'd tried to avoid.

'There's one other matter,' he said, keeping his back to her.

'What's that?'

'I have to sleep on my own for a bit. Separate bedrooms and all that. For a while anyway.'

She bit back her disappointment. 'The wound obviously.'

'That's right.'

'Of course if it's necessary, Geoffrey. Of course.'

Well, at least that was over he thought. The first hurdle. But the second, the truth? God alone knew how he'd summon up the courage to tell her that.

He saw off his second large whisky and poured himself another.

★ ★ ★

It wasn't at all how she'd imagined his first night home, Charlotte thought, staring up at the bedroom ceiling. She'd imagined a night of passion, or if not that, she wasn't daft, it had been a groin injury after all which might still be troubling him, his presence in bed and cuddles, caresses, lovetalk, kisses.

He hadn't kissed her since arriving back. Not once, not even on saying goodnight.

The latter had shocked her, though she'd tried not to show it. When offering herself for a kiss he'd pulled away with a muttered excuse about how dreadfully tired he was.

Was he involved with another woman, one of his nurses? That wasn't what had come across when she'd quizzed him about the hospital. So what was wrong?

It was the long separation, she decided. That and all he'd been through. She'd been expecting too much for him to arrive home and them to immediately take up where they'd left off. Not that they'd had much of married life, they'd only been wed five minutes before he'd been off to war.

And how he'd aged. There was a heaviness about him where there had been lightness before. Again understandable.

She wondered what Peter would have been like if he'd survived. No doubt he would have aged dramatically also.

Dear Peter, her big brother. The last person she would ever have seen as being a soldier.

But wasn't that the case with so many others. They'd been needed and gone off to do their duty, men no more suited to soldiering than she was to what . . . ? Being a navvy she thought, and inwardly laughed, picturing the absurd sight of herself with a pick in her hands. How ridiculous.

Oh, Geoffrey, if only you were here in bed with me, snuggled up close, instead of in another bedroom.

Somehow it was worse with him being in the same house as herself and she still alone.

Much, much worse.

★ ★ ★

Hettie closed the book she'd been reading. 'So how was that?'

'Absolutely splendid. Thank you.'

'We'll have the next instalment tomorrow night.'

He ran a hand over his face, feeling the scarring, loathing it. Vanity, he told himself. Sheer vanity. 'You read extremely well.'

'You mean for an ex-dairy maid?' she commented drily.

He laughed. 'Not at all. You simply read well, ex-dairy maid or no.'

'Why thank you, kind sir. Now would you like a cup of tea or anything else before I trot off?'

He shook his head.

Hettie studied Jack, thinking how much nicer he was since returning from the war. Not that he hadn't been nice, and certainly kind, before,

476

but now he was even nicer and somehow more mellow. Vulnerability she suddenly realised. That was the key, he was now far more vulnerable than he'd ever been previously.

'Will you do what has to be done before you leave?' he said.

'Don't I always?'

He smiled. 'You're a good woman, Hettie. Never think I don't appreciate that.'

'You'll manage as usual.'

'As usual. Darkness is the norm for a blind man.'

That brought a lump to her throat. 'I thought cottage pie for tomorrow. How does that appeal?'

'Very much so.'

'And a crumble afterwards.'

'I can hardly wait.'

She laughed, knowing he was making fun of her. Setting the book aside she rose and went about extinguishing the lights, coming back to him with her coat on and a single lamp in her hand.

'Goodnight, Jack.'

'Goodnight, Hettie.'

'Sleep tight and don't let the bugs bite.'

'If there are any bugs in my bed you're for the sack.'

She laughed again. 'Tyrant!'

'On you go then. I'll sit here a while longer before going up.'

'See you in the morning.'

'I'll be here,' he replied, a trace of bitterness in his voice.

She left him to the darkness and his thoughts.

★ ★ ★

'Do you understand?'

It was Geoffrey's first day at the distillery and Charlotte had begun to teach him what was what.

He stared at the ledger. 'I think so.'

'It's easy really.'

Bookwork, he thought, and inwardly groaned. How could he face bookwork for the rest of his life. He, a man who'd led such an active life. The prospect was appalling. He was sitting at the desk Peter had once occupied.

'Just say if you have any problems,' Charlotte smiled.

He looked at her, thinking how gorgeous she was. How he ached to take her into his arms and smother her with affection. This woman he'd dreamt about so often, whom he desperately loved.

He bowed his head and got on with the task he'd been given which proved every bit as tedious as he'd expected it to be.

★ ★ ★

Charlotte entered the bathroom to find an aghast Geoffrey staring at her from the bathtub. All he could think was he'd stupidly forgotten to lock the door.

'I'm sorry, I — '

'Get out!' he screamed. 'Get out!'

A thoroughly shaken Charlotte fled, banging the door shut behind her.

* * *

'I sincerely apologise for earlier,' Geoffrey said to her over dinner, when they were alone.

'It *was* rather unnecessary, don't you think? You are my husband after all.'

He coloured slightly. 'It's my nerves, Charlotte. Shot to hell. And you did catch me by surprise.'

She was instantly sympathetic. 'I understand.'

Oh no you don't, he thought. You don't even begin to. 'You live on a knife edge for so long when anything can happen any second of the day or night. It has its effects, I'm afraid.'

'I said I understand, Geoffrey.'

'I'm only trying to explain.'

'And you have. Let's forget it now.'

But, despite her smile, she was still shaken nonetheless. She'd never forget his face as he'd screamed at her. It was the face of a man in torment.

* * *

'Cheer up,' Nell said to Wonky, the pair of them in the still room. 'You're so melancholic of late.'

'Am I?' Wonky rinsed a kidney dish. 'It's just not the same since Dale left. I miss him dreadfully.'

Nell put an arm round her cousin. 'He writes

479

regularly. That's the best you can do in the circumstances.'

'I know that. And I write to him too, all the time. I just wish he was still here that's all. Letters aren't the same as being with someone.'

'I know.'

Wonky shook her head. 'He's lost to me, Nell, I'm sure of it. Lost to me for ever.'

'You mustn't say that.'

'But it's what I believe. He and I are as much casualties of this rotten war as those poor souls lying out there on the ward.'

Nell didn't know what to reply to that for Wonky was probably right. So many relationships had been uprooted and torn apart because of the conflict, it was a common enough story. One you almost heard daily.

'We'd better get on with this or Sister will give us a flea in our ear,' she smiled.

Wonky rinsed another kidney dish.

★ ★ ★

'I never realised before how much I really enjoyed stories,' Jack declared to Hettie who'd just finished her evening reading.

'They certainly fill the time.'

His face clouded. 'And that's something I have plenty of. I get so bored with nothing to do, Hettie. There are times when I'm almost suicidal from it.'

'We walk.'

'And lovely that is too.'

480

'We go to the pub where you have a good chaff with people.'

'But it's not enough, Hettie, can't you understand that? I want to be doing things, a job. Keeping my mind occupied.' He smashed a fist into his opposite palm. 'Only I can't work and never will be able to do so again. It's so damned frustrating. I feel like . . . well a bomb that's on the point of explosion.'

He hadn't had to tell Hettie that, she'd been aware of it for ages. If only she could come up with some sort of solution. But Jack was right, what could a blind man do? Nothing. At least nothing she could think of. How her heart went out to him.

'You'd better go,' he said.

'We could have a trip to the pub if you wish?'

He shook his head. 'I'm not in the mood for company. At least not that sort anyway.'

'Would you like me to stay a while longer?'

There was a long pause, then he said very quietly, 'Please.'

She read him more of the book after which they had a drink together.

★ ★ ★

'A letter from Dale?' Nell queried. Rebecca Levi, the only other one present in the tent, was combing her hair of which she was extremely proud. She'd said more than once it was her best feature.

Wonky looked up at Nell, the beginnings of

481

tears in her eyes. 'From my mother.'

'Oh?'

'It's Dad, he's had a stroke.'

Rebecca stopped combing to stare at Wonky in concern.

'That's awful,' Nell said.

'It's worse than that. Ma wants me home. Says she needs me there.'

Nell sat on the cot beside Wonky, took her hand and squeezed it. 'Will you go?'

'I'll have to. If Ma says she needs me then she does.'

'I'm sorry, Wonky,' Rebecca said.

The tears came, floods of them. 'You know what this means, don't you?' she wailed to Nell.

'It won't be so dreadful.'

'Yes it will. There's been some purpose in my life since arriving in France. There's been Dale. Now I'll be going back to total humdrum and boredom. Probably for the rest of my life.'

Nell bit her lip.

'I'll leave you two alone for a while,' Rebecca said tactfully and, setting down her comb, walked from the tent.

'Humdrum and boredom,' Wonky repeated, remembering how she'd hated living at the manse. Now she'd not only be living there again but would have the responsibility of looking after her father. A complete tie.

'How bad is the stroke?' Nell asked softly.

'Fairly bad according to Ma. He'll probably be bedridden until . . . ' She trailed off. 'Whenever.'

'Sweet Jesus,' Nell whispered, thinking of her

Uncle Tom whom neither she nor Charlotte had ever really liked. But how awful.

Wonky shook her head. 'I'll make arrangements as soon as I can. Matron isn't going to be best pleased, but what can I do?'

It was the one question Nell didn't want to ask, but did, 'What about Dale?'

Wonky covered her face with her hands, picturing Dale in her mind. How different things might have been, if only . . .

'I won't answer any more of his letters.'

'Oh, Wonky!'

'For a short while I thought we might have a future together, but how can we now? He's in Angers and I'm here. We don't even see one another any more. And now I'll be returning to Dalneil and at the end of the war he'll be going home to Albany to take up practice there. It's best it's ended now, for both our sakes.'

'You'll write to explain of course?'

'No, I couldn't do that, it would simply be too painful. Let him think I just lost interest.'

It certainly wasn't what Nell would have done had she been in Wonky's position. 'I think he's owed an explanation, don't you?'

'He'll forget me soon enough. Though I'll never forget him. It just wasn't to be, that's all. As Jack Riach and I weren't to be. I'm ill fated, Nell, I tell you that. I'll end up an old maid, I know I will.'

'Nonsense.'

'It isn't nonsense. Let Dale find himself someone else in time, an Albany girl probably. He and I come from two different worlds and if it wasn't for the war would never have met. A short time, that's all we had. All we were ever destined to have. Better a quick severance and happy memories than a long one and regrets.'

'It's your decision,' Nell said disapprovingly.

'Oh, Nell,' Wonky whispered, eyes awash. 'Oh, Nell!'

Wonky left for Scotland exactly one week later with instructions to Nell that Dale's letters were to be torn up unread.

★ ★ ★

Andrew stared at the burnt-out skeleton of Greystones. He was on leave and had decided to spend it in Dublin. The memories of the house and Alice were thick in his head.

It could all have been his, now everything was gone, literally, up in smoke.

Alice, whom he'd loved and who'd loved him. Greystones.

He remounted his horse and rode away, vowing never to return.

★ ★ ★

Charlotte stared at Geoffrey across the office. She didn't recognise this man, he certainly wasn't the Geoffrey she'd married. And why wouldn't he sleep with her? It had been months now.

He was putting on weight, she thought. And thinning on top. His face had become quite podgy.

'Geoffrey?'

He looked up from his work and smiled at her.

'What is it? What's really wrong?'

The smile abruptly vanished.

'You're going to have to tell me sometime. Was there someone else, is that it?'

He shook his head.

'Then what? We can't go on as we are. You've become a stranger to me.'

An icy feeling crept into his belly. He wasn't ready yet. He needed more time. The last thing he wanted to do was hurt her, and yet what was he now doing? Better by far he'd died out there in France than come home to this.

'The wound is still painful. It'll take more time,' he mumbled.

'Are you sure that's all it is?'

'There hasn't been anyone else, Charlotte, I swear. I love you as I've always done.'

'Then why!' she cried.

He glanced away. 'The war does funny things to people. It's hard to explain to someone who's never experienced it. But there has never been anyone else, on my word of honour as an officer and a gentleman.'

'I want you back in my bed,' she declared simply.

'No, not yet.'

'We don't have to make love if that's a problem. You just being there would be enough.'

He laughed inwardly. How that tune would change if she knew the truth.

'Is there something I don't know about?'

He swallowed hard. 'The nerves, Charlotte, the nerves. As I said I need more time.'

'Then let me help instead of keeping me at arms' length the way you do. Do you know you've kissed me only three times since coming back and all three on the cheek.'

He paled.

'Well?'

'Excuse me,' he said and, rising, strode from the office.

He didn't return until that afternoon when the matter wasn't referred to again.

★ ★ ★

'Can I leave promptly at six tonight, Jack?'

'Oh?'

She hadn't thought she'd be embarrassed, but was. 'You see I've been asked out.'

Jack readjusted his dark glasses which didn't need readjusting. 'Of course, Hettie. Am I allowed to enquire who the chap is?'

'Jimmy Carruthers. You must remember him.'

'Oh yes.' A spotty-faced lad, he was about to comment but decided that wouldn't be tactful. 'So why isn't he in the army?'

'Reserved occupation, Jack.'

'Is this . . . ' He coughed. 'The first time you've been out together?'

Hettie could see the hurt on Jack's face. 'Yes.'

'Then I hope you have a good time together.'

'It's only a drink in the pub. There's nothing else to do in Dalneil.'

'No,' he agreed.

'So that's fine then.'

'Naturally.'

'Then if you'll excuse me I want to go through to the kitchen and get on with the ironing. I've let it pile up a bit.'

She left him in a brooding silence.

★ ★ ★

'Hello, Ma.'

Moira Comyn started having been lost in thought. 'Veronica! I didn't hear the door.'

'I let myself in.'

Wonky gazed about her, dismayed by the dreariness of the room and her general surroundings. She felt like a prisoner who'd escaped and now been recaptured and returned to jail. There was a tremendous sinking feeling inside her.

'How's Father?'

Moira went to her daughter and hugged her tightly. 'It's good to have you home again. I can't say how much. As for your father, I'll take you up in a moment and you can judge for yourself.'

Moira disentangled herself and gazed adoringly at Wonky. 'I must say you're looking well.'

Her mother had put on weight Wonky noted. She was even fatter than before. Tom's stroke hadn't affected her appetite.

'And feeling it.'

'Are you hungry?'

Wonky shook her head. 'Not in the least.'

'How about a wee scone? I baked some earlier.'

'No thanks, Ma.'

'Are you sure?'

'Certain, Ma,' Wonky sighed.

'Then would you like to see your father?'

'Of course.'

Moira gripped Wonky by the arm. 'Try not to appear too shocked. There's an awfully big change in him as you can imagine.'

'I've been dealing with frontline casualties, Ma, there's not much would shock me any more.'

How grown up she was, Moira was thinking. There wasn't any real change physically, but certainly in the eyes. There was maturity there which there hadn't been before.

'Let's go on up then. He's expecting you.'

Wonky felt her shoulders slump as she followed her mother out the room.

★ ★ ★

'Can I have a word with you, Miss Charlotte?' Miss McQueen requested.

'Go ahead.'

Miss McQueen had bided her time, waiting till Geoffrey was absent. Now she'd got Charlotte on her own.

'What is it, Miss McQueen?'

'I hope you don't think this presumptuous of me, or impertinent, but it's Mr Geoffrey.'

'Oh?'

'He's not sleeping very well. I've heard him.'

Charlotte frowned. 'Heard him?'

'Prowling. He prowls round the house at night for hours on end. And in his room, walking up and down, up and down into the small hours. I thought . . . Well I just thought it was something you should be aware of if you weren't already.'

'No, I wasn't.'

'Have I done wrong? It is personal, after all.'

'No, Miss McQueen, I'm glad you've told me.'

'Then I'll be getting on.'

'Thank you, Miss McQueen,' Charlotte said as the housekeeper was about to leave.

Well, Charlotte thought, frowning.

Well.

27

CHARLOTTE woke with a start to find someone staring down at her. She gasped in fright and clutched the bedclothes.

'I'm sorry, love,' Geoffrey's voice said. 'I shouldn't have . . . I . . . '

Turning, he fled.

★ ★ ★

Charlotte knocked on the door. 'Geoffrey, can I come in?'

There was no reply.

'Geoffrey?'

The door slowly opened. 'I'm sorry,' he repeated, shamefaced.

'We have to talk, Geoffrey.'

'Not now, I . . . '

She brushed past him into the bedroom. '*Now*,' she stated emphatically.

He groaned. It had been madness going to her, sheer utter madness. But the longing was still there, the terrible longing that tormented him day and night.

'I'll put a light on,' she declared.

'No please, don't.'

She hesitated, then decided to comply. She sat on his bed and patted a spot alongside. 'It's high time you told me what this is all about. I have to know, I'm your wife after all.'

He sat beside her. 'This is difficult, Charlotte. You've no idea how difficult.'

'I'm listening.'

He thought of the hospital in France and the doctor who'd broken the awful news. Probably the worst day of his entire life.

'I'm not a man, any more,' he muttered huskily.

That rocked her. 'How do you mean?'

'There was a grenade. It killed a sergeant and wounded me. In the groin.'

It was beginning to dawn on her what he was getting at. 'Go on.'

'I have . . . I still have . . . ' He fell silent for a few moments, struggling with himself to utter what finally had to be said.

'I still have a penis, Charlotte, or most of one anyway. But not the other bits.'

She was stunned. How stupid of her, how incredibly stupid not to have realised. 'I see,' she breathed.

He leant forward and put his head in his hands, feeling absolutely ghastly. He was in a living, waking nightmare. Better he'd died in France. Oh how he wished he had.

He started to cry. 'You've no idea what it's like to be with you day after day, to want you, and not be able to do anything about it. And know that I never will again.'

She put an arm round him. 'You should have explained sooner.'

'I meant to, I wanted to, but just couldn't.'

Children, she thought. There would never be any now. Nor any more of the lovemaking she'd so enjoyed. What a brief interlude that had been.

'Come on, pull yourself together,' she said sympathetically, squeezing him.

'Oh, Charlotte,' he moaned. 'I love you so.'

'It isn't the end of the world, Geoffrey. We'll manage.'

'Will we?'

'Of course we will. It's simply something that has to be lived with, that's all.'

'And how do you live with it? Knowing your manhood's been taken from you.'

She blanched.

'It's just hanging there, useless.'

'There's more to a marriage, Geoffrey. How little you must think of me to believe that was all I was interested in. I married you for what you are, not simply because of that.'

'But we're both so young. There's a whole lifetime ahead without . . . ' He trailed off.

'I want you to come back to bed with me, Geoffrey. For us to cuddle up. That'll be enough, I promise you.'

'How can it be!' he cried out, wrenching himself from her embrace and throwing himself backwards.

She mustn't show pity, she thought. Not now, not ever. That would surely destroy him.

'You're alive, Geoffrey, that's all I ever prayed for. It's enough, I swear.'

'No it isn't. Better I was dead leaving you the chance to meet someone else who could . . . '

'No it isn't!' she interjected sternly. 'I meant what I said. You are my love, the only one there will ever be. All right, it isn't an easy burden to carry, but one we will. I love you and you love me, that's all that matters.'

He turned a tearstained face to her. 'Do you really mean that?'

'With all my heart. Now let's go to my bed, *our* bed, where you should be. Where I insist you are.'

Later, he fell asleep in her arms. But there wasn't any sleep for her that night.

All she could do was think, remember what had been.

★ ★ ★

'Right, the book,' Hettie declared to Jack, picking up the novel she was currently reading, her other chores for the day finished.

'I don't think we'll bother tonight,' he replied stiffly.

She stared at him. 'But you enjoy it so much.'

He shrugged.

She replaced the book. He'd been in a strange mood all day, irritable. Not snapping at her exactly but not far off it.

'Are you ill?'

'No. I'm right as rain.'

'Then what's the matter, Jack?'

'There's nothing the matter.'

'Yes there is.'

'Don't contradict me. There isn't.'

She knew then what it was all about. Jimmy Carruthers whom she'd been out with several

493

times now. Jack was jealous.

'I'll go then,' she said.

He nodded. 'See you tomorrow morning.'

'I'll do the usual first of course.'

'Fine.'

He harumphed when she said goodbye.

★ ★ ★

God but it was awful, cleaning your own father's bottom. And if it was awful for her what was it like for him?

'I won't be long, Father,' Wonky smiled to Tom whose eyes were shut as they always were when she did this particular job.

His legs were paralysed, as was one arm, his face grotesquely misshapen. It had been a massive stroke.

When she'd finished with his bottom, she began on his blanket bath.

Tom's eyes remained firmly closed.

★ ★ ★

Rory was alone on the heather, a gaunt emaciated figure stumbling forward. He paused for breath and stared about him through eyes filled with pain and defeat.

At least he'd survived the battle, Nell thought. Thank God for that. But what a state he was in.

Rory gulped in several more deep breaths and then, chest heaving, continued on his way.

Oh my love, Nell thought. Oh my dearest love.

★ ★ ★

'I've stopped seeing Jimmy Carruthers,' Hettie announced.

'Oh?'

'He wasn't for me. Nice enough chap really, but boring! I can't tell you how boring. Being with him was one long yawn.'

Jack chuckled. 'I don't remember him as being particularly bright or entertaining. A simple country clod is my recollection.'

Hettie smiled to herself, that had certainly perked Jack up as she'd supposed it would. His entire body had suddenly become more animated.

'I've had an idea,' she said.

'And what's that?'

'I'll only tell you if you take it seriously. I won't have you laughing at me, Jack Riach.'

'As if I would,' he replied drily.

'I may be an ex-dairy maid and your housekeeper but I do have a brain in my head. One I can use when required.'

He folded his hands in front of him. 'Come out with it then.'

'You enjoy stories, right?'

'Very much so. We've already discussed that.'

'And you've nothing to do most of the day except sit on your arse.'

He laughed at that. 'How delicately put.'

'Well, it's true. Apart from our walks and

495

visits to the pub you spend most of your time in that chair. You've also complained to me many times that you wished you had something to do. In other words, a job.'

His interest quickened. 'Go on, my dear Hettie.'

'Why don't you try and write some stories yourself?'

This time his laugh was a roar. 'How can I possibly do that when I'm blind? It's preposterous.'

'No it isn't. Hear me out. You dictate and I'll write it down for you.'

His laugh subsided as he considered that. 'It's a thought,' he conceded eventually. 'Though what sort of thing would I attempt? I mean, I've never written anything other than a composition at school.'

'You'll have to think about it of course. Work it out in your mind. That's still totally functional after all. There's nothing wrong with that, which is your problem.'

Could he? Was it possible? The notion certainly appealed.

'There's the war for a start,' she said. 'You could do a story about that.'

Excitement gripped him. A story about the war.

'Anyway, I'll leave you with it, I have to get on,' she declared and swept from the room.

A bemused Jack started thinking.

★ ★ ★

496

Nell stared at the letter, the sixth one that had arrived now from Dale to Wonky, his name clearly written on the back.

With a sigh she tore it up.

* * *

He was whimpering again in his sleep, waking Charlotte who turned to him in concern. Night after night it was the same. The whimpering, the talking the shaking, the reliving of terror.

'Geoffrey?' she said, tugging his shoulder.

'The wire, all hanging on the wire,' he mumbled.

'Geoffrey?'

He whimpered again, then came awake.

'Geoffrey?'

His chest heaved. 'Was I . . . ?'

'Yes, my darling.'

'I'm sorry.'

'There's no need to apologise. I understand.'

He wished he could have a cigarette but had left his case downstairs. 'Are you certain you want me in bed with you? I disturb you so much, and there's the business to consider.'

She took him in her arms. 'Of course I want you here, even if you do disturb me.'

'It was too . . . unspeakable, Charlotte,' he said in a low, hollow voice. 'I know I'll have nightmares about it for the rest of my life.'

Charlotte cradled him against her breasts which she instantly realised was a mistake when she felt his body stiffen.

'Is there anything I can get you?' she asked,

497

releasing him. 'A cup of tea perhaps?'

'No thank you.'

'Do you want to talk?'

'Not really.'

She smoothed his hair which was wet with sweat. 'My poor darling.'

'So many men . . . so many incidents,' he muttered, and shuddered.

She thought of her brother Peter and others from the village who'd gone off to war and never returned. The whole thing had been catastrophic and was far from over yet. At least the Americans were now in the war, that must hasten its end.

'I think the gas was the worst,' Geoffrey said. 'The effects of that were horrendous.'

'We've a long day tomorrow. Try and get some sleep,' she counselled.

'All right.'

They lay side by side, a couple who weren't really one any more. Fate, war and a grenade had brought that about.

Charlotte wept silently.

★ ★ ★

Wonky stared out of the window at the driving rain lashing the ground. The new minister was due to arrive sometime that day, a bachelor from Glasgow who'd be taking her father's place. Luckily for them they'd been allowed to stay on at the manse which wouldn't have been the case had the new minister been married with a family.

498

She thought of Dale and wondered what he was doing and how he was. Nell had recently been in touch to report that Dale's letters had finally stopped.

'Dale,' she whispered to herself, picturing him in her mind. How she longed to be with him in person. To touch him, kiss . . .

Enough of that, she rebuked herself sharply. Dale was out of her life for ever. She'd never see him again, or he her. Dale was in the past, a lovely memory. One she'd treasure always, no matter what.

'Dale,' she whispered a second time.

★ ★ ★

'You're hurting me,' the girl complained.

An amused glint came into Andrew's eyes. 'Am I? Sorry.'

'There's no need to be so . . . vigorous.'

Andrew laughed inwardly. Of course there wasn't, but he enjoyed hurting her. And a fine-looking Dublin whore she was too, the prettiest in the house.

He withdrew and started to turn her over. This was extra, a great deal extra. But he knew that, although she did it, she hated the experience.

Another way of getting back at them, he thought gleefully as he thrust himself into her again.

The girl's face contorted.

★ ★ ★

499

He was an excellent preacher this John McLean, Charlotte thought, as she and Geoffrey sat in church. The service was the first conducted by the new minister. He had a way with words, an eloquence. And was certainly less 'fire and brimstone' than her Uncle Tom. She approved.

Quite handsome too. How old? she wondered. Late twenties, possibly early thirties. And what beautiful expressive hands. She liked men with nice hands.

Geoffrey glanced sideways at her, bored rigid with the proceedings. He couldn't wait for the service to be over so they could get home again.

McLean concluded his sermon, and departed the pulpit.

The next hymn was one of Charlotte's favourites, 'By Cool Siloam's Shady Rill'.

She sang it with gusto.

★ ★ ★

Geoffrey was already in his pyjamas when Charlotte joined him in the bedroom. 'Another Monday tomorrow, another week,' she sighed.

He wasn't looking forward to work either; like the service it bored him. Far more than he'd ever truly admitted to his wife.

His eyes fastened on Charlotte as she started to undress, the ache of longing heavy within him.

He winced when, for a few brief seconds, she stood naked before slipping into her nightdress.

A few brief seconds that made him want to vomit.

He groaned inwardly and closed his eyes. 'You all right?' she asked, having turned round to catch him like that.

'Fine,' he smiled. 'I was just thinking.'

'About what?'

'Nothing important.'

She gazed at him in concern. 'The war?'

He shook his head.

Charlotte sat at her vanity table and began brushing her hair as she did every night, Geoffrey meanwhile getting into bed.

Another night of her lying beside him, available and yet unavailable. Another night of torture.

Better by far . . . Better by far . . .

★ ★ ★

'How kind of you to call, Mr McLean,' Charlotte smiled at the new minister.

Geoffrey gazed on disconsolately having taken, for no reason he could put his finger on, an instant dislike to the man.

'Will you please order tea, Geoffrey,' Charlotte requested, sitting.

Geoffrey went to the bell pull. How long would McLean stay? he wondered. He certainly couldn't make his excuses and leave, that would be extremely rude and make Charlotte furious.

He mustn't indulge in too many of the scones, teacakes or crumpets, Geoffrey told himself for he was piling on the weight. He'd become quite rotund which distressed him. His hair was also thinning rapidly which was another cause of distress. If he went on at the current rate he'd be bald before he knew where he was, a hateful prospect.

McLean settled himself in a chair facing Charlotte. What a striking female, he was thinking, just as he'd thought it when thanking them for attending the service the previous Sunday. He had stood outside the church having a quiet word with members of the congregation as they left.

'It's my pleasure entirely to call, Mrs Armitage, I assure you,' McLean smiled in return.

'And how are you settling in at the manse?'

'Admirably thank you. I've been made to feel most at home.'

'Good.'

He glanced about him. 'What a lovely room.'

'How sweet of you to say so.'

'Indeed, I've heard a great deal about you and this house from your cousin. She says it's a house she adores.'

Geoffrey slumped into another chair.

'I believe you were invalided out of the war, Mr Armitage?'

Geoffrey went cold, for a horrible moment thinking the minister might know why. But that was impossible, only Charlotte knew the true extent of his injuries. 'That's correct.'

Christine, a new maid, appeared in the room. 'You rang, ma'am?'

That she'd presumed it had been Charlotte

who'd rung irritated Geoffrey. 'No I did. Can we have tea for three?'

'Of course, sir,' Christine replied, and left them.

Charlotte thought Geoffrey's tone had been somewhat harsh. Why shouldn't the girl presume it had been her after all. There again, irritability was fast becoming a common feature with Geoffrey, so unlike his manner of old.

'The war's a terrible business,' McLean declared, shaking his head.

Idiot, Geoffrey thought. What the hell would you know about it, you pious, sanctimonious clown. You've never been in the trenches, seen, experienced what I have.

Geoffrey, not caring what the minister thought, pulled out his cigarette case and lit up.

★ ★ ★

'I've been considering your idea,' Jack said to Hettie. 'And come to the conclusion I'd like to write a play.'

She stared at him in astonishment. 'A play!'

He chuckled. 'It is a bit strange I admit. And I have to confess I know little about plays, though I have seen a few in my time. But that's what I'd like to attempt.'

'Why?'

He folded his hands in front of him. 'I'm not sure I could adequately describe what I went through in the war. Whereas with a play it would be more or less reproducing what I heard. Does that make any sense at all?'

Hettie thought about it. 'Possibly.'

'We could send off to London for some published plays to find out how they're put together, and then go on from there. What do you think?'

Hettie hadn't seen him so animated or enthusiastic since his return home. 'It's worth a try.'

'Good,' he nodded.

★ ★ ★

Geoffrey swore and threw down his pen. 'I find this so damned difficult, I really do,' he fumed.

Charlotte frowned. 'It's only adding up figures.'

'Mathematics was never one of my strong points.'

She laid her own pen aside. He was quite apoplectic. 'I'll do it if you wish.'

'No, it's my job. My responsibility. I'll get it right even if I'm here all night.'

Oh dear, she thought.

'Four times I've added up this column and four times I've come up with different answers.'

Geoffrey lurched to his feet and crossed to a cupboard from which he took a bottle of Drummond. 'A dram might help. God help me, but I need one.'

'In working hours, Geoffrey?' she gently admonished.

He glared at her. 'In working hours if I so

504

choose. I may be deficient in other departments but I'm still capable of making my own decisions and knowing how they'll affect me.'

'That's not fair,' she said softly.

He swore again. Took a glass from the same cupboard and poured a huge measure which he despatched in a single gulp, after which he shuddered.

'Geoffrey?'

He glared at her again, then poured another hefty measure. He then returned the bottle to the cupboard and slammed the door shut.

She didn't know what to do or say.

He returned to his desk and threw himself into his chair, whisky slopping onto the sheet of figures he'd been trying to add up.

'Buggeration,' he said.

Charlotte bit her lip. 'Would you like me to join you?'

'In what?'

'A dram.'

He laughed cruelly. 'You just said it wasn't right in working hours and now you propose to do the same. Isn't that called hypocrisy?'

'I'm only trying to help.'

'I don't need your bloody help,' he snarled.

She sat back in her chair, concern written all over her face. Everything she seemed to do nowadays was wrong. She just couldn't please him. How she yearned for the Geoffrey she'd fallen in love with. Of course she knew the reason for his changing, but that didn't make it any easier to put up with. She'd have done anything to have been able to wave a magic wand and make things as they'd once been. But of course that was impossible.

Geoffrey ran a hand through what was left of his hair, thinking the prospect of a life in this office was completely stultifying. Maybe he should leave, go away somewhere, be on his own for a while. Though how could he possibly suggest that to Charlotte?

'Why don't you take a walk,' she suggested.

He considered that. Anything to get out of the damned office and away from these figures.

'All right.'

'Then off you go.'

His temper flared again. 'Don't talk to me as if I'm a child.' He mimicked her. 'Off you go!' Followed by, 'Yes, mummy dear.'

'I didn't mean it that way, Geoffrey.'

'Well, that's how it sounded.'

'I'm sorry.'

'And so you should be, you patronising bi — '

He stopped himself in time.

He drank the remainder of his whisky. 'I'll be back when I arrive.'

'Fine.'

He gave her a look of utter contempt before leaving, slamming the door as he'd slammed the cupboard.

Charlotte was bereft, as though her insides had been gouged out and only an empty shell remained. It was a full fifteen minutes before she was able to pick up her pen again.

Geoffrey's walk took him straight to the pub.

★ ★ ★

Hettie eagerly opened the packet, knowing what was inside. The six plays that she'd ordered for Jack from London. Three were comedies, three tragedies.

He was delighted when she told him and instructed her to sit down there and then and read one to him.

She began with the description of the set.

28

JACK came to his feet the moment he heard Hettie arrive. 'I'm here!' he called out.

'It's a lovely day,' she smiled on entering the room.

'Yes, I could feel that.'

'I'll get started . . . '

He waved a dismissive hand. 'Forget the housework for the moment. Get pen and paper, I want to make some notes on a few ideas I've had.'

'About the play I take it.'

'That's right. I'm considering setting it in the trenches, in a dugout more specifically. A group of four officers coming and going, mainly talking about what they're going through, how they miss home, loved ones, that sort of thing. That's just how it was. On the surface anyway, but there was a lot more going on underneath.'

'I understand,' she nodded.

'Now get that pen and paper and we'll crack on.'

He spoke for almost an hour while perched on the arm of a chair, Hettie assiduously writing down every word he uttered.

When he'd finished he made her repeat it back to him, at the conclusion of which he grunted.

'Reaction?'

'So far so good, I'd say.'

He beamed.

'You're drunk,' Charlotte accused when Geoffrey staggered into the drawing room. He'd disappeared after work without an explanation of where he was off to.

'Drunk! I should hope so after the amount I've put away,' he slurred in reply.

She stared at him disapprovingly. His tie was askew, his cheeks flushed. His eyes were glazed.

'You missed dinner,' she said. 'We held it for ages and then I ate on my own. Mrs Clark wasn't best pleased.'

'Sod Mrs Clark, she's only a servant after all. Not paid to approve or disapprove.'

Charlotte was shocked. 'The staff may be servants but should be treated with respect, as well they deserve. Pa always said that.'

'Pa!' Geoffrey sneered. 'Well he's dead and gone and won't be saying anything any more.'

Charlotte's eyes blazed. 'You won't speak ill of my father, that's one thing I simply won't allow.'

'Or what?' Geoffrey taunted, swaying on the spot. 'Or what?'

'I simply won't allow it, that's all.'

He threw back his head and laughed uproariously, knowing there was nothing she could do. She certainly wouldn't chuck him out for that would be scandalous in her position. As for divorce, quite out of the question for that would be even more scandalous.

He staggered over and leered into her face.

'I'll say what I like and that's an end of it.'

'But you liked my father.'

'Hardly the point.'

'Then what is the point? That you're trying to assert your masculinity?'

She realised the instant she'd said it that it was a mistake. His hand flashed cracking her hard across the cheek. With a cry she jerked backwards on the sofa.

'That wasn't very nice,' he declared.

'I'm sorry.'

'Being sorry doesn't help matters, Charlotte. For it tells me what you truly think, that I'm only half a man.'

She clutched his arm. 'Geoffrey, I . . . '

He tore himself away. 'Don't touch me. And don't look at me with such pity in your eyes. Have you any idea what it does to me?'

He lurched over to the whisky decanter and poured himself a large dram, spilling some on the floor in the process. How he hated himself, loathed himself. Peter had been lucky, so damned lucky. If there was a hell then he was now living in it, every moment of consciousness sheer torment. He could almost see grinning devils prodding tridents into him.

'Surely you've had enough,' Charlotte forced herself to say.

'Enough! I haven't even started yet, Mrs Armitage. I'll be the judge of when I've had enough.'

She rose. 'I'm going to bed.'

'Yes go. Get out of my sight. And never ever mention my masculinity, or lack of it, again.'

'I won't,' she promised in a quiet voice.

'Good. For your sake, believe me.'

Upstairs she started to shake and it was a long time before it finally subsided.

When Geoffrey eventually joined her in bed she pretended to be asleep.

He soon was, snoring in a drunken stupor.

★ ★ ★

Nell fell onto her cot, totally and utterly exhausted having just come off an eighteen-hour shift. She was due back on duty in six hours' time.

'I don't know how much of this I can take,' she said to Hope Langton.

'Me neither.'

'It's become a nightmare. I'm so tired I hardly know what I'm doing half the time.'

'And the Sisters never let up,' Rebecca Levi chipped in. 'You'd think they'd show a little compassion, but not them. They're all slave drivers.'

Georgina Fletcher sighed. 'I could sleep for a fortnight. No, a month more like.'

'It isn't a hospital any more,' Nell commented. 'A butcher's shop is more apt.'

Hope nodded her agreement. 'It certainly wouldn't do to be squeamish.'

'And that's a fact,' Rebecca added, shuddering at the memory of a particularly grisly amputation she'd witnessed earlier that day.

In the distance a battery of guns opened up.

Nell hardly heard them as her eyes began to droop.

Next thing she knew it was morning with another gruelling day stretching ahead of her.

⋆ ⋆ ⋆

Charlotte woke to find herself alone in bed. Where was Geoffrey? She thought about the situation for a few moments then got up and slipped on her dressing gown. She found him sitting in the drawing room, a single light on, staring into space.

'Geoffrey?'

He blinked, then focused on her. 'What are you doing up?'

'I came looking for you. What's wrong?'

He laughed hollowly. 'The same thing as always.'

She crossed and sat beside him. 'It doesn't do you any good brooding like this.'

'I'd rather brood down here than up there. It's . . . ' He broke off.

'It's what?'

He took a deep breath, and slightly turned away from her. 'It's even worse being in bed with you than it was being in the other bed thinking about you. It's agony, Charlotte, sheer agony.'

She didn't know what to reply to that.

'You're there beside me, driving me to distraction. It's like standing outside a sweetie shop without any money in your pockets staring in. It's all there in front of you but you can't have it.'

512

'Oh, Geoffrey,' she murmured.

'I want to move back to the other room,' he stated. 'At least that way I may keep my sanity.'

'If you wish.'

'I do.'

'I've told you before, Geoffrey, you mustn't worry on my account. A cuddle and kiss is good enough for me.'

He barked out a laugh. 'So you say. But for how long? You're a normal woman, for God's sake. You won't be content to put up with a cuddle and kiss for the rest of your life. And then what?'

'I will, Geoffrey. Because they'll be coming from you whom I love. I suppose women are different to men in that respect. It's not a subject I know a great deal about, but I think it must be true.'

He shook his head. 'Even if you're right, and I doubt it, there's me to consider. What's on offer isn't enough. I'd rather have nothing than a reminder of what's been taken away from me. It's still all there, Charlotte, the urge. An urge I can't satisfy.'

She sighed. 'You'll come to terms with it in time, Geoffrey. I'm sure of it.'

'How long?' he replied sarcastically. 'Five years. Ten. Twenty? Oh, wonderful!'

She wanted to hold him, comfort him, but refrained from doing so knowing it wouldn't be appreciated. 'I'll instruct Miss McQueen that you're moving back to the other room tomorrow. Though she and the others are going to think it strange.'

'I don't care what they think,' he groaned. 'Tell them I'm impossible to sleep with any more, that I'm restless in the extreme because of my wound. Tell them any damn thing you please as long as I move.'

Charlotte got up. 'I'm going back to bed, are you coming?'

He shook his head.

'You'll be tired in the morning and there's work.'

Work! he thought. Revolting, horrible, boring boring work. 'I'll come soon,' he said.

'All right.'

She left him to it, wishing there was something she could do to help.

But what? That was the question she'd asked herself a hundred times.

⋆ ⋆ ⋆

'Is that really her husband?' Charlotte queried of Mrs Ogilvie as they emerged from church. Geoffrey had stayed behind at Drummond House not wishing to attend the service.

'It is indeed,' Mrs Ogilvie giggled. 'He's old enough to be her father.'

He was that, Charlotte thought, glancing back to where the Grahams were talking to John McLean. They'd moved into the area a few weeks previously and this was their first time at church.

'Pretty thing,' Charlotte commented, referring to Mrs Graham.

'Well one thing's for sure, it can't be a love

match. She must have married him for his money. He's substantially well off I understand. Well he'd have to be to buy the old Sneddon place.'

Charlotte was intrigued. 'Are you sure we haven't got the wrong end of the stick and that's not his daughter?'

'His *wife*,' Mrs Ogilvie stated emphatically. 'Take my word for it.'

She'd invite them over some time, Charlotte decided. Welcome them to Dalneil. It would be an excuse to entertain which she hadn't done in a long time. It would be fun to have the house alive again and hopefully Geoffrey would enjoy it.

Charlotte glanced again at Mr Graham. Late fifties, she thought, even early sixties while his wife — well early twenties at the most.

'What does he do?' Charlotte asked.

'Had a firm in Perth I believe which he sold and has retired early. I couldn't tell you what sort of firm though. No doubt we'll hear on the grapevine soon enough.'

No doubt, Charlotte thought.

★ ★ ★

'It's bliss getting out of that house and away from Mother and Father, sheer bliss,' Wonky declared.

Charlotte made a sympathetic face. 'It must be awful for you.'

'And how. You've no idea. Imagine having to look after your father the way I do. He's

515

mortified every time I have to wash his bottom.'

'I can imagine. Not very pleasant for either of you.'

'If only Ma would help, but she refuses point blank to do so. Oh, she'll sit with him for hours on end chattering away, but when it comes to the dirty work that's strictly my province. Says she couldn't possibly do those things.'

'But you can, eh?'

Wonky smiled. 'So it would seem. Anyway, how are you and how's Geoffrey?'

Charlotte desperately wanted to unburden herself about Geoffrey but wouldn't. His secret had to remain strictly between the pair of them. 'He's fine,' she lied.

'And you?'

'Never better.' Another lie.

'That's good then,' Wonky sighed. 'I'm glad somebody's happy for I'm certainly not.'

'It won't last for ever,' Charlotte replied. 'Your father . . . well, without being unkind, there must be an end in sight in the foreseeable future. What does Dr McAllister say?'

'More or less the same. But Father could still last for years and in the meantime I'm hardly getting any younger. I know I'll end up one of those horrible prune-like spinsters, I just know it.'

'It was a pity about Dale,' Charlotte murmured.

Wonky's face clouded. 'There isn't a day goes by but I don't think of him. I miss him terribly.'

'And what about the new minister? He seems personable enough.'

'John's smashing, I like him a lot.'

'Any . . . eh, interest on his part there?'

Wonky laughed. 'None whatsoever. We're just good friends and that's it.'

'Pity.'

Wonky shrugged. 'Maybe. It would be difficult after Dale. He was very special to me.'

Her eyes narrowed in memory. Dale Kutchinsky, whom she'd never see again. How cruel life could be.

Charlotte patted her cousin's hand. 'Cheer up. Things can only get better.'

Wonky smiled in agreement.

★ ★ ★

'Hello, Jack, it's Geoffrey Armitage.'

'Geoffrey, old boy! Have a seat.' Jack patted the space beside him. 'How are you?'

'Oh, fit to middling. And yourself?'

Jack gave a hollow laugh. 'Coping, I suppose. What else can you do.'

Geoffrey wished he was. 'I've been meaning to cut along and see you but between one thing and another . . . ' He trailed off and shrugged.

'I understand,' Jack nodded.

'Can I get you another drink?' They were in the Dalneil pub.

'Sounds like a good idea.'

'Right then. Dram and pint?'

'Please.'

Geoffrey went up to the bar where he gazed around waiting to be served. A group of women whom he recognised from the distillery were at the table next to his and Jack's, the tables separated by a wooden and glass partition. From the looks of them they were far from sober.

Geoffrey returned with a tray. 'Just in front of you,' he said, placing Jack's pint and dram on the table.

'Thank you.'

Geoffrey stood the tray against a table leg. 'They seem to be having a fine old time next door,' he commented quietly to Jack.

'It's a twenty-first. They were here when I arrived and are intent on making a night of it. I've had a few chuckles to myself listening to the conversation. Whoever said women are the fairer sex?'

Geoffrey smiled. 'At least they don't have work in the morning.' For it was a Saturday night.

Jack took off his dark glasses and rubbed empty eye sockets. 'Sorry about that,' he apologised, replacing the glasses. 'They get itchy from time to time.'

'It must be difficult for you,' Geoffrey said softly.

'Well, it certainly isn't easy. At least you came out of it more or less unscathed.'

Geoffrey blanched. If only Jack knew. 'Yes,' he lied.

'Groin, wasn't it?'

'Damage to the thighs. Bad enough for them to discharge me.'

'Can you walk all right?'

'A slight limp on occasions, that's all.'

'Lucky you,' Jack sighed, and tasted his pint.

A raucous shriek went up from the next table. They *were* enjoying themselves, Jack thought.

'And then the swine . . . '

The woman who was speaking dropped her voice to confide in her companions which concluded in a concerted bellow of laughter.

Something dirty, Geoffrey thought correctly.

'I think of Peter a lot,' Jack stated quietly. 'I miss him.'

'You were good pals.'

'Even closer when we were over there. You share so much in a situation like that, as you well know.'

'Yes,' Geoffrey agreed softly.

Jack considered telling Geoffrey about his intended play, then decided against it. That was something best kept between himself and Hettie for the time being.

'Do you manage to get around by yourself?' Geoffrey queried.

'I'm learning. The pub I've got down pat, and the shop, which gives me some freedom. It's so demeaning having to be totally reliant on someone else.'

'You've got a housekeeper, I understand. Charlotte mentioned.'

'A lass who used to work for me before. She's wonderful, looks after me a treat.'

'It was this size, I swear,' a female at the next table declared, that followed by more laughter.

Jack laughed also. 'It's amazing how alcohol loosens the tongue. They're having a whale of a time.'

Something he could do with himself, Geoffrey

reflected. He hadn't had that since . . .

He picked up his whisky and saw it off, shuddering from that and the many memories suddenly crowding his mind.

'It was hysterical on our wedding night. The damn bampot was so pissed he couldn't get it up. Talk about a let down! I could happily have slaughtered him. There was me all eager and champing at the bit and he was absolutely useless.'

Those overheard words were like a knife plunged into Geoffrey's heart. He went rigid, eyes staring fixedly ahead. He jerked slightly when another roar of feminine laughter rang out.

'Working lasses,' Jack mused, shaking his head. 'The salt of the earth.'

'I've got to go, Jack. I was only in for the one.'

'Oh, come on, stay and have another. Keep me company.'

'I'm sorry, I have to be on my way. Another time.'

'Another time then,' Jack agreed with a smile and small salute.

Couldn't get it up! The words screamed in Geoffrey's mind as he hurriedly left the pub.

Couldn't get it up. Followed by a roar of derisory female laughter. He hadn't gone more than a couple of yards when he stopped and vomited.

★ ★ ★

Wonky dropped into the armchair and sighed heavily. Over at the desk where her father had written his sermon for years John McLean was now writing his for that coming Sunday.

He glanced up at her and smiled. 'Tired?'

She nodded.

'It's a hard task you've been set by the good Lord.'

Didn't she know it, she thought.

He laid down his pen and studied her. 'Is there something on your mind? Anything you'd care to talk about?'

'Not really, John, but thank you for your concern.'

'Simply tiredness, is that it?' He regarded her shrewdly, for John was no fool. He had insight into people which was why he was such a good minister. He knew Wonky was a troubled soul, had recognised that shortly after his arrival.

'You're extremely peaceful to be with,' she said. 'I like that.'

'Oh?'

'There's a sort of calmness about you which you exhude. It washes over one.'

'Why thank you, Veronica.'

'Call me Wonky, please. At least when Ma isn't around.'

He smiled again. 'I'm a good listener. And can occasionally offer a decent piece of advice when required.'

She closed her eyes for a moment, then opened them again.

'Is it all getting too much for you?'

'It's not just that,' she heard herself saying.

'Then what is it?'

Ma was with her father and would be there for ages which meant she was able to speak freely if she so chose.

'I met someone in France,' she stated simply.

'I see.'

'Someone I fell in love with.'

'Was he killed?'

'No, at least not to my knowledge. Although who knows what's happened since I last saw him.'

He didn't reply, waiting for her to go on.

She did, telling him all about Dale Kutchinsky. John hadn't lied, he was a good listener.

★ ★ ★

Geoffrey stared at the papers in front of him, seeing nothing. All he could think about was that ghastly overheard conversation in the pub.

Couldn't get it up! Those words had reverberated round and round in his mind ever since. How they'd laughed those distillery women. Cruel laughter that had cut him to the bone. Thank God no one other than Charlotte knew his secret. That would have been too much to bear.

'Geoffrey?'

He glanced up at his wife, suddenly hating her. 'Yes?'

'You've been staring at those invoices for ages.'

'Are you complaining, is that it?' he snapped in reply.

Oh dear, she thought. It was another of those days. 'No, I just wondered if there was anything wrong. Perhaps something you didn't understand?'

He wanted to cross the office and slap her. What satisfaction that would give.

'I understand what I'm doing perfectly,' he replied, managing to control his voice.

'Fine then,' she smiled.

He recalled how it had once been between them, how wonderful those nights. How she'd trembled to his touch, sighed with pleasure as he'd moved within her.

Stop torturing yourself, he thought. That was over, gone. Would never come again, couldn't.

For the umpteenth time he wondered how she really felt about the situation. He didn't believe a word of it when she said a kiss and cuddle were all she needed. Not one bloody word of it.

Not one bloody word.

★ ★ ★

Charlotte had considered having a large dinner party, then decided she wouldn't. There would be just the four of them, she, Geoffrey and the Grahams. That way they'd get to know the Grahams better.

Geoffrey was in a filthy mood, she thought. But then that was nothing unusual nowadays. As for the Grahams, Sandy and Christina, they were perfectly charming.

'I do adore your house,' Christina declared across the table. 'If you don't mind I think I'll steal a few ideas for our place which as you're no doubt aware is being done up.'

'Please feel free,' Charlotte smiled back.

'This lamb is delicious,' Sandy commented. 'Your own?'

'No, bought from a neighbour. I'll give you his name and address before you leave.'

Sandy beamed.

Geoffrey glanced again at Christina, thinking how pretty she was. Ridiculous her married to that old buffoon. There again, Sandy Graham could still no doubt do what he couldn't. The thought of that was depressing in the extreme.

'Terrible trouble getting workmen with the war on,' Sandy said. 'It's quite a job I can tell you.'

Charlotte nodded her understanding.

'You were in the war I believe, Geoffrey,' Christina smiled.

He grunted.

'Invalided out.'

'I don't like to talk about it if you don't mind,' he replied gruffly.

'I understand.'

'Too old myself of course,' Sandy stated. 'Otherwise I'd have been over there as well.'

Geoffrey stared sourly at him. 'I doubt you'd have been so keen if you knew what it's really like.'

Charlotte shot him a warning look.

'Well, it's true.'

Christina changed the subject.

* * *

524

Charlotte was getting out of bed when a distraught Miss McQueen burst unannounced into her bedroom. Charlotte stared at her in astonishment.

'You'd better come, miss, right away. It's Mister Geoffrey. McPhie found him in the garage. He's . . . ' She broke off and took a deep breath.

'Oh, Miss Charlotte, he's hanged himself!'

29

RORY'S wife, standing at a window, suddenly became extremely agitated. Turning to the children who were in the room with her she seemed to snap out an order. Next moment they'd turned and fled leaving her alone.

What was going on? Nell wondered. And where was Rory? Why wasn't he present?

The wife stood stock still, as though waiting for something to happen, eyes wide with fear and anxiety.

And then that something did happen. The door was thrown open and five redcoats came rushing in. Four had muskets with bayonets attached.

The wife was questioned, that was clear, the questioner being some sort of officer. The wife kept shaking her head as she replied.

They were asking about Rory, Nell guessed. And she was right.

The officer's hand flashed, striking the wife on the cheek, spinning her away. The officer then appeared to bark out an order.

His men disappeared into the house, undoubtedly searching it. Nell's heart came into her mouth, fearing for the children.

The wife picked up a kitchen knife and came at the officer like a tiger, her face contorted. The officer quickly disarmed her and threw her contemptuously onto the floor where she lay stunned.

The officer was laughing as he began undoing his britches. When they'd dropped to the floor he squatted over the wife.

Oh dear God no, Nell thought, mesmerised by what she was witnessing. He was going to rape her.

The wife came round as her skirts were thrown up over her waist exposing the lower part of her body. Her mouth opened in a silent scream as the officer plunged into her.

Nell was transfixed with horror. She wasn't only witnessing a rape, but she herself being raped. It made her go icy cold all over.

One by one the other redcoats returned, all laughing at what was going on. When he was finished the officer stood up and gestured to the nearest soldier.

The man began unbuttoning his britches while the wife started trying to crawl away. She was soon stopped and turned onto her back, her skirts once more pulled up to her waist.

A third was enjoying himself when the vision began to fade.

★ ★ ★

'Read that scene to me again,' Jack instructed Hettie.

She did, while he listened intently. 'I think we'll change a couple of lines. The ones . . . '

When that had been done he sat back in his chair, going through the scene in his mind.

The two men involved were himself and Peter, though under different names. He could recall the original conversation with crystal clarity, though he had altered a few of the lines for what he considered better dramatic effect and to tighten it up a bit.

'What do you think?' he asked eventually.

'It seems good to me, Jack.'

'You wouldn't fib, would you?'

'No.'

He believed her.

Jack sighed. 'So many memories. It seems a lifetime away, yet on the other hand as if it was only yesterday.'

'It must have been terrible,' she murmured.

Jack removed his glasses and rubbed his eye sockets. 'Terrible isn't the word for it. It was more than that. Far more.'

Hettie glanced again over the words she'd written to his recent dictation and shuddered. Thank God she wasn't a man. Thank God she hadn't had to go through what they had in France and Belgium.

'It's finished,' Jack announced. 'That's the end.'

Hettie digested that. 'Now what?'

'We'll get the manuscript typed up. We'll have to go to Pitlochry for that — we can't have it done in Dalneil.'

'And then?'

He smiled wryly.

'We send it away and wait to see what happens.'

'You'll want a number of copies done.'

528

'Several I should think.' He suddenly laughed. 'You know, it must be a bit like having a baby. At least that's how I feel about it.'

'You still haven't given it a title,' she said.

'Oh I have. I just haven't mentioned it that's all. It's to be called 'The Long Night'.'

''The Long Night',' she mused.

'For that's what it was. Seeming darkness without end.'

'Oh, Jack,' she whispered.

''The Long Night',' he repeated.

★ ★ ★

'It's Mrs Graham,' Florence the maid announced to Charlotte, sitting by herself in the drawing room.

'Show her in.'

A few moments later Christina Graham entered the drawing room to smile sympathetically at Charlotte who'd risen to greet her.

'How kind of you to call.'

The two women shook hands.

'Please have a seat.'

She looked dreadful, Christina thought. But then what would you expect. 'I would have called before, but . . . well we hardly know one another and you probably wanted to be alone or with close friends.'

Charlotte closed her eyes for a second. 'It's been a difficult time.'

'I can well imagine. What a tragedy.'

'It was the war you know. He never recovered from it.' She paused, then said in a small voice,

'The man who came back wasn't the man who went away. He was entirely different.'

'Sandy and I just wanted you to know how much we feel for you in your grief, and of course if there's anything we can do just say.'

Charlotte smiled. 'That's kind of you.'

'Are you, eh . . . managing at the distillery?'

Charlotte considered that. 'I suppose so. Though most of the time my mind's in a fog. I seem to somehow muddle through the days. The workforce has been magnificent, they've rallied round wondrously.'

'That's excellent.'

'I've been very lucky in that respect. The minister too, the Reverend McLean, he's been to see me on a number of occasions. I've found great solace in his company. He has a soothing presence.'

'We like him also.'

'And my cousin Wonky's been a brick. A tower of strength.'

Christina nodded.

'It's just . . . ' Charlotte hesitated. 'So lonely with Geoffrey gone. It was like that when he was away, but now it's worse. Now I know for certain he won't be coming back. That he's gone for ever. In this lifetime anyway.'

'I'm so sorry,' Christina murmured.

Charlotte thought of Geoffrey and how it had been with him. Perhaps what had happened was all for the best. He'd been a tortured soul since coming back from France. Anguished in the extreme. But how she missed him. She still couldn't really believe he was dead.

'Will you take some tea or coffee?' she smiled.

'No thank you, I must be getting on.'

Pleasant woman, Charlotte thought. Someone who could become a good friend.

'Perhaps you'll come over to us one evening?' Christina suggested. 'We're still in a muddle but it would be lovely to have you if you could put up with that.'

'I'd be delighted,' Charlotte responded.

'Then let's set a date.'

★ ★ ★

'They've arrived, Jack,' Hettie stated, beaming broadly.

'Let me have them.'

She gave him the packet which he carefully opened. He dropped the wrapping paper by his side and clutched the six copies of his play. Slowly, and lovingly, he ran his fingers over the crisp paper of the title page of the top copy.

'Are you proud?'

'Of course I am, Hettie. Even if it isn't put on I feel I've achieved something. And that's thanks to you.'

She blushed.

'The next step is to send them to the managements we've agreed on. Will you do that today?'

'Of course.'

'Just let me keep holding them for a while though. I know it's daft but . . .'

'I fully understand, Jack,' she interjected softly.

It was the Jack of old, she thought. She didn't see his scars any more, or his blindness. It was just Jack Riach. A lump came into her throat.

He continued to run his fingers over the top copy, recalling the scenes the manuscript contained, remembering the dialogue, reliving the reality.

He started when he was suddenly kissed on the cheek.

'Hettie?'

'Well, it wasn't a bloody fairy.'

He laughed, then frowned. 'How can you bring yourself to do that? I mean, considering how I now look.'

'You look fine to me, Jack,' she replied, a choke in her voice, and abruptly left the room.

He went on stroking the top copy while he thought about that.

★ ★ ★

Charlotte stood staring at the spot where Geoffrey had been buried, her heart heavy with memories. Kneeling, she placed a bunch of flowers on the grave.

'Sleep easily, my darling, sleep easily,' she murmured.

'Am I interrupting?' a male voice queried.

She rose and turned to find John McLean standing behind her. 'Not really.'

'One never knows in these situations. Just say and I'll leave you alone.'

She shook her head. 'I'm pleased to see you.'

John gazed sorrowfully down at the grave. 'Pretty flowers.'

'From our own garden.'

John sighed. 'This war has an awful lot to answer for. I've often wondered what God's intention and purpose is. So many millions . . . why?'

'You tell me.'

He smiled. 'I may be a minister, Charlotte, but that doesn't mean I have all the answers. What I do have is faith, faith that there must be a reason behind it all. Not only this war but all wars. And life, the trials and tribulations we all have to go through.'

'How's Wonky?' she asked.

He pulled a face. 'Bearing up, though not finding it easy. We talk at times, she seems to enjoy that.'

Again he was struck by what a handsome, good-looking woman Charlotte was. Not presently at her best, but there again she'd only recently lost her husband.

'I wish you'd known Geoffrey before,' she said. 'You'd hardly have recognised him as the man we buried.'

'The war again,' John murmured.

'If I tell you something will it be in confidence? And I mean exactly that. Strictly between the two of us?'

John nodded.

'Geoffrey's wound was more than he ever let on to people. He . . . well he couldn't make love any more. That was something he could never come to terms with.'

'I see,' John breathed.

'He found it very difficult, as I'm sure you can well imagine.'

John thought of the situation. Being married to Charlotte and not being able to . . . Yes, that must have been excruciating.

'I could cope with the situation, but he never believed me. He simply felt he wasn't a man any longer and in the end couldn't live with that.'

She paused. 'You're the only person I've told this to. Not even Wonky. It was our secret, Geoffrey's and mine.'

Charlotte glanced down at the grave, remembering the first occasion she'd met Geoffrey. Who would have thought then that in such a few short years he and so many others would be dead. Her brother Peter for one, her father for another.

'Are you all right, Charlotte?'

She nodded.

'Perhaps I should walk you home? For company's sake if nothing else.'

How kind he was, she thought. A real gem.

'Let's go,' she said, and moved away from the graveside.

He fell into step beside her.

★ ★ ★

'Are you Scots, lassie? You sound it.'

Nell paused in her rebandaging. The soldier

534

was a Glasgow Highlander who'd been severely wounded.

'I am,' she replied.

He sighed. 'Where frae?'

'A little place called Dalneil in Perthshire.'

'Perthshire,' he breathed. 'I've never been there. Heard of it mind, but never been there. In fact I'd never been out of Glesca until I joined up. I'm Glesca through and through.'

'I like Glasgow, it has some fine shops.'

'Aye, and pubs too. Best pubs in the world I always thought.'

She laughed. 'Well I'm not an expert on pubs, though I am somewhat on whisky.'

He stared at her in amazement. 'Whisky! Get away, you're pulling my leg.'

'No, it's true. My family own a distillery. Ever heard of Drummond whisky?'

'Oh aye, I've drunk a few drams of that in my time. Good stuff.'

'Well I'm Nell Drummond.'

'Would you credit that!' Then, half joking, half serious, 'I don't suppose you'd have a few wee samples tucked away somewhere?'

'I'm afraid not.'

'Ah well,' he sighed. 'No harm in asking.'

He went on to tell her about his life in Glasgow where he'd worked as a coalman before the war. She found some of his anecdotes, the native Glasgow wit shining through, excruciatingly funny.

★ ★ ★

535

Hettie opened the large buff-coloured envelope to find a copy of Jack's play inside with an accompanying letter.

'Well?' he queried.

She perused the letter. 'It's from the Curzon Management, they've turned down the play.'

'Damn!' Jack muttered.

'Oh come on, you mustn't be downhearted, it's only your first reply after all. Your first refusal.'

'I know but . . . ' He trailed off.

'We've still the others to hear from. And even if they all turn it down there are other managements to approach.'

He smiled thinly. 'You're right of course.'

'It might be a case of try, try and try again until you eventually succeed. And succeed you will, I'm sure of it.'

'Oh, are you?' he replied drily.

'Yes I am. Call it female intuition if you like, but I'm certain in my heart of hearts it'll be put on.'

'Come here.'

She approached to stand beside him.

'Give me your hand.'

She did.

'You're priceless, Hettie Campbell. Absolutely priceless. Whatever man lands you is going to be very lucky indeed.'

'Is that a fact?'

'It is. Take it from me.'

She hesitated in saying what she did next, but said it nonetheless. 'And what about you, Jack? What about the woman who gets you?'

He laughed scornfully. 'Me! The state I'm in? No right-minded female would ever take me on now.'

'Maybe you'd be surprised.'

Jack shook his head. 'I doubt it. Very much so. In fact I know so.'

'Do you now?'

'Oh yes,' he replied softly.

'I'll make your morning coffee,' she said, and left him.

* * *

Charlotte stared out of the window, listening to the repeated cracks of thunder and watching the lightning that was zig-zagging across the sky in spectacular fashion. Torrential rain was sheeting down.

It was as though God was making a statement, she reflected. But on what? The war perhaps, humankind in general. Who knew?

How tired she was, absolutely drained. There was so much work at the distillery it was wearing her out. If only she could take a break, go on holiday. But of course that was impossible. There was no one to take her place if she went away.

She started when a particularly loud peal of thunder boomed, or so it seemed anyway, almost directly overhead.

'Oh, Pa,' she whispered. 'I wish you were here to help me.'

* * *

Charlotte had been surprised to find John McLean at the Grahams when she'd arrived, then realised he'd been invited to make up the numbers. There were only to be the four of them.

'As I said to you before we're still in a bit of a muddle,' Christina apologised to Charlotte across the dinner table. 'There's still a great deal to be done.'

Charlotte was enjoying herself, the company excellent. 'And decent workmen hard to come by at present,' Charlotte smiled back.

'*Any* workmen,' Sandy chipped in.

John was trying not to stare too often or too directly at Charlotte. She quite fascinated him. And how elegant she looked in her pale green silk gown with a deep cut, V neckline, this line enhanced by loose, short sleeves.

'You owned a factory I understand, Sandy,' John said.

Sandy nodded. 'Sold it due to ill health. That's why we came to the country, for the quiet life. Suits me down to the ground. I'm not so sure about Christina though. Eh, my dear?'

'Oh I enjoy it well enough. I must admit it takes a little getting used to after Perth, but I feel I'm settling in all right.'

'You mean the country's boring?' Charlotte teased.

'I wouldn't say that, just different. I'm sure I'll find lots to do when I'm settled completely in.'

'There's always the church,' John said. 'We're forever needing people to help out.'

'I'll remember that,' Christina replied, thinking the church was the last thing she wanted to get involved with. They'd go to Sunday service of course, but that was it as far as she was concerned.

Christina glanced sideways at her husband. A sweet man if ever there was, but hardly the most exciting. Still, she'd known what she was getting into. And he'd been well aware of what he was getting in return.

'Tell me about your family, Charlotte,' Sandy requested. 'I believe you lost your father and brother some while back.'

'That's right.' She then recounted the story of Peter's death and how her father had suffered a massive heart attack on learning about it.

Sandy shook his head. 'Very sad indeed.'

'I miss them both dreadfully. We were a lively house before the war, now I'm all on my own until my sister returns from France where she's serving as a VAD.'

'Don't you have a brother left?' John enquired.

'That's correct. Andrew, he's over in Ireland with the army.'

Christina went very still. It couldn't be. Surely not! But the name Andrew Drummond, and he in the army. Just a coincidence, surely?

'Army?' she smiled.

'In Ireland.'

Christina frantically trawled through her memory. 'Which regiment is he with?'

Charlotte told her.

Christina breathed an inward sigh of relief. It wasn't the same man.

'But he used to be with the Black Watch.'

Christina couldn't believe it. 'The Black Watch,' she repeated dully.

'The same regiment my elder brother Peter was in when killed. They're normally based in Perth as you probably well know.'

'Yes,' Christina whispered huskily.

'I say, are you all right?' John queried anxiously. 'You've gone very pale.'

Christina gave him a thin smile. 'I came over all strange there for a moment.' She laughed. 'Probably someone walking over my grave.'

She suddenly realised what she'd said and focused on Charlotte. 'Oh I am sorry. That was tactless when we've just been talking about your father and brother.'

'No offence taken, I assure you. It's a common enough expression. I use it myself.'

It had been a splendid evening, Charlotte reflected later when she was home again. It had bucked her up no end.

★ ★ ★

Sandy Graham came awake to find Christina sitting up in bed worrying at a nail.

'Christina?'

'Go back to sleep, Sandy.'

He rolled onto an elbow. 'Can't you sleep yourself?'

'A bit of indigestion, that's all,' she lied. 'The pudding was rather rich.'

He grunted in acknowledgement; the pudding had been rich. 'No more funny turns?'

'None. It's simply indigestion. Now go back to sleep.'

'If you insist, my dear.'

'I do.'

He yawned.

Christina continued worrying at her nail.

★ ★ ★

'It's another rejection I'm afraid,' Hettie said to Jack.

'Bugger!' he swore.

She smiled in sympathy.

'So much for your female intuition,' he declared.

'It's only the third. You must be patient.'

'I suppose so,' he replied.

'And in the meantime, why not start something else? Another play perhaps?'

He considered that. 'It's an idea.'

'It'll keep your mind occupied, stop you moping.'

'Oh, I mope do I!' he retorted sarcastically.

'You know you do.'

'I know nothing of the sort.'

She sighed. 'Jack Riach, you're a bloody liar. And if you want to sack me for saying that then go ahead.'

Alarm filled him. 'I don't want to sack you, Hettie. Not now, not ever.'

She stared at him. Remembering how it had once been between them, and how it was now all so terribly changed. A softness and warmth engulfed her.

'Would you like to go to bed?' she queried.

He drew in a sharp breath. 'I beg your pardon?'

'You heard me.'

'Bed,' he repeated, a catch in his voice.

'That's what I said.'

He shook his head. 'I won't have your pity, Hettie. Anything but that.'

She went to him and gently stroked his cheek. 'I didn't offer through pity, Jack. You have my word on that.'

'Then why?'

'Because I'd like to.'

'But look at me!' he cried. 'My face is awful and I'm blind.'

'They don't matter to me, Jack. I swear.'

He swallowed hard. 'No?'

'No,' she repeated emphatically.

He took her hand in his and squeezed it. 'I never thought I'd be with a woman ever again, Hettie. I believed that was all over for me.'

'Then you were wrong.'

'Oh, Hettie,' he breathed. 'Are you sure?'

'Yes. I still fancy you, Jack, as I've always done. You still excite me.'

He tried to digest that, finding it amazing. 'We had some good times you and I.'

'And there's nothing to stop us having more. You talk about pity, well you should stop pitying yourself. Now what about it?'

He rose. 'It's been so long.'

'Don't worry. I'll go easy on you.'

He laughed. 'Will you indeed?'

542

'Unless that's unnecessary.'
In the event, it was.

★ ★ ★

Charlotte was at her desk when the church bells suddenly started ringing. She frowned. It was a Monday, not Sunday. So why on earth was it ringing?

And then the office door crashed open and a wild-eyed Isobel flew in.

'Oh, miss!' she gasped. 'Oh, miss. The war's over!'

30

WONKY was in the kitchen helping her mother prepare lunch when their maid Heather appeared. 'Miss Comyn, there's someone at the door to see you.'

'Oh!' Wonky picked up a teatowel and began drying her hands, having been peeling potatoes.

'A Mister . . . ' Heather struggled, trying to correctly remember the strange sounding name. 'Kuzinsky?'

For Wonky it was as though the world had suddenly stopped turning. She came over all faint. 'Kutchinsky?'

'That's it, miss. He has a foreign accent.'

Moira Comyn glanced at her daughter. 'Who on earth is that?'

Wonky had to hold onto the edge of the sink to stop herself from falling over. 'Someone I met in France.'

'Then don't keep him waiting, dear. Manners.'

Moira wondered why someone from France should be calling on Veronica. Another place for lunch she thought. Luckily they had enough in.

Wonky laid the teatowel aside and slowly took off her pinny. She couldn't believe this was happening. Dale in Dalneil!

He smiled wryly at her as she approached him down the hall. 'Hello, Wonky,' he said.

'Hello, Dale. This is a surprise.'

'Not a nasty one I hope?'

She shook her head. 'You'd better come in.'

'Thank you.'

He removed his hat which she took from him and placed on the hallstand. Then his coat when he removed that.

'It sure is beautiful countryside,' he declared.

'We like to think so.'

'Unlike anything I've ever seen before.'

She was so filled with emotion she thought she might burst. Dale, here! It was incredible.

'Come on through,' she said, and led the way.

'This is a bit of a shock,' she declared when they'd both sat facing one another.

'I considered writing, and then . . . ' He broke off and shrugged. 'To be truthful I wasn't sure I'd have the nerve to knock when I arrived here. Or even if I'd have the guts to arrive at all.'

She nodded. 'I understand.'

'Do you?'

She glanced away. 'So, how have you been?'

'Fine. As you can see I survived the war intact. Though I must admit there were a few times when it was touch and go. I got blown up once but walked away. That sure was my lucky day.'

How good it was to see him, she thought. She suddenly felt alive for the first time in a long while. It was like . . . well being reborn Or walking out of a dark room into the light.

'And how are you?' he asked.

She shrugged. 'Managing I suppose.'

'Just that?'

'I have duties at home which keep me occupied.'

'Oh?'

'My father had a stroke which is why I had to come home. He needs constant care and attention.'

'I see.'

No you don't! a voice screamed inside her head. You don't at all.

'Where are you staying?' she heard herself ask.

'At the local tavern. They've fixed me up with a room as long as I want one.'

'And how long will that be for?'

He regarded her steadily, his expression quizzical. 'That depends entirely.'

'On what?'

He didn't reply.

Wonky rose. 'I'm being rude. I haven't offered you anything. Would you care for coffee or tea? We also have whisky in the house if you'd like.'

'Whisky would be just great,' he smiled, hoping his nervousness wasn't showing. He wondered what she'd think if she knew he'd stood a full five minutes outside before summoning up the courage to knock.

'Right,' she declared, and hurried from the room.

He glanced about him. He'd often wondered about where she lived. Now he knew, and wasn't all that impressed. Dreary was the word that came to mind. Dreary and dull.

Wonky returned with the dram and a small jug

of water. 'No soda I'm afraid,' she apologised.

'That's just dandy,' he replied, accepting both dram and jug.

Wonky sat again, gazing at him as though he was a genie who'd just popped out a bottle.

'Your father had a stroke?' he said.

'That's right. And a bad one.'

'I'm sorry to hear that.'

He sipped his whisky and water. Things between them were suddenly difficult, strained.

'You'll stay for lunch of course?'

He waved a hand. 'I wouldn't impose.'

'But you must.'

He had another sip of whisky. 'I came to ask a question,' he stated.

She glanced away again, waiting.

'Why?'

'Why what?'

'I thought you and I had something together. I thought . . . ' He broke off. 'Well no matter. The question is still why?'

'I didn't answer your letters?'

He nodded.

Wonky closed her eyes, remembering their journeys together in the ambulance travelling to and from the CCS. How intimate it had become between them. Of course he was due an explanation. Especially now as he'd come all the way to Dalneil to see her.

'I thought it best,' she stated simply.

'Best?'

She was about to reply when her mother breezed into the room.

'Hello,' Moira smiled at Dale.

Wonky could have killed her.

★ ★ ★

Hours had gone by. Lunch had been taken after which Wonky had dealt with her father. Now she had a little time to herself again.

'Shall we go for a walk?' she asked Dale.

'That would be pleasant.'

'You won't be long I hope?' Moira queried, frowning at the clock.

'No,' Wonky replied with a forced smile.

'In case . . . Well you know.'

Wonky sighed. She knew only too well. 'We won't be long,' she repeated, and ushered Dale from the house.

'Do I get the correct impression you ain't exactly the happiest of bunnies?' he queried when they were outside and alone.

She thought his phraseology amusing, though hardly the content. 'No,' she replied softly.

'When you broke off contact I imagined you must have met someone else.'

She rounded on him. 'There wasn't, and isn't, anyone else, Dale. I swear.'

'Then why the silence?'

They walked a good ten yards before she replied. 'You're an American, I'm Scots. We met under unusual circumstances. We were forced to part, so why continue the pain by writing. You'll go back to Albany and start practising while I'm stuck here nursing my father. You'll no doubt meet an Albany girl and marry. It all seemed very clear to me when I thought it through.'

'So there isn't anyone else?'

'I just said so, didn't I?'

He sighed. 'You're a fool, Wonky Comyn.'

'I'm nothing of the sort.'

He suddenly stopped and took her into his arms. 'It wasn't until after we parted that I realised just how much I'd come to love you and by then it was too late.'

She gulped. Love!

'Wonky?'

'Do you still?'

'No,' he replied drily. 'I only came to Dalneil for the experience.'

She laughed.

'I was a prize fool too. I should have cottoned on earlier.'

'Oh, Dale!' she whispered.

'So what about it?'

Wonky frowned. 'So what about what?'

'Marrying me.'

Tears misted her eyes. 'If only I could, Dale. If only I could.'

★ ★ ★

'Marry you!' Nell exclaimed. 'How wonderful.'

Wonky shook her head in misery. 'How can I marry him? I have my duties at home, my responsibilities. There's Ma and Father to consider.'

'But surely they'd understand?'

'Marrying Dale means going to America, Nell. Who would look after Father if I wasn't there.

549

Ma isn't capable, or refuses to be. So it's down to me.'

'Oh, Wonky,' Nell breathed in sympathy, wishing Charlotte was there to give advice, but her sister was at work.

'I've told him I need time to think about it. Which is a lie, I suppose. My answer is a foregone conclusion.'

'Do you love him?'

Wonky nodded.

'And he loves you obviously.'

'So he said.'

They stared at one another in grim silence.

'I never had any luck with men,' Wonky said tremulously. 'But this takes the biscuit.'

'It's certainly a poser and that's a fact,' Nell declared.

Wonky nodded her agreement.

'Have you spoken to the minister about this?'

Wonky stared blankly at Nell. 'You mean John?'

'Of course. Charlotte says he's very wise for his age and might give you good counsel. If I was you I'd have a word with him.'

Wonky considered that. It was a thought.

She rose. 'I'd better get back and see to Father. He can't be left unattended for too long.'

'I wish I'd been more help,' Nell stated at the door.

Wonky kissed her cousin on the cheek and hurried off.

★ ★ ★

What to do? Dale wondered, sitting on the chair his room at the pub provided. It sure was a problem. And a problem he couldn't, for the time being anyway, see any way round.

Wonky was committed to her parents, that was obvious. And he admired her for that. But it sure as hell made things difficult for the pair of them.

Was it possible for him to stay on in Dalneil, make a living there? He couldn't see how. He was trained as a lawyer and wanted to practise as one. Nor could he practise law in Scotland, that was a whole different system. No, it had to be the States.

Wonky. His heart beat faster just thinking about her. She was the woman he wanted in life, to be his wife, the mother of his children. And yet it seemed, even though she was willing, that was to be denied him.

He swore.

★ ★ ★

John McLean exhaled slowly. 'You are in a bind, aren't you.'

Wonky nodded.

He thought about what she'd told him. 'Time,' he said.

'I beg your pardon?'

'Your father, time. Will Dale wait for you?'

She considered that. 'You mean . . . ?'

John nodded.

'I don't know.'

'I don't see any other way round it. Unless of course you just shrug off your responsibilities and go to America.'

'I couldn't do that,' Wonky replied in a small voice. 'I simply wouldn't be able to live with myself. It would ruin the relationship between Dale and myself.'

John nodded his approval. 'You're a good woman, Wonky. And often that, as being a good man, is hard to be.'

'I want to sleep at nights,' she said. 'At ease with myself and conscience.'

She was far more intelligent than he'd first given her credit for, he decided. 'Then perhaps you must take a chance,' he declared.

'Take a chance?'

'That your Dale might not find someone else in the meantime.'

Would he? she wondered. He was an attractive man after all, and wealthy she knew from certain things he'd let drop. In other words a catch. No doubt when he returned to Albany the available ladies would swarm round him like bees round a honeypot.

'I'm sorry, but I can't think of anything else to say,' John smiled.

What a risk, she thought. But how could she possibly leave her mother alone to look after her father. That, no matter how hard, was out of the question. She was her father's child, brought up in the faith, and it went deep. Deeper than she'd ever previously realised.

They both glanced round when Moira entered

the room. 'Your father needs you,' Moira stated to Wonky.

Wonky dutifully rose and went upstairs.

★ ★ ★

Rory stood staring aghast at the smoking ruins of what had once been his home. He unleashed his broadsword and broke into a loping run.

Nell's heart was in her mouth as she watched, his expression terrible to see.

Rory found his wife first, butchered worse than any animal in an abattoir. He dropped his broadsword and sank onto his knees beside the blackened corpse. Face awash with tears he lifted the body and held it tight against his chest. He then began rocking to and fro. Although she couldn't hear, Nell was certain he was keening his grief.

That was her there, she thought, filled with cold horror. Raped and then brutally, savagely murdered. She felt sick inside.

After a while Rory laid his wife down again, then went in search of his children. He eventually discovered them in what remained of a byre, also dead, burnt beyond recognition.

Nell felt vomit crowding her throat as she continued to witness the vision. Those were her children, the flesh of her own flesh and Rory's. Young lives wiped out.

Rory collapsed, prostrate over the girl, shoulders heaving.

Thank God, thank merciful God, the vision began to fade.

When it had finally gone Nell wept for hours.

'Well?' Dale demanded softly.

Wonky considered them the hardest words she'd ever had to utter. 'I can't,' she whispered.

'You'd have a wonderful life, want for nothing. I promise you that.'

'I know, Dale.'

'And you still won't come with me?'

She wanted to, oh how she wanted to. To be Mrs Dale Kutchinsky. 'It's just not to be,' she replied.

'Surely your mother can make some accommodation. Realise the situation you're in?'

Wonky took a deep breath. 'Ma flatly refuses to deal with Father. She'll talk to him all right, be with him. But when it comes to the nursing side she swears she can't. How can I possibly leave her in a situation like that?'

He knew then it was useless. 'I understand,' he sighed.

'I spoke to the minister about us,' she said.

'And?'

'He said time.'

'Time?'

'Father won't last forever, then I'd be free. It would then be a case of whether or not you were still free and wanted me.'

'I see,' he murmured.

'What do you think?'

He wasn't at all certain. He loved Wonky, there was no doubt about that. But how long did love last? Her father could linger for years and who was to say what would happen in the meantime.

'I honestly don't know,' he replied.

Her heart sank. But hadn't that been the answer she'd been expecting?

'When will you leave?' she asked.

He couldn't look her straight in the face, his insides churning. 'As soon as possible I guess. A few days in London and then passage home.'

'Oh, Dale!' she choked.

He turned and abruptly left the room, collecting his coat from the hallway.

Outside he stood and stared at the manse, believing he'd never see it or Wonky again.

★ ★ ★

Charlotte and Nell stared at their cousin in consternation. 'He's gone then,' Nell said.

Wonky nodded. 'The only man I'll ever love.'

'You can't be certain of that,' Charlotte declared.

'I am. Totally and utterly.'

Charlotte went to Wonky and took her into her arms. 'There there,' she murmured.

Wonky began to shake with grief. 'I love him so, Charlotte. With all my heart and soul.'

'Would you like me to have a word with Aunt Moira? See if I can't talk some sense into her?'

'It's no use. Both she and Father think it's my duty to be doing what I am. And so do I. The dutiful daughter and what have you.'

How unfair life was, Charlotte reflected, thinking of Geoffrey. Now this and Wonky. When would it ever end? Never was the answer. That was simply the way it was.

'I'm going to miss him so much,' Wonky sobbed.

Nell wrung her hands, wishing there was something she could say which would help. But nothing came to mind.

'How about a nice cup of tea?' Charlotte suggested. 'And possibly cake if Mrs Clark has been baking.'

'Please,' Wonky murmured in reply.

Nell hurried off.

★ ★ ★

Hettie's good mood vanished the moment she saw Jack's face. 'What's wrong?' she queried.

He shrugged.

'Come on, what is it?'

'It just seems all . . . so pointless.'

Hettie sighed, and sat facing him. 'You're having trouble with the new play, I appreciate that. But it isn't the end of the world.'

He laughed softly. How true that was. The end of the world was in Ypres, or the Somme, or going back to the Marne. "The Long Night' has been rejected by everybody,' he stated.

'That's true enough.'

'So why go on with this pretence that maybe

556

I can write? Obviously I can't.'

She wasn't sure what to reply to that. 'So are you just going to give up? That doesn't sound like the Jack Riach I used to know.'

'I'm not the Jack Riach you used to know. I'm a different man entirely.'

'Are you now?' she replied caustically.

'You know damned well I am.'

'I know nothing of the sort. Of course you've changed, you've been through a war which is something I can only try and imagine. You've been blinded and had your pretty face damaged. But does that really make you all that different?'

He stared hard in the direction of her voice.

She smiled. 'And apart from anything else you're still wonderful in bed. That hasn't been taken away from you, so be thankful.'

He shook his head. 'What is it about you, Hettie? You always know when to say the right thing to cheer a chap up.'

Her smile widened. 'I suppose you're now going to suggest we go upstairs?'

'It's a thought.'

'Well not before you've earned it. The new play needs working on which is precisely what you're going to do.'

'Bully,' he retorted good humouredly.

★ ★ ★

Wonky ran the sponge over her father's back, then his buttocks. How she hated doing this, positively loathed it. It had been different in

557

France where the men had been strangers, but to be so intimate with her own father.

Tom's eyes were shut as usual while Wonky did these ministrations, he reflecting, for the umpteenth time, that life had indeed come to a sorry pass when your own daughter had to wash your backside.

He began thinking of his courting days. What a happy, glorious time that had been.

Moira had been a tremendous catch, a Drummond and all that went with the name. Not that there had been all that much money, though there had been some. It was the prestige of marrying into a family so well placed in the area.

He hadn't married her just for that of course. Oh no, he'd been genuinely in love with her, and she with him. A match made in Heaven for which he'd be eternally grateful.

Moira, he recalled her as she'd been on their wedding day. A fine figure of a lass. She'd put on weight since then, a lot of it actually. But that had never mattered to him. She was still his Moira, his beloved.

'I'm going to move you over now, Father,' Wonky declared.

He continued keeping his eyes shut and day dreaming of times past.

★ ★ ★

Dale stood on a deck of the S.S. *Paul Jones* watching the English shoreline gradually diminish in the distance. London had been fun, but how much better it would have been if Wonky had been with him.

Wonky.

He shook his head in despair. What a waste for the pair of them. She shackled to her bedridden father, he . . . Well he with a life to get on with. A life he'd wanted Wonky to share and which she never would.

It was best to try and put her out of his mind, he thought. Forget her. There would only be ongoing pain if he didn't.

Wonky.

England finally slipped from view and all that could be seen was green rolling sea.

Turning from the rail he headed for the nearest bar, of which there were four on the liner.

All four of which he came to know well before eventually disembarking in New York.

★ ★ ★

Charlotte was dozing in a chair after another long, hard day at the distillery, when John McLean was ushered in.

'Oh, I'm sorry, am I disturbing you?' he queried.

She buried a yawn behind a hand and sat up straight. 'Not at all, John. I must have dropped off.'

'I can come again if you wish?'

She shook her head. 'I'm delighted to see you. Some company will be most pleasurable.'

'Well, if you're sure.'

She waved a hand at the nearest chair. 'Go and sit down. Now what can I do for you?'

She looked pale and drawn he thought. And there were black smudges under her eyes. Perhaps he shouldn't make his request. It would appear she already had enough on her plate.

'I don't know about you,' she declared, standing. 'But I could use a drink.'

'Wonderful idea,' he smiled.

'How is everyone at the Comyns?'

'The same as usual,' he sighed. 'I've done my best to jolly up Wonky to no avail.'

'Yes, that was very sad. Has she heard from Dale?'

'Not that I know of. Nor if she's written to him. She hasn't said.'

'A dram?'

'Please.'

Charlotte handed him his drink and sat down again, thinking how much she always enjoyed John's company. He was very relaxing to be with.

'I was wondering . . . ' He paused and took a deep breath. 'You mustn't feel obliged about this. But I was wondering if you'd consider reading the lesson from time to time.'

'A woman?'

He laughed at her incredulity. 'I know it's always been the province of a man, but why not?'

Why not indeed, she thought.

'Please don't feel the necessity to give me an answer now. Take a while to think about it if you wish.'

She was about to reply when another male figure strode into the room.

'Hello, sis,' smiled Andrew. 'I'm home for good. Resigned my commission and all that. Back to take over the reins.'

31

'WE haven't had much luck of late you and I,' Andrew said later when John had left. The pair of them were now alone, Nell having earlier gone visiting before his arrival. 'I lost my Alice, you Geoffrey.'

'No,' Charlotte agreed softly.

'Well I'm going to make a go of it. If you don't mind that is. I mean, after all, you've been running the show for a while now. You'll have to teach me of course. I know sod all about the business. But I will be an eager pupil.'

She regarded him steadily. 'I take it you've given up the idea of selling then?'

He nodded. 'That's right.' He thought of Alice, it would all have been so terribly different if she was still alive and they'd married. But she was dead, her inheritance lost to him, so getting involved in the distillery, and eventually taking it over himself when he'd learnt the ropes, seemed the obvious thing to do.

Relief welled through Charlotte. It had been an ongoing anxiety that Andrew, as was his right after all, might sell.

'I'm pleased,' she stated.

'The army was fine and well in the circumstances, second son and all that, but now Peter and Pa have gone it changes things entirely. Also I would have had to wait years for promotion, so many chaps having been promoted over my head because of the war, that it was senseless to stay on.'

She nodded her understanding.

'So here I am. Raring and eager to go.'

'You can start Monday,' she declared quietly. 'At Peter's old desk, the one where . . . ' She broke off.

'Geoffrey sat?'

'Yes.'

'Then Monday it is.'

★ ★ ★

'What do you think?' Jack demanded, Hettie having just read aloud the latest version of his new play.

She stared at him in consternation. 'It lacks something in my opinion, Jack. Don't ask me what, I don't know. But I do feel it lacks something.'

Which bore out his own doubts. His shoulders sagged. It had been a lovely dream, a wonderful idea, but it seemed he just wasn't cut out to be a writer.

'You mustn't give up, Jack. That would be awful.'

'I don't believe in wasting time, Hettie,' he replied sharply. 'My own or anyone else's. I'm just going to forget it. The whole damn thing.'

'Oh, Jack!' she whispered.

'And don't try to argue me out of it. I

can't write worth tuppence and you know it.'

'I know nothing of the sort!' she retorted. 'I thought 'The Long Night' was a smashing play. It really gripped me.'

'Well it didn't grip any of the managements we sent it to. They were most unimpressed.'

'More fool them!' she riposted.

Jack suddenly smiled. 'What an ego booster you are, Hettie. A veritable light in the darkness. God knows what I'd do without you.'

That touched her deeply. 'I'm only telling the truth as I see it, Jack.'

He crooked a finger. 'Come here.'

He reached out a hand when she stood beside him. 'Give me a kiss, wench. I want to taste you.'

'Taste me, is it? What are you, a cannibal?'

Jack laughed. 'I could be where you're concerned. Eat you up each and every day.'

'Indeed.'

'Indeed,' he repeated.

She bent and kissed him lightly on the lips. 'There.'

'That's no good!' he protested.

'Well, it's all you're going to get for now.' And with that she removed her hand and moved away.

'You're becoming more of a tyrant with every passing month, Hettie Campbell.'

And he more adorable, she thought. Their lives had become so intertwined. They might have been a plaited piece of string.

'What are you thinking?' he asked.

'About lunch.'

'Liar!'

'I am not.'

'Whatever, you weren't thinking about lunch. And don't ask me how I know. I just do.'

'Shall we go through the play again?' she queried softly. 'See if you can somehow improve it.'

He shook his head. 'It's a dead duck, Hettie. Chuck it on the fire.'

'I will not.'

'You'll do as you're told,' he replied, pretending anger. A pretence she saw straight through.

There was a few seconds silence between them, then, simultaneously they both broke out laughing.

★ ★ ★

'I'd like to invite a couple to dinner this Saturday,' Charlotte announced to Andrew across the office.

He glanced up. 'Who?'

'You don't know them. They're called the Grahams and are new hereabouts. He's a lot older than she is which has caused some comment, believe me. I like them both.'

Andrew shrugged. 'Suit yourself.'

'Good. I'll have McPhie deliver an invitation.'

Andrew went back to the work in hand, thinking how much easier this all was than he'd expected. He had a tremendous amount to learn about the actual whisky making of course, but the men were being most helpful in tutoring him.

He was also enjoying himself which was a surprise.

★ ★ ★

Sandy Graham read the handwritten note. 'It's an invitation from Charlotte Drummond to dinner this Saturday. How kind. We'll naturally accept.'

Christina went cold all over.

'As you know, her brother Andrew is back from Ireland. It'll be interesting meeting him.'

A true gentleman or not? Christina wondered. She was about to find out.

Pray God he was.

★ ★ ★

'Christina, how are you!' Charlotte exclaimed as the Grahams were shown in. Crossing to Christina she kissed her on the cheek while Sandy beamed on.

Andrew, who'd come to his feet the moment the Grahams appeared, was frowning. This Christina Graham was familiar, but from where if she was new in Dalneil? Certainly far younger than her husband, no wonder it had caused so much comment.

Charlotte made the introductions. 'Delighted to meet you,' Andrew declared, shaking her by the hand.

'And I you, Mr Drummond.'

566

He gazed into her eyes and in that moment it clicked. Tina from Mulligan's, by all that was holy!

* * *

'So what did you think of them?' Charlotte asked Andrew after the Grahams had gone.

'Charming.'

'I'm pleased you like them. I believe Christina and I could become extremely good friends in time. We have an empathy together.'

Andrew smiled inwardly. If only you knew, sis.

If only you knew.

* * *

'I'm so nervous,' Charlotte stated. She, Andrew and Nell were on the way to church in the Rolls.

'You'll be fine,' Andrew assured her, patting her hand.

'A woman has never read in our church before.'

'Well, it's high time one did!' Nell retorted fiercely. 'It doesn't say anywhere in the Bible that only men should read the lesson after all.'

Andrew gave a soft laugh. 'The war certainly changed you, Nell. And I approve.'

'Do you?'

'Oh yes. You have my word on that.'

Charlotte wrung her hands, noting they were sweating. This was turning out to be far more of an ordeal than she'd anticipated. She could just imagine some of those old Presbyterian eyes gazing disapprovingly at her while she stood at the lectern.

Well, she wouldn't let them put her off, she decided. She was a Drummond after all. A pillar of the community even if she was a woman.

She swallowed hard as the Rolls drew up outside the church.

★ ★ ★

Charlotte was in the middle of her reading, and an excellent job she was doing of it too, when Andrew caught Tina's eye. Still as good looking as ever, he thought. More so. The years, and a more expensive, tasteful, grooming had improved her.

He began reminiscing, remembering how it had been between them. How good she'd been in bed. The tricks she'd taught him.

As though realising what was going through Andrew's mind Tina, or Christina as she now called herself, blushed bright red and stared fixedly at her clenched hands.

★ ★ ★

'I came round to repeat how splendidly you read today,' John McLean declared to Charlotte.

'Why thank you. You're very kind.'

'There's nothing kind about it. I mean what I say.'

'And the reaction from the congregation?'

He chuckled. 'There were a few mutterings I must admit. But mutterings to be disregarded as far as I'm concerned. The world moves on, and we must move with it.'

She agreed with that. 'Can I get you something?'

He shook his head. 'Not for the present, thank you. I have other calls to make and certainly mustn't make them smelling of alcohol. As for tea and coffee, I get plied with them all the time to the point where I sometimes wish I'd never see either again.'

She laughed. 'I never thought of that.'

'It's quite a hazard I can tell you. There are occasions when I'm so full of liquid I think I must explode.'

Charlotte waved him to a seat. 'I was very nervous. I hope it didn't show.'

'Not in the least. In fact you came across as most composed.'

What a relief. Despite Nell and Andrew's assurances she hadn't been totally convinced. Now she was.

'May I ask you a personal question? In my capacity as minister that is.'

'Of course.'

'Have you come to terms with your husband's death? Or let me rephrase that, are you coming to terms with it? These things take time you know.'

Charlotte considered that. 'I believe I am. It was a tremendous shock and loss you understand. And a certain sense of guilt.'

'Guilt?'

She looked down into her lap. 'That perhaps I could have done more than I did. Been more understanding in some way. Prevented from happening what did.'

'That's a perfectly normal reaction, Charlotte, I promise you. The bereaved often feel guilty, it's very common.'

She glanced up at him, her expression tortured. 'But he committed suicide, John, that's the difference between me and others. My husband killed himself.'

John sighed. 'I didn't know Geoffrey all that well, but he struck me as someone who knew his own mind. Although I heartily disapprove, though cast no judgement, I'm sure he decided to die because the burden he was carrying was simply too hard to bear. It can't have been easy after all, in fact it must have been intolerable. You're a beautiful woman, Charlotte, and Geoffrey was very much in love with you. Not being able to fulfil his natural desires, and I understand the desires remain even though the body is incapable, must have been terrible for him.'

'Yes,' Charlotte agreed softly.

'You weren't harsh in any way, I take it?'

'No, John, not in the least. I was quite prepared to . . . put up with things as they'd become.'

'Then there shouldn't be any guilt on your part. None at all.'

She found great solace in those words. 'Thank you, John. I appreciate that.'

'If I may give some advice?'

'Naturally.'

'You should try and get out and about more. That would surely help.'

She smiled thinly. 'I might if I had the energy. My work at the distillery takes it out of me. I get so tired nowadays that all I want to do is sleep when I get home.'

'But now you have Andrew to assist that must remove some of the burden from your shoulders?'

'That's true. He's impressing me no end by how fast he's learning. He hasn't been with me that long and already I feel the difference.'

'There then,' John beamed.

He paused, then said slowly, 'Talking of getting out and about. We're having a whist drive in the church hall next Friday evening. The usual light refreshments afterwards. Would you care to attend as my guest?'

Why not, she thought. Why ever not. 'Yes, I'd like that.'

'It'll be a change if nothing else,' he smiled.

★ ★ ★

'What's wrong with you lately?' Sandy Graham queried of Christina. 'You're all of a twitter. Not your usual self.'

Oh dear, she thought. Had it been that obvious? She hadn't been aware.

'Well, darling?'

'I suppose it's just the worry of getting the house finished,' she lied. 'That and . . . well, ladies' things.'

'Oh, I see!'

She went to him and kissed him on the cheek. 'Sorry if I've been a bore or difficult.'

'You could never be either, Christina. If anyone's going to be a bore it's bound to be me.'

'That you're not, Sandy, nor ever will be. You're the most wonderful and entertaining of husbands.'

'Perhaps a holiday?' he suggested. 'We could go away for a few weeks.'

She was tempted, but decided against it. She wouldn't rest easy until she'd spoken to Andrew Drummond. The question was, how did she get to speak alone with him?

'Wait till later when everything's completed here. That'll be the time for us to go away.'

She was right of course, he thought. 'Then that's what we'll do.'

He was such a dear man, she reflected. If it became common knowledge that she'd been what she had, it would hurt him dreadfully. That was why they'd chosen Dalneil, thinking there couldn't possibly be anyone here who'd know of her past. And then Andrew Drummond had turned up.

It was excruciatingly bad luck.

* * *

How alone she felt nowadays, Nell mused, gazing out over the garden from the bench on which she was sitting. She had Charlotte and Andrew to keep her company, but most of

572

the time they were at the distillery.

She smiled, remembering France. She'd never been alone there. There had always been something to do, someone to chat to. Coming home was like walking out of a whirlwind into a dead calm.

France, how exciting that had been, though terrible at the same time. How she missed it.

She must write to some of the others she decided. Rebecca Levi for one, Hope Langton for another. Find out how they were doing.

Were they finding readjusting as difficult as she, she wondered, rising and going back into the house.

★ ★ ★

'OK, kiddo, tell me all about it?'

Dale focused on his mom, having been lost in thought. 'About what?'

'Whatever's troubling you. And something certainly is. I'm your mother don't forget. I know you inside out.'

Dale gave a small smile. 'I'd forgotten that.'

'Is it the war?'

Dale sighed. 'Partly, Mom.'

'Something happened, didn't it?'

'Lots of things happened, Mom. Things I never wish to speak about.'

She nodded her understanding. 'But I take it there was something in particular?'

'Someone,' he replied slowly.

'Ah!'

'A girl.'

She'd guessed as much, Nancy Kutchinsky reflected. 'Want to talk about it?'

'Her name is . . . '

Nancy sat back in her chair when Dale finally finished his story. 'That's very sad,' she stated.

'I can't get her out of my mind, Mom. I try to but she just keeps popping back in again.'

'Do you want to return to England and see her again?'

'Scotland, Mom, she lives in Scotland. The Scots get very upset if you refer to the whole country as England.' He paused. 'I've considered it, but what's the point? There isn't one.'

How hurt he looked, Nancy thought. And that hurt her. He might be a grown-up man but he was still her little boy, and always would be. His hurt was hers.

Dale lapsed into a moody silence.

'Have you run into Marybeth Schneider since you got back?'

'No.'

Nancy smiled. 'Maybe I'll invite her and her folks round for supper one night.'

'Mom!' Dale protested. 'Are you trying to matchmake?'

'Not me,' Nancy lied. 'But you should see Marybeth nowadays. She quite transformed while you were away.'

'Transformed?'

'She was always a bit of a dumpy little thing, and then suddenly, wow! She ain't half something I can tell you.'

Dale was curious. 'Really?'

'Knock your eyes out. And lovely personality to go with it. She's a piece of cake all right.'

Dale recalled the kid he'd known, finding it hard to believe that what his mother said was true.

'No matchmaking, son, I promise you. But this Wonky . . . crazy name that . . . is in the past. You got to think of the future, make a new start. If having Marybeth to supper is that start then why not? It doesn't have to go any further after all. Where's the harm in supper, for Pete's sake?'

'OK, Mom,' Dale capitulated. 'You arrange it.'

Wait till he saw Marybeth, Nancy thought with glee. Just wait!

★ ★ ★

John excused himself from the group surrounding him and hurried over to Charlotte who was preparing to leave.

'Did you enjoy yourself?'

'Very much so. Thank you for asking me.'

'How are you getting home?'

'It's McPhie's night off so I'll walk, which won't be a hardship as it's a lovely night. At least it was when I arrived.'

'May I escort you?'

She stared at him, her expression curious.

'To ensure you're all right. We don't want anything happening to you after all.'

She laughed. 'In Dalneil! It's hardly Glasgow.'

'Nonetheless, I'd feel better seeing you to your door. Ravening wolves and all that.'

She laughed again. 'There hasn't been a wolf, ravening or otherwise, in Scotland for hundreds of years.'

He winked conspiratorially. 'Who said all wolves have four legs There are quite a few of the other sort in this parish, believe me.'

She found that funny. 'What a cynic you are, John.'

'Not so. Merely a realist.'

She considered his suggestion. 'I'd be delighted if you'd accompany me.'

'Good. Because I have a proposal to make.'

An eyebrow rose. 'Oh?'

'Regarding the church,' he qualified hastily.

'Then shall we?'

He glanced about, knowing he really should hang on a while longer. 'Let's,' he said.

A number of disappointed females watched them depart.

★ ★ ★

Dale couldn't believe this was the same Marybeth Schneider. His mom hadn't been exaggerating when she'd used the word transformed.

'Hello, Dale. How are you?'

She was gorgeous, he thought. Talk about the ugly duckling. 'Just fine. And you?'

'Fine also.'

'It's been a while.'

'Well, you were off in France enjoying yourself.'

That chilled him slightly. 'I'd hardly call it enjoying myself. It was a war after all.'

'I used the wrong word then. I simply meant you've been away while I've been stuck here in ole Albany.'

Her figure was stupendous he reflected. Where before she'd been dumpy she was now all curves. And what spectacular curves, enough to make a man . . . Well enough of that.

'You've matured,' she stated.

'You've changed somewhat yourself.'

She laughed. 'So I'm told.'

He stopped himself adding, and *how*. He gazed into her dark liquid brown eyes and felt he was drowning in them.

'Are you cold, Dale?'

He shook his head.

'I swear you're trembling.'

With a shock he realised he was. 'I do that from time to time,' he lied. 'Aftermath of France. It soon stops.'

Her expression became one of concern. 'You poor thing.'

He basked in her sympathy. 'Can I get you a drink, Marybeth? A martini perhaps. Or how about a Tom Collins?'

'A juice would be lovely.'

'Then a juice it is.'

He needed a drink himself, he reflected. And it wasn't a juice he had in mind.

★ ★ ★

577

Hettie tore open the bulky letter and read the top page, the rest being documents of some kind. A smile lit up her face. This was wonderful. Absolutely marvellous.

'Why don't you forget the housework and all that malarkey for a while,' Jack said when he heard her enter the room. 'And read to me.'

'What would you like me to read?'

'I don't know. What's available.'

A little teasing, she thought. Then she was going to take him up to bed and give him the time of his life. He deserved it. God knows he did.

She reeled off the titles of a few books she'd acquired in the past week.

'Hmmh,' Jack mused. 'Difficult there.'

'Or I could read you a contract.'

He frowned. 'A what?'

'You've heard of a contract, haven't you?'

'Of course.'

'Well I could read you one of those, Jack Riach.'

He leant back in his chair and stared in the direction of her voice. 'What are you up to, Hettie?'

'Me?' she replied, pretending astonishment. 'Why nothing.'

'Then what's all this about a contract?'

'Remember Curzon Management?'

He nodded.

'It seems they've changed their minds and decided to stage 'The Long Night'.'

His jaw literally dropped. 'You're joking!'

'They intend doing a short pre-London tour

and then putting it on at the Savoy Theatre. They say they have a brilliant new young actor who they intend casting in the lead.' She glanced again at the accompanying letter.

'Someone called Noel Coward.'

32

'HELLO, Tina.'
She started, and turned away from the coconut shy where she'd been watching a youth trying his luck. 'Why, hello, Mister Drummond.'

He smiled in amusement. 'Enjoying the fête?'

'Very much so.'

'They suspended them during the war you know. Not a time for frivolity and games. This is the first one since.'

'So I understand.'

He closed his eyes for a brief second, drinking in the scent of her, remembering . . .

'I thought we'd got to first-name terms,' he said.

She glanced quickly about her. 'I've been wanting a word. It's important.'

'I thought you might. Shall we stroll?'

They fell into step beside each other.

'Does Sandy know?' he queried quietly.

'Oh yes. He was a client. That's how we met.'

'Well, well,' Andrew muttered. Sandy Graham didn't at all look the type to be frequenting Mulligan's, far less going upstairs. It just went to show how you could misjudge someone.

'Please promise me you'll never blab about our secret, Andrew. It would devastate Sandy.'

'I can imagine,' Andrew replied drolly.

580

'He's such a nice, kind man. I owe him a great deal.'

Andrew smiled again. 'Quite a change in lifestyle, what?'

Her heart sank. She'd always known Andrew could be a bit of a bastard. It had been a side of him that had rather attracted her.

'Quite,' she agreed, spotting Sandy about a hundred yards off chatting to some people.

'Tart to lady,' Andrew chuckled. 'Still, I suppose it's not the first time that's happened.'

'I'm a different person, Andrew, I swear. Sandy has given me respectability for which I'll be eternally grateful.'

'And what do I get in return?'

She stopped and stared at him blankly. 'How do you mean?'

'For keeping your secret. What do I get in return?'

Her heart sank even further. 'Are you trying to blackmail me?'

He pretended astonishment. 'Me?'

'Yes you,' she snapped crossly.

'A bargain goes both ways, Tina. You don't get something for nothing, at least not in my experience.'

She was appalled, this was the last thing she'd expected. 'I thought you were a gentleman,' she said.

'How wrong of you.'

'But I'm a married woman now. You can't ask that.'

'Ask what?' Oh but he was enjoying this. Her discomfiture was delicious.

She swallowed hard. '*That*,' she replied in a small voice.

He felt himself becoming aroused and knew he could have taken her there and then if they'd been alone. 'What Sandy doesn't know won't bother him.'

'But it would be wrong, Andrew, a betrayal on my part. Can't you understand that?'

He shrugged.

She felt she was going to burst into tears and fought not to. All the good fortune that had come her way was about to be put in jeopardy because of Andrew Drummond. A bit of a bastard? She'd been wrong, a *total* one. And yet, strangely, the idea of sleeping with Andrew again excited her. Damn his eyes! Truth was, Sandy wasn't very good in bed, hardly adequate. Whereas, she recalled, Andrew had been excellent with great staying power. A far younger man of course.

'It's impossible,' she stated.

'Nothing's that, Tina.'

'Christina, please.'

'Christina then.'

Sandy noticed her and waved. She waved back and was infuriated when Andrew did too.

'Well?' Andrew queried.

'Please don't insist on this. I beg you.'

'How's the house coming along?'

The sudden change of subject startled her. 'Fine, why?'

'Almost finished?'

'More or less.'

'And I believe Sandy enjoys it here. Feels

you're both settling in well. It would be a shame if he had to move again. Especially after all the work you've had done on that house of yours. All that inconvenience.'

She knew Sandy would hate moving again, positively loathe it. But would feel they had to if their secret got out.

'You're a swine,' she hissed.

'Oh, through and through.'

'You wouldn't really blab, would you?'

He felt like an angler with a fish wriggling on the end of his hook. He had her, and knew it. He couldn't wait to again enjoy that body he remembered so well.

'You can bet your life on it,' he stated.

She'd have given anything to have been able to slap him with all the strength she could muster. But that, in the circumstances, was out of the question. Her excitement was increasing, much to her disgust.

'When?' he queried softly.

She thought about that. 'Sandy and I are supposed to be going away for a few days next month, back to Perth to visit some friends. I can always feign illness at the last moment, though whether or not he'll go without me I don't know.'

'Insist,' Andrew said.

'And then what?'

'I'll no doubt bump into you before then. We'll arrange something.'

The damnable thing was, she reflected, she was looking forward to it.

★ ★ ★

'It's going well, don't you think?' John smiled to Charlotte, who was also at the fête.

'Extremely.'

He beamed about him. 'I always think these are such jolly occasions, especially if you get the weather.'

'Yes,' she agreed.

'May I say you're looking splendid. Quite the belle of the fête, to coin an expression.'

Charlotte laughed. 'You are an old flatterer.'

'Less of the old please.' His expression softened. 'And it isn't flattery, I assure you. I mean every word.'

She turned away in embarrassment.

John coloured slightly. 'Sorry.'

'For what?'

'Being forward. I shouldn't have been.'

Charlotte found herself thinking of Geoffrey, and what a tragic end he'd come to. As much a casualty of the war as her brother Peter. How halcyon those early days had been, and how short in duration before the conflagration.

'Excuse me,' John said. 'I'm being summoned.'

She watched him as he strode away, a picture of Geoffrey in her mind. Geoffrey as he'd once been, not as he'd become.

★ ★ ★

God, did she never stop talking, Dale thought as Marybeth babbled on. The woman was all mouth.

'And so I said . . . '

Dale glanced down at the remainder of his meal in distaste, having completely lost his appetite. They were in the best restaurant Albany had to offer, and how he wished he hadn't invited her. She might be stunning to look at, but was irritating in the extreme.

He started thinking of Wonky and how much he missed her.

'Dale?'

He glanced up. 'Sorry?'

'I just asked you a question.'

He hoped his smile wasn't as artificial looking as it actually was. 'My mind strayed for a moment,' he apologised.

'I said . . . '

He groaned inwardly, wondering how soon before he could take her home.

★ ★ ★

Nell was dumbfounded. 'Is that so?'

'Well, that's how it appears,' Charlotte replied.

'I see.'

Charlotte sank into a chair. 'He's a pleasant enough man, I can't deny that. Good fun, and . . . soothing to be with. In fact more than that.'

'Ah!' Nell smiled. 'Do I detect the beginnings of interest?'

Charlotte considered that. 'Much as I loved Geoffrey I don't, and God forgive me, wish to remain a widow for ever. That prospect is just too ghastly.'

Nell thought of herself. Not a beau in sight, not even the glimmerings of one. Was she destined to be an old maid? As Charlotte said, the prospect was just too ghastly, not to mention downright frightening. She shuddered inwardly.

'It's too soon after Geoffrey though,' Charlotte declared. 'Far too soon.'

'I'm sure John appreciates that and is biding his time, if what you assume is correct. He hasn't actually said anything, has he?'

Charlotte shook her head. 'He doesn't have to. It's becoming more and more obvious.'

'You could do a lot worse,' Nell stated.

'I suppose.'

'How do you feel about him?'

Charlotte sighed. Good question, she thought. 'I don't love John, there was no instant attraction the way there was with Geoffrey. And yet . . . ' She trailed off.

'And yet what?' Nell prompted.

'I suppose I'm realist enough to know you can't fall head over heels every time. He'd certainly be a good husband, of that I've no doubt.'

'And father?'

Charlotte coloured slightly. 'Yes.'

'And you want children.'

Charlotte thought back to the one she'd lost and how empty she'd been afterwards. 'If possible,' she breathed.

'I certainly think you should give it some consideration. In other words don't give him the cold shoulder but a little encouragement.

That seems the intelligent thing to me to do.'

Nell paused, then added, quietly, 'I'm sure Geoffrey would have approved. He wouldn't want you to remain on your own either. He loved you too much.'

True, Charlotte reflected.

The new minister and Charlotte, Nell mused. Now there was a turn up for the book.

★ ★ ★

Wonky was sitting alone in her room, in darkness, tears streaming down her face. How she'd come to hate her father. If it wasn't for him her life would be completely different. She'd never have lost Dale and would now be Dale's wife living in America.

She sobbed into her hands. There wasn't a day went by when she didn't think of Dale, when he wasn't with her in imagination. Oh how it might have been.

If only . . . if only.

★ ★ ★

The ship was a three-master flying the French flag. A forlorn Rory stood on deck staring into the distance.

He'd escaped, Nell thought with relief. He'd lost his family but he himself had got away. Clearly going off into exile, as so many Jacobites who'd survived Culloden had done.

His face was wretched, contorted with pain and grief. He was no doubt thinking of his wife, children and lost homeland. Nell's heart went out to him.

Suddenly she knew this was the last vision she'd ever have, knew it with absolute certainty. This was her goodbye to the man who, in another life, had been her husband.

He turned, and for a moment their eyes met, though there wasn't any recognition of seeing her in his.

'Goodbye, my darling,' she whispered. 'Stay safe.'

And then the vision began to fade.

* * *

Andrew watched in admiration as Christina started to undress. How he'd been looking forward to this. Fairly champing at the bit.

'We must keep quiet,' Christina said. 'The servants . . . '

'I understand.'

She was furious with herself for being so excited at the prospect of going to bed with Andrew again. It was all so wrong. So very very wrong.

Andrew also began to undress, meanwhile never taking his eyes off Christina. It had been so long since he'd had a woman, he positively ached for one. And Christina . . . Tina . . . well he knew what he was in for with her.

He smiled at the memory of creeping in through the back door, of she anxiously waiting for him. Her reassurances that Sandy had gone to Perth and the servants were fast asleep. It had all, so far anyway, gone exactly as planned.

He sucked in a breath when she was finally naked, having forgotten just how magnificent she was. His arousal was instantaneous.

'Come here,' he commanded huskily.

She came into his arms, he closing his eyes as he drank in the scent of her. What memories were invoked, memories of the sweetest and most erotic kind.

He undid the comb holding up her hair which now tumbled over her shoulders. It took all his willpower not to thrust into her there and then.

His hand caressed a breast, her nipple immediately responding. She felt her legs turn to jelly as his hardness pressed into her.

'Oh, Tina,' he whispered. Then they were on the bed, his mouth covering hers, a hand roaming freely.

How she wanted him, Christina thought, despising herself at the same time. She couldn't help moaning when the roving hand slipped between her thighs.

Andrew bided his time, tuning her up as one would a fine instrument.

Christina stifled a scream as he entered her. And that was only the beginning.

★ ★ ★

'Christ,' Christina muttered afterwards. 'I'd almost forgotten what it was like.'

Andrew grinned at her. 'Good, was it?'

'Don't be stupid. You know it was.'

He inwardly preened.

Christina closed her eyes, revelling in the aftermath of their lovemaking. She felt as replete as any woman could. How tame Sandy now was by comparison.

'I often thought about you after you left so mysteriously,' she said, eyes still closed.

'Oh?'

'You just stopped coming.'

'Hardly,' he smiled.

She biffed him on the arm. 'You know what I mean.'

'I was posted. It all happened very quickly.'

She rolled onto her side. 'I thought you might have said goodbye.'

Tell her the truth or not? For she obviously didn't know. Not, he decided. 'As I said, it was sudden. There simply wasn't time to pay my farewells.' He paused, then queried softly, 'Why, did you miss me?'

'You were slightly special, Andrew. Don't ask me why, but you were. I was hurt when you just vanished without a word.'

'Sorry. Couldn't be helped.'

'So what happened to you?'

'I went to Ireland, you know that. And there . . . ' He trailed off.

'What?'

'I met someone,' he confessed.

She could see the distress on his face. 'And?'

'The Fenians killed her. They torched her house and she was killed.'

'Oh, Andrew,' Christina breathed. 'That's awful.'

He took a deep breath, the pain of memory strong within him. 'They paid though. I saw to that. They paid all right.'

'How?'

He shook his head. 'That I won't tell you. But take my word, they paid for it.'

Christina felt a sudden chill creep over her. 'And you were directly responsible for the reprisal or reprisals?'

He came out of his reverie. 'I never said that. Only that those responsible paid.'

'What was her name?'

'Alice.'

'Pretty?'

'As a picture. And worth a bloody fortune. Though in the end the money was secondary. It was Alice herself. We could have been so happy together.'

'I am sorry,' Christina said.

'Not half as much as I was. It was like having the whole world in your hands and then somehow letting it slip through. I was . . . well distraught to say the least.'

'Are you over it yet?'

Andrew thought about that. 'It's hard to say. I don't think you ever get over something like that. It stays with you for ever.'

Sympathy welled within her. 'You were obviously very much in love with your Alice.'

'Very. Strange, it didn't start out that way, but that's how it became. When she died it was as if I'd lost part of myself.'

'I'm so sorry,' Christina repeated.

He turned to her and smiled. 'Anyway, that's

in the past. It's the here and now which is important.'

She watched in fascination as he twitched in renewed arousal. With Sandy . . . She put that from her mind.

'This is going to be a regular thing,' he declared quietly.

She wanted to protest, to argue against that, but couldn't. For in her heart of hearts it was what she too wanted. Though God help the repercussions if Sandy ever found out.

Andrew reached for her.

★ ★ ★

'When are you taking Marybeth out again?' Nancy Kutchinsky enquired casually. 'It's been a week now since your date.'

Dale stared dejectedly at his mother. 'I'm not.'

Nancy was genuinely shocked. 'But why?'

'Because she bores the pants off me.'

'But Marybeth's so beautiful.'

Dale sighed. 'That's as may be. She still bores the pants off me. The date I had with her was excruciating in the extreme. I couldn't wait to offload her.'

Nancy bit back her disappointment. 'Is it still this Wonky?'

Dale nodded. 'I don't say I won't take up with someone else, but it certainly won't be Marybeth.'

Nancy sat facing her son. 'Don't you think it's time you went to work? I appreciate you've been through a war and all, but you have had a good rest and recuperation. Dad's just waiting for you to say the word to welcome you into the practice.'

Dale had been resisting going to work because somehow he felt it would for ever sever his ties with Wonky. Why he should think that he didn't know, but think it he did.

'I suppose,' he replied sourly.

'Then speak to your dad.'

Dale thought for a moment. 'I feel . . . I feel . . . ' He trailed off.

'Yes?'

He shook his head. 'Nothing. I'll have that word with Dad tonight.'

'Good, son. It's all for the best.'

Was it? he wondered. He wasn't at all sure.

★ ★ ★

Andrew capped his fountain pen and stood up. 'I'm going for a wander round the distillery, sis,' he declared.

She stared at him in mild astonishment. 'For a reason? Is there something wrong I don't know about?'

He came from behind his desk and perched on the front of it. 'I don't think I really ever understood Pa until I came here, concerning the distillery that is.'

Charlotte frowned. 'Could you explain that?'

'His love for the place and what we do. If I was married I'd say it's almost like having another wife.'

Charlotte couldn't believe she was hearing this from Andrew of all people, the original Philistine. 'Graphically put,' she smiled.

'Well it is.'

She knew then the distillery was safe, for their generation at least. And her shoulders sagged with relief.

She closed her eyes for a brief second. How pleased Pa would have been. How very pleased. She could almost see Murdo shaking Andrew by the hand and clapping him on the back.

'Sis?'

'Go and have your wander,' she said quietly.

'Won't be long,' he declared, striding to the door.

'Take as long as you like, Andrew,' she further smiled.

★ ★ ★

'Is something wrong, dear?'

Christina glanced across at her husband, her mind having been filled with thoughts of Andrew. 'No.'

'You seem so . . . preoccupied.'

'Am I?' she queried innocently.

'And not for the first time of late either.'

He came over and sat on the sofa beside her, taking her hand in his. 'You're not ill are you?'

'Not in the least, Sandy.'

'Then is something bothering you? A domestic matter perhaps?'

She gazed into his face, remembering what

594

had passed for lovemaking the night before, and how different it was with Andrew. God how she ached to be with Andrew again, to experience all those wonderful sensations which Sandy was simply incapable of arousing in her.

She flushed slightly from embarrassment, the sense of betrayal great within her.

'Darling?' he queried with a frown.

She removed her hand and ran it over his cheek. 'You're a lovely man, Sandy Graham. I owe you so much.'

Now it was his turn to colour. 'We'll have less of that. I always consider I got the best of the bargain. What other young thing would have taken on an old fuddy duddy like me. I'm the lucky one and no mistake.'

'You're still a lovely man. Kind, generous, all that a girl could wish for. And if you are that bit older, what of it. It doesn't matter.'

An enormous warmth welled within him. 'Thank you, my dear,' he replied softly.

She kissed him tenderly on the lips.

★ ★ ★

Hettie appreciated the irony of the situation. All those years she'd so desperately wanted it to happen, and now that it had she didn't. It upset everything.

'Jack, I have to speak to you.'

'Speak away,' he beamed.

'I'm, eh . . . ' She took a deep breath. Damn but this was difficult. 'I'm afraid I'm going to have to leave your service.'

His beam abruptly vanished. 'What!'

'Leave your service,' she repeated.

He stared in the direction of her voice, thunderstruck. 'But why? Aren't I paying you enough, is that it?'

'The pay's fine, Jack.'

'Then why, for God's sake?'

'Because I'm pregnant.'

'You're . . . ' He broke off and swallowed hard.

'There's no doubt about it. I'm three months gone.'

'Well, bugger me,' he swore, trying to digest her news.

'I'm hoping . . . Well I'm hoping you'll keep to the bargain we once had and see me right. Moneywise that is.'

'Of course, of course.'

She hadn't thought for a moment that he'd renege on her, still it was a relief to have it confirmed. But now . . . well, once it had all seemed so important, but not any more. Although she didn't stay overnight she'd come to think of Jack's cottage as her own. The cottage and garden she'd always wanted.

How would he manage without Hettie? Jack was wondering. He'd come to rely on her so much. That he could easily replace her he had no doubt, but it wouldn't be the same. Never could be.

'When?' he asked despondently.

'Sometime after we've been to London for your first night. I think that would be about right.'

596

'Surely you can continue on longer than that?' he protested.

'Well . . . if you insist.'

'I do.'

He had a thought. 'Is there someone else?'

That angered her. 'No, Jack bloody Riach. You're the father. Believe me.'

He heard her blunder from the room and when he went in search of her couldn't find her anywhere.

33

WONKY glanced at the clock. Time to administer to her father again.

With a heavy heart, she climbed the stairs to his room. She forced a cheery smile onto her face before entering.

Tom was lying on his back, staring at the ceiling. There was something different about him, Wonky thought, crossing to the bed. Though she couldn't think what.

'Hello, Father, ready for . . . '

She broke off to stare at Tom in consternation. Then gasped. A quick feel of his neck pulse confirmed he was dead.

She hurried from the room in search of John.

★ ★ ★

Moira had hysterics when John broke the news to her. 'Dear God, dear God!' she screamed, and covered her face with her hands.

'Surely it's a welcome release for him, Moira. You must think of it that way.'

Moira's whole body was shaking, her ample bosoms jiggling from side to side.

'The doctor's been sent for. Heather's gone for him.'

A shaken Wonky came into the kitchen where her mother and John were. John grimaced at her over Moira's head.

Wonky went to Moira and put a comforting arm round her shoulders. 'There there, Ma,' she crooned.

The hysterics suddenly subsided, leaving Moira gulping in deep breaths of air. 'It's such a shock,' she choked.

Wonky had already entertained the selfish thought that her father's death let her off the hook. What a relief that was.

'Come and sit down,' John proposed. Together he and Wonky led Moira to a chair.

Moira sat, then abruptly stood up again. 'I want to see him. I want to see my Tom.'

'Is that wise right now? Perhaps a little later,' John counselled.

'No, now!' Moira stated emphatically.

Wonky and John took her up.

★ ★ ★

'He suffered a second massive stroke,' Doctor McAllister informed Moira and Wonky.

'Would he have suffered, doctor?'

'I doubt it,' McAllister replied. 'The end would have been quick.'

'Praise the Lord,' Moira declared.

'I'll arrange the death certificate and then we can go from there,' McAllister stated. 'Now I'd better be on my way.'

'I'll see you to the door,' Wonky said.

Moira began to weep.

Jack couldn't sleep. He'd been tossing and turning for hours thinking about Hettie and her child. *Their* child.

She hadn't gone to bed with him since announcing her pregnancy, or suggested it. He'd already decided if that was what she wanted then he wouldn't suggest it either.

He was so confused. He didn't want to lose her, she'd become such an integral part of his life. And yet . . . what?

That was the question. Bloody what?

★ ★ ★

'You will write to Dale of course and tell him the news,' Nell said to Wonky a week after the funeral.

Wonky shook her head.

'Why ever not?'

'Who knows what his situation is now, Nell. It's been long enough for him to find someone else. And he'll have his work.' She shook her head again. 'No, our time is gone.'

'I think you're being extremely foolish if you don't mind me saying so.'

Wonky gave her cousin a weak smile. 'I don't. Dale's gone out of my life for ever and that's that. A situation I accepted quite some time ago.'

Her expression became wistful. 'I do miss him though. He and I . . . we just got on so well together.

'And loved one another.'

'I beg you, reconsider, Wonky. What have you got to lose?'

Wonky considered that. 'It would break my heart if he wrote back saying there was another woman. That he was engaged or something, or even married.'

'It's hardly been that long!' Nell protested.

'But you never know, do you. No, I simply can't risk that humiliation.'

Nell sighed. 'I still think you're being foolish.'

'And I still don't. Now, can we change the subject please?'

★ ★ ★

'Will you take charge of a stall at the bring and buy sale, Charlotte? It would be wonderful if you could.'

The more she saw of John McLean the more she liked him.

'Let me consider it, John. I've never done that sort of thing before.'

'Perhaps you think you're too grand?' he teased.

She smiled, not taking the slightest offence, realising it was a tease. 'Maybe I do.'

'Then you're not the woman I think you to be.'

'And what sort of woman is that?'

He glanced away. 'A rather lovely one actually.'

'Indeed.'

He wondered how far he could go. 'And

intelligent. I admire that in you. As I admire the way you took over your father's business. That was splendid. Showed enormous character and grit. You also have a big heart.'

Initially she'd thought John McLean something of a weakling, but as she'd come to know him better had found out there was a steely side to his nature. John was certainly no namby pamby man of the cloth.

'I thought you might do cakes,' he said.

'Do I have to supply any?'

'It would be helpful.'

'Well, actually we've always supplied things to the bring and buy. I'd have thought you'd have known that.'

'I did.'

She burst out laughing.

'I'd take it as a . . . personal favour, Charlotte.'

She knew then she would help out, but wouldn't say so there and then. She'd keep him dangling for a few days at least.

★ ★ ★

A British stamp, Dale mused. He then opened the letter that had just arrived. He frowned as he started to read.

The letter was from Nell, Wonky's cousin.

★ ★ ★

'I don't see that it's a problem, Moira. You'll still be getting Tom's pension so there's no reason whatever that things can't continue on as they are.'

Relief flooded her face. 'Thank you, John. You're a most Christian man.'

He laughed. 'I should hope so. I am a minister after all.'

'I've been so worried that you might wish Veronica and me to leave now that Tom's gone.'

'Then you've been worrying yourself unnecessarily. Now I must get on, I have a call to make.'

He sighed. 'More tea and scones I suppose.'

They both laughed.

★ ★ ★

'Why don't you take a couple of days off, sis. You're looking peaky.'

'Do you think so?'

Andrew nodded. 'I do.'

A couple of days off, Charlotte reflected. That would be lovely. 'Are you sure you can manage by yourself.'

He gave her a pained look.

'All right,' she said. 'I shall.'

'Good.'

'Tomorrow and the next day then.'

She'd start with a long lie-in, she decided. Sheer luxury. And breakfast in bed.

★ ★ ★

'Charlotte!'

She'd decided to go for a long walk to blow

the cobwebs out of her head and put some colour back into her cheeks. Andrew had been right, she was peaky.

She stopped and turned to find John McLean hurrying towards her.

'Why, hello,' he smiled when he reached her. 'What are you doing out here?'

'I've been to visit the Hendersons who live a few miles back the way. Not an easy place to get to.'

She knew the Hendersons and their house. 'No,' she agreed.

'And you. Shouldn't you be at the distillery?'

She explained about taking a few days off.

'Quite right too. I did think you were looking a touch pale at the bring and buy last week. I said to you afterwards, but thank you again for your help. It was most appreciated.'

'My pleasure.'

They strolled on together.

John took a deep breath. 'Charlotte, I've been waiting an opportunity to speak to you. And this seems perfect.'

'Oh?'

'It's difficult.'

She didn't reply to that.

'You must be aware by now that I'm . . . well, attracted to you.'

Again she didn't reply.

'And I get the impression you like me well enough.'

She remained silent.

'You're not making this easy for me.'

She smiled inwardly. 'Go on, John.'

'Is it too soon after Geoffrey for me to call on you? Not as the minister, you understand, but as a gentleman calling on a lady.'

Too soon? she wondered. She wasn't sure. Certainly an appropriate amount of time had passed for comment not to be made in the village. As for herself, would she feel any different about the situation this time next year, or the year after that?

'Of course, perhaps I've misinterpreted things. If I've caused offence I do apologise.'

'John, stop wittering.'

'Sorry.'

They walked a short way in silence. 'Why don't you come to tea this Saturday,' she suggested.

His face lit up.

Charlotte suddenly felt lighter inside, somehow buoyed up.

It was a good sign.

★ ★ ★

The stage curtains closed to deafening silence. Jack's heart sank. They didn't like his play. It was a disaster. He of course hadn't seen it but had listened intently to every word. He felt Hettie's hand squeeze his.

And then the audience erupted and a huge wave of applause filled the theatre.

Robert De la Noy of Curzon Management who was sitting on Jack's other side, clapped him on the shoulder. 'Well done, old boy. Well done.'

Hettie couldn't have been more pleased or delighted for Jack.

And then the curtains parted again and the cast began taking their bows.

The applause rose to a crescendo.

'We've a sure-fire hit on our hands,' Robert De la Noy declared to Jack a little later over drinks. 'There's no doubt about it. 'The Long Night' is in for an extensive run.'

That was music to Jack's ears.

'Young Coward was quite outstanding. That chap has a big future ahead of him.'

'He sounded excellent to me,' Jack replied.

Robert hesitated for a moment, having forgotten Jack wouldn't have been able to see the play. 'Quite.'

The cast were milling about, chattering away like so many demented parrots. The atmosphere in the crush bar, which had stayed open for them, was adrenaline charged.

Robert glanced at his watch, then called out, 'Drink up, everybody. We're due in The Grill in a few minutes.'

What a night, Jack thought. What an amazing, incredible night.

They all proceeded to The Grill where they remained wining and dining until the early hours.

* * *

'This is your room, Jack,' Hettie declared with a yawn. 'Do you want me to come in and see you're all right?'

'Please. I wanted you to come in anyway. I wish to speak to you.'

'Oh? Something wrong?'

'Hardly.'

They entered the room and she guided him to the bed where he sat.

'Now what's bothering you, Jack? Surely nothing after a night such as this?'

He smiled. 'It was stupendous, wasn't it?'

'Very.'

His smile turned to a frown. 'Hettie, I've something to ask you.'

The tone of his voice told her this was important. 'Yes, Jack?'

He patted the bed. 'Sit beside me.'

She did, wondering what this was all about.

'Would you consider marrying me, Hettie?'

Her jaw dropped open. 'Marry you?' she croaked a few seconds later.

'That's what I said.'

'But, Jack, I can't possibly.'

'Why not? You told me my blindness and face didn't matter. Was that a lie?'

'No it wasn't. They don't. And they have nothing at all to do with my refusal.'

'You just don't care for me enough then.'

She ran a hand tenderly over a scarred cheek. 'Now you know that's nonsense. I think the world of you, Jack Riach. You've always been very special to me.'

'Then why won't you marry me?'

'Jack, you're a rich man and come from a different class to me. Somebody like you doesn't marry an ex-dairy maid or even a housekeeper. It simply isn't done. Think what folk would say.'

'I don't give a damn what folk would say!' he retorted angrily. 'If they didn't like it they could lump it.'

Marry Jack? Her mind was reeling with shock. His proposal was the last thing she'd ever expected.

'It's just not on, Jack. If you marry it's got to be with someone from your own situation in life.'

Jack took the hand still on his cheek and held it. 'First of all, Hettie, I'm my own man. Always have been. I don't wish to offend others but they're certainly not going to influence how I run my life. You and I are good together. And you're carrying my child. A child I'd like to be a proper father to.'

'You really are serious about this, aren't you?'

'I wouldn't joke about marriage, Hettie. Not on your Nellie Duff.'

'Or your Grizelda McPherson,' she teased.

Jack tensed. 'She was a terrible mistake. God alone knows what I was thinking about. A weak, shallow lassie not worth tuppence. You're ten times the woman she is. No, a hundred.'

'Am I really?'

'Yes you are. The Grizeldas of this world are pale shadows compared to the real thing. And believe me, you're the real thing.'

Hettie thought about marrying Jack. It was tempting, so very tempting. A dream come true. She'd be living in his cottage which she'd already come to think of as almost hers, looking after the garden she'd come to adore. It all seemed so right somehow. If it wasn't for the gossip and rumour-mongering that would inevitably take place. There again, the latter and former would eventually die down, they always did. Die down perhaps, but never quite go away.

'So where would we tie the knot?'

Elation leapt in him. 'There's a place in London called Caxton Hall, a Register office. We could make the arrangements and get married there so that when we arrived back in Dalneil you would already be my wife. It would be what's known as a *fait accompli*.'

Dare she? she wondered. Dare she?

'Well?' he demanded.

Hettie took a deep breath. 'All right, we'll do it.'

A huge smile lit up Jack's face. 'We'll go out first thing in the morning and start making the arrangements.'

He took her in his arms and kissed her deeply, savouring the scent of her.

When the kiss was over he said, 'I swear I've never been happier in my life than I am at this moment.'

'Me neither. And that's the truth.'

★ ★ ★

Sandy Graham switched off the engine of his car and sighed from exhaustion. It had been a damnably long drive, the weather conditions not the best, and he was exhausted. He glanced up at the house which was in darkness. As it should be at that late hour. He promised himself a large dram before going up.

The dram became two during which he almost fell asleep in the chair. This won't do, he thought, rousing himself and finishing off his whisky.

He stopped outside their bedroom door, the bedroom at the rear of the house, and frowned for there was light showing underneath. Christina must still be awake.

He opened the door and went in, stopping dead in his tracks at the sight which greeted him. In that instant his heart was broken.

'Get dressed and come downstairs, you two,' he said quietly, barely able to control his voice.

Turning, he left the appalled lovers.

★ ★ ★

'How long has this been going on for?' Sandy demanded when Andrew and Christina joined him a short while later.

'Not too long, Sandy,' Andrew replied.

'*Mr* Graham to you from now on. *Mr* Graham. Understand?'

Andrew nodded.

'You weren't supposed to be back until tomorrow,' Christina said in a quiet voice.

'I managed to conclude my business and get home early. I was missing you.'

Christina blushed bright red.

'Once a tart always a tart, I suppose. I should have known better,' Sandy declared, knowing that would hurt. From the look on Christina's face it had.

'We've known each other a long time, since before she met you,' Andrew explained. 'I was also a client of hers at Mulligan's.'

'Indeed.'

'So as someone who's used tarts as well I shouldn't take such a high moral tone.'

Sandy drank more whisky, having no intention whatsoever of offering Andrew any. 'The difference between you and me though is, I not only paid for her services, I married her and gave her respectability. The only thing you gave her is money and what's between your legs.'

Andrew swallowed hard.

'I thought that by coming here we'd be safe from her past, that no one would ever know. How wrong I was. It's ironic really if you think about it. I must have been mad to marry her in the first place.'

'Oh, Sandy, I'm so sorry.'

'I'll bet you are. Sorry for having an affair and betraying me or sorry for being found out?'

Christina didn't reply to that.

Sandy pointed a finger at Andrew. 'Now, you, get out of my house.'

Andrew glanced at Christina who didn't meet his gaze, continuing to stare at the floor. He proceeded to do as he'd been told.

When Andrew had gone Sandy placed his glass aside and crossed to Christina. Taking her by the chin he raised her face till it was looking into his.

His other hand suddenly flashed to crack

against her cheek. With a cry Christina went tumbling backwards to end up on her bottom.

Sandy picked up his glass again and the whisky decanter. He left Christina where she'd fallen and headed for a spare room.

★ ★ ★

Robert De la Noy and his wife Tatiana acted as witnesses at Jack and Hettie's wedding. When it was over they all went to a restaurant for a celebratory lunch.

'So how does it feel being an old married man?' Robert teased Jack as the car got under way.

'Just fine.' He groped for Hettie's hand, found and squeezed it. 'You all right?'

She'd transferred the posy she was carrying to her other hand. 'I couldn't be better, Jack.'

Tatiana beamed on, thinking again how splendid Hettie looked in the stylish charcoal grey jacket and matching ankle-length skirt. The lapels of the jacket were edged in black piping. Initially she'd thought it rather severe for a wedding but somehow it worked.

Robert rubbed his hands together. 'Can't wait to get to the champagne and toast the happy couple.'

The meal was a rip-roaring success at the conclusion of which Jack and Hettie returned to the suite they'd reserved at the Savoy, where they'd be spending the next week on honeymoon.

★ ★ ★

Sandy hadn't spoken to Christina for three days now. The atmosphere was chill in the extreme.

Sandy finished his breakfast, this the morning of the fourth day, and carefully laid his knife and fork together on his plate. After which he wiped his mouth with a napkin.

'I've made a decision,' he announced.

She went very still. Here it was, what she'd been dreading.

He stared steadily at her. 'I'm leaving you and returning to Perth where I shall initiate divorce proceedings.'

He waited for comment on that, but there wasn't one.

'As you no doubt know, divorce in Scotland can be lengthy so until it actually comes through I shall allow you to stay on here in this house. Until that date I shall continue to maintain the house, you and the staff.'

'That's very kind of you, Sandy,' she murmured.

For a moment his expression softened. 'The act of an old fool no doubt, but I was fond of you, Christina. Very much so.'

'Can't we . . . patch things up?'

'Don't be ridiculous. With that man living just up the road? I'd be reminded of what happened every time I saw him.' Sandy shook his head. 'No, I can't live with that.'

He paused, then asked, 'Why, Christina. The age difference?'

How could she hurt him further by telling

him that Andrew was a far better lover than he. That would be sticking another knife in his back.

'Andrew and I were quite close when I knew him. I don't know, it just happened,' she prevaricated.

'I see.'

Christina laid down her own knife and fork having lost what little appetite she'd had.

'Within a week of the divorce coming through I shall expect you to move out, taking whatever of your belongings you wish. And the house will be put up for sale.'

She nodded.

'Where you go is of course entirely up to you.' He couldn't resist the jibe, 'Probably back to that hovel I rescued you from.'

She blanched.

'Further, I shall settle a small amount of money on you. And I mean small. I don't want you to leave penniless.'

'Thank you, Sandy.'

He closed his eyes for a brief moment. How good it had been between them he thought. At least he'd believed so. Her deception had been the cruellest thing that had ever happened to him.

'Any questions?'

She shook her head.

'I shall be leaving here as soon as I can get organised.' He paused, then said, 'When I do leave I never want to see or hear from you again.'

'I understand,' she croaked.

Sandy rang the small bell that would summon his coffee.

★ ★ ★

'There's a gentleman here to see you, miss,' Heather declared.

Wonky wondered who this could be. 'Show him in.' She was darning John's socks, a job she loathed. But you could hardly expect a man to darn his own socks when there were two able-bodied women available. Besides, John had been so good to her and Moira he deserved a lot more in return than merely having his socks darned.

She was laying her darning aside when the gentleman strode into the room. When she saw who it was her expression became one of sheer incredulity.

'Hello, Wonky, I told Heather not to let on who it was. I wanted to surprise you.' Dale Kutchinsky smiled.

34

THE stars were bright in the sky, the moon full, as Wonky and Dale gazed up at them. It was a perfect evening.

'So how did you find out?' Wonky queried.

'Your cousin Nell. She wrote to me about your father's death. As that changed everything I immediately hot-footed it back here.'

Nell, Wonky thought. Trust her to do something like that.

'She explained why you hadn't written yourself.'

'I take it there isn't anyone else then?'

'Oh sure, I got married on my return and we now have four kids with another on the way.'

'You're a fast worker,' she grinned.

'Aren't all of us Yanks? At least that's the rep we've got.'

'Rep?'

'Reputation.'

He took her into his arms. 'I've been looking forward to this all the way across the Atlantic. So brace yourself, kid, you're gonna be kissed like you've never been kissed before.'

He was right. The kiss was spectacular.

'Oooh!' she murmured when their lips finally parted.

'As sweet as I remembered. Sweeter even.'

A thrill ran through her to hear that.

He gazed into her eyes, sparkling in the

moonlight. 'I'm gonna ask you a second time, Wonky, and I hope you won't let me down. I didn't come all this way for another refusal. Will you marry me?'

The breath caught in her throat. 'Oh, Dale.'

'Well?'

'What about Ma? She'd be left all alone.'

'That isn't a problem. She can come with us. We'll find her a nice little place and see she's taken care of.'

Wonky doubted Moira would agree to that.

'There's sacrifice and stupidity, Wonky. I could understand the business with your father. If she stays she's perfectly capable of looking after herself.'

Moira was, Wonky thought. Moira would be upset at losing her of course, perfectly natural. She'd let Dale slip through her fingers once, she'd be the fool Nell had called her if she allowed it to happen again.

'What is it you Americans say? OK.'

Dale threw back his head and roared with laughter. 'Goddamn! Yahoo!'

Now Wonky laughed. How did she feel? Incredibly excited. A door had just opened, a door she was going to walk through into an entirely new life. Walk through with the man of her dreams. She shivered at the prospect.

★ ★ ★

'Get married?' Moira gasped.

'That's right, Mrs Comyn.'

'I had no idea that . . . ' Moira stumbled to

617

a chair and sat. This was a bolt out the blue.

'Veronica will be returning to the States with me and we'll get married there. We're hoping you'll accompany us and stay on if you care.'

Moira was having trouble focusing on Dale. 'Oh, I couldn't do that. It's impossible.'

'You mean come for the wedding or stay on?'

'Both. I, eh . . . Well I've never been outside Scotland.'

'Then it would be a big adventure for you, think of it that way.'

Wonky went and knelt beside her mother. 'I appreciate this must be a shock for you.'

'Shock isn't the word. I'm . . . I don't know what I am.'

'I sure could use a Scotch if you have any in the house,' a still jubilant Dale declared.

Wonky told him where he could find some.

'Your father not long gone, and now you. I'll be all alone,' Moira sobbed in self pity.

'You won't be, Ma. You've all your friends. You know everyone.'

'But that's not the same.'

'Ma, if Dale could remain here he would, but he can't make a living in this country. He has to be in the States and I'm going back with him.'

'You selfish girl,' Moira spat.

Dale stared appalled on hearing that.

'No, Ma, it's not me who's being selfish, but you. I'm not giving up Dale merely to sit around and keep you company of an evening. I'm sorry, but that's how it is.'

Moira sagged, reluctantly accepting the inevitable. 'When will you leave?'

Wonky glanced at Dale.

'A couple of weeks,' he informed them.

'So soon?'

'I have my work to get back to, Mrs Comyn. The trip here was unplanned as you'll appreciate.'

'Unplanned?'

Wonky explained about Dale proposing when he'd been there previously and how she'd turned him down because of her father and that responsibility.

'I didn't know.'

'Because I never told you, Ma.'

Moira took a deep breath. 'This is going to take a while to get used to. In the meantime can I have some of that whisky, young man. All us Drummonds are brought up on the stuff.'

Wonky knew then it was going to be all right.

★ ★ ★

'Time,' John beamed when Wonky told him the next day. 'That's what I said, time.'

'And you were right, as it's turned out.'

He held her at arm's length. 'I'm so happy for you. The only regret is I won't be marrying you myself.'

'Dale and his family want it in America and that's how it'll have to be.'

John pecked her on the cheek. 'Congratulations from the very bottom of my heart.'

Andrew was sitting in the pub lost in thought, thinking about Christina and her new situation. Rather than calling on him personally she'd written to him at Drummond House explaining what had happened between her and Sandy, and that Sandy had now left. A letter to which he hadn't yet replied.

What was he to do about her, if anything? The road was now open for him to pay as many secret visits to her as he liked, if she agreed that was. He wasn't at all sure she would.

What a farce that had been. He and she right in the middle of . . . And then Sandy walking in. A farce in hindsight, there had been nothing funny about it at the time.

He had a swallow from his pint and was putting the glass down again when he heard a familiar name mentioned at the bar. He began listening.

'Imagine Jack Riach marrying an ex-dairy maid! Who would believe it. What a come down for him.'

There was a murmur of agreement.

The speaker winked. 'She went for his money I shouldn't wonder. What other reason could there be?'

That was greeted with various sniggers.

Andrew's eyes narrowed. 'Archie Douglas!' he called out.

Archie, the speaker, turned to face Andrew who'd been so quiet in the corner they'd forgotten he was there.

'You find Jack Riach marrying Hettie Campbell funny I take it.'

Archie became wary. 'Yes, sir. Who wouldn't.'

Andrew leant forward fractionally, his now hard gaze boring into Archie's. 'I would remind you that Jack went 'over there' to fight for Dalneil and Scotland. Coming back with appalling injuries as we all know. Do you think it's right to make fun of a man like that?'

Archie swallowed.

'A man who's not only been blinded but horribly scarred into the bargain.'

Archie swallowed again.

'If Jack's found happiness with Hettie, and she with him, then he's earned it. More than earned it in my book. As for the money — nonsense! Jack's far too astute to be taken in by a gold digger, believe me.

'Regarding a 'come down' as you call it, Hettie may be a working-class girl but there's nothing wrong with that. It isn't the first time the gentry have married into the working class and it won't be the last.'

'Yes, sir,' Archie mumbled, and shuffled his feet.

Andrew's gaze swept over the small knot of men. 'You work for me, Tod Gemmill.'

'That's correct, Mr Drummond.'

'Well, let me remind you now that the war's over there isn't the shortage of labour there was. You and any other member of the workforce at the distillery can be replaced.'

Tod went pale.

'And you, Archie Douglas, you work for James Semple. Isn't that so?'

Archie nodded.

'A word from me to James, who incidentally is a good friend of Jack's, and you too could find yourself suddenly unemployed.'

Archie dropped his gaze to stare at the floor.

'There will be no more gossipping about Jack and Hettie, you pass that on to your wives and friends and neighbours. Because if there is, and I get to hear about it, then the gossiper and his or her family will pay the consequences. Do I make myself clear?'

The group nodded in unison.

'Jack's a bloody brave man who doesn't deserve to be laughed at. And I shall personally see that he isn't.'

'We understand, Mr Drummond,' Archie croaked.

'I only hope you do for I don't make idle threats. Not only will you lose your jobs but won't find another in the area. You have my word on that.'

Andrew rose and strode from the pub leaving a stunned silence behind him.

★ ★ ★

'Andrew!' Charlotte burst out the moment he entered the room. 'Wonderful news. Wonky and Dale are to be married.'

Andrew smiled, then crossed to Dale and shook him by the hand. He'd taken a liking to the American during their previous meetings.

'Congratulations! When did you get back?'

'Today.'

'I see.'

Andrew kissed Wonky on the cheek. 'Congratulations, cuz.'

'We're to be married in America. Isn't it exciting?'

'I'll say.'

Andrew rounded on Charlotte. 'Where are your manners? We should be toasting the happy couple.'

'I was getting round to that.'

'Leave it to me.' And with that he headed for the whisky decanter.

'It's all thanks to Nell,' Wonky said as he poured. 'She wrote and told him about Father's death.'

'She was always an interfering lassie,' Andrew replied drily.

'Andrew! I am not. Quite the contrary.'

Andrew began distributing drams. 'That's all right, Nell. I was only joking.'

When they all had a glass Andrew raised his in a toast. 'Here's to Wonky and Dale. May their marriage be a long and joyous one. And may there never be a single day when they regret the dirty deed.'

Everyone laughed.

When Dale and Wonky had gone Andrew took himself off to the study, now his, where he continued the ruminations that had been disturbed in the pub.

It was hours before he re-emerged.

‘Sit down,’ Christina said to Andrew, indicating a chair. She sat opposite him.

She was far from looking her best, Andrew observed. She was pale and drawn with the hint of dark smudges under her eyes. He doubted she'd been sleeping very well, understandable in the circumstances.

‘I was beginning to think I wasn't going to hear from you again,’ she stated matter-of-factly.

He smiled. ‘Well, here I am.’

‘What did you think of my letter?’

He shrugged. ‘Sandy clearly took it very badly indeed. Poor chap.’

‘Wouldn't you have done?’

‘I'd hope I'd never find myself in that situation.’

‘Would you care for some tea?’

He shook his head. ‘So, what are your plans?’

‘To stay on here until the divorce comes through and then return to Perth. What else can I do?’

‘You mentioned that Sandy was going to settle some money on you.’

‘A small amount, he was quite specific about that. But hopefully it'll be enough to tide me over in Perth until I get myself sorted out.’

‘Hmmh,’ Andrew mused. ‘What sort of work do you have in mind?’

‘Certainly not the sort I had at Mulligan's. Those days are over. Perhaps I can find a position as a shop assistant, that sort of thing.'

He closed his eyes for a brief second, again tempted. But only for that brief second. 'I feel guilty about all this, Tina. Please believe that.'

'I was as much to blame as you, Andrew. What I did was foolish in the extreme.'

'And has cost you everything.'

She turned her head, unwilling to meet his gaze.

'I had thought . . . considered . . . ' He broke off and took a deep breath.

'Yes?' she queried softly.

He shook his head. 'It would be impossible, Tina. If your background ever got out . . . well, I'm a Drummond after all. Head of the family now. A position of responsibility, of respect.'

'I understand, Andrew,' she replied, a small cynical smile drifting onto her face. 'You've no need to explain.'

He thought of their times in bed together and how wonderful they'd been. 'I don't suppose you'd . . . '

'No,' she stated emphatically, interrupting him, having correctly guessed what he'd been about to say. 'That's over. I simply couldn't, not after what's happened.'

He nodded. That was the answer he'd expected. What a pity. He'd miss the delightful Tina and her lovely body. Still, he reflected philosophically, everything had to come to an end sometime. And there were other fish in the sea. Others more acceptable to one day be the wife of Andrew Drummond.

'Let me know what Sandy settles on you and

I'll match it,' he declared.

That surprised her. 'Thank you.'

'It's the least I can do.'

Christina suddenly felt very tired, lost and alone. She'd lie down after he'd gone she decided.

Andrew rose. 'I'd better be getting on my way.'

She rose also. 'I'll see you out.'

At the door they paused, each uncomfortable, unsure what to say next.

'Good luck, Tina,' Andrew said, forcing a smile onto his face. 'And don't forget to let me know about the money.'

'I won't. And thank you again.'

He hesitated, then pecked her on the cheek.

There was a huge lump in her throat as she shut the door behind him.

★ ★ ★

It was a highly charged emotional farewell as they'd all expected. Wonky and Dale were to travel to Pitlochry station in the Rolls-Royce. Their luggage was already on board and carefully strapped down by McPhie.

She wasn't going to cry, Moira told herself. She'd save that for after they'd gone. Oh, but this was hard, so very very hard. To see her only child off to a foreign country far away across the ocean. Would she ever see Veronica again? She had no idea. Her heart was swollen almost to bursting.

Andrew and Charlotte had come over from

the distillery, Nell from Drummond House.

'Well, this is it,' Wonky declared to Charlotte and Nell, a huge lump in her throat.

'Have a safe journey,' Charlotte replied.

'Write to us when you get there,' Nell added.

Then Wonky was in Charlotte's arms with Nell hugging the two of them. A few more words were quietly exchanged after which the girls broke apart.

'Goodbye, old sport, take care,' Andrew said to Dale, solemnly shaking hands.

Wonky glanced about her, imprinting what she saw in her memory. Despite all the years of wanting to be away from Dalneil she would miss it dreadfully.

Andrew kissed Wonky on the cheek. 'You look after yourself now, cuz.'

'I don't need to, Andrew. Dale will do that for me.'

Andrew smiled. 'Of course he will. And a fine job he'll do of it too.'

Dale spoke to Moira, again reassuring her that all would be well.

Now it was the moment both women had dreaded, the farewell. 'Goodbye, Ma.'

'Goodbye, Wonky.'

Wonky started. It was the first time her mother had ever called her that. She laughed, and Moira did too.

'Now get on with you, you've a train to catch.'

They kissed, had a final hug, and then Wonky fled to the refuge of the Rolls. Dale joined her and moments later the Rolls purred into life. Moira was proud of herself. The car was almost out of sight before she burst into tears to be helped inside by a consoling Charlotte and Nell.

★ ★ ★

It was now a year since John had started to pay court to Charlotte. A year during which they'd grown closer and closer.

They were out for their weekly stroll together, which had become, weather permitting, a highlight in both their lives.

'Charlotte?'

She smiled at him.

'How would you feel about . . . ' He sucked in a deep breath. 'Getting engaged?'

She stopped and turned to face him, having known for quite some time this would eventually be coming.

'Are you proposing, John?' she teased.

He coloured. 'Yes.'

He was such a dear man, she thought, having already made up her mind months before. It would mean leaving her work at the distillery, a minister's wife having a great deal to do in the parish if the job was done properly. Something she'd always considered Aunt Moira to be somewhat lax about. As for Andrew, he was entirely capable now and she'd always be on hand to give advice if required. She thought of Andrew who, to her amazement, was becoming more and more like their father every day. That was a turn up for the book. Andrew who'd become quite settled back in Dalneil.

'I don't know,' she further teased. 'I don't know.'

John's face fell. 'Please, Charlotte. I love you so.'

Love was a strange animal, she reflected. It came in many forms. She didn't love John the way she had Geoffrey, but love him she did in another way. A gentler, less intense way. John had become an integral part of her life, someone she'd be content to spend the rest of her days with.

'Charlotte?'

She gazed into his eyes and saw happiness there. 'Yes, I'll marry you.'

The face that had fallen now lit up. 'Oh, Charlotte!'

Children, she thought. She wanted many of those.

★ ★ ★

Nell was excited, having been looking forward to this day for weeks, ever since receiving a letter from Hope Langton whom she had known in France. Hope had written saying she and her brother Philip would be in the area and could they come and visit. It would be wonderful talking over old times.

Nell had immediately replied saying she'd be delighted to see them and why didn't they stay a few days. Hope had written accepting Nell's invitation.

Nell picked up a book, then laid it down again when she found she couldn't concentrate. She sighed, wishing Hope would hurry up and arrive.

It was a pity that Wonky wasn't there for the reunion, she'd have adored it.

Nell started when she heard voices out in the hall. They'd arrived at last! She hastily rose and smoothed down her dress.

Christine the maid entered the room. 'A Mister and Miss Langton,' she announced.

Hope breezed in. 'Nell!' she squealed, and the two women flew into each other's arms.

'You're looking so well,' Hope gushed.

'And you.'

'We've lots to talk about.'

'Lots,' Nell agreed, and they both laughed.

The laugh died in Nell's throat the moment she caught sight of the man accompanying Hope. She'd heard of the expression poleaxed; well, that was exactly how she felt.

'Nell, I'd like you to meet my brother Philip. Philip, this is Nell Drummond.'

Philip came forward and formally shook Nell's hand. 'How do you do, Miss Drummond. I trust we're not inconveniencing you in any way.'

She tried to speak and couldn't.

Hope frowned. 'Nell?'

'I, eh . . . I'm pleased to meet you, Mister Langton.'

He was staring at her quizzically. 'I don't mean to be rude, but have we met before? You seem strangely familiar.'

Oh yes, she thought. They had indeed met

before. For Philip Langton was the spitting image of Rory, her Highlander husband in another life.

'I doubt it,' she lied in reply.

A feeling of calmness and peace descended on her. Rory had been returned to her. The outcome of this meeting was inevitable.

The circle was complete.

THE END

CHINESE ALICE
Pat Barr

The story of Alice Greenwood gives a complete picture of late 19th century China.

UNCUT JADE
Pat Barr

In this sequel to CHINESE ALICE, Alice Greenwood finds herself widowed and alone in a turbulent China.

THE GRAND BABYLON HOTEL
Arnold Bennett

A romantic thriller set in an exclusive London Hotel at the turn of the century.

SINGING SPEARS
E. V. Thompson

Daniel Retallick, son of Josh and Miriam (from CHASE THE WIND) was growing up to manhood. This novel portrays his prime in Central Africa.

A HERITAGE OF SHADOWS
Madeleine Brent

This romantic novel, set in the 1890's, follows the fortunes of eighteen-year-old Hannah McLeod.

BARRINGTON'S WOMEN
Steven Cade

In order to prevent Norway's gold reserves falling into German hands in 1940, Charles Barrington was forced to hide them in Borgas, a remote mountain village.

THE PLAGUE
Albert Camus

The plague in question afflicted Oran in the 1940's.

THE RESTLESS SEA
E. V. Thompson

A tale of love and adventure set against a panorama of Cornwall in the early 1800's.